Enterprising America

A National Bureau
of Economic Research
Conference Report

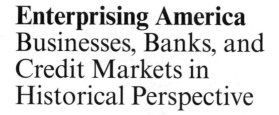

Enterprising America
Businesses, Banks, and
Credit Markets in
Historical Perspective

Edited by **William J. Collins
and Robert A. Margo**

The University of Chicago Press

Chicago and London

WILLIAM J. COLLINS is the Terence E. Adderly Jr. Professor of Economics at Vanderbilt University and a research associate of the NBER. ROBERT A. MARGO is professor of economics at Boston University and a research associate of the NBER.

The University of Chicago Press, Chicago 60637
The University of Chicago Press, Ltd., London
© 2015 by the National Bureau of Economic Research
All rights reserved. Published 2015.
Printed in the United States of America

24 23 22 21 20 19 18 17 16 15   1 2 3 4 5
ISBN-13: 978-0-226-26162-1
ISBN-13: 978-0-226-26176-8
DOI: 10.7208/chicago/9780226261768.001.0001

Library of Congress Cataloging-in-Publication Data

Enterprising America: Businesses, Banks, and Credit Markets in Historical Perspective (Conference) (2013 : Nashville, Tenn.)
Enterprising America : businesses, banks, and credit markets in historical perspective / edited by William J. Collins and Robert A. Margo.
    pages cm. — (National Bureau of Economic Research conference report)
    Papers of the conference "Enterprising America: businesses, banks, and credit markets in historical perspective", held at Vanderbilt University, Nashville TN, on December 14, 2013.
    Includes bibliographical references and index.
    ISBN 978-0-226-26162-1 (cloth : alk. paper) — ISBN 978-0-226-26176-8 (e-book)
1. Business enterprises—United States—History—Congresses. 2. Business enterprises—United States—Finance—History—Congresses. 3. Commercial credit—United States—History—Congresses. 4. Bank loans—United States—History—Congresses.
I. Collins, William J. (William Joseph), 1971– editor. II. Margo, Robert A. (Robert Andrew, 1954– editor. III. Vanderbilt University, host institution. IV. National Bureau of Economic Research, organizer. V. Title. VI. Series: National Bureau of Economic Research conference report.
HD2356.U5E58 2013
338.0973—dc23
                                                                    2015001694

Relation of the Directors to the
Work and Publications of the
National Bureau of Economic Research

1. The object of the NBER is to ascertain and present to the economics profession, and to the public more generally, important economic facts and their interpretation in a scientific manner without policy recommendations. The Board of Directors is charged with the responsibility of ensuring that the work of the NBER is carried on in strict conformity with this object.

2. The President shall establish an internal review process to ensure that book manuscripts proposed for publication DO NOT contain policy recommendations. This shall apply both to the proceedings of conferences and to manuscripts by a single author or by one or more co-authors but shall not apply to authors of comments at NBER conferences who are not NBER affiliates.

3. No book manuscript reporting research shall be published by the NBER until the President has sent to each member of the Board a notice that a manuscript is recommended for publication and that in the President's opinion it is suitable for publication in accordance with the above principles of the NBER. Such notification will include a table of contents and an abstract or summary of the manuscript's content, a list of contributors if applicable, and a response form for use by Directors who desire a copy of the manuscript for review. Each manuscript shall contain a summary drawing attention to the nature and treatment of the problem studied and the main conclusions reached.

4. No volume shall be published until forty-five days have elapsed from the above notification of intention to publish it. During this period a copy shall be sent to any Director requesting it, and if any Director objects to publication on the grounds that the manuscript contains policy recommendations, the objection will be presented to the author(s) or editor(s). In case of dispute, all members of the Board shall be notified, and the President shall appoint an ad hoc committee of the Board to decide the matter; thirty days additional shall be granted for this purpose.

5. The President shall present annually to the Board a report describing the internal manuscript review process, any objections made by Directors before publication or by anyone after publication, any disputes about such matters, and how they were handled.

6. Publications of the NBER issued for informational purposes concerning the work of the Bureau, or issued to inform the public of the activities at the Bureau, including but not limited to the NBER Digest and Reporter, shall be consistent with the object stated in paragraph 1. They shall contain a specific disclaimer noting that they have not passed through the review procedures required in this resolution. The Executive Committee of the Board is charged with the review of all such publications from time to time.

7. NBER working papers and manuscripts distributed on the Bureau's web site are not deemed to be publications for the purpose of this resolution, but they shall be consistent with the object stated in paragraph 1. Working papers shall contain a specific disclaimer noting that they have not passed through the review procedures required in this resolution. The NBER's web site shall contain a similar disclaimer. The President shall establish an internal review process to ensure that the working papers and the web site do not contain policy recommendations, and shall report annually to the Board on this process and any concerns raised in connection with it.

8. Unless otherwise determined by the Board or exempted by the terms of paragraphs 6 and 7, a copy of this resolution shall be printed in each NBER publication as described in paragraph 2 above.

Contents

Acknowledgments

The coeditors (William Collins and Robert Margo) would like to express their appreciation to the National Bureau of Economic Research and Vanderbilt University for financial support of the "Enterprising America" conference and the conference volume and to the National Bureau of Economic Research conference department and Vanderbilt University for their assistance with conference management.

We also thank the following scholars who served as formal discussants or gave prepared remarks at the "Enterprising America" conference:

Margaret Blair, Vanderbilt University (Lamoreaux)
William Collins, Vanderbilt University and NBER (Margo)
Alan Dye, Barnard College (Hansen)
Larry Neal, University of Illinois and NBER (Bodenhorn and White, and prepared remarks)
Claudia Rei, Vanderbilt University (Hilt)
Thomas Weiss, University of Kansas and NBER (Olmstead and Rhode)
David Wheelock, Federal Reserve Bank of Kansas City (Atack, Jaremski, and Rousseau)

Introduction

William J. Collins and Robert A. Margo

This book is a collection of seven research papers that were presented at a conference held at Vanderbilt University in December 2013 and revised in light of suggestions from conference participants and outside reviewers. Sponsored by the National Bureau of Economic Research and Vanderbilt University, the conference was entitled "Enterprising America: Businesses, Banks, and Credit Markets in Historical Perspective."[1] In this introduction, we provide a discussion of the background context that motivated the conference, summarize each chapter, and conclude with a brief recapitulation of the main findings and suggestions for further research.

Background Context

The American economy's ascendance from a colonial outpost into one of the world's most sophisticated and productive economies was an event

William J. Collins is the Terence E. Adderley Jr. Professor of Economics and professor of history at Vanderbilt University and a research associate of the National Bureau of Economic Research. Robert A. Margo is professor of economics at Boston University and a research associate of the National Bureau of Economic Research.

This is the introductory chapter to the NBER conference volume *Enterprising America: Businesses, Banks, and Credit Markets in Historical Perspective*. The conference was held at Vanderbilt University, Nashville, TN, on December 14, 2013. Conference support from the NBER and Vanderbilt University's Adderley Chair and Douglas Grey gift is gratefully acknowledged. We are grateful for detailed comments from two referees that greatly improved the exposition of the introduction and the organization of the volume. For acknowledgments, sources of research support, and disclosure of the authors' material financial relationships, if any, please see http://www.nber.org/chapters/c13130.ack.

1. Coinciding with the conference were lunch and evening events celebrating the scholarly contributions of Jeremy Atack, whose research has done much to advance understanding of the general subject matter of the essays in this volume. The lunch and dinner events were sponsored by Vanderbilt University's Adderley Chair and Douglas Grey gift.

of singular historical importance. From a global perspective, by the end of the nineteenth century, the American economy had become a major force driving international trade, migration, capital flows, and business cycles. Although international comparisons of production are imprecise for the nineteenth century, it is clear that the United States rose from a peripheral position in 1800 to a leading position in the world's economic order by 1913 (Kindleberger 1996; Landes 1998; Maddison 2001).[2] Even as the world's economic output grew at an unprecedented rate, the American economy's growth nearly surpassed all others.

From a domestic perspective, there is no single metric that captures the scope of economic change and its implications for the American people, but salient features of the transformation are clearly visible. Between 1800 and 1900, the share of the labor force in agriculture declined by half (Carter 2006, 2–18), coinciding with the steady rise of towns and cities. At the same time, the geographic center of the population shifted dramatically westward, from near Baltimore to near Indianapolis (US Census Bureau 2011). Within the manufacturing sector, the rise of the factory system and subsequent business consolidations led to "huge corporations mass producing standardized products for a national market" (Atack and Bateman 2006, 4–575). This was encouraged and facilitated by the new network of railways, which sharply cut interregional transportation costs and physically tied markets together into a large, open, commercial space. Finally, the development of the banking and financial sector, despite several crises, provided credit and capital to firms, farms, and consumers, thereby fueling economic growth while in turn benefiting from it.

A basic starting point for understanding the history of American economic growth is to model total output as a function of technology and "factors of production," including labor, capital, and other resources. With certain assumptions and macroeconomic data, technological improvements and additions to the stock of factors provide a comprehensive "accounting" for economic growth (Denison 1962). Such an accounting reveals, for example, that growth in factors of production played a larger explanatory role in accounting for growth in the nineteenth century than in the twentieth.

Behind the growth-accounting framework is the economist's conventional model of industry demand and supply. In the workhorse version of this model, production in the long run is characterized by constant returns to scale. As such, the identities and characteristics of production units— pointedly, their size and location—are ignored in the interest of focusing on the aggregate outcome, and little or no attention is paid to the underlying institutional setting. Indeed, an assumption of "atomistic" production, in

2. Maddison (2001, appendix B), for example, estimated that between 1820 and 1913, the two benchmark dates closest to the start and end of the nineteenth century, the US share of global GDP increased from below 2 percent to nearly 20 percent.

which each unit is very small and produces a tiny share of aggregate output, is often made because it greatly simplifies the analysis.

Economic historians know that the textbook model only scratches the surface of the actual process of economic growth. In particular, the editors and authors in this volume, along with many other scholars, believe that understanding the growth process requires unpacking the historical context in which individuals came together to form voluntary associations whose goal was to provide goods and services to markets and, in doing so, to earn profits.[3] We use the common English word *enterprise* to refer to such associations.[4]

For an enterprise to be economically successful, certain problems of internal organization had to be solved, and factor inputs—capital, labor, real estate, raw materials—had to be assembled and put to productive use. These activities were (and are) pursued within a framework of laws and institutions that set the ground rules for the organization and operation of economic entities. Effective laws and institutions form the foundation, if not the sole motivation, for modern economic growth. Ideally, if not always in reality, they are designed to encourage enterprise when it is in society's interest and also to constrain undesirable behaviors, such as those associated with principal-agent problems in corporate governance or the powers of the state itself. They change, sometimes slowly and sometimes abruptly, as economic and political environments change. Indeed, some laws and institutions that fostered certain types of enterprise in the past are no longer viewed as morally acceptable and have been repudiated and discarded. Chattel slavery is the obvious example.

Enterprises in American history have come in many different forms and structures, depending on the nature of the productive activity, the state of technology, and the laws and institutions governing them. At one end of the spectrum in the nineteenth century there is the family farm—small production units consisting almost entirely of workers bound together by family ties that produced for their own consumption and, increasingly over time, for the market. At the other end there are enterprises like Carnegie Steel or Standard Oil, very large firms that sought to exploit their size to enrich their owners to levels unimaginable, and often feared, by ordinary citizens. In between are many other enterprises, including entities that were formed to complete infrastructure projects in conjunction with state and local govern-

---

3. We recognize that many enterprises are nonprofit associations and that government is also a form of enterprise. Our focus in this volume, however, is on enterprises formed for the purpose of seeking profit.

4. Our use of "enterprise" is flexible but always in keeping with standard definitions of the word. For reference, the American Heritage Dictionary defines "enterprise" as "an undertaking, especially one of some scope, complication, and risk"; "a business organization"; "industrious, systematic activity, especially when directed toward profit"; and "willingness to undertake new ventures; initiative." *American Heritage Dictionary of the English Language*, 5th ed., s.v. "enterprise."

ments, railroad and canal companies, wholesale and retail establishments, and banks and other financial firms.

Within the framework of laws and institutions, enterprises interact with one another in ways that can be productivity enhancing because they complement one another across sectors, such as banks that provide credit to farmers, or because they compete with one another within sectors, such as firms within manufacturing that vie to offer goods at lower costs or to invent entirely new goods. The ensuing processes of innovation, investment, and factor accumulation connect enterprise-level, profit-seeking initiatives with macrolevel economic growth. Because the legal framework in the United States emerged from a deep colonial history and continued to evolve at the state level throughout the nineteenth century, there is institutional variety across space and time and, in some places, exceptionally detailed enterprise-level data. This history, in turn, provides ample opportunity to study institutions, their evolution, and their ramifications for business organization and performance.

It is this historical context that motivated our conference. To be sure, the issues sketched above are hardly undiscovered territory. American economic historians have written extensively about the history of business law and business enterprise; changes in the scale of production in manufacturing; the shift of labor out of small scale, family agriculture and its implications for aggregate labor productivity growth; the evolution of banking and capital markets; and many related issues, such as growth of government regulation. No single volume can hope to cover all of these topics in depth or provide a comprehensive overview of all the relevant economic history literature.[5] Indeed, that is not what we are attempting to accomplish in this volume of research papers. Rather, the authors whose work appears in this volume have made important contributions to the economic history of American enterprise in their prior scholarship, and all have current research projects that engage key features of this history. The conference, therefore, provided a convenient and productive association of scholars—an enterprise, if you will—in which to take stock of ongoing work, to exchange knowledge and ideas that could further advance their research, and to find parallels and complementarities in each other's projects.

Volume Summary

The volume is organized into three sections: Business Organization and Internal Governance, Bank Behavior and Credit Markets, and Scale Economies in Nineteenth-Century Production. We summarize each chapter below and highlight connections among them. Since each chapter represents new

---

5. Readers seeking a broad historical overview of some of these themes may consult Neal and Williamson (2014).

and original research, we do not expect them to dovetail with one another seamlessly. Instead, they provide multiple, often overlapping, perspectives on the organization and operation of "enterprise" during the period of American economic ascendancy.

Section I: Business Organization and Internal Governance

Section I consists of three chapters that focus on the economic history of business organization and internal firm governance. Chapter 1, by Naomi R. Lamoreaux, examines the evolution of law governing the formation of business enterprises in the nineteenth century. Chapter 2, by Eric Hilt, studies how the corporate form of business organization diffused among manufacturing establishments during the second half of the nineteenth century. Chapter 3, by Howard Bodenhorn and Eugene N. White, studies changes over time in the corporate governance of New York state banks.

In a series of important articles and books Lamoreaux (see the citations in her chapter) has explored, solely and with collaborators, the evolution of the legal frameworks governing the types of organizational forms that businesses could adopt in the United States and Europe. These frameworks circumscribed many of the specific features of the enterprises, conferring on them certain rights and privileges that, when necessary, could be defended in a court of law—that is, rights and privileges analogous to, if different from, those enjoyed by actual persons. Broadly speaking, the constraints imposed by the legal framework set the menu of organizational forms that could be legally adopted and also the extent to which the forms might be modified contractually to suit the special needs of the parties.

It is a stylized fact of modern economics that the economies of countries whose legal frameworks originated in the common law seem to have performed better in the long run than those whose legal frameworks originated in civil code as evidenced, for example, by cross-country growth regressions. This would include those aspects of the frameworks governing organizational form in business. Under common law, for example, one might suppose that the available organizational forms provided for more contractual flexibility than under civil law, which was more rigid, and that contractual flexibility was growth enhancing.

In cross-country regressions, common-law countries are usually grouped together, and the difference in long-run performance is measured by the coefficient of the common law dummy variable. Yet a crude categorization of this nature may obscure more than it reveals if there are consequential differences in legal frameworks within groups. Lamoreaux argues that the United States and Great Britain are examples of highly successful common law countries that, nevertheless, diverged significantly in the evolution of the legal framework governing business organizational form. These differences did not arise because of differences in geography, climate, or other "fundamentals," but rather in politics. Specifically, suffrage was more inclusive earlier in the United States than in Great Britain and the widening of the electorate materially influenced the evolution of law governing business organizational forms. Broadly speaking, laws were more restrictive in allowable forms and in the flexibility permitted to parties to contractually modify these forms in the United States than in Great Britain. The historical evolution of the relevant law in both countries follows the give and take of democratic politics, and careful attention to the politics provides essential insights into the behavior of voters, legislatures, lobbyists, and others regarding tensions between equity and efficiency.

Lamoreaux begins by noting that Americans in the early nineteenth century wanted "progress" and knew that individuals alone generally could not make it happen. Rather, progress depended on profit-seeking associations of individuals, but such enterprises would not be formed unless the parties to them were conferred certain legal rights and privileges. No one would invest capital in an enterprise, for example, if someone else could abscond with the investment with impunity. Yet at the same time, Americans were keenly aware that conferring such rights and privileges generally and easily to a fictional business "person" under the law might lead to abuses and an undue concentration of economic power and wealth. The most important example is the corporation, with its characteristic of limited liability. On the one hand, corporations might be able to undertake large-scale infrastructure projects or production, allowing the public to benefit and investors or shareholders to reap profit. But what might happen if the enterprise became too large or too powerful, or if the investors were unable to monitor effectively the actions of the managers and employees? The tensions between efficiency (the desire for business to be of optimal size and structure) versus equity (the desire that the "moneyed elite" not become too powerful) sharpened during the nineteenth century as the transportation revolution opened up new lands and economic opportunities and as technological change increased the optimal scale of production, particularly in manufacturing.

Lamoreaux illustrates this point through a detailed examination of the historical process by which one state, Pennsylvania, modified its incorporation statutes over the nineteenth century. Corporations were a "hot button issue" in Pennsylvania in the late eighteenth and early nineteenth centuries. As in other states at the time, only special charter of the legislature could create corporations in Pennsylvania. From the standpoint of those wishing to form a corporation, securing a charter was a costly and protracted endeavor. Pennsylvanians who were wary of the corporate form approved of the restricted supply but were also keenly aware that those who were granted corporate charters might wish to protect their privileges, for example, by insisting on monopoly power or campaigning against new charters, and hence competition, in the same industry.

These concerns came to the fore during the constitutional convention held in Pennsylvania in 1837, a time of general financial crisis in the country.

Some delegates wished to impose severe restrictions on existing corporations and the ability to form new entities, but they faced opposition from those believing that such restrictions would be an infringement on property rights and a drag on economic development. In the end, the convention adopted additional restrictions on the length of charters for banks and gave the legislature the power to modify or abrogate existing charters under specified conditions. Other than these, the convention did not restrict the ability of the legislature to issue charters, but neither did it take the additional step of passing a general incorporation law. The legislature did begin passing laws pertaining to certain industries and economic activities.[6] Enacting a chapter every time a corporation wished to be set up was costly not only for those wishing to incorporate but also for the legislature. The industry-specific laws relaxed some of this pressure and also provided experience in drafting legislation. But the laws were still very restrictive, so much so that prospective incorporators continued to seek special charters, again prompting charges that the legislature was granting special favors and advantages. Another convention was held in 1872–1873, leading eventually to the replacement of special charters with the adoption of a general incorporation statute in 1874.

Title notwithstanding, the general incorporation law pertained only to specific activities and imposed restrictions on liability and governance structure. Those delegates desiring greater flexibility, however, fashioned a way out with an 1874 statute permitting a type of limited partnership similar in some ways to a modern limited liability corporation (LLC). But the limited partnership was still subject to various restrictions, and it took time for the courts to sort out the implications for partner liabilities under the new form. When this happened in the 1890s, the form was initially popular, but enthusiasm quickly waned. This was the era of the first great merger wave in American industry, and states such as Delaware began to compete to have companies incorporate within their boundaries, finding the fees to be a profitable source of revenue, or what Lamoreaux calls "corporate charter mongering."

The upshot of Lamoreaux's narrative is that the history of law governing business organization in Pennsylvania seems hardly to be a tale of "efficient" institutional change. Rather, it is a tale where politics took center stage. Politics continued to play an important role in shaping the law's evolution well into the twentieth century, so much so that British observers in the 1950s marveled at the apparent inflexibility of American corporation law, which the British treated as the province of contractual negotiation between the parties. However, as Lamoreaux goes on to show, the history of British "laissez-faire" policy toward business organization is full of examples of company charters written in ways that rewarded self-dealing, duplicity, and other "bad" behavior difficult for outsiders to observe, let alone police.

---

6. In manufacturing these were first passed in 1849, and in banking in 1860.

When universal suffrage was finally extended in Britain in the early twentieth century, British corporation law began to be more favorable to the interests of shareholders and other stakeholders, such as employees.

The implications of Lamoreaux's argument are striking. On the one hand, it is easy to imagine that the roadblocks to forming business entities in Pennsylvania in the nineteenth century might have prevented or diverted elsewhere some worthwhile corporate investment, with consequences for growth and development. As the chapter by Eric Hilt (chapter 2, this volume, see the discussion below) shows, the corporate form was used more frequently by large-scale, capital-intensive enterprises. On the other hand, it is difficult to argue with the evidence of corporate abuses in Britain that Lamoreaux and her collaborators have uncovered. It is conceivable, in other words, that the more restrictive nature of American law in the nineteenth century was more protective of shareholder rights and, therefore, encouraged greater investment and growth.

The struggles in the Pennsylvania legislature over the statutory treatment of business organization played out in other northeastern states at the same time and against the same backdrop of industrialization. If manufacturing establishments had remained tiny, as they were at the start of the nineteenth century, then the history of incorporation law might have played out very differently. But this was not to be because the growth of the manufacturing sector was associated with dramatic changes in the distribution of firm sizes and in production methods. Manufacturing firms, on average, became much larger and more capital intensive, especially after the development of steam power and (late in the century) electricity, primarily as a result of growth among the largest enterprises.

Larger, more capital-intensive firms had greater financing needs and more difficult problems of internal governance to solve. Economic historians believe that the corporate form helped in both respects and that the diffusion of the form must have been positively related to size and capital intensity. In this regard, the prevailing wisdom is heavily influenced by the classic study by Berle and Means (1932), which pointed to the fundamental corporate governance issue of "ownership versus control." In the modern corporation, which Berle and Means asserted emerged around the turn of the twentieth century, ownership is widely dispersed among passive investors, and decisions are instead made by managers whose incentives are not necessarily aligned with shareholders.

Economic historians have long been aware of counter examples to the timing cited by Berle and Means, especially among the large textile firms in New England that incorporated early and also made early use of equity financing. However, as Eric Hilt emphasizes in chapter 2, the broader economic history of incorporation is not as well documented or understood as it should be. Hilt's chapter takes an important step forward by analyzing a novel source of data, so-called "certificates of condition," which recorded the nature of firm ownership, lists of stockholders and directors, and certain accounting data. Beginning in the 1870s, Massachusetts required all business enterprises in the state to submit these certificates annually. Hilt analyzes the extant certificates for 1875, a year in which Massachusetts also conducted an industrial census, which provides useful correlates for an empirical study of variation in the use of the corporate form.

Hilt's analysis is in three parts. In the first part, he uses business directories to classify establishments listed in the certificates into the industrial categories used in the 1875 Massachusetts census. Because the census reported the total number of establishments by industry and other industry characteristics, Hilt is able to compute incorporation rates by industry and explore correlations between incorporation rates and average establishment characteristics. Although the sample sizes are small, he shows that incorporation rates were higher in industries with larger establishments, measured either by capital or total employees. He also demonstrates that industries that utilized more steam power, unskilled labor, and fixed capital had higher incorporation rates. These characteristics are associated with factory production, and the patterns suggest that the growth of the factory system and incorporation were closely tied, at least in Massachusetts.

Next, Hilt examines more closely the ownership and governance patterns among corporations. He looks first at textile firms listed on the Boston Stock Exchange, finding that ownership was typically dispersed across passive investors and that day-to-day operations were under the control of hired managers (rather than the owners per se). The textile firms were unusual, however, and the typical manufacturing firm had relatively few shareholders and a high degree of ownership among those operating and managing the business. Turning to the determinants of ownership structure, Hilt finds a positive association between establishment size and the degree to which establishments were widely held. Conditional on size, establishments with characteristics that are associated with factory production had more concentrated ownership. Hilt argues that in Massachusetts, "incorporators and investors responded to the challenges posed by the complex role performed by managers" and engaged in factory production by establishing "adequate ownership incentives to monitor and supervise management."

The issues of organizational form and corporate governance were hardly confined to the growing industrial sector of the American economy in the nineteenth century. If anything, they were more important in the financial sector because from time to time—indeed, to our present day—problems in banks had a way of spilling over powerfully to the rest of the economy, causing financial panics and economic downturns. Yet, economic historians know more about the long-term evolution of governance in the nonfinancial sector than in the financial sector.

In chapter 3, Howard Bodenhorn and Eugene N. White take a step toward remedying this deficiency by presenting a first look at a large, new body of archival evidence on the changes in bank governance over time. The evidence pertains to the state of New York, which required banks to file detailed "articles of association" describing their governance features, such as the time and place of shareholder meetings, shareholder voting rights, and many others. Some of these features are also found in the "certificates of condition" analyzed by Hilt. Bodenhorn and White's analysis uses a sample of the surviving articles for state-chartered banks in New York beginning in 1838 in conjunction with two other sources of information: the annual reports of New York's Bank Superintendent and city directories for New York City, Albany, Buffalo, and Rochester, which provide lists of banks and their directors.

Bodenhorn and White begin their analysis with an overview of the key legislative changes in New York banking history. This provides a broad dating of regime shifts in banking regulation: the eras of chartered banking (1789–1837), free banking (1838–1863), the National Banking System (1864–1913), the early Federal Reserve (1914–1933), New Deal banking (1934–1970s), and the current period (1970s to the present). They use this taxonomy as a frame of reference for their analysis of two features of bank governance: separation of ownership from control, and the size of the board. They report two key preliminary findings. First, during both the free banking and National Banking System eras, bank directors tended to hold a large fraction of bank shares, considerably more than was required by law. In effect, the bank managers must have had a significant fraction of their personal portfolios at stake, which, in Bodenhorn and White's view, properly incentivized their behavior. Ownership and control, in other words, were effectively the same in New York's banks throughout the long nineteenth century.

Second, Bodenhorn and White observed a decline over time in the size of bank boards. While some of this decline can be attributed to an "aging" process within each bank—the longer that a bank was in business, the smaller was its board—a significant portion appears to have been a long-term trend in the banking sector. They suggest that some of this decline may reflect changes in the composition of the boards and the degree of specialization of their members, but they also speculate that regime shifts in bank regulation played a role. It remains for future research to parse out the relative contributions of changes in banking practice versus regulation, as well as the implications for economic performance of the decrease in board size.

Section II: Bank Behavior and Credit Markets

The middle section of the volume presents two chapters that make use of geographic information to study bank behavior and the evolution of capital markets. Both chapters develop and analyze new, richly detailed data sources. Chapter 4, by Jeremy Atack, Matthew S. Jaremski, and Peter L. Rousseau, studies how bank behavior and stability responded to the spread of the transportation network before the Civil War. Chapter 5, by Mary Eschelbach Hansen, uses microlevel data drawn from bankruptcy records to characterize credit market relationships in the 1930s, including the physical distance between borrowers and creditors.

By passing laws to regulate organizational form and internal governance, states could hope to influence the economic behavior of businesses and banks in ways that would promote economic growth and the efficient allocation of resources. Economically virtuous behavior, however, might also have arisen endogenously in response to technological and other nonstatutory changes associated with economic growth and development. One possible causal linkage of this sort involves the so-called "transportation revolution." Starting well before the Civil War, the United States developed a geographically dispersed network of inland waterways and railroads that profoundly and permanently shaped the pace and pattern of economic activity. Although there is a long tradition in economic history of studying the aggregate resource-saving effects of transport innovations, it is only recently that economic historians and other scholars have been able to study other types of impacts, making use of detailed information on transportation access at a disaggregated level. This has been made possible by the development of geographic information systems (GIS) software that permits the construction of statistical databases embodying complex spatial relationships from digitized historical maps and other sources with spatial information. These databases can then be linked to other historical databases with information on local economic characteristics and outcomes, typically at the county level.

Atack (2013) has been a pioneer in the application of GIS methods to the construction of county-level databases that document the spread of the transportation infrastructure in the nineteenth-century United States. Atack's databases have been used to study the county-level effects of gaining rail access on population density and the rate of urbanization (Atack et al. 2010); the proportion of establishments meeting a definition of "factory" status (Atack, Haines, and Margo 2011); per-acre land values in agriculture, agricultural improvements, and the rate of landownership (Atack and Margo 2011, 2012); and other aspects of the transportation revolution (Donaldson and Hornbeck 2013).

In chapter 4, Atack, Jaremski, and Rousseau consider the intriguing possibility that better transportation, specifically railroad access, led to improved bank stability and performance before the Civil War. The point of departure for their analysis is the observation that antebellum banks did business by issuing bank notes. The notes were redeemable for their face value at the issuing bank, and states required banks to hold collateral equal to the notes' value. Until they were redeemed, those bank notes also functioned as a medium of exchange, usually trading at a discount that, among other factors, varied with transportation costs to the issuing bank.

Atack, Jaremski, and Rousseau further point out that monitoring of bank behavior by regulators during the antebellum period appears to have been much looser than today, and the incentives of bankers did not necessarily align with their liability holders. This led to unsound practices known as "wildcat banking" in the colorful language of the period. As a consequence, banks would sometimes fail, meaning that they were unable to redeem their notes.

The authors posit two reasons why an improved transportation network might have reduced bank failure rates. First, better transportation might generate greater local economic activity, leading to higher bank loan rates, profits, and possibly, more diversified loan portfolios. Second, improved transportation might make it easier and less costly for a bank's customers to redeem their notes, and more generally, increase the effective monitoring of the bank to the extent that transportation improvements facilitated access to information about bank activities. Of course, it is possible that a correlation between proximity to transportation and bank stability is merely a reflection of other factors. For instance, there could be selection across locations such that less scrupulous bankers might have gone to the frontier where they could operate more freely (that is, with less scrutiny) while more honest bankers might have gone to settled areas that happened to be served by railroads or navigable waterways.

To explore these hypotheses, Atack, Jaremski, and Rousseau assemble a remarkable panel data set that links information on individual-level banks with information on the diffusion of the railroad system over time. The authors know the location of each bank, and so they are able to measure its distance from the nearest improved means of transportation (steamboat-navigable river, canal, or railroad). Their primary interest is in the effect of the railroad specifically, and so availability of other means of transportation acts as a control variable in their analysis. Crucially, the information is available at sufficient frequency that they are able to observe banks in operation prior to the arrival of a railroad in an area as well as banks that entered after the railroad's arrival. The authors also observe a number of indicators of bank performance and balance sheet-type variables. In particular, they are able to observe bank failures, defined to occur when banks were not able to redeem notes at full value.

The chapter contains two main econometric analyses. The first uses hazard models to study the factors associated with bank failure. The main finding is that proximity to a railroad is associated with a statistically significant, reduced likelihood of bank failure. The negative association between bank failure and rail access is shown to be robust to a number of modifications to the base sample, such as restricting the sample to banks that were present prior to the arrival of a railroad. The negative association between failure and transportation is observed only for railroads, not for inland waterways like navigable rivers or canals. The hazard model analysis reveals that the negative association of bank failure and railroad proximity is reduced when county-level controls for economic characteristics (for example, population or urbanization) or bank balance sheet variables are included, but the estimated effect remains negative and significant.

In the second main analysis, the authors estimate regressions relating bank characteristics to rail access. While not definitive, the results suggest that some of the lower failure rates can be attributed to the effect of railroads on local economic activity, which banks responded to in ways that made them less vulnerable. The authors find suggestive evidence that, after the arrival of a railroad in close proximity, banks reduced excess reserves, the number of notes in circulation and their bond holdings, and increased their loan/asset ratios relative to other banks in the same area that were not as physically proximate to rail service. The authors interpret decreased note circulation as consistent with a "presumed increase in the ease and likelihood that notes would be presented for payment when the railroad made travel easier and faster." Overall, they conclude that, "railroads seem to [have] lowered failure rates by encouraging banks to operate more safely through increased loan as well as lowered bond holdings and circulation." While further research will be necessary to pin down the precise causal mechanisms behind the apparent impact of rail access, an important implication of Atack, Jaremski, and Rousseau's chapter is that by improving the stability of the banking system, the railroad encouraged economic development in ways that are not reflected in traditional measures of the social savings of the rail network (Fogel 1964; Fishlow 1965).

Banks were but one component of a wide variety of organizations that made up the American credit market as the economy grew in the nineteenth and into the twentieth century. Economic historians have studied the evolution of the structure of this market (for example, the varying mix of different types of financial institutions) and its efficiency at allocating resources between competing uses as measured by interest rate differentials. One set of competing uses concerns geography and, specifically, interest rate differences across regions (Davis 1965; Bodenhorn and Rockoff 1992). Such differences are important because the United States economy and its frontier expanded westward from the eastern seaboard, and any impediments to capital mobility could slow the extension of economic activity. Economic historians have established that interest rate differentials narrowed across regions as improvements in transportation and communications increased the information available to financial intermediaries and enabled arbitrage to take place. However, another set of competing uses involves sectors, such as manufacturing versus the agricultural or service sector. Differences in rates of return between sectors were large in the late nineteenth and early twentieth centuries, suggesting that capital did not flow as freely as it might have between sectors (Atack, Bateman, and Weiss 1982). Differences across sectors are important because a central feature of American development has been a relentless shift of resources out of agriculture and into other sectors.

In chapter 5, Mary Eschelbach Hansen takes a fresh look at these differences across sectors using as her lens a large sample of archival records of bankruptcies filed under federal law, a source of exceptionally detailed data that has received only limited attention from economic or financial historians. It has long been known that these records, which date back to the late nineteenth century when the first permanent bankruptcy law was passed, provide remarkable details on borrowers, creditors, and their loan arrangements. Hansen's project involves collecting and digitizing a sample of the extant bankruptcy records. Although the project is still at a relatively early stage, her chapter illustrates the promise of these records and provides substantive new insights into differences in credit relationships across sectors.

Hansen focuses her attention on the experience of one state, Mississippi, over the period 1929 to 1936. A general concern with using bankruptcy filings is their representativeness of the population of borrowers (or potential lack thereof) and, therefore, our ability to generalize on the basis of evidence drawn from such records. Individuals or businesses who file for bankruptcy are unlikely to be a random sample of borrowers, and their creditors may also differ systematically from the relevant population. Such concerns are mitigated to the extent that bankruptcies arise from bad luck as opposed to strategic behavior, which is more likely during an economic downturn such as the Great Depression. As Hansen shows in an illuminating comparison using aggregate data for Mississippi from R. G. Dun and Company for 1929 and 1931, her sample of 780 bankruptcy files looks similar to all Mississippi firms covered by Dun with respect to industry and size.

Hansen begins her chapter with a succinct overview of what economic historians believe to be the evolution of capital markets in the nineteenth and early twentieth centuries. As she points out, it is believed that banks during this period did little in the way of direct lending to manufacturers. Instead, capital needs for manufacturing were met through the formation of organizational structures that facilitated investment from private individuals and related sources, or from retained earnings. Banks did play an important role through the emergence of a national market in trade credit and bankers acceptances (short-term debt issued by a firm and backed by a bank). Merchants also played key roles through the extension of trade credit on book account. By the late nineteenth and early twentieth centuries, banks and related financial entities began lending directly to consumers and to large businesses, but it was not until after World War II that commercial lending to small- and medium-sized businesses became common. Although much of the lending that took place was local, it is thought that the distances between borrowers and creditors grew over time.

The general contours of this evolution are known, but documenting the frequency and magnitude of credit relationships has been difficult because it requires detailed knowledge of the borrowers and lenders. Hansen's approach can advance our knowledge because the information included in the bankruptcy filings is so detailed that she can study the type of loans (for example, trade credit), the amounts involved and purpose, the characteristics of the creditors and borrower, and their location. She finds that a solid majority of bankruptcy filings in her sample pertain to business enterprises (60 percent; see her table 5.1), and the overwhelming majority of debts were owed to commercial lenders, though their relative importance depends on whether the count of debts is weighted by their value.[7] The data also show that manufacturers in the 1930s rarely incurred debt from financial institutions and that long-distance credit was far from uncommon. Long-distance credit was more common than average among merchants, however, than was the case for manufacturers.

Although the generality of Hansen's quantitative findings remains to be established, her preliminary results are broadly consistent with previous beliefs about the evolution of American capital markets. She points out that, for the most part, financial institutions did not facilitate production by lending directly to manufacturers, but rather did so indirectly through the consumer and wholesale credit channels. Credit expansion, in turn, fueled demand, providing incentives to capture economies of scale in production.

Section III: Scale Economies in Nineteenth-Century Production

The final two chapters study economies of scale in production in the nineteenth century.[8] Chapter 6, by Robert A. Margo, addresses manufacturing, and chapter 7, by Alan L. Olmstead and Paul W. Rhode, examines agriculture.

Industrialization was an important driver of economic growth in the nineteenth-century United States. It had its roots in New England but spread to the rest of the nation by the late antebellum period. Productivity growth in manufacturing was so rapid that by the late nineteenth century, American manufacturing workers were more productive than their counterparts in Europe, where the Industrial Revolution began. Coinciding with the growth of manufacturing was a shift in production from small to large establishments, that is, from "artisan shops" to "factories" (Chandler 1977). According to the conventional view among economic historians, factories enjoyed a productivity advantage over artisan shops through the exploita-

7. Nearly three-quarters of all recorded debts were to commercial businesses, but the average value per debt owed to commercial businesses was relatively small, such that only one-third of debts weighted by value were owed to commercial businesses (table 5.2).

8. Our use of the term "economies of scale" is standard: a disproportionate increase in output that occurs when the size of the enterprise grows. Economies of scale are realized typically through greater division of labor or, alternatively, capital equipment (for example, powered machinery) that is "lumpy"—use of the equipment cannot be scaled down so the enterprise needs to be a certain size before it can be profitably employed.

tion of economies of scale achieved through division of labor and mechanization. In turn, the shift toward larger-scale production was facilitated by legal changes that made it easier for establishments to incorporate (see chapter 1 by Lamoreaux and chapter 2 by Hilt); improvements in the functioning of the financial system (as discussed in chapter 3 by Bodenhorn and White and chapter 4 by Atack, Jaremski, and Rousseau), which helped support industrial expansion (Rousseau and Sylla 2005); improvements in transportation that created incentives to expand production and, therefore, implement division of labor and mechanization (Atack, Haines, and Margo 2011); and the development and diffusion of steam power, which provided an expandable source of power and surpassed the productivity gains achievable though division of labor alone (Atack, Bateman, and Margo 2008).

For some economists, the mere shift toward larger-scale production in manufacturing is tantamount to evidence of economies of scale in some form. However, alternative explanations are possible, and even taking the shift at face value one cannot quantify its importance as an explanatory factor in aggregate productivity growth without first measuring the difference in the level of productivity between small and large manufacturing establishments.

In this context, many economic historians cite and teach an iconic paper by Kenneth Sokoloff (1984) as evidence in favor of the conventional wisdom that larger manufacturing establishments were more productive than smaller establishments. Using samples of establishment-level data from the 1820 and 1850 censuses of manufacturing, Sokoloff presented econometric estimates of economies of scale from production functions. His results reveal economies of scale for "nonmechanized" establishments that relied entirely on hand power rather than steam or water power. The interpretation of this result is that such firms must have been able to capture scale economies through the division of labor alone.

A crucial feature of Sokoloff's analysis is an adjustment he made for a specific measurement problem in the original census data—the alleged underreporting of the labor input provided by the establishment's owner or owners. This issue is critical because the labor input of owners was a larger fraction of the total labor input in small establishments than in large establishments. In very small shops, the owner might be the only worker (a sole proprietor) or might work alongside an apprentice or two. In a somewhat larger establishment, the owner (or owners) might eschew production work and instead concentrate on management, marketing, record keeping, or other nonproduction tasks. If the firm was large enough, such as the textile mills studied by Hilt in his chapter, the owners might have little or no involvement directly in production or nonproduction activities. That is, hired employees provided labor of every type. In effect, Sokoloff was arguing that the early censuses of manufacturing did a good job of counting the number of hired employees but systematically ignored the labor input of owners. If this argument is correct, then labor productivity in small establishments, as measured by the census, would be biased upward relative to large establishments, possibly masking the presence of economies of scale. Sokoloff solved this problem by devising protocols to impute the labor input of owners in 1820 and 1850. The protocol for 1850 was particularly simple—he added one to the count of workers.

Although Sokoloff did not investigate economies of scale for years after 1850, the measurement of the "entrepreneurial" or owner's labor input is still germane because it was not until 1890 that the federal census included separate questions on production and nonproduction workers. In chapter 6, Robert A. Margo explores the implications of this particular measurement issue using the Atack and Bateman (1999) samples of the 1850 to 1880 censuses of manufacturing. Margo first demonstrates that parametric estimates of economies of scale for these census years are "knife-edge" with respect to the measurement issue raised by Sokoloff and his proposed solution to the problem. That is, if Sokoloff's solution for imputing the labor of owners is implemented, then there is evidence of broad-based economies of scale in manufacturing between 1850 and 1880, including nonmechanized establishments, but if the imputation is not adopted, there is no such evidence.

Next, Margo assesses the textual and statistical distribution evidence bearing on Sokoloff's claim that the censuses undercounted the labor input of owners. Margo shows first that the census recognized the issue in its formal instructions to enumerators, specifying the conditions under which the owner was to be included in the count of workers.[9] Margo also argues that if the owner's input were not counted routinely there should be considerable numbers of establishments reporting zero employees in the Atack-Bateman samples because sole proprietorships were very common at the time; however, the number of such establishments is very small. Contrary to Sokoloff, Margo concludes that, by and large, the census did count the labor input of owners when it was supposed to do so.

That said, Margo also shows that the labor input, as measured by the census, was underreported in small establishments for a reason entirely different from that asserted by Sokoloff. This bias arises because the labor input in the nineteenth-century manufacturing censuses refers to the number of workers present during a typical day of operation, not a literal (or true) average. However, throughout the year manufacturing establishments would add or shed workers to meet temporary production needs. For larger establishments, the distribution of workers employed on any given day appears to have been more or less symmetric around the typical number, whereas for small establishments, it is right-skewed. Correcting for this problem does lower the measured labor productivity in smaller establishments relative

---

9. The condition was that the labor input of owners was sufficiently frequent and large enough for the owner to be considered part of the work force present on a typical day of operation.

to larger ones, but the correction is much smaller in magnitude than that implied by Sokoloff's imputation. Margo demonstrates these points by using unpublished data collected by the 1880 census and argues that it is plausible that his findings apply to earlier census years because the census questions on employment in manufacturing were fundamentally similar across years.

One might be tempted to read Margo's findings as showing that the smallest manufacturing establishments were more productive than previously thought and, therefore, worthy of more careful scrutiny by economic historians. As Margo notes, while this avenue is worth pursuing, it seems more likely that the consensus view is still correct, but the nineteenth-century manufacturing censuses are simply not well suited to the parametric estimation of scale economies. To address the measurement issue, therefore, sources of data with more detailed information on production and input use than the census are needed to assess the productivity implications of the shift to large-scale production (see Griliches and Ringstad [1971] for a similar argument for twentieth-century data). Indeed, in ongoing work Atack, Margo, and Rhode (2014) are examining one such alternative source, a large-scale study conducted by the US Bureau of Labor Statistics in the 1890s that collected data on hand production and mechanized (machine) production of very specific goods. Their preliminary work shows strong and robust evidence that larger firms were, indeed, more productive than smaller firms, and that both division of labor and powered machinery explain the productivity differential with respect to establishment size.

To this point the volume has primarily focused on the nonfarm sector of the American economy, yet farms were the most ubiquitous form of American enterprise in the nineteenth century. Most, as we noted earlier, were small, family-run operations, using hired labor only occasionally (for example, the harvest) or if no family members were available. To be sure, the family farm had its share of internal governance problems and needs for external finance, but these were quite different from industrial enterprises. Economic historians believe that, for the most part, scale economies in nineteenth-century agriculture were either nonexistent or else exhausted at quite low levels of output (and by extension, number of workers). Substantial scale economies in farm production and the rise of corporate agriculture came in the twentieth century, for the most part after World War II.

The most important and perhaps the only exception to the above characterization was the slave plantation in the antebellum South. These were among the largest and most sophisticated businesses of their time. According to Fogel and Engerman (1974; see also Fogel 1989), plantations enjoyed substantial economies of scale that came about, in part, through the use of the so-called gang system. In Fogel and Engerman's view, the gang system involved division of labor, but instead of taking place on the shop floor, it took place in the field. The evidence for economies of scale derives from extensive and detailed (and controversial to some) econometric analysis of the so-called Parker-Gallman sample, which provides evidence on outputs and inputs for approximately 5,000 free and slave farms on the eve of the Civil War.

Fogel and Engerman were not the first to address the issue of economies of scale in slave agriculture. Rather they took as their starting point an extensive literature in history that viewed the antebellum plantation as "factories in the field" (see, for example, Stampp 1956). But is this metaphor justified and, by inference, is there support for Fogel and Engerman's explanation for the slave productivity advantage? In chapter 7, Alan L. Olmstead and Paul W. Rhode take the "factories in the fields" analogy at face value and then dig deeper into a wide range of historical sources to see whether the supposed similarities hold up under closer scrutiny. Collections of data from nineteenth-century census manuscripts—the Parker-Gallman sample of southern farms, the Bateman-Foust sample of northern farms, and the Atack-Bateman samples of manufacturing establishments—form the basis for their quantitative comparisons of the inputs and outputs of farms and factories. They also draw from a variety of primary and secondary sources, including a fresh reading of surviving plantation records, to characterize the operation of antebellum cotton plantations, to compare and contrast their management and operation with that of contemporary factories, and to challenge some influential descriptions of cotton production under slavery.

Olmstead and Rhode's conclusions are mixed. In some respects, such as their use of professional managers, relatively large labor forces, and share of output, plantations were similar to factories, or at least were more similar to factories than to family farms in the North. But in many other respects, including methods of production or the comparison of slaves to machinery, plantations were fundamentally different from factories. The analogy between plantations and factories, it would appear, served the rhetorical purposes of the historians who introduced it, and subsequently those of economic historians studying the relative efficiency of slave agriculture (Fogel and Engerman 1974). However, Olmstead and Rhode argue that the analogy obscures more than it reveals and is, in any case, misleading as an organizing principle in studying the economics of American slavery. Within agriculture, and certainly between agriculture and manufacturing, enterprises varied greatly in their design and operation so as to maximize profit while producing fundamentally different goods under widely different environmental and institutional conditions (for example, with and without slaves). The variety and flexibility of enterprises defy easy analogies made across sectors, such as "factories in the fields."

Concluding Remarks and Suggestions for Further Research

In summary, the chapters in this volume make contributions to the scholarly literature in three areas. The first is the economic history of corporate governance. Lamoreaux (chapter 1) shows that the process by which state law pertaining to business organization came into being was long and protracted, reflecting fundamental and persistent trade-offs between equity and efficiency concerns. Hilt (chapter 2) shows that the diffusion of the corporate form was connected to the spread of mechanized (steam) factory production in manufacturing. Bodenhorn and White (chapter 3) document how various features of internal governance changed over time in American banking, using New York as a case study.

Second, the volume contributes to the literature on the historical behavior of financial enterprises and the growth of credit markets. Atack, Jaremeski, and Rousseau (chapter 4) show that the diffusion of the rail network, one of the central technological and infrastructure improvements of the nineteenth century, appears to have contributed to a better functioning and more stable banking system, an important external economy of the transportation revolution. This chapter also demonstrates that the internal behavior of enterprise (banks in this case) could be shaped by external forces other than just legislation and regulation. Hansen's pioneering and creative use of bankruptcy records (chapter 5) shows that, even in a place as remote as Mississippi in the 1930s, long-distance debtor-creditor relationships existed. For the key sector of manufacturing, however, the use of long-distance credit networks was relatively uncommon and relatively few loans originated from banks.

Third, the volume contributes to the literature on scale economies in production in the nineteenth century. In the case of manufacturing, the incentive to reap profit by exploiting scale economies was surely a major impetus behind the evolution of state legislation on incorporation; as Hilt shows, the corporate form was adopted disproportionately in industries with larger than average size and greater use of steam power. Robert A. Margo (chapter 6) revisits the analysis of the key evidentiary bases for prior studies of economies of scale in nineteenth-century manufacturing, the federal censuses, shows that the evidence from this source is fragile, and suggests that economic historians need to look elsewhere to bolster the conventional wisdom. Alan L. Olmstead and Paul W. Rhode (chapter 7) revisit another iconic example of scale in the nineteenth century, large slave plantations. They show that analogies to factory production, so-called "factories in the field," are not particularly helpful in understanding how these historically important enterprises operated.

A book of this nature, consisting of original research papers on a diverse but clearly related set of topics, cannot attempt to review and synthesize the literature on all aspects of American economic enterprise. It does attempt to provide multifaceted and interconnected accounts of how businesses, banks, and credit markets promoted the transformation of the American economy through the lens of how these enterprises were organized and operated. In this sense, the studies presented here and others like them illuminate a layer of economic history that rests beneath more than the abstract aggregates of macroeconomic growth accounting. Many opportunities for future research could build upon the studies that comprise this volume. For instance, our understanding of the political economy of incorporation statutes would be enhanced by additional case studies beyond Lamoreaux's investigation of Pennsylvania. Economic historians have much to learn about the causal effects of the organizational innovations elucidated by Hilt and by Bodenhorn and White in their investigations of manufacturing firms and banks, respectively. Atack, Jaremski, and Rousseau's exploration of the impact of the diffusion of railroads on the stability of the banking system raises the obvious question as to whether later technological innovations had similar or very different effects. Hansen's fascinating window on what one can learn about creditors and borrowers from bankruptcy records begs to be extended to a broader geography and to other economic times. Finding out precisely how and why production differed in small versus large enterprises in the nineteenth century, be it in manufacturing (Margo) or agriculture (Olmstead and Rhode), requires that economic historians bring new data and methods of analysis to the table. In all cases, further excavation of the history of American enterprise promises to yield a better understanding of the origins, distinctive and otherwise, of American economic development.

References

Atack, Jeremy. 2013. "On the Use of Geographic Information Systems in Economic History: The American Transportation Revolution Revisited." *Journal of Economic History* 73:313–38.

Atack, Jeremy, and Fred Bateman. 1999. "Nineteenth-Century American Industrial Development through the Eyes of the Census of Manufactures: A New Resource for Historical Research." *Historical Methods* 32:177–88.

———. 2006. "Manufacturing." In *Historical Statistics of the United States*, vol. 4, edited by S. B. Carter, S. S. Gartner, M. R. Haines, A. L. Olmstead, R. Sutch, and G. Wright, 573–78. New York: Cambridge University Press.

Atack, Jeremy, Fred Bateman, Michael Haines, and Robert A. Margo. 2010. "Did Railroads Induce or Follow Economic Growth? Urbanization and Population Growth in the American Midwest, 1850–1860." *Social Science History* 34:171–97.

Atack, Jeremy, Fred Bateman, and Robert A. Margo. 2008. "Steam Power, Establishment Size, and Labor Productivity in Nineteenth-Century American Manufacturing." *Explorations in Economic History* 45:185–98.

Atack, Jeremy, Fred Bateman, and Thomas Weiss. 1982. "Risk, the Rate of Return, and the Pattern of Investment in Nineteenth-Century Manufacturing." *Southern Economic Journal* 49:150–63.

Atack, Jeremy, Michael Haines, and Robert A. Margo. 2011. "Railroads and the Rise of the Factory: Evidence for the United States, 1850–1870." In *Economic Evolution and Revolution in Historical Time*, edited by P. Rhode, J. Rosenbloom, and D. Weiman, 162–79. Palo Alto, CA: Stanford University Press.

Atack, Jeremy, and Robert A. Margo. 2011. "The Impact of Access to Rail Transportation on Agricultural Improvement: The American Midwest as a Test Case." *Journal of Transport and Land Use* 4:5–18.

———. 2012. "Landownership and the Coming of the Railroad to the American Midwest, 1850–1860." In *Railroads in Historical Context: Construction, Costs, and*

Consequences, vol. 1, edited by A. McCants, Eduardo Biera, Jose M. Lopes Cordeiro, and Paulo Lourenco, 151–78. Gaia, Portugal: Inovatec: V. N.

Atack, Jeremy, Robert A. Margo, and Paul Rhode. 2014. "The Division of Labor and Economies of Scale in Late Nineteenth-Century American Manufacturing: New Evidence." Unpublished Manuscript, Department of Economics, Boston University. May.

Berle, Adolf, and Gardiner Means. 1932. *The Modern Corporation and Private Property*. New York: Harcourt, Brace, and World.

Bodenhorn, Howard, and Hugh Rockoff. 1992. "Regional Interest Rate Differentials in Antebellum America." In *Strategic Factors in Nineteenth-Century American Economic History: A Volume to Honor Robert W. Fogel*, edited by C. Goldin and H. Rockoff, 159–87. Chicago: University of Chicago Press.

Carter, Susan B. 2006. "Labor Force." In *Historical Statistics of the United States*, vol. 2, edited by S. B. Carter, S. S. Gartner, M. R. Haines, A. L. Olmstead, R. Sutch, and G. Wright, 13–35. New York: Cambridge University Press.

Chandler, Alfred. 1977. *The Visible Hand: The Managerial Revolution in American Business*. Cambridge, MA: Harvard University Press.

Davis, Lance E. 1965. "The Investment Market, 1870–1914: The Evolution of a National Market." *Journal of Economic History* 25:335–99.

Denison, Edward F. 1962. *Sources of Economic Growth in the United States and the Alternatives Before Us*. New York: Committee for Economic Development.

Donaldson, Dave, and Richard Hornbeck. 2013. "Railroads and American Economic Growth: A 'Market Access' Approach." NBER Working Paper no. 19213, Cambridge, MA.

Fishlow, Albert. 1965. *American Railroads and the Transformation of the Antebellum Economy*. Cambridge, MA: Harvard University Press.

Fogel, Robert William. 1964. *Railroads and American Economic Growth: Essays in Econometric History*. Baltimore: Johns Hopkins University Press.

———. 1989. *Without Consent or Contract: The Rise and Fall of American Slavery*. New York: W. W. Norton.

Fogel, Robert William, and Stanley L. Engerman. 1974. *Time on the Cross: The Economics of American Negro Slavery*. Boston: Little, Brown and Company.

Griliches, Zvi, and Vidar Ringstad. 1971. *Economies of Scale and the Form of the Production Function*. Amsterdam: North Holland.

Kindleberger, Charles P. 1996. *World Economic Primacy, 1500–1990*. New York: Oxford University Press.

Landes, David S. 1998. *The Wealth and Poverty of Nations: Why Some Are So Rich and Some So Poor*. New York: W.W. Norton Company.

Maddison, Angus. 2001. *The World Economy: A Millennial Perspective*. Paris: Organisation for Economic Co-Operation and Development.

Neal, Larry, and Jeffrey G. Williamson, eds. 2014. *The Cambridge History of Capitalism*. Cambridge: Cambridge University Press.

Rousseau, Peter, and Richard Sylla. 2005. "Emerging Financial Markets and Early US Growth." *Explorations in Economic History* 42:1–26.

Sokoloff, Kenneth. 1984. "Was the Transition from the Artisan Shop to the Mechanized Factory Associated with Gains in Efficiency? Evidence from the US Manufacturing Censuses of 1820 and 1850." *Explorations in Economic History* 21:351–82.

Stampp, Kenneth. 1956. *The Peculiar Institution: Slavery in the Ante-Bellum South*. New York: Vantage Books.

US Census Bureau. 2011. "Mean Center of Population for the United States, 1790–2010." http://www.census.gov/geo/reference/centersofpop/animatedmean2010.html.

I

Business Organization and Internal Governance

Revisiting American Exceptionalism: Democracy and the Regulation of Corporate Governance
The Case of Nineteenth-Century Pennsylvania in Comparative Context

Naomi R. Lamoreaux

1.1 Introduction

The idea of American exceptionalism, particularly the notion that American institutions should be held up as a model to the rest of the world, has fallen out of favor among historians in recent decades. The idea had its roots in the Puritans' vision of their settlement in the Massachusetts Bay Colony as a "city on the hill" and in early nineteenth-century Americans' belief in their "manifest destiny" (Murrin 2000; Onuf 2012). Writing in the late nineteenth century, historians George Bancroft and Frederick Jackson Turner transformed this belief into a story of the growth of democracy and the spread of liberty (Ross 1984; Tyrrell 1991). Although there was always a counter narrative that emphasized the limits of this achievement and the extent to which progress depended on hard-fought struggles waged by those on the bottom of society, the idea of American exceptionalism retained considerable influence on historical writing through much of the twentieth century. More

Naomi R. Lamoreaux is Stanley B. Resor Professor of Economics and History and chair of the history department at Yale University and a research associate at the National Bureau of Economic Research.

This chapter builds on collaborative work with Timothy Guinnane, Ron Harris, and Jean-Laurent Rosenthal. I am grateful for the comments of Jeremy Atack, Margaret Blair, William Collins, Stanley Engerman, Louis Galambos, Carl Gershenson, Timothy Guinnane, Leslie Hannah, Robert Margo, Eric Rasmusen, an anonymous referee, participants in the NBER-Vanderbilt conference on "Enterprising America," the University of California, Santa Barbara, symposium on "The New History of Capitalism," and the Harvard Workshop in History, Culture, and Society. Thanks also to Guillaume Frencia, Sasha Nichols Geerdes, Thao Nguyen, and Erinn Wong for their able research assistance and to the National Science Foundation, the University of California, Los Angeles, and Yale University for financial support. For acknowledgments, sources of research support, and disclosure of the author's material financial relationships, if any, please see http://www.nber.org/chapters/c13131.ack.

recently, however, historians have stressed the dark side of these trends, in particular the extent to which increases in the rights and status enjoyed by common white men came at the expense of women, blacks, native peoples, and immigrants. As a result, the notion that we should study American history for lessons that other countries might profitably emulate has largely disappeared from historical writing, although the idea continues to exert considerable hold on the popular imagination (Tyrrell 1991).

Economists are more likely than historians to hold the United States up as a model for the world to emulate, though they do not typically use the language of American exceptionalism. Instead, they discuss the American advantage as the product of a set of measurable characteristics that quantitative analysis (mainly in the form of cross-country regressions) has shown to be significantly related to economic performance. These characteristics include geographic factors that are largely outside history (such as climate or topography); institutional or cultural characteristics that, though they are products of history, generally are taken as givens (such as a country's ethnic or religious makeup); and institutional or cultural variables that, though they are products of history, could at least in theory be adopted by any country (such as democratic elections or a free press).[1] It is mainly this last category that leads economists to treat US institutions as the standard to which other countries should aspire.

Cross-country regressions, however, are at best crude analytical tools. The need to collect the same types of measures for a large sample of countries means that key variables must often be represented by highly imperfect proxies. Moreover, there is often an element of circularity in the choice of explanatory variables. Scholars start with knowledge of which countries are successful, pick variables that contemporary observation would suggest are causally associated with that success, and then see if the correlations withstand further scrutiny. But here they encounter the further problem that many of the variables that they hypothesize are important for economic development might also be endogenous products of that development or of other circumstances causally related to it. To deal with that possibility, economists search for some other variable that allows them to isolate causation—an "instrument" that is plausibly exogenous and related to economic development only through the posited channel. That search typically leads to a measure that is either outside of history completely, such as a geographic indicator, or outside the historical processes being analyzed because it long predated them. What then all too frequently happens is that these "instruments" irresistibly become explanations in and of themselves, and the chan-

1. The literature is voluminous, but see, for example, Barro (1997); Barro and McCleary (2003); McCleary and Barro (2006); Bloom and Sachs (1998); Gallup, Sachs, and Mellinger (1999); Sachs and Warner (2001); Acemoglu, Johnson, and Robinson (2001); Rodrik, Subramanian, and Trebbi (2004); Papaioannou and Siourounis (2008). For an approach that does not involve cross-country regressions, see Engerman and Sokoloff (2011).

nels they were supposed to help identify fade into the background.[2] The result has been a flurry of "historical" studies in which history itself plays little or no role. Instead, these studies emphasize the persistent effects of the instrumental variable and treat what happened in the intervening centuries as if it were of little consequence.[3]

The larger purpose of this chapter is to argue that we ignore the intervening history at our peril. To make this case I focus on the history of the law of business organizational forms, particularly the corporation. Studies based on cross-country regressions have argued that Anglo-American common law is much more conducive to financial development than the code-based legal systems of the European continent, particularly those modeled on the French code.[4] I show, to the contrary, that until recently corporate law in the United States was fundamentally different from that in the other major common-law country, Great Britain, which had more in common with the law on the European continent. The different character of business law in the United States, I would like to propose, was related to characteristics that have been traditionally considered markers of US exceptionalism, particularly the early achievement of universal (white) manhood suffrage. In Britain and on the European continent, general incorporation laws were enacted long before the expansion of the suffrage, which meant that they were largely written by and in the interests of the business people who would use them. By contrast, in the United States the expansion of suffrage came much earlier. The various state legislatures wrote their general incorporation laws in the context, on the one hand, of a mass political movement aimed at preventing "the moneyed few" from using the corporate form to gain unfair economic advantages and, on the other, of efforts by the elite to prevent democratically elected legislators from tampering with property rights. How these countervailing pressures played out on the ground varied from one state to the next, but as a general rule they resulted in significant restrictions on the use of the corporation and related forms.

Although it might be tempting to think of the extension of the franchise as another initial condition that could be added to cross-country regressions, this chapter aims to document the importance of ongoing historical processes in shaping the law of business organizational forms. To this end, after setting up the general context, this chapter focuses on the experience of Pennsylvania, where democratic politics kept the state's general incorporation laws remarkably restrictive, and where creditor-oriented (pro-property rights) courts hamstrung an effort to create an early version of a limited

2. On this point, see especially Rodrik, Subramanian, and Trebbi (2004).

3. Examples include Nunn (2008), Nunn and Wantchekon (2011), Alesina, Giuliano, and Nunn (2013).

4. See especially La Porta et al. (1997, 1998). These articles sparked an enormous literature that has been surveyed in La Porta, Lopez-de-Silanes, and Shleifer (2008) and Roe and Siegel (2009).

liability company (LLC). It focuses in particular on the latter third of the nineteenth century in order to emphasize the importance of moving beyond initial conditions to examine the interaction of democratic politics and business needs. The chapter then returns to the general context, comparing developments in Pennsylvania with those in other states and drawing out the implications of these parallel histories for our understanding of US exceptionalism. The case of Delaware in particular highlights the importance of looking beyond initial conditions. Delaware started out on much the same path as Pennsylvania, and by the middle of the nineteenth century its corporate law had moved in an even more restrictive direction. Only at the very end of the century, when New Jersey's liberalization of its general incorporation laws sparked a national charter-mongering competition, did Delaware shift to a different path and enact the more permissive law for which the state is famous. Although other states then began to copy Delaware's example, convergence was much slower than is generally realized. Moreover, as late as the 1950s, even in Delaware US law was still much more prescriptive than its British counterpart. Visiting at Harvard during that decade, the prominent British company-law specialist L. C. B. Gower was stunned to observe that although British law is "essentially contractual[,] . . . the American statutes tend to lay down mandatory rules" (Gower 1956, 1376).

There was no single, archetypal American story of the development of business institutions in the nineteenth century. Rather, there was a Pennsylvania story, a Delaware story, a New Jersey story, a Massachusetts story, an Ohio story, a Virginia story, a California story, and so on.[5] Nonetheless, as I argue in this chapter, the conflict over elite privileges versus property rights that resulted from the early expansion of the franchise drove the evolution of business organizational forms throughout the United States in broadly similar ways. The trick to getting the history right is to understand how different local manifestations of essentially the same initial conditions interacted with each other to shape the path of institutional change.

1.2   The Distinctive Character of the Corporate Form in the United States

Virtually everywhere in the world in the early nineteenth century, business people could only form corporations with the specific authorization of the state, which meant that those who were closely connected with the ruling elite had privileged access to the form. By the end of the century, however, in the United States and most Western European countries access to the corporate form had been opened up, so that almost anyone who wanted to could form a business corporation by a simple process of registration (North, Wallis, and Weingast 2009; Lamoreaux and Wallis 2012). General incorporation came

---

5. One important implication of this argument is that we need a new generation of state-level studies of the corporate form such as the one by Eric Hilt (chapter 2, this volume).

somewhat later to the European continent than to England and the United States, but that was largely because the Napoleonic code enabled businesses to achieve some of the benefits of incorporation in other ways (Lamoreaux and Rosenthal 2005; Guinnane et al. 2007). For example, in France and other countries that adopted Napoleonic law, business people could form limited partnerships in which the general partners bore unlimited liability but the limited partners risked only their investments. Limited partnerships could even have tradable shares, making them reasonable substitutes for corporations. In Britain, by contrast, the only alternative to the corporation that multiowner enterprises could employ was the ordinary partnership in which all members were unlimitedly liable. In the United States, most states passed laws in the early nineteenth century allowing businesses to organize limited partnerships, but the form never became widespread because creditor-oriented courts interpreted the law in ways that increased the risk that limited partners would be found unlimitedly liable (Lamoreaux and Rosenthal 2005; Guinnane et al. 2007).[6]

Although in both Britain and the United States the lack of alternatives to the ordinary partnership increased demand for the corporate form, the political contexts in which two countries enacted their general incorporation laws were very different, and as a result the statutes were poles apart in the way they functioned. In Britain, the Reform Act of 1832 had shifted representation in Parliament in favor of cities (and hence business interests) without dramatically expanding the franchise, so still less than half of adult males were formally eligible to vote and less than 10 percent actually voted (Flora et al. 1983; O'Gorman 1993; Phillips and Wetherell 1995). When Parliament finally responded to the pent-up demand for corporate charters by passing a general enabling law, it was mainly the people involved in organizing and financing companies who shaped the content of the legislation.[7] The first statute, passed in 1844, protected investors' interests by making shareholders unlimitedly liable for their corporation's debts. Otherwise, however, it treated the relationship between a company's organizers and investors as contractual. The law provided companies with a basic governance template, but permitted incorporators to add any "provisions for such other purposes (not inconsistent with Law) as the parties to such Deed shall think proper."[8] When Parliament passed additional legislation in 1855 and 1856, making it possible for companies to opt for limited liability, it increased the extent

6. In France, moreover, even ordinary partners could control the extent of their liabilities by writing contracts that restricted partners' ability to encumber the firm without the explicit approval of the other partners. Under the Napoleonic Code, such agreements were fully enforceable so long as they were registered. Under the British or American common law, by contrast, they were not enforceable against third parties that had not been notified in advance about their terms. See Lamoreaux and Rosenthal (2005).

7. On the transition to general incorporation in Britain, see Harris (2000), Taylor (2006), and Freeman, Pearson, and Taylor (2011).

8. Companies Act 1844 7&8 Vict. C. 110 Section VII.

of incorporators' contractual freedom by replacing the basic template with a set of default governance rules included in a table appended to the act (Thring 1856). This table was formalized in the Companies Act of 1862 as Table A. If a company did not submit its own articles of association at the time of registration, the detailed governance rules in Table A applied. However, a company could reject any or all of the clauses of the table and write its own rules from scratch. The only governance rules that the law mandated were that the company hold a general meeting at least once a year and that the articles of association be amendable by a three-quarters vote of the shareholders (Guinnane, Harris, and Lamoreaux 2014).[9]

The contractual flexibility that characterized British company law contrasted sharply with the much more prescriptive statutes passed by the various US states around the same time (Gower 1956; Harris and Lamoreaux 2010). These statutes were enacted in the very different political environment produced by the early achievement of nearly universal manhood suffrage. In the decades following independence, state governments had faced insistent demands to provide their citizens with the infrastructure needed for economic development, from transportation improvements to financial services. The same citizens did not want to pay taxes, however, so states solved the problem of financing such projects by granting corporate charters to private groups that promised to undertake them in their stead (Seavoy 1982; Majewski 2000). These charters usually included an array of special privileges, sometimes as inducements to invest in projects of uncertain profitability and sometimes in response to the lobbying of politically well-connected incorporators.[10] Charters for turnpike, bridge, and canal companies typically conveyed a monopoly right to levy tolls, as well as powers of eminent domain. Perks granted to incorporators of the Society for Useful Manufactures (SUM), a textile company chartered in New Jersey in 1791, included permission to raise funds through a public lottery and exemptions for the company's employees from taxes and military service (except in the case of invasion) (Maier 1993). Bank charters conveyed the right to issue currency in the form of bank notes (Handlin and Handlin 1969; Lamoreaux 1994). This latter privilege turned out to be so valuable that control of entry into banking became an important way of solidifying political power in the years following the American Revolution. Whichever party dominated the legislature kept tight control of bank charters, awarding them exclusively to prominent political supporters (Lu and Wallis 2014; Bodenhorn 2006).

The boons that legislatures awarded to recipients of corporate charters generated a tremendous amount of resentment, most obviously among the

---

9. British law set the minimum number of incorporators at seven, but in many closely held companies at least some of the seven were nominal. This practice was upheld by the House of Lords in *Salomon v. A. Salomon and Co. Ltd* (1897) AC 22.

10. Political officials were often large shareholders in early corporations. See, for example, Hilt and Valentine (2012) on New York.

members of the general population who bore the cost, but also among entrepreneurs seeking the chance to compete away some of the monopoly rents. As corporations became a lightning rod for political discontent, some states passed constitutional amendments that imposed outright bans on chartering certain types of corporations. In other states, however, legislatures began instead to liberalize their chartering policies. In Massachusetts, for example, the General Court responded to popular pressure by handing out charters to rival interests. In 1828, it granted a charter of incorporation to a company that proposed to build a bridge over the Charles River right next to one that had been awarded the original monopoly (Kutler 1971). It also granted numerous charters for banks in competition with existing financial institutions—so many, in fact, that when the state finally passed a general incorporation law in 1851, almost no banks organized under it (Lamoreaux 1994; Lu and Wallis 2014).

In most states, however, popular pressure led directly to the passage of general incorporation laws. When the political turmoil that followed the Panic of 1837 dislodged New York's democratic political machine (the Albany Regency) from power, the legislature passed the first "free banking" act (Bodenhorn 2006). A number of other states soon passed similar legislation, and the New York statute subsequently became the model for the National Banking Acts passed by the US Congress during the Civil War (Bodenhorn 2002). Even earlier, New York had enacted the first general incorporation act for manufacturing as a way of encouraging domestic industry during the run-up to the War of 1812, but few states followed suit until the late 1840s. The Panic of 1837 and the depression that followed a second major financial crisis in 1839 led a number of states to default on their debts. The political realignments that followed led to major constitutional reforms and also to the spread of general incorporation laws, so that by 1860 the vast majority (twenty-seven out of thirty-two) states and territories had enacted them for manufacturing (Hilt 2014; Wallis 2005; Hurst 1970).

Not surprisingly, given this political context, most of the early general incorporation laws imposed strict limits on what corporations could do, how big they could grow, how long they could last, and what forms their internal governance could take. The extent of these regulations varied from state to state (see table 1.1). Ohio's 1846 law, Massachusetts's 1851 statute, and Illinois's 1857 act all put ceilings on the amount of capital a corporation could raise, but neither New York's 1848 statute nor Pennsylvania's 1849 law imposed such a limit. Pennsylvania set the term of a corporate charter at twenty years, Ohio at forty years, and New York and New Jersey at fifty years, while Massachusetts allowed corporations perpetual life. All of these states except Ohio limited the amount of debt that corporations could take on to some multiple of their capital stock (usually one). Pennsylvania had the most generous multiple, but it severely restricted the amount of real estate that corporations could own. The Massachusetts and New Jersey

Table 1.1   **Restrictions on manufacturing corporations in early general incorporation statutes**

State	Year of statute	Restrictions on capital stock	Restrictions on borrowing or assets	Restrictions on duration	Governance structure	Voting rule	Shareholders' liability
Massachusetts	1851	Must be at least $5,000 but not more than $200,000	Debts cannot exceed paid-in capital	None	Managed by at least three directors, one of whom is president; must also elect clerk and treasurer	None	Stockholders jointly liable for all debts until capital is fully paid in; then for debts to workers
New York	1848	None	Debts cannot exceed amount of capital stock	Fifty years	Managed by three to nine trustees, one of whom is president	One vote per share	Stockholders individually liable for debts up to amount of subscription until capital is fully paid in; jointly liable for debts to workers
New Jersey	1849	Must be at least $10,000	Debts cannot exceed paid-in capital	Fifty years	Managed by at least three directors who must be stockholders; majority must be residents of state; president must be a director and resident of state	None	Stockholders' liabilities limited to amount of subscription
Pennsylvania	1849	Must be at least $20,000	Liabilities cannot exceed three times paid-in capital; can't own more than 2,000 acres of land	Twenty years	Managed by five to thirteen directors; majority must be citizens of state; president must be a director; treasurer and secretary elected by stockholders but cannot be directors	One vote per share, but no shareholder can vote more than one-third of total	Stockholders jointly liable for amount of debts up to amount of subscription until capital is fully paid in
Ohio	1846	Must be at least $5,000 but not more than $200,000	None	Forty years	Managed by three to seven directors; president chosen by directors	One vote per share	Stockholders' liability limited to amount of subscription, except are fully liable for debts to workers
Illinois	1857	Must be at least $10,000 but not more than $500,000	Debts cannot exceed the amount of capital stock	Fifty years	Managed by three to seven directors who must be stockholders; directors choose other officers	One vote per share	Stockholders liable for debts up to amount of subscription until capital is fully paid in
California	1850	None	Debts cannot exceed amount of paid-in capital	Fifty years	Managed by three to nine trustees, one of whom chosen president	One vote per share	Unlimited individual proportional liability; also jointly liable for debts to workers

Sources: Massachusetts (1854, vol. 1, 660–64); Massachusetts (1836, 327–34, 362–66); New York (1848, 54–61); Elmer (1855, 456–62); Pennsylvania (1849, 563–69); Ohio (1846, 37–40); Illinois (1857, 161–65); California (1850, 347–76).

statutes did not specify a voting rule for shareholders, but New York, Ohio, and Pennsylvania mandated one share one vote, and Pennsylvania added a restriction that no shareholder could vote more than one-third of the total number of shares. The laws generally prescribed the number of directors, sometimes requiring them to be shareholders and/or citizens of the state. The statutes often also imposed additional liabilities on shareholders under specified circumstances.

The flip side of this democratic concern about corporate privileges was elites' anxiety about the security of their property rights. From the nation's earliest years, James Madison and other prominent political leaders had worried that if the poor had political power, they would use it to redistribute property from the rich (Nedelsky 1990). As late as 1821, in a speech to New York's constitutional convention, Chancellor James Kent had opposed abolishing property qualifications for voting for state senators on the grounds that "[t]he tendency of universal suffrage is to jeopardize the rights of property, and the principles of liberty." It was human nature, Kent declared, for the poor to covet the wealth of the rich, the debtor to wish to avoid the obligation of contracts, and "the indolent and the profligate to cast the whole burthens of society upon the industrious and virtuous." Democratic politics provided "ambitious and wicked men" with the opportunity "to inflame these combustible materials," so it was critical to preserve at least one branch of the legislature "as the representative of the landed interest" (New York 1821, 221). Legislatures were already bowing to popular demands to the disadvantage of the wealthy, enacting stay laws to protect debtors from foreclosure during financial crises and passing adverse possession laws that made it easier for squatters to claim the property of landowners who had legitimate titles (Hartz 1948; Gates 1962; Aron 1992; de Soto 2000; Balleisen 2001; Van Atta 2008).[11] Expanding the franchise, conservatives like Kent worried, would only make the problem worse.

Legislatures also responded to popular pressures by reneging on privileges that earlier bodies had imbedded in corporate charters. In Massachusetts, for example, complaints that the original 1784 charter of the Massachusetts Bank was too expansive led the General Court to pass an "Addition" in 1792 that placed greater limits on the bank's operations (Maier 1992). The Virginia legislature intervened in a dispute between urban and rural members of the incorporated Mutual Assurance Society against Fires on Buildings, passing an act in 1800 dictating that legislators would represent absent members at general meetings. With the assistance of these legislative representatives, the country members were able to reorganize the company so that it better suited their interests (Campbell 1975). After the Virginia assembly chartered the Richmond James River Company in 1804,

---

11. It should be noted, however, that elite owners of mills, mines, and transportation companies also used their influence in legislatures to take property from farmers and other small holders using eminent domain proceedings. See Lamoreaux (2011).

a deluge of complaints led the legislature to amend the charter and, over the objections of the company, exempt small boats from having to pay tolls (Campbell 1975).

The Supreme Court temporarily put a stop to such actions when Chief Justice John Marshall famously declared in *Dartmouth College v. Woodward* (1819)[12] that a corporate charter was a contract that the state could not unilaterally abrogate, but legislatures quickly learned to imbed reservation clauses in charters that gave them the authority to alter the terms at will (Hartz 1948; Wells 1886). Moreover, under the leadership of Chief Justice Roger Taney, a Jacksonian Democrat, the court moved to construe corporate charters in the narrowest possible terms. When the Massachusetts legislature authorized the construction of the second bridge across the Charles River at Charlestown, proprietors of the original Charles River Bridge sued to block construction. In the words of their attorney, Warren Dutton, chartering the new bridge was "an act of confiscation" that threatened "all sense of security for the rights of persons and property."[13] Similarly, Justice Joseph Story warned that if the proprietors had foreseen "such a total insecurity of all rights of property" as the legislature's actions signified, "the project would have been dropped, still born," and the growth in commerce that the bridge had made possible would never have occurred.[14]

These arguments did not carry the day in the Charles River Bridge case, but wherever and whenever they could, conservative jurists used the power of the courts to protect the rights of creditors and of property holders more generally. One important consequence of these efforts was to compress further the menu of organizational forms available to business enterprises. As already noted, the Napoleonic code enabled French entrepreneurs to organize limited partnerships, but English common law did not permit an equivalent form. In an early attempt to reduce the extent of the privileges associated with the corporate form, most of the US states passed enabling statutes for limited partnerships during the 1820s and 1830s (Kessler 2003; Hilt and O'Banion 2009). The courts soon eviscerated these statutes, however, interpreting them, in their zeal to protect creditors, in ways that potentially exposed limited partners to liability. For example, judges gave notice that they would view deviations from the declarations contained in the partnership certificate as sufficient cause to hold all of the partners unlimitedly liable for the firm's debts—even partners who were innocent of error, and

12. *Dartmouth College v. Woodward*, 17 U.S. 518 (1819).
13. *Charles River Bridge v. Warren Bridge*, 36 U.S. 420 (1837). The quotation is from pp. 73–74 of the 1837 U.S. LEXIS 180 edition of the case.
14. *Charles River Bridge v. Warren Bridge*, 36 U.S. 420 at 615. Taney in turn justified his decision against the monopoly with the claim that it was necessary for economic development. He conjured up a nightmarish vision of proprietors of old turnpike corporations "awakening from their sleep" to claim similar rights, putting in jeopardy "the millions of property which have been invested in railroads and canals" along adjacent routes (552–53). For an extended analysis of this case, see Kutler (1971).

even if the substance of the deviation was inconsequential (Lewis 1917; Warren 1929, ch.6; Howard 1934). Not surprisingly, the form was used much more rarely in the United States than in France or elsewhere on the European continent.[15] The end result of the political battles of the early nineteenth century, therefore, was that business people in the United States had much less contractual flexibility in the way they could use the corporate form and also an effectively smaller menu of organizational forms than their counterparts in Britain and on the European continent.

1.3   Pennsylvania: A Tale of Two Statutes

1.3.1   Early Nineteenth-Century Background

Pennsylvania is a particularly good case for studying the effect of popular distrust of corporations and elite distrust of democracy on the availability and flexibility of business organizational forms. First, the expansion of the franchise occurred in Pennsylvania especially early. The state abolished property qualifications for voting even before the ratification of the Constitution, and Pennsylvania entered the new United States with a tax qualification that seems to have been quite minimal.[16] Second, controversy over the privileges that the legislature had granted to the Bank of North America, the financial arm of the national government under the Articles of Confederation, made corporations a hot-button political issue at the very time the franchise was expanding. Indeed, a populist-oriented legislature repealed the bank's Pennsylvania charter in 1785, raising concerns about property rights in corporate stock. Although a political swing back toward the elite led to the reissuance of the charter two years later, the new version was less generous than the original, and the bank's supporters continued to feel under siege (Maier 1993; Hartz 1948; Hammond 1957; Schocket 2007).[17]

The reincarnated Bank of North America had a monopoly on banking in the state, and its leaders fought to maintain that position. They did not completely succeed; the legislature chartered three additional banks, all in Philadelphia, during the next couple of decades. These charters all went

15. Hilt and O'Banion (2009) found "a surprising number" of limited partnerships in New York City in the early nineteenth century, counting 1,098 registrations between 1822 and 1858. However, Howard (1934) searched the records of five New Jersey counties from the 1830s until the 1930s and found only 140 registrations for limited partnerships. I compiled a sample of partnerships reported in the R. G. Dun credit ledgers for Boston for the 1840s and 1850s and found that only 2 out of 164 were limited. For the details of the sample, see Lamoreaux (1997).

16. Fully 71.5 percent of the state's adult white male population voted in the 1808 presidential election, and 77.4 percent voted in 1840. See Engerman and Sokoloff (2005).

17. Farley Grubb (2003) has shown that prominent officers and shareholders in the Bank of North America sought to protect the bank's position as a monopoly issuer of currency in Pennsylvania by pushing successfully for the provision in the US Constitution that banned paper money issues by the states. Paper money issues generally had broad popular support, but were regarded by the elite as a threat to property rights.

to supporters of the then dominant political coalition, known as the Federalists, and the banks' leaders joined together to lobby against additional applications for charters (Schwartz 1987; Majewski 2006; Schocket 2007). The vehemence with which the incumbents sought to block entry fueled suspicion that they were reaping exorbitant returns from their control of the credit market and insured that the issue of corporate privileges would remain a subject of heated public debate. As the political balance in the legislature shifted in the wake of the War of 1812, this anger about corporate privileges, coupled with the dire need for banking facilities in other parts of the state, spurred the passage in 1814 of an omnibus banking bill that chartered about two score new banks (Majewski 2006; Schocket 2007). Then the political balance shifted back again, and the movement for additional charters stalled. The relatively few banks incorporated over the next several decades had to pay hefty bonuses to the state in exchange for their charters, leading to charges of a corrupt bargain between banks and the legislature and raising the specter of more nefarious exchanges of money behind the scenes (Hartz 1948).

These charges provided the backdrop for Pennsylvania's constitutional convention of 1837, which opened in May, the same month as a massive financial panic forced all the banks in the state to suspend specie payments. The financial crisis dominated the convention's debates, focusing attention on banks almost to the exclusion of other types of corporations. Nonetheless, in their arguments over bank charters, delegates gave voice to all the same concerns that inflected discussions of corporations more generally—in particular, the fear that the unfair advantages that corporations obtained through their charters perpetuated the dominance of the moneyed elite. As one delegate put it, "the power now exercised by corporate bodies" was a threat to "equal rights." It must "be limited or abolished," and the only sure way to do that was increase the power of the people over their representations. Hence the delegates pushed to extend "the elective franchise . . . as widely as possible" and, at the same time, subject all members of government, including judges, to election, so that "an immediate and direct action of the people may occur in the choice of those who are to administer that government" (Pennsylvania 1837, vol. 1, 321–22). Defenders of corporations responded by raising the specter of insecure property rights. "Mark my words!" one delegate warned. "If ever our republic falls, it will be by the destruction of the confidence of our citizens in the security of individual rights," a consequence that "will necessarily follow" if democratically elected governments were allowed to countenance "the violation of contracts, the destruction of private rights, or the uprooting of charters" (Pennsylvania 1837, vol. 5, 562–63).

The prodemocratic, anticorporate forces made some gains at the convention, but only modest ones. They failed in their effort to eliminate tax qualifications for voting once and for all, though they did manage to secure a reduction in the residency requirement from two years to one—perhaps a more significant change, given the highly mobile character of the population and the small magnitude of the tax qualification (Akagi 1924; Keyssar 2000; Pennsylvania 1837, vol. 2, 470–96, 500–61, vol. 3, 113–45, 148–73). They also failed in their demand that bank charters that perpetrated "a fraud upon the people" be considered "repealable" by the legislature (Pennsylvania 1837, vol. 6, 434). Instead, all they obtained from the convention was a provision in the 1838 constitution limiting future bank charters to twenty years and requiring that each charter contain a clause "reserving to the legislature the power to alter, revoke, or annul the same, whenever in their opinion it may be injurious to the citizens of the commonwealth," a directive that was softened by the addition of language requiring that any such action be accomplished in "such manner . . . that no injustice shall be done to the corporators" (Section 25).[18]

From the perspective of hindsight, what is most striking about the debate over corporations that raged at the convention is how narrow it was. Delegates fought at great length over the issue of whether a corporate charter was a contract that future legislatures had to honor, even though this principle had presumably already been settled by the Supreme Court's Dartmouth College decision.[19] At the same time, there was surprisingly little discussion of the possibility of general incorporation. Delegates made a few attempts (all unsuccessful) to nudge the state toward a system of general laws (see, for example, Pennsylvania 1837, vol. 1, 129, vol. 2, 172, and vol. 6, 384), with proponents of general incorporation arguing that open access to the corporate form would counteract the inequality that the special charter system had exacerbated: "The principle of corporate or joint associations . . . enabled the many, with small means, to compete with the few who were wealthy," and it would improve their position even more "if the monopoly principle of our present corporations were abolished, and all men left free to associate with shares, large or small, at their pleasure" (Pennsylvania 1837, vol. 1, 385). Such proposals gained few adherents, however, probably because of the convention's focus on the banking crisis. Most delegates seem to have shared the view that allowing anyone who wanted to organize a bank to do so would undermine the soundness of the financial system. Thus one delegate blamed the 1814 omnibus statute, which had granted charters to about forty banks, for inflicting "on the commonwealth an evil of a more disastrous nature than has ever been experienced by its citizens" (Pennsylvania 1837, vol. 5, 528).[20]

18. The constitution was amended in 1857 to extend this clause to all corporations. The other major achievement of the convention was to bar the state from continuing to invest money in corporations. For the text of Pennsylvania's 1838 constitution and subsequent amendments, see the NBER/Maryland State Constitutions Project, http://www.stateconstitutions.umd.edu/index.aspx, accessed 8 June 2014.

19. *Dartmouth College v. Woodward*, 17 U.S. 518 (1819).

20. The expansion of the number of banks in 1814 received much blame for the Panic of 1819. See Majewski (2006).

To this point, moreover, the delegates simply did not have much experience with general laws for business corporations.[21] New York had enacted the first such statute for manufacturing in 1811 to encourage domestic production during the embargo on trade with Britain and France.[22] Only Ohio and New Jersey had followed suit, and both states later repealed their acts (Hilt 2014). Even in New York there was enough uncertainty about the principle of general incorporation for business that the 1811 statute was initially enacted for only five years, though it was subsequently renewed before being made permanent in 1821 (Kessler 1940; Seavoy 1982). At the time of the Pennsylvania convention, New York's pioneering free banking law was still a year in the future (Bodenhorn 2006). Some states, like Massachusetts and Rhode Island, had already loosened access to bank charters, but they had done so simply by regularizing the process of granting special charters, enabling the legislature to continue to deny applications to incorporators whose character they thought suspect (Handlin and Handlin 1969; Lu and Wallis 2014; Lamoreaux 1994). Pennsylvania would not adopt a general incorporation statute for banking until 1860 (Hartz 1948).

Just the year before the constitutional convention, Pennsylvania's legislature had taken a first, very small, step in the direction of general incorporation by enacting a law that allowed companies that manufactured iron using processes fueled by coke or mineral coal to form corporations by a simple registration process.[23] Not even other kinds of iron companies were allowed to avail themselves of the act. As Section 7 emphatically stated, "nothing herein contained, shall be construed to empower such corporation to manufacture iron which has not been manufactured from the ore, with coke or mineral coal," and the legislature only extended the act to companies manufacturing iron with charcoal in 1852.[24] This first general incorporation law for manufacturing was highly restrictive in other ways as well. Charters for companies organized under the 1836 act were limited to twenty-five years duration. The companies had to have a capital of at least $100,000 but not more than $500,000, and they would forfeit their charters if at any time they contracted "debts to a greater amount than that of the capital subscribed." Companies could hold no more than 2,000 acres of land divided into no more than three parcels, all of which had to be in the same county or in "two counties which shall adjoin each other" (Sections 1, 3, and 6). Furthermore,

21. Certainly, there was no aversion per se to the idea of general incorporation laws, for the Pennsylvania legislature had passed such laws for other purposes. As early as 1791, for example, it had enacted a statute enabling groups formed for "any literary, charitable, or for any religious purpose" to incorporate by a simple registration process (Pennsylvania 1810).

22. "AN ACT relative to Incorporations for Manufacturing Purposes," passed March 22, 1811. All acts cited by their titles are from the Session Laws of the respective state, available at www.heinonline.org.

23. "AN ACT To encourage the manufacture of Iron with Coke or Mineral Coal" June 16, 1836.

24. It was extended to companies that made steel as well as iron in 1864. See Eastman (1908, vol. 1, 6).

companies were to be managed by a board of directors elected by the stock-holders according to a proportional voting rule that limited the number of votes large shareholders could cast (Section 3).

The legislature continued in this prescriptive spirit when it enacted a law "to encourage manufacturing operations in this commonwealth" in 1849. Despite the opening words of the bill, the act initially applied only to a lim-ited set of companies formed "for the purpose of carrying on the manufac-ture of woolen, cotton flax, or silk goods, or of iron, paper, lumber or salt,"[25] though coverage was gradually extended over the next couple of decades to "the manufacture of glass" (1850); "articles made from salt, except in Philadelphia" (1851); "printing and publishing" (1851); the "manufacture of enameled and vitrified iron, and articles made of cast or wrought iron, coated with glass or enamel, within the County of Allegheny" (1852); "oil and other products of rosin" (1852); "mining and manufacturing of mineral paints and artificial slates and other articles made by the use of said painting materials except in Philadelphia" (1852); "manufacture of artificial manures, and of articles made out of iron and other metals, or out of wood, iron and other metals" (1853); "mining coal, mining, quarrying and preparing for market lime, marl, soda, hydraulic cement, or other minerals, smelting copper, lead, tin or zinc ores, quarrying marble, stone or slate, and manu-facturing lumber" (1853); "manufacture of flour in Philadelphia and Beaver counties" (1853); "quarrying, preparing for market and vending marble, sandstone and other stone used for building purposes" (1853); "common carriers, without the capacity to hold real estate" (1854); "manufacture of leather in certain counties" (1859); "manufacture of oils, hydro-carbon fluids and all other products resulting from subjecting coal of any kind to the action of heat or the process of distillation" (1859); "manufacture of oil from mineral coal in Beaver County" (1859); "the mining, manufacturing and refining of carbon oil" (1860); "manufacture of fuel" (1860); "manu-facture and preparation of lubricating oil and material, out of and from mineral oils, and other oils or fatty substances, whether mineral animal or vegetable" (1863); and the "manufacture of leather in the county of Elk" (1865) (Eastman 1908, vol. 1, 8–9).

Like the original 1836 law, the 1849 act and its supplements imposed substantial restrictions on the activities and internal governance structures of companies chartered under their auspices. Although companies faced no ceilings on capital and could incur liabilities up to three times the amount of their paid-in stock, they could not hold more than 2,000 acres in real estate and their duration was limited to twenty years. They were to be managed by a board of five to thirteen directors, the majority of whom had to be citizens of the United States. The president had to be a director, but the secretary and treasurer could not be. Stockholders had one vote per share, but no indi-

25. "AN ACT To encourage manufacturing operations in this commonwealth" April 7, 1849.

vidual stockholder could cast votes amounting to more than one-third of the issued shares. Directors had the power to make bylaws "subject however to the revision and approval of the stockholders." Elaborate rules governed voting by proxy (for example, "no stockholder, females excepted, residing within ten miles of the place appointed for such general meeting or election, shall vote by proxy"), the powers of directors (they could not use the company's funds "for any banking purposes whatever, nor in the purchase of any stock in any other corporation," nor to make loans to any stockholder or officer on the security of the company's own stock), the calling of special meetings, and procedures for increasing or decreasing the company's capital.[26]

Because Pennsylvania's general incorporation laws were so restrictive, companies continued to petition for special charters from the legislature in the hopes of securing better terms. Five years after the passage of the 1849 law, less than a dozen companies had incorporated under it (Hartz 1948). Yet in 1855 alone the legislature passed 196 private bills chartering or amending the charters of for-profit business corporations (Pennsylvania 1855). A significant proportion of these bills pertained, of course, to types of enterprises that could not incorporate under the general laws, but many companies that could incorporate by registration still sought special charters in order to escape some of the restrictive features of the general laws. For example, in the iron industry one can observe companies obtaining special charters in order to buy stock in other companies, engage in related lines of business (such as building a railroad or a telegraph), borrow money in greater amounts than allowed by the general statute, institute nonstandard voting rules for elections for directors, and even occasionally escape the limits on real estate holdings.[27]

Incorporators resented having to lobby the legislature to secure provisions they regarded as reasonable or to be able to incorporate in the first place if their industries were not covered by general laws. Moreover, in some politically sensitive industries, charters were difficult to get under any circumstances. In coal mining, for example, the legislature adopted a policy of chartering corporations only in areas where the industry was not yet established, and so it refused almost all requests for charters in anthracite-rich areas such as Schuylkill County (Adams 2006). In other sectors, like bank-

26. "AN ACT To encourage manufacturing operations in this commonwealth" April 7, 1849.
27. See, for example, "AN ACT To enable the Sharon Iron Company, of Mercer county, to subscribe to the Stock of the Pittsburg and Erie Railroad Company" April 5, 1855; "AN ACT to incorporate the Hopewell Coal and Iron Company" May 7, 1855; "AN ACT To incorporate the Saucona Iron Company, in the county of Northampton" April 8, 1857; "AN ACT To incorporate the Sullivan Coal and Iron Company" March 2, 1868; "AN ACT To incorporate the Emaus Iron Company" March 2, 1870; "AN ACT Relative to the Bloomsburg Iron Company" March 12, 1870; "A Further Supplement To an act, entitled 'An Act to incorporate the Emaus Iron Company'" April 2, 1872. The evidence in many of the charters and supplements is contrary to Hamill's (1999) claim that special charters were generally little different in their salient features than charters obtained under general laws.

ing, charters were simply expensive to obtain (Hartz 1948), and those seeking to form corporations had to hire agents, variously known as "middle housemen," "lobby members," or more graphically "borers," to advance their cause (Pennsylvania 1837, vol. 6, 92). The activities of these lobbyists fueled complaints about corruption and increased antipathy both to corporations and the legislature. It was almost impossible, critics charged, to get a bill through the assembly "without the aid and influence of that class of men called '*borers*,' whose business it is to flatter, cajole, treat, and, perhaps, bribe the members. . . . These are the men who procure charters for banks, rail roads, &c., and, who offer for every vote they get, a consideration in some form or other" (Pennsylvania 1837, vol. 6, 434). The sight of legislators "beset by borers," wielding not "the power of the sword, but, what is a thousand times more mischievous, the power of the purse" (Pennsylvania 1837, vol. 6, 183) reinforced in the public's mind the idea that corporate power was illegitimate and had to be restrained for the survival of the Republic. As one delegate to the 1837 convention put it, there was a critical need for constitutional restrictions on banking "to guard our legislature from the importunities of such men" (Pennsylvania 1837, vol. 6, 92). When that effort bore little fruit, the conviction grew that it was necessary to tie the hands of legislators so far as the chartering of corporations was concerned.

1.3.2   The 1872–1873 Constitutional Convention

The passage by Congress of the National Banking Acts during the Civil War took the issue of bank charters off the table for at least the next couple of decades. These statutes instituted a general incorporation system for banks at the federal level and, by taxing the notes of state-chartered banks, made it unattractive for banks to seek state charters.[28] Nonetheless, veterans returned from the fighting to find Pennsylvania's economy seemingly transformed by the large number of corporations the legislature had chartered during the war. In Schuylkill County, for example, the number of coal-mining corporations had increased from one to fifty-two, and corporations suddenly accounted for about half of the county's output (Adams 2006, 2012). Although Pennsylvania loosened its general incorporation law during the Civil War, nearly 40 percent of the new coal-mining corporations in the state had obtained special charters from the legislature and almost an equivalent number of companies secured charter supplements that expanded their privileges. Not surprisingly, critics raised questions about the legislative bargains that allowed these "soulless monsters" suddenly to play such a prominent role in the state's economy (Adams 2012).

---

28. This situation would change during the 1880s, when deposits grew relative to currency issues on banks' balance sheets, but at least through the 1870s relatively few banks sought state charters. Pennsylvania had enacted a general incorporation law for banking in 1860 (Hartz 1948), but the law was scarcely operational before the National Banking Acts stripped it of any significance.

The issue came to a head in 1872 when it came time for Pennsylvania to again rewrite its fundamental law. As the delegates gathered in November of that year to draft a new state constitution, it quickly became apparent that the central reform impulse of the convention would be to get the legislature out of the business of passing "local or special" laws of all types. First and foremost among the types of legislation the delegates singled out for prohibition were special charters of incorporation. But if businesses were no longer going to be able to secure special charters that met their needs, then the restrictive character of the state's general incorporation laws posed serious problems. How would companies in industries not covered by the general laws obtain charters? Would all companies now have to conform to the restrictive features of these laws?

Worried industrialists found a champion at the convention in the person of Henry C. Carey, the well-known writer on political economy. Carey, a Republican delegate at large,[29] chaired the Committee on Industrial Interests and Labor, and he embedded his views in the committee report he presented to the convention (Pennsylvania 1873, vol. 5, 470–81). The new constitution, he proclaimed, should guarantee "[t]he right of the people of the State to associate together for all lawful purposes, and for trading on principles of limited or unlimited liability" (Pennsylvania 1873, vol. 5, 481). In other words, it should embody the principle that Douglass North, John Wallis, and Barry Weingast (2009) have called "open access," where the government no longer determines who can form such organizations or what the organizations can do.

Carey complained that in Pennsylvania, in contrast to Great Britain and a few of the other US states, "the right of association, for any purposes of trade or profit, has never been admitted" (Pennsylvania 1873, vol. 5, 479). He offered as an example a so-called general incorporation law enacted by the legislature the previous year. The statute applied only to iron and steel and other enumerated types of manufacturing enterprises, but more importantly, it imposed significant disadvantages on enterprises that chose to limit their liabilities. Limited enterprises had to pay a higher "bonus" to the state at the time of their formation. In addition, their shareholders remained unlimitedly liable "for debts due for labor or services" (Pennsylvania 1873, vol. 5, 480). Because Pennsylvania's general laws routinely imposed such taxes and liabilities on members of corporations that formed under them, Carey pointed out, they have "remained almost, if not absolutely, a dead letter" (Pennsylvania 1873, vol. 5, 480). Businesses could only get reasonable terms by seeking instead to incorporate under special acts, but now that alternative was going to be foreclosed.

Carey's committee did not have jurisdiction over the parts of the constitution that concerned corporations, so it overstepped its authority in propos-

29. Information on the political affiliations of the delegates and the districts they represented is from Harlan (1873).

ing that the new constitution include a right to associate. The committee that had jurisdiction, the "Committee on Private Corporations," did not include any similar principle in the article it initially drafted. However, on the article's second reading, the committee's chair, George W. Woodward (Chief Justice of the Pennsylvania Supreme Court and a Democratic delegate at large), proposed an amendment that Carey accepted as a close substitute:

> It shall be the duty of the Legislature to provide by general enactment that any five or more persons, citizens of this Commonwealth, associated for the prosecution of any lawful business, may, by subscribing to articles of association and complying with all requirements of law, form themselves into an incorporated company, with or without limited liability, as may be expressed in the articles of association, and such publicity shall be provided for as shall enable all who trade with such corporations as adopt the limited liability to know that no liability exists beyond that of the joint capital which may have been subscribed. (Pennsylvania 1873, vol. 6, 17)

After an extensive discussion, the convention agreed provisionally to a revised version of the amendment that cut the phrase about the legislature's duty and simply conferred the right of association on "any two or more persons, citizens of this Commonwealth" (Pennsylvania 1873, vol. 6, 27).

This amendment, however, was stricken from the draft article on its third reading. Despite Woodward's support, the amendment had been added mainly with Republican votes. Republicans had overwhelmingly supported the measure on second reading, with forty in favor and only eleven opposed, whereas the Democratic delegates had been evenly divided, with twenty-three for and twenty-five against (Pennsylvania 1873, vol. 6, 27).[30] After the debate heated up on the third reading, Democrats voted to strike the amendment by a three-to-one margin, thirty-three to eleven. The Republican vote was closer, but Republicans also favored striking the amendment by a vote of twenty-seven to twenty-three (Pennsylvania 1873, vol. 7, 779).[31]

If Republican delegates had continued to support the proposition in the original proportions, the amendment would have passed, but Democratic opponents of corporations shrewdly and successfully played on Republican fears about the security of property rights. When the amendment had been originally proposed, a few Democratic delegates had spoken against it on the grounds that it was "class legislation in favor of capitalists" (Pennsylvania 1873, vol. 6, 23). On the third reading, however, these opponents moved beyond their general antipathy to corporations to expound on the dangers

---

30. One Liberal Republican and two unaffiliated at-large delegates also voted for the amendment. Thirteen Democrats, seventeen Republicans, and one unaffiliated at-large delegate were absent at the time of the vote.

31. One Liberal Republican voted to delete the amendment and three unaffiliated at-large delegates voted to keep it. Seventeen Democrats and eighteen Republicans were absent at the time of the vote.

to creditors of making limited liability so broadly accessible to small firms. Thus S. C. T. Dodd warned that "we shall have no more partnerships; individuals cannot do business; it will be all done by corporations . . . and every one knows that the moment men form themselves into a corporation they lose their moral responsibility in their business" (Pennsylvania 1873, vol. 7, 765).[32] Such expressions of concern for creditors of small businesses were somewhat disingenuous. As the convention's subsequent actions make clear, the positions of many of the Democratic representatives were driven by fears about the economic power of large-scale business and the wealthy individuals who dominated them. Their warnings about the dangers of limited liability resonated, however, with a certain type of Republican worried about protecting creditors' rights. As one Republican delegate who had originally supported the amendment fretted, the clause would enable any two persons to "set up a grocery on the corner in any town, advertise that they have put in a thousand dollars, spend it all, and leave their creditors minus" (Pennsylvania 1873, vol. 7, 763). As a consequence, the vote on striking the amendment was much less split along party lines than other votes on corporations.

Not only did Democrats in the convention oppose embodying in the constitution a right freely to form corporations, but they went further and imbedded in that document rules that restricted what corporations could do and how they could be governed (Pennsylvania 1874a). These rules were of a specificity that one normally might expect to be reserved for statutes. Their presence in the state's fundamental law signaled the delegates' continued commitment to the idea that the corporate form facilitated a dangerous concentration of economic power that had to be controlled. Hence the 1873 Constitution specified such details as a corporation could not hold real estate beyond what was "necessary and proper for its legitimate business" (Article XVI, Section 6), "no corporation shall issue stocks or bonds except for money, labor done, or money or property actually received" (Article XVI, Section 7), and increases in capital within the ceilings allowed by law required "the consent of the persons holding the larger amount in value of the stock" obtained at a meeting "held after sixty days notice" (Article XVI, Section 7). The constitution even imposed a uniform voting rule for "all elections for directors or managers of a corporation" in order to give minority shareholders a better change to secure representation on the board. It mandated that "each member or shareholder may cast the whole number of his votes for one candidate, or distribute them upon two or more candidates, as he may prefer" (in other words, the constitution required what is known as cumulative voting) (Article XVI, Section 4).

The most vocal supporters of including these restrictions in the constitution spoke about the evils of corporate privileges and the corrupting influence

---

32. Ironically, about a decade later, Dodd would, as lawyer for Standard Oil, engineer the formation of the Standard Oil Trust.

that corporate lobbyists had on the legislature. Thus Charles R. Buckalew, a Democratic delegate from a largely rural part of the state, countered an objection that the requirement that corporations adopt cumulative voting bypassed the legislature and stripped it of its authority to set corporate governance rules by claiming that legislators had been so corrupted by large corporations that they could not be trusted to use their powers for the public good:

> Yes, sir, it does take away the power from the Legislature to give undue power to dominating men or cliques who undertake to run corporations in their own special interests and to the disadvantage of the stockholders. It is a check upon the Fisks and the Vanderbilts of the country in manipulating Legislatures to the injury of the general stockholders of a company; and that is all the effect that it has. The Legislature ought not to have this subject in charge. It ought to be settled as one of the fundamental arrangements concerning these corporate bodies. (Pennsylvania 1873, vol. 5, 759)

Rallying to this kind of traditional anticorporate rhetoric, Democratic delegates voted overwhelmingly (thirty-seven to seven) in favor of inserting into the constitution the requirement that corporations adopt cumulative voting. A large majority of Republican delegates opposed the measure (the Republican vote was fourteen to twenty-seven), but that was not enough to prevent its passage on second reading (Pennsylvania 1873, vol. 5, 768),[33] and the provision easily withstood a motion to delete it on the third reading of the bill (Pennsylvania 1873, vol. 7, 760–61).

Pennsylvania's 1873 Constitution stripped the legislature of much more than the right to regulate voting procedures in corporations (see Pennsylvania 1874a). The revulsion that Delegate Buckalew expressed about the corrupt use of legislative power permeated the entire convention. As a result, Article III, Section 7 contained a long list of categories of special legislation that the legislature was henceforward prohibited from enacting, ranging from the political (laws "locating or changing county seats, erecting new counties or changing county lines," "creating offices, or prescribing the powers and duties of officers in counties, cities, boroughs, townships, election or school districts," "for the opening and conducting of elections, or fixing or changing the place of voting"), to the judicial (laws "changing the venue in civil or criminal cases" or "regulating the practice or jurisdiction of, or changing the rules of evidence in, any judicial proceeding"), to the personal (laws "changing the names of persons or places," "authorizing the adoption or legitimation of children," or "granting divorces"). Prominent on the list, however, was the prohibition against special charters of incorporation: "The General Assembly shall not pass any local or special law . . .

---

33. The one Liberal Republican voted for cumulative voting, and two unaffiliated at-large delegates voted against. One unaffiliated at-large delegate was absent at the time of the vote, as were seventeen Democrats and twenty-seven Republicans.

Creating corporations, or amending, renewing or extending the charters thereof [or] Granting to any corporation, association or individual any special or exclusive privilege or immunity."[34] No longer would the legislature have the power to enact private bills that enabled corporations to evade the restrictive provisions of the general laws.

1.3.3   Pennsylvania's 1874 General Incorporation Law

Now that there was no escape hatch through private legislation, the content of the public laws governing corporations became critically important. When the new legislature convened in early 1874, the senate immediately got to work on a revision of the state's general incorporation law. The senators who tackled the assignment understood the stakes involved. As one member put it, "While we agree that the prohibition against special legislation creating corporations is wise, we also agree that we must be careful of the ground upon which we are walking." He went on to warn against writing a statue that will "build up a Chinese wall around our great State" that will scare off foreign capital (Pennsylvania 1874b, 541). The Speaker of the Senate, Butler B. Strang (a Republican from Tioga County) put the matter even more bluntly. Referring to the undeveloped parts of the state, he proclaimed, "[I]n my judgment, the question [is] whether that provision of the new Constitution . . . is to operate so as to entirely blot out the enterprise and the investment of capital" (Pennsylvania 1874b, 541).

Although Republicans dominated both houses of the Pennsylvania legislature in 1874, the statute that finally passed on April 29, 1874, fell dramatically short of what Carey and his allies in the constitutional convention had wanted.[35] Rather than a liberal statement of the right of association, the statute restricted access to corporate charters to a list of specifically enumerated types of enterprises.[36] Rather than simply granting members of corporations limited liability, it continued to burden them with additional liabilities. Rather than a statute that allowed incorporators a great deal of contractual flexibility like the British law Carey so admired, the act mandated important aspects of every corporation's governance structure. In addition, the law placed strict limitations on the size of many types of corporations, as well as the extent of their real estate holdings and indebtedness.

---

34. Many other states enacted similar constitutional prohibitions around the same time. See Hennessey and Wallis 2014.

35. See "AN ACT To provide for the incorporation and regulation of certain corporations" enacted April 29, 1874.

36. Section 2 listed the types of "Corporations Not for Profit" that could be formed under the act and also the types of "Corporations for Profit." The latter included narrow categories, such as "the supply of ice to the public," or "the construction and maintenance of a bridge over streams within this state," but also broad categories, such as "the carrying on of any mechanical, mining, quarrying or manufacturing business." "The manufacture of iron or steel" was listed separately from other manufacturing activities, and the statute imposed some different rules on corporations in this category, as it did for other specific types of corporations.

More specifically, the statute directed that the business of any manufacturing, mining, or quarrying company must "be confined exclusively to the purpose . . . specified in its charter, and no such company shall manufacture or sell any commodity or articles of merchandise other than those therein specified" (Section 43).[37] Shareholders were subject to double liability. That is, in addition to their investment, they were individually liable "to the amount of stock held by each of them, for all work or labor done, or materials furnished, to carry on the operations" of their company (Section 14). Shareholders in iron and steel companies were fully liable as individuals for "debts due to the laborers, mechanics, or clerks, for services" provided in the past six months (Section 38, Clause 8). Those in manufacturing companies more generally were jointly and severally liable for the company's debts "[i]f any part of the capital stock . . . [was] withdrawn and refunded to the stockholders." Directors were also personally liable for dividends declared when the company was insolvent or if they encumbered the enterprise beyond the statutory ceiling (Section 39, Clause 5).

Corporations could enact bylaws for their governance, but the statute specified that the business of every corporation "shall be managed and conducted by a president, a board of directors or trustees, a clerk, a treasurer," and such other officers as the corporation authorizes. Directors or trustees were to be chosen annually by the stockholders. There must be at least three, and a majority had to be present for the board to act (Section 5). As mandated by the state constitution, stockholders had the right to cumulate their votes for specific directors or trustees (Section 10). Corporations could borrow money but, except as otherwise provided by the act, only to an amount "not exceeding one-half of the capital stock . . . paid in, and at a rate of interest not exceeding six per centum" (Section 13). Corporations could issue preferred stock with the "consent of a majority in interest of its stockholders, obtained at a meeting to be called for that purpose" (Section 16). The law required a similar majority vote of the stockholders to increase or decrease a corporation's capital and specified in elaborate detail the method of conducting such a ballot (Sections 19–21).

With a few exceptions, corporations chartered under the act were limited to $1 million in capital (Section 11). Iron and steel companies could have a capital of up to $5 million and could issue bonds amounting to three times paid-in capital ("bearing interest not exceeding six per centum"), but they could not hold more than 10,000 acres of land within the state, "including leased lands" (Section 38, Clause 1). As a general rule, it was not lawful for corporations to use their funds to purchase stock in any other corporation

37. Legislators were especially concerned to prevent corporations from establishing company stores, and the section went on to restrict buying and selling on company premises and to prohibit companies from withholding employees' wages in payment for goods. See for example, Pennsylvania (1874b, 1019, 1134, 1145).

"or to hold the same, except as collateral security for a prior indebtedness" (Section 11), but iron and steel companies were specifically exempted from this prohibition (Section 38, Clause 6). "Companies incorporated . . . for the carrying on of any mechanical, mining, quarrying, or manufacturing" business also faced a ceiling on capital of $5 million, but these companies, upon the vote of three-quarters of their stockholders, could also issue a second kind of stock called "special stock" up to two-fifths of their total capital. Special stock resembled bonds in that it was "subject to redemption at par, after a fixed time, to be stated in the certificates." It also bore a fixed rate of dividend, "not exceeding four percentum." Holders of special stock bore no personal liability beyond their investment. Mechanical, mining, quarrying, and manufacturing corporations could hold real estate, but only so much as was "necessary for the purpose of its organization," and they could borrow up to the amount of their paid-in capital (Section 39, Clause 7).

The prescriptive features of the bill were present when it was first reported out of committee (as Senate Bill no. 44) on February 11, 1874, and they survived the amendment process largely intact. Most of them did not even generate any discussion. The main exception was a provision limiting the amount of land that iron and steel companies could own or lease to 10,000 acres. Thomas Chalfant, a Democratic senator who represented Columbia, Montour, Lycoming, and Sullivan counties, proposed an amendment that would reduce the figure to 5,000 acres, and his motion generated a heated exchange about the need to attract capital to develop the state's resources versus the danger of allowing corporations to monopolize those resources. Chalfant's motion was defeated by a vote of fifteen to ten (eleven Republicans and one Liberal Republican voted against the amendment and six Republicans voted in favor of it).[38] What is most striking, however, is that no one in this Republican-dominated senate argued that the limitation on land holdings should be removed altogether. Rather the debate was over whether the provision should be even stricter than the one in the original draft.

1.3.4 Pennsylvania's 1874 Statute for Partnership Associations

The Republicans, it seems, had something else up their sleeves, for a few days after the legislature passed the new general incorporation law, the senate began consideration of an enabling statute for another form of limited liability company that would not be called a corporation and hence would not push any of the same political buttons.[39] Senate Bill no. 295, "An act

38. Three Republicans were absent. The Democrat vote was four in favor, three opposed, and five absent. For the vote, see Pennsylvania (1874b, 542). The party affiliations of the senators are from Smull (1874).

39. As Edward H. Warren later cynically commented, "it would seem to be probably that those who favored the principle of liability limited to the capital subscribed thought that the legislature would be more likely to pass a law sanctioning such a limitation if the term 'corporations' were avoided in framing the law." See Warren (1929, 512).

authorizing the formation of partnership associations " was introduced in the legislature on May 4 and became law on June 2.[40] The statute passed with overwhelming bipartisan support and generated little debate in either house en route to passage.[41]

In many respects the bill was opposite in spirit to the general incorporation act. It was only three pages long, as opposed to thirty-five pages for the corporation bill, and the business form it enabled was remarkably flexible. The bill's simple language allowing "any three or more persons . . . to form a partnership association, for the purpose of conducting any lawful business or occupation within the United States or elsewhere" was similar to Carey's original proposal to the constitutional convention. Although the term of a partnership association was limited to a maximum of twenty years, there were no ceilings on capital or on the amount of real estate that could be owned and no restrictions on the types of business in which the firm could engage, the state of citizenship of the incorporators, or where the company could conduct its business (so long as it maintained a headquarters in Pennsylvania). Any three people could form a partnership association simply by registering with a local county official. A supplementary act passed on May 1, 1876, allowed the capital to be paid "in real or personal estate, mines or other property, at a valuation to be approved by all the members subscribing."[42]

The main difference between the bill and Carey's proposal was a provision that linked the new form to the ordinary partnership by enabling the existing membership to determine whether or not to admit new members. Section 4 of the act provided that interests in a partnership association, like those in a corporation, were to be considered "personal estate" and hence transferrable, but it also specified that "no transferee of any interest . . . shall be entitled thereafter to any participation in the subsequent business of said association, unless he or she be elected thereto by a vote of a majority of the members in number and value of their interests." The statute thus explicitly allowed (indeed, required) members of partnership associations to do something that members of corporations could not easily do at this time—control the identity of their associates.[43] In Pennsylvania, as elsewhere in the late

40. As will become clear, the new form was much like a modern LLC. See "AN ACT Authoring the formation of partnership associations, in which the capital subscribed shall alone be responsible for the debts of the association, except under certain circumstances" June 2, 1874.

41. In the senate, Republicans voted fourteen to one in favor (five absent) and Democrats, six to two in favor (four absent). In the House, Republicans voted seventy-four to two in support of the bill (eight absent), and Democrats, twenty-three to thirteen (seven absent). For the roll call votes, see Pennsylvania (1874b, 1982). Party affiliations are from Smull (1874).

42. "AN ACT Supplementary to the act, approved the second day of June, Anno Domini eighteen hundred and seventy-four, . . . providing for the contribution of real and personal estate to the capital stock" May 1, 1876.

43. However, a supplementary statute enacted on June 25, 1885, enabled organizers of a partnership association to opt out of this provision. See "A SUPPLEMENT To an act, entitled 'An act authorizing the formation of partnership associations, . . .' regulating the transfer of interests in said partnerships associations."

nineteenth century, courts did not permit corporations to enact bylaws that impeded the transferability of shares. They generally refused to uphold rules that limited in any way shareholders' ability to sell their property, including those that required shareholders to give each other a first right of refusal.[44]

In other respects, the enabling act for partnership associations was highly permissive with respect to internal governance. The act specified procedures for winding up the company, required partnership associations to hold at least one general meeting each year at which the membership would elect three to five managers, including a chairman, a secretary, and a treasurer (or a chairman and a secretary-treasurer) (Section 5), and forbid a partnership association from lending "its credit, its name or its capital" to any of its members (or to anyone else without "the consent in writing of a majority in number and value of interest") (Section 7). Otherwise, all governance rules were up to the members.[45]

The limit on the transferability of shares should have made it more difficult for partnership associations to raise capital from external investors and thus may have been what made the form palatable to Democrats fearful of concentrations of capital. Intriguingly, however, the greater flexibility of the form seems to have heightened its appeal to some very large enterprises. Although there are no general counts of the numbers and types of firms that adopted the form, I collected the registrations of all partnership associations filed in the county of Philadelphia for every fifth year beginning in 1877.[46] As table 1.2 shows, most of the firms adopting the new form were small, but especially early on a significant number of larger enterprises found the partnership-association form appealing. As late as 1887, approximately one-fifth of the registrants had capitalizations of $100,000 or more, and several had considerably more.[47]

44. For Pennsylvania cases recognizing that the transfer rules for partnership associations was different than for corporations, see *Eliot v. Himrod*, 108 Pa. 569 (1885) and *Carter v. Producers' Oil Co., Ltd.*, 182 Pa. 551 (1897). A Maryland Court of Appeals articulated the general principle in 1896, when it ruled that any such bylaws constituted "an unreasonable and a palpable restraint upon the alienation of property." See *Bloede Co. v. Bloede*, 84 Md. 129 (1896, 141). For further discussion and additional case citations, see Harris and Lamoreaux (2010).

45. About two decades later, the legislature imposed a voting rule of a "majority in value of interest" for the choice of managers and a "majority in number and value of interest" to adopt bylaws. By then, however, the popularity of the form had peaked. See "A SUPPLEMENT To an act, entitled 'an act to authorize the formation of partnership associations, . . . providing for the continuance of such associations after the expiration of the original term, prescribing the manner of electing managers thereof" June 8, 1895.

46. Partnership Books, 1836–1955, RG 5.23, City Archives, City of Philadelphia, Department of Records. There are tax ledgers in the state archives beginning in 1880 that include partnership associations, but I could not find in them many of the partnership associations that I know existed. See State Treasurer, Capital Stock Tax Ledgers, 1876–1900. These records were indexed in two volumes mislabeled as Corporate Endorsement Index, Nos. 7–8, 1909–13. For later years, see Bonus Ledgers for Limited Partnerships and Associations, No. 1, 1914–16. These volumes are all in Record Group 28, Records of Treasury Department, Pennsylvania State Archives, Harrisburg, Pennsylvania.

47. Partnership associations initially had more advantageous tax treatment than corporations, but the legislature eliminated that difference in 1879 (Freedley 1883).

Table 1.2   Number and size of partnership associations registered in Philadelphia County, 1877–1927

Year	Number of firms	Percent with 3 owners	Percent with 4–9 owners	Percent with 10+ owners	Average capital in $$	Percent with capital ≤ $10,000	Percent with $10,000 < capital < $100,000	Percent with capital ≥ $100,000
1877	31	45.2	45.2	9.7	113,300	35.4	38.7	25.8
1882	47	59.6	36.1	4.3	43,700	46.8	38.3	14.9
1887	59	57.6	37.3	5.1	69,600	45.8	32.2	22.0
1892	69	69.6	29.0	1.4	111,800	56.5	37.7	5.8
1897	65	69.2	27.7	3.1	48,400	67.7	18.5	13.8
1902	30	83.3	13.3	3.3	6,400	80.0	20.0	0.0
1907	12	75.0	16.7	8.3	8,000	83.3	16.7	0.0
1912	5	80.0	20.0	0.0	6,000	100.0	0.0	0.0
1917	0	n/a	n/a	n/a	0	n/a	n/a	n/a
1922	1	0.0	100.0	0.0	10,000	100.0	0.0	0.0
1927	2	50.0	50.0	0.0	2,700	100.0	0.0	0.0

Source: Partnership Books, 1836–1955, RG 5.23, City Archives, City of Philadelphia, Department of Records.

An important example of a large partnership association (though not one registered in Philadelphia) was the Carnegie Steel Company, Limited, capitalized at $25 million. At the time of its organization in 1892, the company included four major steel plants, several iron furnaces and mills, two coke works, and an assortment of other properties. The form appealed to the owners because of Andrew Carnegie's dominant position in the company. A few years earlier Carnegie had been so seriously ill that it appeared he would die, and his partners in the company's predecessor firms (all ordinary partnerships) had faced the dire prospect that the companies would be bankrupted by the cost of settling Carnegie's estate. Although they could have protected themselves by organizing their enterprise as a corporation, Carnegie was not willing to go along. He wanted to be able to control who could be a member of the firm, reward talented managers with ownership shares, and rid the firm of partners who did not share his strategic vision. The solution, the so-called "Iron Clad" agreement, was possible under the flexible partnership association statute but not under Pennsylvania's general incorporation law. In the event of Carnegie's death, his partners got the right to buy out his interest at book value over an extended period of time (fifteen years). In exchange, Carnegie got a clause that enabled him (upon the vote of three-quarters of the members in number and value of shares) to force a partner to sell out his interest in the company at book value.[48]

Another example of an important firm that took the partnership association form was the Bessemer Steel Company, Limited, the patent pool that controlled the process of making Bessemer steel in the United States. This company filed its registration papers in Philadelphia in 1877. It had an initial capital of $825,000 and a membership consisting of five individuals (the association's managers) and eleven major steel companies. The firms that belonged to the association had the right to use patents held by the pool at the cost of a specified royalty per ton of steel produced. Profits from the royalties were then divided among the members in the form of dividends. The partnership-association form allowed members of the pool to develop a set of enforceable rules to control access to steel technology. Members that did not adhere to the rules, that failed to give a proper accounting of their production, or that refused to pay royalties they owed could be expelled by a two-thirds vote of the "members present at a meeting called for the purpose . . . and shall thereafter have no rights in the Association or in the property which it owns and controls."[49]

48. The threat of Carnegie's death gave all the partners an interest in keeping the company's book value below market value, so the agreement had considerable bite. The details of the agreement became public when Carnegie tried to force Henry Clay Frick out, and Frick sued to get the company revalued. See Wall (1970, 491–93); Livesay (1975, 171–72); Bridge (1903, 336–38).

49. Articles of Association of the Bessemer Steel Company, Limited, 1 March 1877, in Limited Partnerships, F. T. W., 1873–1879 (LP4), Partnership Books, 1836–1955, RG 5.23, City Archives, City of Philadelphia, Department of Records.

The ability to control access to valuable property also explains the attractiveness of the form for the Producers' Oil Company, a partnership association created by an organization of oil producers (the Producers' Protective Association) with the aim of liberating well owners from their dependence on the Standard Oil Trust. The whole purpose of the enterprise was to gain control of oil supplies and keep them out of Standard's hands. If the company had been organized as a corporation, the producers would never have been able to prevent some of their number from selling out to Standard; they had suffered such defections before. The partnership-association form gave them the necessary means, however, because the simple purchase of shares was not sufficient to convey membership in the company (Tarbell 1904, vol. 2, ch. 15). Transferees also had to be voted in by the continuing membership. In fact, parties associated with Standard managed to buy up a huge block of the shares in the Producers' Oil Company, but they were not admitted to the company. John J. Carter, the member of the company who took possession of these shares on behalf of the Standard interests, sued to be allowed to vote the additional interest, but he was not successful. On appeal, the Supreme Court of Pennsylvania ruled in favor of the partnership association. "We cannot assent," the justices declared, "to the plaintiff's claim that the defendant company is a corporation restricted, in the adoption of by-laws, rules and regulations for its government, to such as it is within the power of the latter to prescribe. It may be conceded that the defendant company has some of the qualities of a corporation, but it is nevertheless a partnership association, governed by the statutes and articles under which it was organized."[50] Under Pennsylvania law corporations had to adhere to governance rules imposed by the statute and could not restrict the transferability or voting rights of shares. But partnership associations had much more contractual flexibility, and by means of carefully worded bylaws the Producers' Oil Company was able to prevent Standard Oil from buying control.[51]

The courts' willingness to treat partnership associations differently from corporations could also be a disadvantage, however. In an 1885 debt case involving the Keystone Boot and Shoe Company, Limited, the Pennsylvania Supreme Court used this same feature of partnership associations to justify piercing the veil of limited liability and holding the members unlimitedly liable as general partners. Although for convenience partnership associa-

---

50. *Carter v. Producers' Oil Co., Ltd.*, 182 Pa. 551 (1897, 573–74).

51. The company had adopted a bylaw prohibiting any member from selling or transferring "any interest in capital or shares of stock to any person not a member in good standing of the Producers' Protective Association, unless with the approval in writing of a majority of the board of managers." The bylaw also specified that "[n]o transferee of any interest in capital or shares of stock shall be entitled to participate in the subsequent business or profits of the association, or to vote on such interest or shares so transferred, unless elected to membership therein by a vote of a majority of the members in number and value of their interests." *Carter v. Producers' Oil Co., Ltd.*, 182 Pa. 551 (1897), "Prior History."

tions were "clothed with many of the features and powers of a corporation," the court ruled that in a partnership association, unlike a corporation, "no man can purchase the interest of a member and participate in the subsequent business, unless by a vote of a majority of the members in number and value of their interests." Partnership associations were thus in a fundamental way different from corporations. Moreover, the state did not grant a charter to a partnership association; its privileges rested entirely on the statement submitted at the time of registration. Because a corporation was a chartered entity, its "existence and ability to contract [could not] be questioned" in a suit brought against a corporation for payment of a debt. But the legitimacy of a partnership association rested on the truthfulness of its filing. As a result, it was "competent" for a plaintiff suing for payment of a debt "either to point to a fatal defect" in the statement "or to prove that an essential requisite, though formally stated, is falsely stated."[52]

This type of procreditor judicial reasoning had earlier, in Pennsylvania and elsewhere, severely curtailed the appeal of the limited-partnership form by increasing the risk that limited partners would be held fully liable as general partners for their firm's debts.[53] The lower court judge who tried the Keystone Boot and Shoe case made a valiant attempt to prevent the partnership-association form from suffering the same fate. Counsel for the plaintiffs had cited the case law on the earlier form in support of their claim that the members of Keystone Boot and Shoe Company, Limited, should be considered general partners who were individually liable for the company's debts. But the judge did not accept this line of reasoning, instead ruling that the 1836 enabling act for limited partnerships was so different from the 1874 act for partnership associations, "that the decisions under the former are not to be taken as conclusive of the rights and liability of the parties under the latter Act." For example, the 1836 act explicitly listed a set of circumstances in which failure to conform to the terms of the statute would cause limited partners to be held fully liable, but the 1874 statute included no similar provisions. "We must presume," the judge declared, "that the Act of 1836 and the decisions under it were well known to the law-makers at the time the Act of 1874 as passed," so the omission of similar penalties "is good reason for concluding that no such liability was intended." The 1874 act authorized the formation of partnership associations in which the capital subscribed "shall alone be liable for the debts of the association except under certain circumstances," and the judge pointed out, "in no instance do the excepted circumstances impose a liability as general partners on the members of the association."[54] The Pennsylvania Supreme Court, however, reversed the judge's decision on appeal. The high court justices acknowledged that the Act of

---

52. *Eliot v. Himrod*, 108 Pa. 569 (1885, 580).
53. A key Pennsylvania case was *Andrews v. Schott*, 10 Pa. 47 (1848).
54. *Eliot v. Himrod*, 108 Pa. 569 (1885).

1874 bore "little resemblance to the Act of 1836" and was far less stringent in its terms. Rushing to the defense of creditors, however, they insisted "that the statute demands a true statement of capital" at the time of registration, because the filing is what informs the public "of the strength of the association."[55]

This idea that creditors could rely on the initial statement of capital for information about the credit worthiness of companies that potentially lasted twenty years is dubious to say the least and certainly formed no part of the jurisprudence on corporations, even though corporate capital could also be paid in real or personal estate.[56] Nonetheless, the Pennsylvania Supreme Court enforced this principle increasingly stringently in a series of decisions holding members of partnership associations liable for their company's debts.[57] Most of the opinions were written by James P. Sterrett, an upright Republican judge from Alleghany County, who first joined the court in 1877 (Jordan 1921, 153–56). The composition of the court seems to have shifted in Sterrett's favor during the late 1880s with four new justices (out of a total of seven) elected in 1887 and 1888. Three were Republicans and one was a Democrat.[58] Two of the justices leaving the court had dissented in the first case holding members of a partnership association unlimitedly liable because of a defective filing.[59] With these justices gone, Sterrett faced little opposition to his strict construction of the statute. The court began rigorously to assess registration filings to determine whether creditors could "form any estimate of its quantity, character or value,"[60] and the justices showed no compunction about holding members of partnership associations unlimitedly liable as general partners in cases where the statements were insufficiently detailed. Under Sterrett's leadership, the court insisted that property put into an association as capital had to be accurately and fully described. That was more important than valuing it precisely because if the valuation "is excessive, the creditor can decline to give the company credit." By contrast, "if the description be so defective or inaccurate that the creditor may be misled, he has no means of forming an accurate judgment."[61]

55. *Eliot v. Himrod*, 108 Pa. 569 (1885, 579).

56. See Section 17 of Pennsylvania's 1874 general incorporation act.

57. See *Hill, Keiser & Co. v. Stetler*, 127 Pa. 145 (1888); *Vanhorn v. Corcoran*, 127 Pa. 255 (1889); *Sheble v. Strong*, 128 Pa. 315 (1889); *Gearing v. Carroll*, 151 Pa. 79 (1892); *Haslet v. Kent*, 160 Pa. 85 (1894); *First National Bank of Danville v. Creveling*, 177 Pa. 270 (1896); *Lee & Bacchus v. Burnley*, 195 Pa. 58 (1900).

58. See "Historical List of Supreme Court Justices" on the website of the Unified Judicial System of Pennsylvania, http://www.pacourts.us/learn/history/historical-list-of-supreme-court -justices, accessed 24 September 2014. See also Williamson et al. (1898, 41–43); Blanchard (1900, 943–44); *The Twentieth Century Bench and Bar of Pennsylvania* (1903, 210–12); "Williams, Henry W., Assoc. Justice," *PA-Roots*, http://www.pa-roots.org/data/read.php?690,502081, accessed 3 Oct. 2014.

59. See *Maloney v. Bruce*, 94 Pa. 249 (1880).

60. *Vanhorn v. Corcoran*, 127 Pa. 255 (1889, 266).

61. *Cock v. Bailey*, 146 Pa. 328 (1892, 340). See also *Rehfuss v. Moore*, 134 Pa. 462 (1890).

As a result of this emphasis on an accurate description of personal estate paid in as capital, the registration documents filed for both limited partnerships and partnership associations grew longer and longer in the early 1890s. The most extreme example was the filing for Wanamaker's department store, a limited partnership, which took up an entire ledger volume and part of a second and seems to have included a complete inventory of the store's goods. But many other registrations went on for scores of pages.[62] Moreover, even the most painstaking filing was no guarantee against creditors' attempts to pierce the veil, as members of the National Electric Company, Limited, found to their chagrin. At the time of its registration in 1890, the company had a capital of $8,500, most of which had been paid in as items of personal estate. Although the company filed a long inventory that included such detail as 109 8" flat porcelain shades valued at 13¢ each, and 34 boxes of no. 8 screws valued at 35¢ each, the trial judge did not find the inventory sufficiently detailed and ruled in favor of creditors who were suing the members personally to recover a debt. This time, however, the Pennsylvania Supreme Court reversed. Justice J. Brewster McCollum, a Democrat, wrote the opinion. Noting that the company's filing "consisted of a hundred and fifty-one items, the integrity and valuation of which were not questioned," he ruled that "this schedule was sufficient to enable parties dealing with the company to readily ascertain the kind, amount and value of the property contributed to its capital" and that "the defendants in forming the National Electric Company, Limited, honestly sought to comply with the statutes."[63]

In fact, the justices had begun to back away from their extreme position in 1892, declaring that "[i]t was never intended" that the filing requirements "should be used as a trap to catch persons who have honestly complied with their substantial requisites, and impale them upon a meaningless technicality."[64] But the damage was done. As the cost of filing mounted along with the length of the required descriptions, the popularity of the partnership-association form declined. As table 1.2 shows, in Philadelphia use of the form peaked during the 1890s and then dropped precipitously, so that by the 1920s hardly any partnership associations were being registered.[65] This decline was not likely a result of a lack of desire to form private limited

62. The Wanamaker's filing was in Limited Partnership, vols. 10–11 (LP10–LP11), Partnership Books, 1836–1955, RG 5.23, Philadelphia City Archives. I examined all registrations of limited partnerships and partnership associations filed during every fifth year and found no long inventories before the 1890s. This time pattern suggests that the already strict construction of the limited partnership statute was becoming even stricter as a result of the litigation over partnership associations.

63. See *Robbins Electric Co. v. Weber*, 172 Pa. 635 (1896, 644–45).

64. *Cock v. Bailey*, 146 Pa. 328 (1892, 342). See also *Laflin & Rand Co. v. Steytler*, 146 Pa. 434 (1892).

65. Fifty-three percent of the partnership associations registered in Philadelphia registrations during 1892 and 1897 had capital paid in the form of personal or real estate. The proportion fell to 36 percent in 1902 and 1907. None of the few partnerships registered in the 1920s had capital in this form.

liability companies. When similar types of entities were introduced in Germany and France, they quickly established themselves. Within two decades of the passage of enabling legislation in Germany more than one-third of all new firms registered as private limited liability companies, and in France the figure was more than 75 percent (Guinnane et al. 2007). Moreover, in the United States today, LLCs are quickly becoming the form of choice for the majority of new enterprises, even though the corporate form is much more flexible now than it was in Pennsylvania in the late nineteenth century.[66]

If the partnership association form was so useful, why did contemporary business people not demand that the legislature fix the problem? In part, I think, the answer is that the small-scale enterprises that made the greatest use of the form did not yet constitute an organized interest group capable of lobbying for changes in the law. It would not be until the second half of the twentieth century, when high income tax rates encouraged them to make common cause, that small businesses would join together and lobby for changes in the menu of organizational forms (Lamoreaux 2004). Another part of the answer is federalism. Only a small number of states followed Pennsylvania's lead and passed enabling legislation for the partnership-association form: Virginia in 1874, Michigan in 1877, New Jersey in 1880, and Ohio in 1881 (Warren 1929; Stransky 1956; Schwartz 1965; Gazur and Goff 1991). There was consequently a great deal of uncertainty about how partnership associations would be treated by courts in other states. An 1897 case in which a Massachusetts court held a Pennsylvania partnership association to be an ordinary partnership helped kill off interest in the form.[67]

The corporate charter-mongering competition that developed at the end of the nineteenth century in response to the rise of large-scale business enterprises also undercut the partnership-association form (Chandler 1977; Lamoreaux 1985). Before this rivalry erupted in the 1890s, nearly all corporations obtained charters from the states in which they originated. New Jersey's famous amendments to its general incorporation laws in 1888 and 1889 broke the pattern. Under existing state laws corporations generally could not own stock in other companies, and two corporations could merge only if one of them dissolved and the other purchased its assets. The New Jersey revisions not only created a streamlined process for mergers but facilitated the creation of holding companies by allowing one corporation to own shares in another (Grandy 1989). Over the next two decades, most of the enterprises involved in the period's successively larger waves of mergers switched to New Jersey charters, and the state, which taxed corporations on the basis of their authorized capital stock, found its revenues soaring. New Jersey's

---

66. For the number of registrations of LLCs relative to corporations in each state, see the International Association of Commercial Administrators, *Annual Report of Jurisdictions.*
67. *Edwards v. Warren Linoline & Gasoline Works*, 168 Mass. 564 (1897).

flush treasury inspired a number of other states (most notably Delaware, but also West Virginia, Maryland, Maine, and New York) to compete for the business of chartering corporations by enacting still more liberal laws (Butler 1985; Grandy 1989).

Although the literature has focused on the advantages of New Jersey's amendments for consolidations formed by merger, the charter-mongering competition also highlighted other benefits of New Jersey's general incorporation laws. Like Pennsylvania, New Jersey had revised its generation incorporation law in the mid-1870s in response to a new constitutional ban on special charters (Cadman 1949). New Jersey's general incorporation act was much less restrictive, however. It allowed corporations to be formed for any lawful purpose and placed no limits on the amount of capital they could raise, the sums they could borrow, or the acreage of real estate they could own. Incorporators also had more freedom to shape the governance structure of their companies. The act included a number of default rules, but the certificate, charter, or bylaws could specify alternatives. For example, each member of a corporation had one vote for each share owned, unless otherwise specified (Section III. 38). The quorum for stockholders' meetings was a majority of the shares, unless the bylaws indicated otherwise (Section II. 21). Similarly, although the New Jersey law required a two-thirds vote to increase a corporation's capital beyond the amount specified in its certificate, issue a new class of preferred shares, or voluntarily dissolve the corporation, the certificate could specify a different voting threshold to move into a new line of business or decrease capitalization (Section II. 33). More significantly, the certificate could include "any limitation upon the powers of the corporation, the directors, and the stockholders that the parties signing the same desire," so long as these limitations did not "attempt to exempt the corporation, the directors, or the stockholders, from the performance of any duty imposed by law" (Section V). Hence large corporations in Pennsylvania or elsewhere that wanted more contractual flexibility than their state allowed could take out charters in New Jersey instead. There was no need any longer to battle their legislatures for more permissive laws.[68]

1.4   Pennsylvania in Comparative Perspective

Before its foray into corporate charter mongering, New Jersey's nineteenth-century political history had much in common with Pennsylvania's. The state maintained a property qualification for voting until 1807 and a tax qualification until 1844, but these barriers seem to have been quite minimal, and throughout the first half of the century a large fraction of adult white males voted—more even than in Pennsylvania (Engerman and Sokoloff 2005). In New Jersey, as in Pennsylvania, corporations were an ongoing subject

---

68. For the text of the act, see Corbin (1881).

of heated debate, and Democrats continually pushed to restrict corporate privileges and level the economic playing field. At the 1844 state constitutional convention, they failed to secure a provision requiring a two-thirds super majority in the legislature to charter corporations, but the general incorporation law for manufacturing that the legislature enacted in 1846 was highly restrictive. By 1849, however, the political balance in the state shifted and the legislature rewrote the law. Although the revised statute still included a number of restrictive provisions (see table 1.1), it was generally more permissive than that of neighboring states, and the gap would grow again in 1875 when the legislature responded to a constitutional ban on special charters by passing a new general incorporation law (Cadman 1949; Harris and Lamoreaux 2010).

The famous 1888–1889 amendments seem to have been an opportunistic response to a tax problem rather than a logical extension of the trend toward permissiveness. Before the Civil War, New Jersey's residents paid almost no property taxes, and levies on railroad corporations constituted the bulk of the state's revenues. The state emerged from the war with a large burden of bonded debt that the railroads resisted assuming in a variety of ways, including merging with corporations chartered elsewhere (Grandy 1989). Astute contemporaries seem to have noticed that the more liberal provisions of New Jersey's general incorporation laws were inducing a growing trickle of firms to take out charters in the state (Yablon 2007). Corporate attorney James Brooks Dill, in particular, saw that there was money to be made increasing this flow. Dill helped to guide the amendments through the legislature and then actively promoted the advantages of a New Jersey charter, setting up a new firm, The Corporation Trust Company, to handle the paperwork of companies headquartered outside the state and to serve as their legal representatives in New Jersey. Dill's efforts paid off handsomely both for himself and for the state of New Jersey. Combinations that had previously resorted to the trust device now took out New Jersey charters, as did virtually all of the giant consolidations formed during the merger waves of the period. Much of this business, as well as that of other firms flocking to New Jersey, went through Dill's firm. At the same time, tax revenues soared. By the end of the so-called Great Merger Movement in 1904, fully 60 percent of New Jersey's income came from incorporation fees and franchise taxes. Not only did New Jersey's budget move from deficit to surplus, but the state was able to completely pay off its bonded debt and abolish property taxes on its citizens (Grandy 1989; Yablon 2007).

New Jersey's success in luring the charters of many of the nation's largest businesses stimulated a backlash within the state—a resurgence of anticorporate politics—that helped elect Democratic candidate Woodrow Wilson governor in 1910 and climaxed with the passage of a set of antitrust statutes in 1913 that effectively undid the liberal amendments of the late 1880s. The state's revenues from chartering corporations immediately plunged, and the legislature reversed course again. But the damage was done. The state never regained its previous position, and Delaware emerged victorious from the charter-mongering competition (Grandy 1989; Rutledge 1937; Wells 2000).

Delaware's rise to be the domicile of choice for the nation's largest businesses could never have been predicted from its nineteenth-century political history. Like Pennsylvania, Delaware had broadened its franchise in the late eighteenth century by shifting from a property to a tax qualification for voting (Engerman and Sokoloff 2005). As in Pennsylvania, moreover, opposition to corporate privileges was an important issue around which the new mass democratic movements of the early nineteenth century formed. If anything, these movements were stronger in Delaware than in Pennsylvania or New Jersey at the same time, and Democrats in Delaware succeeded where their counterparts in the other two states had failed, securing a tough constitutional provision requiring a two-thirds vote in both houses of the legislature to charter a corporation.[69] Delaware did not even enact a general incorporation law until an amendment to the state's constitution in 1875 specially authorized one, and even then the procedure the legislature set up was so cumbersome that few businesses took advantage of it and instead turned to paid lobbyists (and perhaps bribery) to get special charters through the legislature.[70] Delaware's permissive 1899 general incorporation law was thus, for all practical purposes, its first. Enacted in response to a ban on special charters embodied in the state's new 1897 constitution (itself a response to what was perceived to be the corruption of the legislative process), it seems to have been shepherded through the legislature by a group of individuals alert to the revenue possibilities of charter mongering, as well as to the profits that could be earned by serving as local agents for out-of-state corporations. It essentially copied the New Jersey statute but charged lower fees, and the resulting flow of revenues changed the course of the state's corporate politics permanently. In contrast to New Jersey's experience, anticorporate forces in Delaware never regained the upper hand (Arsht 1976; Larcom 1937; Grandy 1989).

As more and more large firms took out charters in New Jersey, Delaware, and the other charter-mongering states, legislatures elsewhere reacted to the resulting loss of revenue by liberalizing their own general incorporation statutes, generating fears of a regulatory race to the bottom (US Commissioner of Corporations 1904). This response, however, was less full-throttled than

69. Such a measure was repeatedly proposed by delegates to Pennsylvania's 1837 constitutional convention, but did not succeed. See, for example, Pennsylvania 1837, vol. 2, 224–25. As noted above, a similar measure also failed in New Jersey.

70. Under Delaware's 1875 general incorporation law the application for a charter had to be filed with the local county judge and notice of the filing published for three weeks in a newspaper. The judge then determined whether the application was lawful and the corporation not injurious to the community. If the decision was positive, another period of public notice followed before the ruling could take effect. An 1883 revision of the law streamlined the process somewhat but still required the local judge's approval. See Arsht (1976).

is generally recognized.[71] Some states, it is true, responded by undertaking complete revisions of their statutes. Massachusetts, for example, created a special commission in 1902 that concluded that Massachusetts's general incorporation law was unsuited to modern business conditions (Massachusetts 1903b). The commissioners drafted a completely new statute that the legislature adopted in 1903 almost as proposed (Massachusetts 1903a). The act eliminated a number of the old law's most prescriptive features, including ceilings on the amount of capital a corporation could raise, but it retained other restrictions that provided more substantial protection for shareholders than Delaware's law (Dodd 1936).

Other states (Pennsylvania is a good example) did not undertake a complete revision of their general incorporation statutes until much later, instead meeting the charter mongerers' challenge with a series of amendments that gradually moved the law in the new direction. For example, a supplement to Pennsylvania's 1874 law passed in 1901 authorized a corporation "to buy and own the capital stock of, and to merge its corporate rights, powers and privileges with and into those of, any other corporation."[72] Another amendment removed all ceilings on the capital or indebtedness of corporations chartered in the state.[73] However, most other features of the 1874 statute remained in effect until Pennsylvania finally adopted a new general incorporation law in 1933. Only then did the state give up the practice of listing the types of businesses that could avail themselves of the law, eliminating most, but not all, of the special regulations imposed on different industries. But even then, the act retained a number of governance prescriptions, including the requirement, still mandated by the state constitution, that shareholders be permitted to cumulate their votes when electing directors.[74]

When states revised their general incorporation statutes, moreover, they often deliberately distinguished them in important respects from Delaware's (Wells 2000). Illinois touted its 1933 law as offering superior safeguards for investors (Dodd 1936; Wells 2000), and the committee that drafted the Model Business Corporation Act based its 1946 prototype on the Illinois statute, bragging that "not a single member of the committee thought it desirable to use the Delaware statute as a pattern" (Campbell 1956, 100).

71. Only small states like Delaware could cut incorporation fees and still gain enough revenue relative to their needs to make it worthwhile to compete for charters. Moreover, corporations that shifted their domiciles to Delaware did not also move their production facilities, so the cost of losing the charter-mongering competition was relatively low. See Carruthers and Lamoreaux (2015).

72. "AN ACT Supplementary to an act, entitled 'An act to provide for the incorporation and regulation of certain corporations,' approved the twenty-ninth day of April, one thousand eight hundred and seventy-four; providing for the merger and consolidation of certain corporations" May 29, 1901.

73. "AN ACT To amend section one of the act, entitled 'An act to provide for increasing the capital stock and indebtedness of corporations,' approved the ninth day of February, Anno Domini one thousand nine hundred and one; authorizing corporations to increase their capital stock and indebtedness" April 22, 1905. For other changes, see Whitworth and Miller (1902, 1905).

74. "AN ACT Relating to business corporations" May 5, 1933. See also Pennsylvania (1931).

However, the model act was in some ways more permissive than the Illinois statute. In particular, it eschewed one of the Illinois law's most restrictive features—a prohibition against the creation of shares with limited voting rights that derived from the legislature's interpretation of a provision in the Illinois constitution (Campbell 1956, 101).

Decades after New Jersey's opening salvo in the charter-mongering competition, the general incorporation statutes of Pennsylvania, Illinois, and other states retained important vestiges of the anticorporate politics of the nineteenth century, often in the form of restrictions on corporate governance that had been written into their constitutions. Even Delaware's statutes struck observers as much more prescriptive than British company law at the same time. As Gower noted when he visited the United States in the 1950s, "To an Englishman it seems strange that corporate codes, such as that of Delaware, which are notoriously lax in failing to provide important safeguards against abuses, should nevertheless be strict in matters which seem to us to be essentially for the parties themselves to settle." British law was contractual to the core. Whereas "the British Companies Act . . . [provides] a standard form which applies only in the absence of contrary agreement by the parties," the American statutes "tend to lay down mandatory rules" and, as a result, are "much less flexible" (Gower 1956, 1372, 1376–77).

These differences mattered. Gower's complaint about the lack of safeguards in the Delaware statute notwithstanding, the flexibility of British company law allowed corporations to disenfranchise shareholders to an extent that was inconceivable in the United States, even in Delaware. Timothy Guinnane, Ron Harris, and I have collected the articles of association filed by three random samples of British companies (from 1892, 1812, and 1927, respectively) to observe how incorporators used the contractual freedom that British company granted them (Guinnane, Harris, and Lamoreaux 2014). We found a growing tendency over time for British companies to write rules that isolated the directors from shareholders' oversight. In most companies, for example, directors obtained the power to name one or more of their number "managing directors" who did not have to stand for election by the shareholders during their term of service. Moreover, an increasing proportion of the companies (fully half of the firms in the 1927 sample) named in their articles one or more permanent directors who never had to stand for election.[75] A good example is Dymock's Patent Twine Company, Limited, registered in 1912. Clause 21 of the company's articles of association specified that it would have two to five directors. Clause 22

---

75. James Foreman-Peck and Leslie Hannah (2013) have argued that British companies that traded on the London Stock Exchange voluntarily adopted more stringent governance rules to attract external investment, but they do not check this contention by examining systematically the provisions of the companies' articles of association. Reports from the period in the *Financial Times* and the *Economist* suggest that shareholders were effectively disenfranchised in many listed firms as well. See Guinnane, Harris, and Lamoreaux (2014).

named three of them (a majority), declaring that they "shall be permanent Directors of the Company, and each of them shall be entitled to hold such office so long as he shall live" and meet certain basic qualifications. The articles then went on to lay out procedures that allowed the men's executors to choose successors in the event of their death, again without needing to secure shareholders' approval.[76]

How much power shareholders in corporations should have over management is a hotly debated issue to the present day. Scholars from both ends of the political spectrum have advocated shifting the balance toward shareholders—one side on democratic grounds, and the other on the principle that companies should be run in the interest of their shareholders.[77] But others have argued that too much shareholder control leads to pressure for short-term gains that discourages executives from developing firm-specific human capital and, more generally, is detrimental to innovation.[78] Whatever the merits of these different views, I would suggest that the balance of power between shareholders and directors in corporations has been determined more by political forces in the larger society than by any dispassionate assessment of these ideas (on this point, see also Roe [1994]). In particular, the early achievement of universal (white) manhood suffrage in the United States shaped the evolution of corporate law in a way that gave American shareholders, at least on paper, considerably more power in corporations than their counterparts in Britain (and elsewhere in Europe) in the nineteenth and early twentieth centuries. Intriguingly, the spread of the franchise in Britain ultimately reversed the shift in power away from shareholders that occurred in the late nineteenth and early twentieth centuries.[79] Although the change took a long time, when the Labour Party finally gained control of the government in the years following World War II, it not only nationalized some of Britain's largest corporations but enacted a revised Companies Act that gave shareholders the power to dismiss directors by a simple majority vote. Scholars have recently touted this provision as granting shareholders in Britain extraordinary power to discipline directors (Bruner 2013; Nolan 2006; Cheffins 2008), but it is important to recognize the extent to which this law was a product of the new mass democratic politics of the twentieth century.[80]

76. Company no. 124849, BT 31, Board of Trade: Companies Registration Office: Files of Dissolved Companies, National Archives, Kew, United Kingdom.

77. The literature ranges from Berle and Means (1932) and Bebchuk (2007) to La Porta et al. (1997, 1998) and Baker and Smith (1998).

78. See, for example, Stout (2007) and Lazonick (2007).

79. The percent of the adult male population that was formally enfranchised trended up to about 75 percent in the last third of the century and then reached nearly 100 percent after World War I. Before the Great War, however, less than 30 percent of adult males actually voted. See Flora et al. (1983).

80. Similar changes in the political environment in Germany led to requirement of labor representation on corporate boards. See O'Sullivan (2001) and Roe (1994).

To reiterate, the early achievement of universal (white) manhood suffrage in the United States shaped American corporation law in an exceptional way. I have developed this argument by focusing on the case of Pennsylvania, where a powerful political movement formed in the early nineteenth century around opposition to the special privileges the legislature had granted to corporations. One result of the movement's success was the early adoption of general incorporation laws, but another was the implanting in those laws of a number of restrictions on what corporations could do and how they could be governed. Businesses attempted to escape these restrictions by lobbying the legislature for special charters. This practice, however, only ensured that corporate privileges would continue to be a hot-button political issue until the constitution finally outlawed private charters in 1873. Pennsylvania's general incorporation laws nonetheless remained highly prescriptive, and an attempt to make an end run around the restrictions in the form of an enabling statute for partnership associations, an early form of LLC, ran afoul of a court system whose vigilant defense of creditors' rights was another consequence of the democratic politics of the nineteenth century.

The general outlines of the Pennsylvania story were essentially the same as those of other US states, but political pressures played out in each case in ways that varied according to local circumstances. As a consequence, although general incorporation statutes in the United States were on the whole much more prescriptive than in Britain, they were still quite heterogeneous in the extent and type of the rules they imposed. Although it is beyond the scope of this chapter to analyze the determinants of these differences and how they came to shape the evolution of the law, I would caution against approaching the problem simply by running cross-state regressions that include a measure of the early extent of the franchise on the right-hand side. As the different histories of Pennsylvania, New Jersey, and Delaware's general incorporation statutes suggest, initial conditions may bound the set of likely outcomes, but they are not fate.

References

Acemoglu, Daron, Simon Johnson, and James A. Robinson. 2001. "The Colonial Origins of Comparative Development: An Empirical Investigation." *American Economic Review* 91 (December): 1369–401.
Adams, Sean P. 2006. "Promotion, Competition, Captivity: The Political Economy of Coal." *Journal of Policy History* 18 (1): 74–95.
———. 2012. "Soulless Monsters and Iron Horses: The Civil War, Institutional Change, and American Capitalism." In *Capitalism Takes Command: The Social Transformation of Nineteenth-Century America*, edited by Michael Zakim and Gary J. Kornblith, 249–76. Chicago: University of Chicago Press.

Akagi, Roy H. 1924. "The Pennsylvania Constitution of 1838." *Pennsylvania Magazine of History and Biography* 48 (4): 301–33.

Alesina, Alberto, Paola Giuliano, and Nathan Nunn. 2013. "On the Origins of Gender Roles: Women and the Plough." *Quarterly Journal of Economics* 128 (May): 469–530.

Aron, Stephen. 1992. "Pioneers and Profiteers: Land Speculation and the Homestead Ethic in Frontier Kentucky." *Western Historical Quarterly* 23 (May): 179–98.

Arsht, S. Samuel. 1976. "A History of Delaware Corporation Law." *Delaware Journal of Corporate Law* 1 (1): 1–22.

Baker, George P., and George David Smith. 1998. *The New Financial Capitalists: Kohlberg Kravis Roberts and the Creation of Corporate Value.* New York: Cambridge University Press.

Balleisen, Edward J. 2001. *Navigating Failure: Bankruptcy and Commercial Society in Antebellum America.* Chapel Hill: University of North Carolina Press.

Barro, Robert J. 1997. *Determinants of Economic Growth: A Cross-Country Empirical Study.* Cambridge, MA: MIT Press.

Barro, Robert J., and Rachel M. McCleary. 2003. "Religion and Economic Growth across Countries." *American Sociological Review* 68 (October): 760–81.

Bebchuk, Lucian A. 2007. "The Myth of the Shareholder Franchise." *Virginia Law Review* 93 (May): 675–732.

Berle, Adolf A., and Gardiner C. Means. 1932. *The Modern Corporation and Private Property.* New York: Macmillan.

Blanchard, Charles, ed. 1900. *The Progressive Men of the Commonwealth of Pennsylvania,* vol. 2. Logansport, IN: A. W. Bowen & Co.

Bloom, David E., and Jeffrey D. Sachs. 1998. "Geography, Demography, and Economic Growth in Africa." *Brookings Papers on Economic Activity* 1998 (2): 207–73.

Bodenhorn, Howard. 2002. *State Banking in Early America: A New Economic History.* New York: Cambridge University Press.

———. 2006. "Bank Chartering and Political Corruption in Antebellum New York: Free Banking as Reform." In *Corruption and Reform: Lessons from America's Economic History,* edited by Edward L. Glaeser and Claudia Goldin, 231–57. Chicago: University of Chicago Press.

Bridge, James Howard. 1903. *The Inside Story of the Carnegie Steel Company: A Romance of Millions.* New York: Aldine Book Co.

Bruner, Christopher M. 2013. *Corporate Governance in the Common-Law World: The Political Foundations of Shareholder Power.* Cambridge: Cambridge University Press.

Butler, Henry N. 1985. "Nineteenth-Century Jurisdictional Competition in the Granting of Corporate Privileges." *Journal of Legal Studies* 14 (January): 129–66.

Cadman, John W., Jr. 1949. *The Corporation in New Jersey: Business and Politics, 1791–1875.* Cambridge, MA: Harvard University Press.

California, State of. 1850. *Statutes of California, Passed at the First Session of the Legislature.* San Jose: J. Winchester.

Campbell, Bruce A. 1975. "John Marshall, the Virginia Political Economy, and the *Dartmouth College* Decision." *American Journal of Legal History* 19 (January): 40–65.

Campbell, Whitney. 1956. "The Model Business Corporation Act." *Business Lawyer* 11 (July): 98–110.

Carruthers, Bruce G., and Naomi R. Lamoreaux. 2015. "Regulatory Races: The Effects of Jurisdictional Competition on Regulatory Standards." *Journal of Economic Literature,* forthcoming.

Chandler, Alfred D., Jr. 1977. *The Visible Hand: The Managerial Revolution in American Business.* Cambridge, MA: Harvard University Press.

Cheffins, Brian R. 2008. *Corporate Ownership and Control: British Business Transformed*. Oxford: Oxford University Press.

Corbin, William H. 1881. *The Act Concerning Corporations in the State of New Jersey Approved April 7, 1875 with all the Amendments to January 1, 1881*. Jersey City, NJ: Frederick D. Linn & Co.

de Soto, Hernando. 2000. *The Mystery of Capital: Why Capitalism Triumphs in the West and Fails Everywhere Else*. New York: Basic Books.

Dodd, E. Merrick, Jr. 1936. "Statutory Developments in Business Corporation Law, 1886–1936." *Harvard Law Review* 50 (November): 27–59.

Eastman, Frank M. 1908. *A Treatise on the Law Relating to Private Corporations in Pennsylvania*, 2nd ed., 2 vols. Philadelphia: George T. Bisel Co.

Elmer, Lucius Q. C. 1855. *A Digest of the Laws of New Jersey: Containing All the Laws of General Application, Now in Force, from 1709 to 1855, Inclusive, with the Rules and Decisions of the Courts*, 2nd ed. Philadelphia: J. B. Lippincott & Co.

Engerman, Stanley L., and Kenneth L. Sokoloff. 2005. "The Evolution of Suffrage Institutions in the New World." *Journal of Economic History* 65 (December): 891–921.

———. 2011. *Economic Development in the Americas since 1500: Endowments and Institutions*. New York: Cambridge University Press.

Flora, Peter, Jens Alber, Richard Eichenberg, Jürgen Kohl, Franz Kraus, Winfried Pfenning, and Kurt Seebohm. 1983. *State, Economy, and Society in Western Europe, 1815–1975, Vol. 1: The Growth of Mass Democracies and Welfare States*. Frankfurt: Campus Verlag.

Foreman-Peck, James, and Leslie Hannah. 2013. "Some Consequences of the Early Twentieth-Century British Divorce of Ownership from Control." *Business History* 55 (4): 543–64.

Freedley, Angelo T. 1883. *The Limited Partnership Association Laws of Pennsylvania, with Notes, Forms and Index*. Philadelphia: T. & J. W. Johnson & Co.

Freeman, Mark, Robin Pearson, and James Taylor. 2011. *Shareholder Democracies? Corporate Governance in Britain and Ireland before 1850*. Chicago: University of Chicago Press.

Gallup, John Luke, Jeffrey D. Sachs, and Andrew D. Mellinger. 1999. "Geography and Economic Development." *International Regional Science Review* 22 (August): 179–232.

Gates, Paul W. 1962. "Tenants of the Log Cabin." *Mississippi Valley Historical Review* 49 (June): 3–31.

Gazur, Wayne M., and Neil M. Goff. 1991. "Assessing the Limited Liability Company." *Case Western Reserve Law Review* 41 (2): 387–501.

Gower, L. C. B. 1956. "Some Contrasts between British and American Corporation Law." *Harvard Law Review* 69 (June): 1369–402.

Grandy, Christopher. 1989. "New Jersey Corporate Chartermongering, 1875–1929." *Journal of Economic History* 49 (September): 677–92.

Grubb, Farley. 2003. "Creating the US Dollar Currency Union, 1748–1811: A Quest for Monetary Stability or a Usurpation of State Sovereignty for Personal Gain?" *American Economic Review* 93 (December): 1778–98.

Guinnane, Timothy W., Ron Harris, and Naomi R. Lamoreaux. 2014. "Contractual Freedom and the Evolution of Corporate Governance in Britain, 1862 to 1929." NBER Working Paper no. 20481, Cambridge, MA.

Guinnane, Timothy W., Ron Harris, Naomi R. Lamoreaux, and Jean-Laurent Rosenthal. 2007. "Putting the Corporation in its Place." *Enterprise and Society* 8 (September): 687–729.

Hamill, Susan Pace. 1999. "From Special Privilege to General Utility: A Continuation of Willard Hurst's Study of Corporations." *American University Law Review* 49 (October): 81–180.

Hammond, Bray. 1957. *Banks and Politics in America: From the Revolution to the Civil War.* Princeton, N.J.: Princeton University Press.

Handlin, Oscar, and Mary Flug Handlin. 1969. *Commonwealth: A Study of the Role of Government in the American Economy,* rev. ed. Cambridge, MA: Harvard University Press.

Harlan, A. D. 1873. *Pennsylvania Constitutional Convention 1872 and 1873: Its Members and Officers and the Result of their Labors.* Philadelphia: Inquirer Book and Job Print.

Harris, Ron. 2000. *Industrializing English Law: Entrepreneurship and Business Organization, 1720–1844.* Cambridge: Cambridge University Press.

Harris, Ron, and Naomi R. Lamoreaux. 2010. "Contractual Flexibility within the Common Law: Organizing Private Companies in Britain and the United States." Unpublished Manuscript.

Hartz, Louis. 1948. *Economic Policy and Democratic Thought: Pennsylvania, 1776–1860.* Cambridge, MA: Harvard University Press.

Hennessey, Jessica L., and John Joseph Wallis. 2014. "Corporations and Organizations in the United States after 1840." Unpublished Manuscript.

Hilt, Eric. 2014. "General Incorporation Acts for Manufacturing Firms, 1811–1860." Unpublished Manuscript.

Hilt, Eric, and Katharine O'Banion. 2009. "The Limited Partnership in New York, 1822–1858: Partnerships Without Kinship." *Journal of Economic History* 69 (September): 615–45.

Hilt, Eric, and Jacqueline Valentine. 2012. "Democratic Dividends: Stockholding, Wealth, and Politics in New York, 1791–1826." *Journal of Economic History* 72 (June): 332–63.

Howard, Stanley E. 1934. "The Limited Partnership in New Jersey." *Journal of Business of the University of Chicago* 7 (October): 296–317.

Hurst, James Willard. 1970. *The Legitimacy of the Business Corporation in the Law of the United States, 1780–1970.* Charlottesville: University Press of Virginia.

Illinois, State of. 1857. *Laws of the State of Illinois, Passed by the Twentieth General Assembly Convened January 5, 1857.* Springfield: Lanphier & Walker.

Jordan, John W. 1921. *Encyclopedia of Pennsylvania Biography.* New York: Lewis Historical Publishing Co.

Kessler, Amalia D. 2003. "Limited Liability in Context: Lessons from the French Origins of the American Limited Partnership." *Journal of Legal Studies* 32 (June): 511–48.

Kessler, W. C. 1940. "A Statistical Study of the New York General Incorporation Act of 1811." *Journal of Political Economy* 48 (December): 877–82.

Keyssar, Alexander. 2000. *The Right to Vote: The Contested History of Democracy in the United States.* New York: Basic Books.

Kutler, Stanley I. 1971. *Privilege and Creative Destruction: The Charles River Bridge Case.* Philadelphia: Lippincott.

Lamoreaux, Naomi R. 1985. *The Great Merger Movement in American Business, 1895–1904.* New York: Cambridge University Press.

———. 1994. *Insider Lending: Banks, Personal Connections, and Economic Development in Industrial New England.* New York: Cambridge University Press.

———. 1997. "The Partnership Form of Organization: Its Popularity in Early Nineteenth-Century Boston." In *Entrepreneurs: The Boston Business Community,*

1750–1850, edited by Conrad E. Wright and Katheryn P. Viens, 269–95. Boston: Massachusetts Historical Society.

———. 2004. "Partnerships, Corporations, and the Limits on Contractual Freedom in US History: An Essay in Economics, Law, and Culture." In *Constructing Corporate America: History, Politics, and Culture*, edited by Kenneth Lipartito and David B. Sicilia, 29–65. New York: Oxford University Press.

———. 2011. "The Mystery of Property Rights: A US Perspective." *Journal of Economic History* 71 (June): 275–306.

Lamoreaux, Naomi R., and Jean-Laurent Rosenthal. 2005. "Legal Regime and Contractual Flexibility: A Comparison of Business's Organizational Choices in France and the United States during the Era of Industrialization." *American Law and Economics Review* 7 (Spring): 28–61.

Lamoreaux, Naomi R., and John Joseph Wallis. 2012. "The Economics of Civil Society." Unpublished Manuscript.

La Porta, Rafael, Florencio Lopez-de-Silanes, and Andrei Shleifer. 2008. "The Economic Consequences of Legal Origins." *Journal of Economic Literature* 46 (June): 285–332.

La Porta, Rafael, Florencio Lopez-de-Silanes, Andrei Shleifer, and Robert W. Vishny. 1997. "Legal Determinants of External Finance." *Journal of Finance* 52 (July): 1131–50.

———. 1998. "Law and Finance." *Journal of Political Economy* 106 (December): 1113–55.

Larcom, Russell Carpenter. 1937. *The Delaware Corporation*. Baltimore: Johns Hopkins Press.

Lazonick, William. 2007. "The US Stock Market and the Governance of Innovative Enterprise." *Industrial and Corporate Change* 16 (December): 983–1035.

Lewis, William Draper. 1917. "The Uniform Limited Partnership Act." *University of Pennsylvania Law Review* 65 (June): 715–31.

Livesay, Harold C. 1975. *Andrew Carnegie and the Rise of Big Business*. Boston: Little Brown.

Lu, Qian, and John Wallis. 2014. "Banks, Politics, and Political Parties: From Partisan Banking to Open Access in Early Massachusetts." Unpublished Manuscript.

Maier, Pauline. 1992. "The Debate over Incorporations: Massachusetts in the Early Republic." In *Massachusetts and the New Nation*, edited by Conrad Edick Wright, 75–81. Boston: Massachusetts Historical Society.

———. 1993. "The Revolutionary Origins of the American Corporation." *William and Mary Quarterly* 50 (January): 51–84.

Majewski, John. 2000. *A House Dividing: Economic Development in Pennsylvania and Virginia before the Civil War*. New York: Cambridge University Press.

———. 2006. "Toward a Social History of the Corporation: Shareholding in Pennsylvania, 1800–1840." In *The Economy of Early America: Historical Perspectives & New Directions*, edited by Cathy Matson, 294–316. University Park: Pennsylvania State University Press.

Massachusetts, Commonwealth of. 1836. *The Revised Statutes of the Commonwealth of Massachusetts, Passed November 4, 1835*. Boston: Dutton & Wentworth.

———. 1854. *General Laws of the Commonwealth of Massachusetts Passed Subsequently to the Revised Statutes*. Boston: Dutton & Wentworth.

———. 1903a. *Acts and Resolves Passed by the General Court of Massachusetts in the Year 1903*. Boston: Wright & Potter.

———. 1903b. *Report of the Committee on Corporation Laws, Created by Acts of 1902, Chapter 335*. Boston: Wright & Potter.

McCleary, Rachel M., and Robert J. Barro. 2006. "Religion and Political Economy in an International Panel." *Journal for the Scientific Study of Religion* 45 (June): 149–75.

Murrin, John M. 2000. "The Jeffersonian Triumph and American Exceptionalism." *Journal of the Early Republic* 20 (Spring): 1–25.

Nedelsky, Jennifer. 1990. *Private Property and the Limits of American Constitutionalism: The Madisonian Framework and Its Legacy*. Chicago: University of Chicago Press.

New York, State of. 1821. *Reports of the Proceedings and Debates of the Convention of 1821, Assembled for the Purpose of Amending the Constitution*. Albany: E. and E. Hosford.

———. 1848. *Laws of the State of New-York Passed at the Seventy-First Session of the Legislature*. Albany: Charles Van Benthuysen.

Nolan, R. C. 2006. "The Continuing Evolution of Shareholder Governance." *Cambridge Law Journal* 65 (March): 92–127.

North, Douglass C., John Joseph Wallis, and Barry R. Weingast. 2009. *Violence and Social Orders: A Conceptual Framework for Interpreting Recorded Human History*. New York: Cambridge University Press.

Nunn, Nathan. 2008. "The Long-Term Effects of Africa's Slave Trades." *Quarterly Journal of Economics* 123 (February): 139–76.

Nunn, Nathan, and Leonard Wantchekon. 2011. "The Slave Trade and the Origins of Mistrust in Africa." *American Economic Review* 101 (December): 3221–52.

O'Gorman, Frank. 1993. "The Electorate before and after 1832." *Parliamentary History* 12 (Pt. 2): 171–83.

Ohio, State of. 1846. *Acts of a General Nature Passed by the Forty-Fourth General Assembly of the State of Ohio, Begun and Held in the City of Columbus, December 1, 1845*. Columbus: C. Scott and Co.

Onuf, Peter S. 2012. "American Exceptionalism and National Identity." *American Political Thought* 1 (Spring): 77–100.

O'Sullivan, Mary. 2001. *Contests for Corporate Control: Corporate Governance and Economic Performance in the United States and Germany*. New York: Oxford University Press.

Papaioannou, Elias, and Gregorios Siourounis. 2008. "Democratization and Growth." *Economic Journal* 118 (October): 1520–51.

Pennsylvania, Commonwealth of. 1810. *Laws, Statutes, etc., 1700–1800*, 4 vols. Philadelphia: Bioren.

———. 1855. *Laws of the General Assembly*. Harrisburg: A. Boyd Hamilton.

———. 1837–1838. *Proceedings and Debates of the Convention to Propose Amendments to the Constitution*, 14 vols. Harrisburg: Packer, Barrett, and Parks.

———. 1873. *Debates of the Convention to Amend the Constitution of Pennsylvania*, 9 vols. Harrisburg: Benjamin Singerly.

———. 1874a. *The Constitution of the Commonwealth of Pennsylvania Adopted December 16, 1873*. Harrisburg: Benjamin Singerly.

———. 1874b. *The Legislative Journal for the Session of 1874*. Harrisburg: Benjamin Singerly. (Available on microfilm at the Pennsylvania State Library in Harrisburg.)

———. 1931. *Proposed Business Corporation Law Prepared by the Department of Justice*. Harrisburg: n.p.

Phillips, John A., and Charles Wetherell. 1995. "The Great Reform Act of 1832 and the Political Modernization of England." *American Historical Review* 100 (April): 411–36.

Rodrik, Dani, Arvind Subramanian, and Francesco Trebbi. 2004. "Institutions Rule: The Primacy of Institutions over Geography and Integration in Economic Development." *Journal of Economic Growth* 9 (June): 131–65.

Roe, Mark J. 1994. *Strong Managers, Weak Owners: The Political Roots of American Corporate Finance*. Princeton, NJ: Princeton University Press.

Roe, Mark J., and Jordan I. Siegel. 2009. "Finance and Politics: A Review Essay Based on Kenneth Dam's Analysis of Legal Traditions in *The Law-Growth Nexus*." *Journal of Economic Literature* 47 (September): 781–800.

Ross, Dorothy. 1984. "Historical Consciousness in Nineteenth-Century America." *American Historical Review* 89 (October): 909–28.

Rutledge, Wiley B., Jr. 1937. "Significant Trends in Modern Incorporation Statutes." *Washington University Law Quarterly* 22 (April): 305–43.

Sachs, Jeffrey D., and Andrew M. Warner. 2001. "The Curse of Natural Resources." *European Economic Review* 45 (May): 827–38.

Schocket, Andrew M. 2007. *Founding Corporate Power in Early National Philadelphia*. DeKalb: Northern Illinois University Press.

Schwartz, Anna J. 1987. "The Beginning of Competitive Banking in Philadelphia, 1782–1809." In *Money in Historical Perspective*, edited by Anna J. Schwartz, 3–23. Chicago: University of Chicago Press.

Schwartz, Edward R. 1965. "The Limited Partnership Association—An Alternative to the Corporation for the Small Business with 'Control' Problems?" *Rutgers Law Review* 20 (Fall): 29–88.

Seavoy, Ronald E. 1982. *The Origins of the American Business Corporation, 1784–1855: Broadening the Concept of Public Service during Industrialization*. Westport, Conn.: Greenwood Press.

Smull, John A. 1874. *Rules and Decisions of the General Assembly of Pennsylvania, Legislative Directory, Together with Useful Political Statistics, List of Post Offices, County Officers, &c.* Harrisburg, PA: Benjamin Singerly, State Printer.

Stout, Lynn A. 2007. "The Mythical Benefits of Shareholder Control." *Virginia Law Review* 93 (May): 789–809.

Stransky, George E., Jr. 1956. "The Limited Partnership Association in New Jersey." *Rutgers Law Review* 10 (Summer): 701–15.

Tarbell, Ida M. 1904. *The History of the Standard Oil Company*, 2 vols. New York: McClure, Phillips & Co.

Taylor, James. 2006. *Creating Capitalism: Joint-Stock Enterprise in British Politics and Culture, 1800–1870*. Woodbridge, UK: Royal Historical Society/Boydell.

Thring, Henry. 1856. *The Joint Stock Companies Act, 1856: With an Introduction, Practical Notes, and an Appendix of Forms*. London: Stevens & Norton.

The Twentieth Century Bench and Bar of Pennsylvania, vol. 1. 1903. Chicago: H. C. Cooper, Jr., Bro. & Co.

Tyrrell, Ian. 1991. "American Exceptionalism in an Age of International History." *American Historical Review* 96 (October): 1031–55.

US Commissioner of Corporations. 1904. "Report." House Doc. 165, 58th Cong., 3rd Sess. Washington, DC: Government Printing Office.

Van Atta, John R. 2008. "'A Lawless Rabble': Henry Clay and the Cultural Politics of Squatters' Rights, 1832–1841." *Journal of the Early Republic* 28 (Fall): 337–78.

Wall, Joseph Frazier. 1970. *Andrew Carnegie*. New York: Oxford University Press.

Wallis, John Joseph. 2005. "Constitutions, Corporations, and Corruption: American States and Constitutional Change, 1842 to 1852." *Journal of Economic History* 65 (March): 211–56.

Warren, Edward H. 1929. *Corporate Advantages without Incorporation: An Examination of the Law Relating to Ordinary Partnerships, Limited Partnerships, Partnership Associations, Joint-Stock Companies, Business Trusts, ...* New York: Baker, Voorhis.

Wells, Harwell. 2000. "The Modernization of Corporation Law, 1920–40." *University of Pennsylvania Journal of Business Law* 11 (Spring): 573–629.

Wells, William P. 1886. "The Dartmouth College Case and Private Corporations." In *Report of the Ninth Annual Meeting of the American Bar Association*, 229–56. Philadelphia: Dando.

Whitworth, John F., and Clarence B. Miller. 1902. *Statutory Law of Corporations in Pennsylvania, Including Annotations and a Complete Set of Forms.* Philadelphia: T. & J. W. Johnson & Co.

———. 1905. *The Corporation Laws of Pennsylvania, 1903–1905, . . . , Being a Supplement to Statutory Law of Corporations.* Philadelphia: T. & J. W. Johnson & Co.

Williamson, Leland M., Richard A. Foley, Henry H. Colclazer, Louis N. Megargee, Jay H. Mowbray, and William R. Antisdel, eds. 1898. *Prominent and Progressive Pennsylvanians of the Nineteenth Century: A Review of their Careers*, vol. 1. Philadelphia: Record Publishing Co.

Yablon, Charles M. 2007. "The Historical Race: Competition for Corporate Charters and the Rise and Decline of New Jersey: 1880–1910." *Journal of Corporation Law* 32 (Winter): 323–80.

Corporate Governance and the Development of Manufacturing Enterprises in Nineteenth-Century Massachusetts

Eric Hilt

2.1 Introduction

The ownership structure of public companies in the United States is unique. Relative to those of other countries, American corporations are less likely to have a parent company or be part of a family business group, and more likely to be widely held (LaPorta et al. 1999). The historical origins of the distinctive patterns of corporate ownership in the United States are the subject of some debate, and a number of competing theories have been offered, ranging from populist politics (Roe 2004) to the protections of investors resulting from the early origins of the American legal system (LaPorta et al. 1998). But the historical evolution of corporate ownership in the United States is poorly documented, and the timing of the emergence of the distinctively American style of corporate ownership, along with the factors that may have been responsible for its emergence, are not well understood.

Most accounts of the history of American corporate ownership tend to echo the influential work of Berle and Means (1932), who argue that prior to the rise of "big business" around the turn of the twentieth century, American industrial corporations were owned by limited numbers of investors who participated actively in the governance of their

Eric Hilt is associate professor of economics at Wellesley College and a research associate of the National Bureau of Economic Research.

I would like to thank Jeremy Atack, Carola Frydman, Robert Margo, Claudia Rei, and William Collins for helpful comments. For acknowledgments, sources of research support, and disclosure of the author's material financial relationships, if any, please see http://www.nber.org/chapters/c13132.ack.

firms.[1] More recent work has challenged this view, arguing from early nineteenth-century data that the separation of ownership from control occurred much earlier (Hilt 2008). The contradictory and fragmentary findings of this literature reflect the frustrating scarcity of data on early American corporations, particularly industrial firms, which were subject to relatively few disclosure requirements in most states' corporation laws.

This chapter presents new, comprehensive data on the ownership and governance of industrial corporations from the third quarter of the nineteenth century—before the rise of "big business"—from the state of Massachusetts. At the time, Massachusetts was among the most heavily industrialized states. Entrepreneurs in Massachusetts were pioneers in the textile industry, and developed the first "integrated" cotton textile mills in the United States in the early nineteenth century (see Ware 1931). Dozens of enormous textile corporations were eventually founded in the state, and the shares of many of these enterprises were traded on the Boston Stock Exchange, which was then the premier market for American industrial securities (Atack and Rousseau 1999). In the second half of the nineteenth century, a number of new industries developed in Massachusetts, including chemicals, fabricated metals, and machinery, and entrepreneurs in these industries also made heavy use of the corporate form.

Relative to those of nearly all other states, Massachusetts's corporation law included an unusually strict disclosure requirement that mandated that several different classes of firms submit "certificates of condition" to the state government, which listed the names of their directors and stockholders.[2] In this chapter, I use the certificates filed for the year 1875 to construct a comprehensive data set of operating manufacturing corporations in the state, which includes detailed ownership information. I then classify each corporation by industry and match them to data from the state's 1875 manufacturing census, which recorded information on production methods, total numbers of firms and employees, and wages in different industries. These data present a detailed and comprehensive picture of corporate ownership among manufacturing firms in the third quarter of the nineteenth century. With the matched data I am able to analyze the variation in incorporation rates as well as the differences in corporate ownership structures across industries. In particular, I can document the extent of the separation of ownership from control among the prominent textile corporations in the state, and compare them to corporations operating in other industries.

---

1. For example, Becht and Delong (2005, 614) argue that the unusually diffuse ownership of American corporations "is not a long-standing historical tradition." Likewise, Cantillo Simon (1998) argues that prior to 1890 American stock markets did not function actively, since corporate ownership was so concentrated in the hands of company founders. See also Dodd (1938), Hovenkamp (1991), Hurst (1970) and Coffee (2001). An important exception is Werner (1986).

2. The corporations subject to this requirement included manufacturing firms, utilities, and cooperatives. Banks, insurance companies, and railroads were subject to different regulations.

The analysis proceeds in three steps. First, I study the adoption of the corporate form across industries. The data reveal substantial variation in incorporation rates, ranging from a high of more than 60 percent among producers of chemicals and of glass, to zero among producers of carriages and wagons. Perhaps unsurprisingly, an analysis of the determinants of incorporation rates reveals that they were higher among industries where average firm size, measured by either capital or total employees, was large. However, conditional on firm size, industries that made greater use of steam power and unskilled labor, and industries in which a relatively large proportion of firms' capital was accounted for by fixed assets, were incorporated at higher rates. This is consistent with the notion that the corporate form found heaviest use among those industries in which production was undertaken within factories, rather than artisanal shops.[3] The data suggest that the corporation was used not only to achieve greater scale, but also to adopt mechanized, factory-based production methods.

In the second step I analyze the ownership of the corporations, and calculate a variety of statistics comparable to those commonly used in the analysis of modern corporate governance. The data indicate that the degree of ownership dispersion in general, and managerial ownership in particular, varied widely across industries. The great textile corporations, whose shares were traded on the Boston Stock Exchange, were "widely held" at even higher rates than those of modern American publicly traded corporations.[4] The degree of the separation of ownership from control among those firms was comparable to large modern publicly traded firms, and Berle and Means (1932) would have characterized nearly all of them as subject to "management control." The ownership structures of those firms certainly contradict any simplistic narrative of the evolution of American corporate ownership in which the separation of ownership from control suddenly occurs at the turn of the twentieth century.

However, the data also indicate that the great textile mills were rather atypical of the state's industrial corporations: they were larger, had greater numbers of shareholders, and lower degrees of managerial ownership. Entrepreneurs were able to use the flexibility of Massachusetts's corporation law to configure their enterprises in a variety of ways, according to their needs and circumstances. Most corporations had relatively few shareholders and high levels of managerial ownership, but the degree of ownership concentration observed across industries, and also among firms within particular industries, varied significantly.

---

3. On the distinction between the two, see Katz and Margo (2013) and the references cited therein. On the significance of steam power for productivity, see Atack, Bateman, and Margo (2008).

4. La Porta, Lopez-de-Silanes, and Shleifer (1999) document that 80 percent of their sample of large modern American public companies are widely held in the sense that they do not have an owner holding 20 percent or more of their stock. In contrast, 98 percent of the manufacturing corporations traded on the Boston Stock Exchange were widely held by that definition.

Finally I analyze the determinants of ownership concentration and managerial ownership. Unsurprisingly, larger firms were more widely held. But the results indicate that, conditional on firm size, corporations that made greater use of steam power and unskilled labor had more concentrated ownership. That is, relative to corporations of similar sizes in industries that relied more on skilled labor and less on steam power, those in industries that organized production within factories, rather than large artisanal shops, had fewer shareholders, and a greater proportion of the shares were held by the directors. Investors responded to the complex role performed by the managers of those firms by ensuring that there were adequate ownership incentives to monitor and supervise management.

This chapter contributes to three interrelated lines of research. First, it complements the large and growing literature on the development of manufacturing in New England.[5] Much of this work has focused narrowly on textiles and the very large corporations that were formed within that industry (for example, McGouldrick 1968). This chapter complements that work by presenting an account of how the corporate form was utilized within manufacturing. The data reveal that in the third quarter of the nineteenth century, the corporation had proliferated well beyond textiles into a broad range of industries, and that across those industries somewhat different "styles" of ownership were adopted.

Second, the chapter contributes to a literature that documents the history of corporate ownership, both in the United States and elsewhere.[6] This chapter complements that literature by presenting comprehensive statistics on the ownership of nineteenth-century industrial corporations, prior to the rise of "big business."

Finally, the chapter also contributes to the literature on the adaptability of the corporate form to the needs of small- and medium-sized enterprises (SMEs). The early corporation laws of many American states were quite rigid, and regulated firms' internal governance institutions in ways that may have been unattractive to SMEs.[7] Some contributions to this literature have argued that innovations in the menu of organizational forms available to American firms in the later twentieth century, such as what have been termed the private limited liability company (PLLC), created alternatives that were superior to the corporation for the needs of SMEs (Guinnane et al. 2007). The results of this chapter show that Massachusetts was somewhat of an

---

5. See, for example, Temin (2000) and Handlin and Handlin (1974).

6. Recent work on British corporations, for example, includes Acheson et al. (2014); Cheffins, Chambers, and Koustas (2013); Freeman, Pearson, and Taylor (2011); and Hannah (2007). Work on the historical ownership of American corporations includes Bodenhorn (2012, 2013), Davis (1958), Hilt and Valentine (2012), Majewski (2006), and Wright (1999).

7. Lamoreaux (2014) details the origins and consequences of the restrictive elements of Pennsylvania's corporation laws. Hilt (2014) presents detailed tabulations of the terms of the American states' general incorporation acts.

exception. The laws of Massachusetts were unusually flexible with regard to the internal governance of corporations, and entrepreneurs were able to successfully adapt the form into a wide range of enterprises, including small closely held firms.

2.2   The Massachusetts Legislature and Corporation Law, 1790–1850

As in most American states, during the first half of the nineteenth century the corporate form was not freely available to entrepreneurs in Massachusetts. Instead, incorporation was only possible if the state legislature passed a law granting a charter to a business. These "special act charters" were probably not accessible to entrepreneurs who lacked a fair measure of legal sophistication and financial resources. Nonetheless, over the first half of the nineteenth century, Massachusetts granted charters to nearly 550 manufacturing firms. The terms of these charters were initially restrictive in some respects, but they quickly became quite liberal, particularly with regard to the internal governance of the firms they created. This flexibility was unusual, relative to the terms of other states' corporation laws, and may have contributed to the heavy use of the corporate form in Massachusetts.

Beginning in the early national period, the state government actively used the law to promote economic development, offering public support to private enterprises that would furnish transportation infrastructure or develop the capacity for manufacturing (see Handlin and Handlin 1974). When entrepreneurs sought charters to incorporate manufacturing businesses, they were generally accommodated. As the state industrialized and new companies proliferated, demand for corporate charters grew rapidly, and the state showed a clear willingness to meet that demand. In the first half of the nineteenth century, Massachusetts granted the highest number of corporate charters of all the American states and territories. Figure 2.1 presents the charters granted by the state in a comparative perspective. By 1850 Massachusetts had granted more than twice the number of corporate charters relative to its population than the national average.

Especially in the period before 1830, however, these charters often did not contain all the terms sought by entrepreneurs. For example, the petition for the Boston Manufacturing Corporation, the firm that would become the first to create an integrated cotton mill, sought banking powers for their enterprise, which were refused (McGouldrick 1968). The great success of that firm and the other Waltham-Lowell mills that followed demonstrated quite clearly that banking powers were unnecessary. Yet those firms' charters lacked another important power that was routinely granted to manufacturing corporations in other states: limited liability for the shareholders. The state refused to grant limited liability to any manufacturing corporation in the 1810s and 1820s. All charters granted to such enterprises explicitly made shareholders subject to an 1809 statute, which made them personally

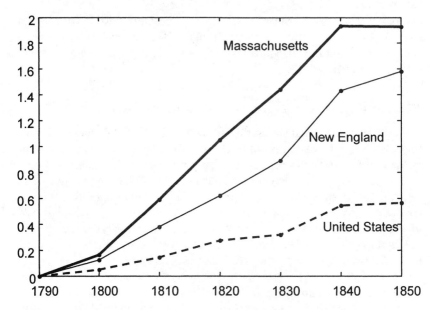

Fig. 2.1 Cumulative corporate charters per 1,000 persons

Sources: Corporate charters from Sylla and Wright (2013); population figures from the decennial federal census.

Note: The data do not include corporations created through general acts.

liable for their firms' debts.[8] When it was later objected that shareholders could circumvent this provision by selling their shares to "men of straw," the legislature strengthened its requirement of individual liability by passing legislation that made shareholders liable for any debts incurred while they were shareholders, *even if they subsequently sold their shares*.[9] Yet in spite of this restriction, manufacturing enterprises sought to incorporate in Massachusetts at very high rates; from 1800 to 1809, fifteen charters were granted to manufacturing enterprises, and from 1810 to 1819, 133 were granted. In the 1820s, another 146 were granted.[10]

The burden of unlimited liability for shareholders ultimately came to be perceived by many to be limiting economic development. In 1829, a year of high numbers of business failures, the personal liability of many households owning corporate stock led to "wide spreading and irretrievable ruin

8. This general regulating act for manufacturing companies to some extent standardized many of the terms in subsequent charters, and helped reduce the scope for special privileges to be granted in particular charters (*Massachusetts Laws*, 1809, ch. 65). The special privileges granted to some very early Massachusetts manufacturing corporations, ranging from lottery tickets to grants of land, are described in Davis (1917).

9. *Massachusetts Laws* (1822, ch. 38).

10. *Massachusetts Senate Documents* (1836, no. 90).

to individuals."[11] Ultimately the governor, Levi Lincoln, took up the cause and despite the vigorous opposition of some influential merchants, a new law granting limited liability to manufacturing enterprises was passed in 1830.[12] This law, a "general regulating act" that dictated virtually all of the terms of subsequent manufacturing charters, stated that the shareholders of these enterprises would have unlimited liability for debts until their capital subscriptions were fully paid in, at which point their liability would be limited to the amount of their shares. The act included various other safeguards for the creditors of corporations; for example, limiting total indebtedness and prohibiting the payment of dividends from the capital stock or loans to stockholders.

The 1830 act did not, however, include any terms relative to the governance of the corporations subsequently created, other than imposing the requirement that each corporation have a president, a clerk, a treasurer, and at least three directors. The voting rights of the shareholders, and their method for choosing these officers, were left to the corporations themselves to decide. The silence of the law on these issues was quite unusual; most states' early corporation laws strictly regulated director elections and shareholder voting rights (Hilt 2014). All subsequent manufacturing charters were quite brief, stating only the name of the firm, the nature of its operations, and the size of its capital stock, and then simply indicating that the firm was subject to the 1830 act. In the twenty years between 1830 and 1850, Massachusetts granted more than 400 charters to manufacturing firms.[13]

Finally, in 1851 Massachusetts took the important step of passing a general incorporation act for manufacturing enterprises.[14] Rather than applying to the legislature for a charter, the act provided that any three or more people could form a corporation, in virtually any manufacturing or mining industry, by simply filing the certificates required in the act with the Secretary of the Commonwealth and with their county.[15] Following the precedent of the 1830 general regulating act, the 1851 general incorporation act was mostly silent regarding the internal governance of the corporations, beyond requiring that the firms have a president and a treasurer—the act did not even specify a minimum or maximum number of directors. The act required that corporations created through its terms have a minimum of $5,000 in capital, and also imposed a maximum of $200,000, which was far smaller than the capital of many chartered corporations. The statute therefore served as an alternative route to incorporation for small firms, while large firms were still required to

11. Governor's message, January 1830, in Massachusetts Resolves, 1830.

12. *Massachusetts Laws* (1830, ch. 53).

13. Author's calculations from the charters themselves, obtained from *Massachusetts Laws* (1830–1850).

14. *Massachusetts Laws* (1851, ch. 133).

15. Massachusetts was relatively late to adopt a general incorporation act; see Hilt (2014) for a comprehensive tabulation of general incorporation acts for manufacturing firms.

seek charters from the legislature. In 1855, the maximum capital permitted for corporations formed under the general act was raised to $500,000, but the legislature continued to retain control over access to the corporate form for the largest enterprises.[16]

The 1851 general act imposed one significant burden on the corporations created through its terms that chartered corporations were not subject to, and that was an annual report known as a certificate of condition, which stated the names of the officers and shareholders, and provided financial information such as the amount of paid-in capital and the total indebtedness.[17] In 1870 the state formally imposed a requirement that a more detailed certificate of condition be submitted annually by all industrial corporations in the state, whether they were chartered or incorporated through the general act. These certificates of condition form the basis for the data analyzed in this chapter.

2.3   The Adoption of the Corporate Form in Massachusetts

The corporate form was utilized with great frequency, but many multiowner firms remained unincorporated, effectively choosing the partnership form. The privileges of incorporation should have been most attractive to firms seeking to raise relatively large amounts of capital from investors. For example, the transferability of shares, the governance structure of a board of directors to whom control over day-to-day management would be delegated, and the limitation of personal liability for shareholders would all seem to be well suited to the needs of passive, outside investors. For a firm with a small number of owners, who were perhaps from the same family or had been in business together previously, the formalities of an annual meeting and director elections and the requirement of detailed annual disclosures probably represented a substantial nuisance. On the other hand, the corporation laws of Massachusetts were relatively flexible, and effectively permitted incorporators to configure their enterprises' voting rights and decision-making procedures as they wished. Did small firms, or firms with small numbers of owners, actually incorporate?

One way to address these questions is to examine the industries in which incorporation rates were relatively high, and compare them to industries in which incorporation was uncommon. Massachusetts's manufacturing censuses reported detailed information on the total numbers of establishments, their capital, and their employees, by industry. These records can be compared to the filings of manufacturing corporations, whose certificates of condition stated their capital and other information. The certificates unfortunately do not specify the industry of the corporation or its products or

16. *Massachusetts Laws* (1855, ch. 68).
17. Unfortunately, the certificates of condition submitted prior to 1870 do not survive.

revenue. However, the corporate names (e.g., "Bay State Faucet and Valve Company") often provide a relatively clear indication of the firm's industry. For those with names that do not provide identifying industrial information (e.g., "Paul Whitin Manufacturing Company") contemporary business directories were used to classify most corporations into the categories of the state census.[18] The earliest year for which totally comprehensive corporation records are available, and a manufacturing census is available, is 1875.[19] In that year, the manufacturing census listed more than 10,000 manufacturing establishments in Massachusetts, and the certificates of condition of 601 corporations could be classified into the industrial categories of the census.[20]

The resulting data are presented in table 2.1.[21] The data in the table show quite clearly that incorporation rates differed significantly across industries. Several of the state's largest industries (measured by the number of establishments), such as boots and shoes, clothing, food preparations, and printing and publishing, had very few incorporated firms at all, and vanishingly low incorporation rates. At the other end of the spectrum, there were smaller industries with relatively small numbers of establishments, such as chemicals, glass, jute baggings, and textile printing ("print works"), where the corporate form was quite dominant. The various categories within the textile industry, as expected, had large numbers of corporations and relatively high incorporation rates. But there were also relatively large numbers of incorporated firms producing machinery, metallic goods, paper, and brick and stone.

The data in the table also seem consistent with the notion that incorporation rates were higher in industries with higher average capital per firm. The industries with the smallest capital, such as tobacco, lumber, vessels, and carriages and wagons, all had incorporation rates of 2 percent or less,

---

18. In particular, the *Massachusetts Register and Business Directory* (1878) and the *New England Business Directory and Gazetteer* (1877) were consulted, along with directories of individual towns. The industries of eleven of corporations could not be identified and were excluded from the analysis.

19. The collection and analysis of the data for the 1875 census was overseen by the chief of the Massachusetts Bureau of Statistics of Labor, Carroll D. Wright, who would later become the US Commissioner of Labor and oversee the 1890 Federal Census. The 1875 Massachusetts Census was designed and implemented using relatively sophisticated methods, and represented a substantial improvement over earlier state censuses. See Wright (1877).

20. The state did not require a minimum for revenues or size for establishments to be included in the census (Wright 1877, 103). However, excluded from these data are around 11,000 firms engaged in what the census categorized as "occupations," rather than manufacturing. These occupations included blacksmithing, coopering, butchering, painting, sewing machine repairing, fish curing, cobbling, tinsmithing, roofing, plumbing, and related tasks. These firms had been classified as engaged in manufacturing in earlier state censuses.

21. The average capital of all establishments, column (2) in the table, is calculated by dividing total capital in the industry by the number of establishments. There is not sufficient data to calculate median capital from the census data. The table excludes industry categories with very few firms, and industry categories where the census reports did not present data on firm characteristics.

Table 2.1   Establishment size and incorporation rates: Industry averages, Massachusetts (1875)

	All establishments		Corporations		
	N (1)	Average capital (2)	N (3)	Average capital (4)	Incorporation rate (5)
Clothing					
Boots and shoes	1,461	12,795	12	125,707	0.01
Other clothing	1,088	8,442	23	202,174	0.02
Food and tobacco					
Food preparations	783	12,580	16	175,875	0.02
Liquors and beverages	155	26,802	1	150,000	0.01
Tobacco	264	3,076	4	14,088	0.02
Instruments					
Clocks and watches	14	132,425	3	588,533	0.21
Scientific instruments and appliances	52	8,244	7	107,382	0.13
Musical instruments and materials	71	54,163	8	122,363	0.11
Metals, metallic goods, and machinery					
Agricultural implements	38	30,118	6	190,833	0.16
Arms and ammunition	20	48,215	1	9,398	0.05
Artisans' tools	124	17,956	12	118,133	0.10
Machines and machinery	311	44,565	69	157,666	0.22
Other metals and metallic goods	768	28,526	87	171,375	0.11
Oils and chemicals					
Chemical preparations	9	34,644	6	106,935	0.67
Fertilizers	9	136,722	2	218,000	0.22
Oils and illuminating fluids	33	69,311	7	112,929	0.21
Paints and colors	20	55,790	2	35,500	0.10
Paper and paper goods					
Paper	120	90,502	38	119,314	0.32
Printing and publishing	533	12,033	11	69,755	0.02
Textiles					
Carpetings	24	160,665	6	520,567	0.25
Cotton goods	220	290,203	107	449,478	0.49
Linen	5	184,800	2	550,000	0.40
Print works	9	285,556	5	185,200	0.56
Silk	6	81,333	1	120,000	0.17
Woolen goods	183	94,044	32	198,005	0.17
Other textiles	28	169,700	15	140,173	0.54
Vessels and carriages					
Carriages and wagons	356	6,777	1	84,000	0.00
Vessels	163	5,733	1	350,000	0.01
Wooden goods					
Furniture	294	16,836	6	237,807	0.02
Lumber	579	4,697	7	35,971	0.01
Other wooden goods	460	9,728	10	67,975	0.02

Table 2.1   (continued)

	All establishments		Corporations		
	N (1)	Average capital (2)	N (3)	Average capital (4)	Incorporation rate (5)
Other industries					
Bricks	104	15,939	9	186,222	0.09
Glass	13	119,615	8	247,963	0.62
Jute	6	72,833	3	119,000	0.50
Leather	495	16,969	10	164,110	0.02
Rubber	23	151,509	4	115,000	0.17
Stone	151	11,020	21	90,468	0.14
Miscellaneous					
Miscellaneous manufactures	1,250	21,396	37	113,103	0.03

whereas those with the highest firm capital, such as cotton goods, textile printing, linen, and "other textiles," all had incorporation rates of more than 40 percent. The data in table 2.1 also indicate that in all but one industry the average capital of corporations was larger than the average capital of all establishments, sometimes by as much as a factor of ten. In at least a few cases it seems very likely that the corporations were effectively operating in a slightly different industry, even though according to the rough classification system of the census they were grouped into the same category.

How consistent is the relationship between average firm size and incorporation rates at the industry level? An analysis of this relationship is presented in figure 2.2. The scatterplot in the figure indicates that industries with higher levels of capital per firm (in logs) indeed had higher incorporation rates. The regression line included in the figure illustrates the strong tendency toward higher incorporation rates among firms in industries with higher than average capital. However, the residuals of many industries are also high, and in particular, there are several industries with relatively high incorporation rates and relatively low levels of average capital. The lower panel illustrates the same pattern, using the log of total employees, rather than capital, as a measure of firm size.

The census recorded detailed data on certain elements of manufacturing firms' capital, workforce, and operations. These data, which are summarized in table 2.2, provide some insight into the production methods utilized by firms in different industries. For example, some industries appear to have been dominated by artisanal shops, with relatively small numbers of workers and little fixed capital. Producers of tobacco products, scientific instruments, and food preparations on average had fewer than six employees, and less than $10,000 in capital. Firms in each of these industries also made relatively

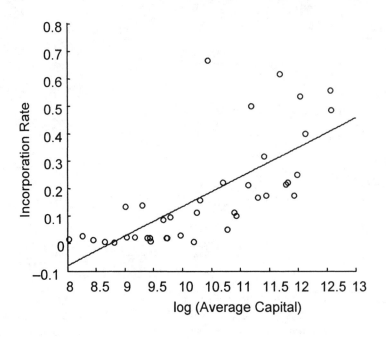

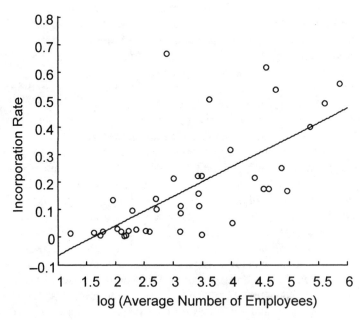

Fig. 2.2 Incorporation rates and firm characteristics by industry

Table 2.2   **Industry characteristics**

	Mean	SD	Min.	Max.
Incorporation rate	0.178	0.193	0	0.670
Capital				
Log capital	10.340	1.270	8.031	12.578
Capital-output ratio	0.618	0.305	0.171	1.497
Steam engines per establishment	0.342	0.253	0	0.889
Fraction assets machines and buildings	0.589	0.133	0.388	0.933
Labor				
Log total employees	3.286	1.208	1.220	5.873
Fraction workforce female	0.215	0.238	0	0.815
Log annual wage, all employees	6.273	0.273	5.521	6.764
Log annual wage, adult male employees	6.381	0.211	5.727	6.782
Growth rate of output, 1865–1875	0.433	0.699	–0.849	2.020

little use of steam power, with around 0.10 steam engines per establishment or less. In contrast, print works, as well as producers of cotton goods or of linens, typically had well over 200 employees and $200,000 or more in capital, and in these industries there were 0.8 steam engines per establishment. Establishments in these industries are best characterized as factories.

Likewise the workforce of some industries consisted of a relatively large proportion of skilled labor, whereas others relied heavily on unskilled labor. The table presents proxies for the share of skilled labor, based on wages and the gender composition of the labor force. A higher wage is consistent with a greater level of skill; the fraction of the labor force that was female is an indicator for the proportion that was unskilled. The table presents wages for all workers, which reflects the mix of skilled and unskilled labor (in the form of women and children) and also the wage for adult male workers only. The industries with the highest levels of wages were musical instruments and clocks and watches, whose adult male workers earned $876 and $882 per year, respectively. The lowest wages of adult males were in jute baggings ($307) and linen ($390), and in these industries female workers represented more than 50 percent of total employees.

We can gain some insight into the purposes for which the corporate form was utilized by analyzing how incorporation rates varied with these industry characteristics. In addition to achieving a greater scale, incorporation facilitated the creation of firms that utilized particular kinds of assets or production processes, and the variation in incorporation rates across industries reflected these patterns. Table 2.3 presents regressions of incorporation rates on industry characteristics. Panel A presents univariate regressions, and since many of these characteristics may be correlated with firm scale, in panel B the regressions are repeated with a measure of scale included—the log of the number of employees per establishment.

Table 2.3   **Determinants of industry incorporation rates**

	(1)	(2)	(3)	(4)	(5)	(6)	(7)
			A. Univariate regressions				
Capital-output ratio	0.236**						
	(0.086)						
Steam engines per establishment		0.492**					
		(0.116)					
Fraction assets machines and bldgs.			0.596*				
			(0.235)				
Percent workforce female				0.230			
				(0.137)			
Log wage, all employees					−0.322**		
					(0.086)		
Log wage, adult male employees						−0.368**	
						(0.123)	
Growth rate of output, 1865–1875							−0.083+
							(0.046)
Constant	0.0364	−0.0065	−0.166	0.137**	2.196**	2.521**	0.195**
	(0.0542)	(0.0324)	(0.136)	(0.0433)	(0.540)	(0.792)	(0.0409)
R-squared	0.138	0.475	0.156	0.077	0.202	0.158	0.113
			B. Controlling for average firm scale				
Capital-output ratio	0.090						
	(0.069)						
Steam engines per establishment		0.368*					
		(0.146)					

Fraction assets machines and bldgs.							
Percent workforce female			0.373+	−0.058			
			(0.213)	(0.120)			
Log wage, all employees					−0.140		
					(0.099)		
Log wage, adult male employees						−0.214*	
						(0.099)	
Growth rate of output, 1865–1875							−0.018
							(0.028)
Log total employees	0.098**	0.053*	0.099**	0.112**	0.096**	0.100**	0.103**
	(0.016)	(0.021)	(0.020)	(0.018)	(0.020)	(0.018)	(0.015)
Constant	−0.199**	−0.132**	−0.362**	−0.174**	0.747	1.223+	−0.170**
	(0.055)	(0.042)	(0.088)	(0.048)	(0.648)	(0.639)	(0.045)
R-squared	0.459	0.561	0.504	0.444	0.450	0.469	0.574
Observations	38	35	35	36	33	33	34

Note: Robust standard errors in parentheses.

**Significant at the 1 percent level.

*Significant at the 5 percent level.

+Significant at the 10 percent level.

The estimates in panel A indicate that incorporation rates were higher in industries in which production took place primarily within factories, rather than artisanal shops. The capital-output ratio, the use of steam power, and the use of unskilled labor (reflected in both lower average wages and a higher percentage of female labor, although the latter estimate is not statistically significant) were all substantially higher among industries with higher incorporation rates. The incorporation rate also varied with the composition of firms' capital. Column (3) presents a regression of the percentage of firms' assets represented by "fixed assets"—buildings and machinery—rather than stock on hand. This measure was also positively correlated with incorporation rates, which likely reflects the fact that the capital of incorporated firms was used to finance fixed investments.[22]

Finally, column (7) regresses the growth rate of industry output in Massachusetts between the 1865 and 1875 censuses on incorporation rates. If the corporate form facilitated investments in rapidly growing, new, or innovative industries, then one would expect that this measure would be positively correlated with incorporation rates. However, the estimated correlation is negative, and even significant at the 10 percent level. This is likely due to the negative correlation between industry growth rates and average firm size—industries with larger firms grew more slowly.[23]

In panel B of table 2.3, the same regressions are estimated, but with log total employees included as a measure of scale. That is, in these regressions the relationship between industry characteristics and incorporation rates are analyzed, conditional on average firm size. Some of the estimated relationships change substantially, implying that the correlations in panel A were simply due to the greater scale in industries that had higher incorporation rates. In particular, the estimated correlations with the capital-output ratio (column [1]), the percentage of the labor force that was female (column [4]), the log wage for all employees (column [5]), and the growth rate of industry output following 1865 (column [7]) all show substantial decreases in absolute magnitude and statistical significance. Evidently these relationships were driven by scale. Interestingly, the log average wage paid to adult male employees—which should reflect the degree of skill among those workers, rather than the overall mix of skilled and unskilled labor—continues to

---

22. In contrast, working capital ("stock on hand') was likely financed by commercial credit. All else equal, borrowing terms for unincorporated firms, whose owners faced unlimited liability, may have been more favorable than those faced by incorporated firms, and this may have contributed to the lower incorporation rates among firms in which stock on hand represented a substantial portion of total assets.

23. The correlation between the industry growth rate and log total employees was –0.36. It should also be noted that over the 1865–1875 period many industries in Massachusetts contracted significantly, and this contraction may have been related to the end of the Civil War. In addition to the arms and ammunition industry, which contracted by more than 70 percent, the oils and illuminating fluids, glass, and woolen goods industries, all of which had relatively high incorporation rates, saw substantial contractions in their output.

indicate a strong negative relationship, although the magnitude of the estimate is diminished. Likewise the estimated effects of the use of steam power and the fraction of firm assets represented by fixed capital, both of which were likely correlated with factory production, were robustly correlated with incorporation rates, even conditional on firm scale.

Unfortunately it is impossible to infer from these data whether access to the corporate form facilitated the creation of firms that could not otherwise have existed, or if it enabled firms to achieve a greater scale or adopt different production methods than would have been possible otherwise. It is worth noting that *if* the corporate form enabled firms to increase their scale or adopt steam power, relative to what was attainable as a partnership, then these results imply that the corporate form increased productivity. Using data from the federal census, Atack, Bateman, and Margo (2008) find strong productivity gains associated with the adoption of steam power, and that these gains were increasing in firm size.

But overall these results indicate that corporations were formed in industries in which establishments resembled factories more than artisanal shops. Even conditional on average firm size, industries with high incorporation rates were more likely to utilize steam power and relied on less skilled male workers, relative to their peers. In what follows, I analyze the ownership of corporations and how their governance may have responded to these industry characteristics.

2.4   Ownership and Governance of Massachusetts's Corporations

Concentrated corporate ownership imposes costs, and also presents some benefits. The most obvious cost is that the wealth of investors holding large blocks of stock will be illiquid and poorly diversified. In cases where a shareholder holds a controlling stake, an additional cost may arise, namely that the controlling shareholder may engage in self-dealing or other actions that benefit himself at the cost of the other owners, and those other owners may have little recourse. On the other hand, concentrated ownership creates incentives for investors to monitor the management of the firm. In the nineteenth century many corporate directors likely participated directly in management (they *were* the managers), implying that large stakes held by the board would create strong ownership incentives for diligent effort. One of the main arguments of Berle and Means (1932) is that when there are no large blockholders, control falls into the hands of management, who become unaccountable to the shareholders, except in rare circumstances.

The historical record indicates that among the very large textile corporations in the state, there was an absence of substantial owners who would have had strong incentives to monitor management, and this appears to have been a source of some concern. Sophisticated merchants often expressed skepticism that the managers of early corporations would be capable of performing as well as those who operated on "an individual basis." For example, Henry Lee, a Boston merchant, complained in his correspondence that many major textile corporations were "in danger of being ruined by extreme salaries and high wages in all the departments," a problem he attributed to weak performance incentives for managers (Porter 1937, 125). But the most clear and direct evidence of such managerial opportunism is found in the early 1860s, when an activist investor named J. C. Ayer initiated a campaign to reform the governance institutions of the major textile corporations. He produced a pamphlet, *On the Usages and Abuses in the Management of Our Manufacturing Corporations* (1863) that argued that opportunism by directors was rampant: they engaged in self-dealing in their transactions with firms to whom the purchase of raw materials or the sale of finished products were delegated, and paid excessive fees; they hired their relatives for important supervisory positions; they drew excessively high salaries; and they concealed the effects of these practices from the shareholders. Ayer specifically argued that "relations of owners and managers" had changed since the founding of the companies. Unlike the original investors, the existing owners decades later were completely passive, and bought their shares "in the hope that somebody interested in it can and will take care of it." He also argued that the directors perpetuated their control over their firms by soliciting proxy votes from the shareholders through duplicitous means, and, where necessary, by holding the annual meetings of companies with many shareholders in common simultaneously, thereby preventing the larger shareholders from participating in more than one.

Although it is impossible to verify many of Ayer's claims, it is possible to discern the level of shareholder participation in annual meetings for at least a handful of companies and thereby assess whether or not the scope for managerial opportunism was as broad as Ayer claimed. Indeed, it does appear to be the case that stockholders participated in annual meetings only infrequently.[24] The Massachusetts legislature responded to the complaints of Ayer and other stockholders by enacting a statute in 1865 intended to limit the power of directors to utilize proxy votes to perpetuate their control.[25] In particular, the statute limited the number of proxy votes that a sitting director could exercise to twenty, a very small fraction of the total of around 1,000 shares that were typically outstanding.

2.4.1   Ownership Structures of Manufacturing Companies

Whether or not these problems were representative of those faced by investors in early manufacturing corporations generally depends, at least in

---

24. For example, between 1850 and 1875, the number of stockholders in the Pepperell Manufacturing Company grew from 117 to 321. At the annual meetings during that period, the number of stockholders present generally ranged from ten to twenty-five (Knowlton 1948, 16). See also McGouldrick (1968).

25. *Massachusetts Laws* (1865, ch. 236).

Table 2.4   **Ownership of manufacturing corporations**

	Mean	Median	SD	Min.	Max.
A. All manufacturing corporations					
Total paid-in capital	210,638	100,000	323,753	1,000	2,500,000
Total shareholders	47	18	87	2	730
Board size	4.06	4	1.44	2	13
Percent owned by directors	0.45	0.44	0.29	0.01	1
Percent held by largest shareholder	0.28	0.24	0.21	0.01	0.99
Widely held	0.42	0	0.49	0	1
B. Manufacturing corporations traded on Boston Stock Exchange					
Total paid-in capital	912,742	750,000	589,363	100,000	2,500,000
Total shareholders	261	237	182	60	730
Board size	4.90	5	1.08	3	7
Percent owned by directors	0.10	0.07	0.06	0.02	0.26
Percent held by largest shareholder	0.07	0.05	0.07	0.01	0.36
Widely held	0.97	1	0.18	0	1

part, on how unusual the ownership structures of the great textile corporations were, relative to other firms. Panel A of table 2.4 presents data on the degree of ownership concentration among all manufacturing corporations. The average manufacturing corporation had around $210,000 in paid-in capital and forty-seven shareholders. It had a relatively small board consisting of four directors, who owned around 45 percent of the shares. Its ownership was relatively concentrated by the standards of modern public companies, with the largest investor holding 28 percent of the shares. By the definition of La Porta, Lopez-de-Silanes, and Shleifer (1999), only about 42 percent of Massachusetts's corporations were "widely held," in the sense of not having a 20 percent owner. For the average firm, the complaints of Ayer seem unlikely to have been relevant.

In contrast, panel B of the table presents the same statistics for the thirty-one manufacturing corporations in the sample whose shares were traded on the Boston Stock Exchange.[26] Those firms included most of the great Waltham-Lowell textile mills, as well as a few other major industrial firms from other regions in the state. The data reveal that the Boston Stock Exchange firms were quite unusual. Their capital was more than fourfold greater than

26. *Martin's Boston Stock Market* indicates that in 1875, the stocks of around forty-four New England manufacturing companies were traded regularly on the Boston Stock Exchange. Among those forty-four, at least eleven were located in states other than Massachusetts. See Atack and Rousseau (1999) on the performance of Boston Stock Exchange traded shares during this period.

average, and their numbers of shareholders were fivefold greater. Ownership by management was less than one-fourth that of the average corporation, as was the size of the largest stake held. These were huge corporations with an extraordinary degree of diffusion in their ownership. The problems faced by the shareholders of these firms were likely unique.

A more detailed portrait of the structure of ownership of manufacturing corporations is presented in table 2.5, which shows averages for each industry group where there was more than one operating corporation. The data in the table indicate that in nearly every industry managerial ownership was on average quite significant, and typically the largest investor owned more than 20 percent of the shares. Concentrated ownership was the norm, and the managers' own stakes were likely sufficiently large so that they would at least partly internalize the costs associated with shirking or taking other actions harmful to the performance of the firm. On the other hand, their stakes were often so large that they held majority control and could not be removed from their positions by the other shareholders. This suggests that oppression of minority shareholders by dominant owners was likely to have been a potential problem among a substantial portion of the corporations.[27]

What explains the variation in ownership structures across industries? Why did some firms have much larger managerial ownership and smaller numbers of outside shareholders than others? The data in table 2.5 suggest that scale played a role: in the industries with the largest average capital, the degree of ownership concentration appears to be lower. This was likely driven, at least in part, by the constraints of raising large sums of money—it was probably necessary in the case of very large firms for a group of founding investors to seek investments from large numbers of outsiders.

The relationship between average firm scale and ownership across industries is explored more systematically in figure 2.3. The scatter plots in the figure clearly indicate that the number of shareholders was increasing, and the degree of managerial ownership was decreasing, in the average scale of the firm. However, scale was not the only driving force behind the variation in ownership concentration. Across industries and firms, ownership was likely more concentrated where the resulting benefits were greater. The next section analyzes the variation in ownership concentration and investigates the circumstances in which there may have been greater benefits to more concentrated ownership.

2.4.2   Ownership Structures and Production Methods

Incorporators chose the governance institutions of their firms endogenously, which renders any analysis of the relationship between those governance institutions and firm performance empirically problematic. But the

---

27. Hilt (2008) argues that early corporate governance institutions were often focused on addressing this problem.

Table 2.5   Corporate ownership: Industry averages, Massachusetts (1875)

	Total capital	Total shareholders	Share owned by directors	Largest stake held	Share widely held
Clothing					
Boots and shoes	125,707	25	0.48	0.28	0.44
Other clothing	202,174	64	0.42	0.24	0.43
Food and tobacco					
Food preparations	175,875	32	0.32	0.17	0.62
Tobacco	14,088	8	0.66	0.15	1.00
Instruments					
Scientific instruments and appliances	107,382	25	0.60	0.37	0.00
Musical instruments and materials	122,363	10	0.56	0.29	0.20
Metals and metallic goods					
Agricultural implements	190,833	54	0.43	0.22	0.40
Arms and ammunition	9,398	7	0.71	0.63	0.00
Artisans' tools	118,133	68	0.40	0.31	0.29
Machines and machinery	157,666	26	0.52	0.28	0.27
Other metals and metallic goods	171,375	25	0.45	0.29	0.40
Oils and chemicals					
Chemical preparations	89,076	25	0.40	0.28	0.25
Fertilizers	218,000	30	0.41	0.41	0.50
Oils and illuminating fluids	112,929	27	0.52	0.21	0.40
Paints and colors	35,500	16	0.27	0.27	0.25
Paper and paper goods					
Paper	119,314	22	0.58	0.37	0.22
Print works	185,200	12	0.66	0.48	0.25
Printing and publishing	69,755	18	0.72	0.42	0.17
Textiles					
Carpetings	520,567	113	0.41	0.26	0.50
Cotton goods	449,478	100	0.41	0.27	0.53
Linen	550,000	36	0.55	0.41	0.00
Woolen goods	198,005	39	0.54	0.31	0.28
Other textiles	140,173	17	0.51	0.32	0.31
Vessels and carriages					
Carriages and wagons	84,000	6	0.91	0.39	0.00
Vessels	350,000	42	0.45	0.23	0.50
Wooden goods					
Furniture	237,807	15	0.59	0.43	0.00
Lumber	35,971	13	0.56	0.30	0.50
Other wooden goods	67,975	35	0.56	0.26	0.50
Other industries					
Brick	186,222	35	0.44	0.27	0.50
Glass	247,963	109	0.25	0.22	0.57
Jute	119,000	14	0.49	0.28	0.33
Leather	164,110	41	0.47	0.33	0.25
Rubber	115,000	19	0.35	0.29	0.00
Stone	119,194	31	0.44	0.31	0.43
Miscellaneous					
Miscellaneous manufactures	113,103	29	0.36	0.20	0.61

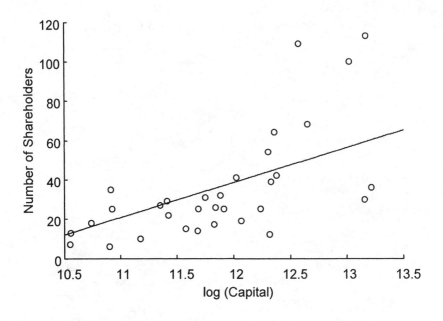

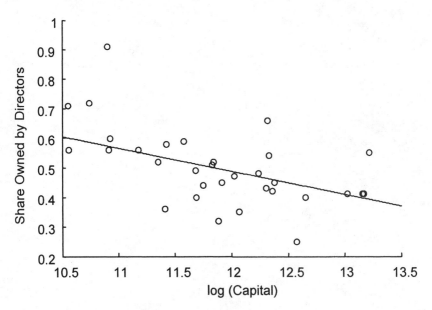

Fig. 2.3 Firm size and ownership structure by industry

corporate form was adapted into a broad range of industries, and if industry characteristics can be taken as exogenous for individual incorporators, then they can be used to empirically analyze some of the determinants of firms' governance institutions.

In what follows, I analyze how the degree of ownership concentration, which is likely to be correlated with owners' incentives to monitor management, varied with the production methods used across industries. The corporate form was sometimes adapted into industries dominated by establishments resembling artisanal shops, but it was much more commonly chosen within industries dominated by factories. Factories made greater use of steam power and unskilled labor, and their production processes likely created a greater division of labor and specialization of tasks among employees (see the discussion in Katz and Margo [2013]). Among these firms, managers likely performed a complex supervisory role that was critically important to the success of the firm. Although the organizational structure of most manufacturing corporations in 1875 was rather simple, some of the larger and more complex firms may have begun to develop new managerial systems and organizational structures (Chandler 1977). The complexity and importance of the role of managers within these firms, and the potential difficulties outsiders may have faced in monitoring and evaluating their performance, likely presented a challenge for their governance. Concentrated ownership may have been a solution.

From the certificates of condition, we cannot observe the production process or managerial structure of the corporations. However, the industry averages available from the census, which reflect the typical production methods used among all firms, can be used as a proxy for the firms' own process. To the extent that they reflect the available choices of production methods given the state of technology and knowledge of management techniques, these industry averages can be taken as exogenous determinants of the governance institutions of individual corporations within each industry. In order to analyze this relationship, I estimate the following model:

$$y_{ijc} = \alpha + \delta_c + \gamma \text{prod}_j + \theta \log k_i + X\beta + \varepsilon_i,$$

where y_{ijc} is the governance measure of interest for firm i in industry j in county c, δ_c is a county fixed effect, prod_j is the average production method (such as the rate of use of steam power) in industry j, $\log k_i$ is the log level of capital of firm i, and X is a vector of other characteristics observed at the firm level. Thus the model estimates the relationship between industry-average production methods and the governance of individual firms, conditional on firm scale. Controls for geographical locations, in the form of county fixed effects, are included in order to address the possibility that different production techniques (again, such as the use of steam power) may have shifted the location of production into places that may have independently influenced firms' governance structures. In order to address potential problems associ-

Table 2.6   **Determinants of ownership structures**

	Dependent variable			
	Log total shareholders (1)	Fraction owned by directors (2)	Board size (3)	Largest stake held (4)
Steam engines per establishment	−0.581*	0.105+	−0.616+	0.0860+
	(0.249)	(0.0526)	(0.313)	(0.0459)
Log paid-in capital	0.449**	−0.0558**	0.224**	−0.0257*
	(0.0859)	(0.0163)	(0.0592)	(0.00945)
Constant	−1.969*	1.065**	1.701**	0.544**
	(0.949)	(0.187)	(0.597)	(0.113)
Observations	459	461	461	460
R-squared	0.291	0.142	0.093	0.105
Log wage, adult male employees	0.689*	−0.135*	0.583+	−0.123**
	(0.269)	(0.0511)	(0.334)	(0.0357)
Log paid-in capital	0.467**	−0.0579**	0.231**	−0.0267*
	(0.0918)	(0.0182)	(0.0639)	(0.0108)
Constant	−6.829**	1.997**	−2.375	1.372**
	(2.161)	(0.425)	(2.563)	(0.279)
Observations	453	455	455	454
R-squared	0.289	0.138	0.086	0.106
Fraction workforce female	−0.163	0.0945*	−0.224	0.0715+
	(0.238)	(0.0398)	(0.297)	(0.0371)
Log paid-in capital	0.452**	−0.0589**	0.216**	−0.0266*
	(0.0884)	(0.0176)	(0.0651)	(0.0109)
Constant	−2.258*	1.127**	1.549*	0.578**
	(0.989)	(0.203)	(0.687)	(0.127)
Observations	464	466	466	465
R-squared	0.282	0.136	0.079	0.096

Note: Robust standard errors, adjusted for clustering by firm county, in parentheses. All specifications include county fixed effects.
**Significant at the 1 percent level.
*Significant at the 5 percent level.
+Significant at the 10 percent level.

ated with the use of industry-averages for the production method variables used in the regression, the standard errors will be adjusted for clustering by industry. The governance characteristics used as dependent variables in these regressions are the log number of shareholders, the fraction of the firm owned by the directors, the size of the board, and the size of the largest stake held.

Table 2.6 presents the results for specifications using steam power, the log annual wage paid to adult male employees, and the fraction of the workforce that was female—the first an indication of factory production; the second an indication of a greater degree of skilled labor, less consistent with factory production; and the third a measure of the use of unskilled labor, consistent with factory production. The results of all specifications are clear and broadly consistent. The use of factory production methods, conditional on firm scale, was associated with more concentrated ownership and stronger governance by shareholders. In particular, the upper panel of table 2.6 indicates that in industries that relied more heavily on steam power, the corporations had fewer shareholders, were owned to a larger extent by their directors, had smaller board sizes, and the size of the largest stake held in their equity was greater.[28] In contrast, corporations in industries where the wages paid to adult male workers were higher, which likely utilized more skilled labor in their production, had larger numbers of shareholders, lower ownership by directors, larger boards, and smaller maximum ownership stakes. The estimates for the share of the workforce that was female, although smaller and less statistically precise, are of the same sign as those for the use of steam power.

One potential source of concern with these results could be that an omitted variable, firm age, may be partly responsible for the observed correlations. If newer corporations tended to be formed in industries that utilized factory production methods, and newer corporations also had more concentrated ownership structures, as their founders had not yet sold off parts of their stakes (and the shares generally had less time to diffuse among investors), then the observed correlations between production methods and firm governance could be driven by firm age. In order to address this possibility, the date of incorporation of each firm was obtained from the Massachusetts Tax Commissioner's Annual Report, and from it the log age of each firm was calculated.

Table 2.7 presents the results of regressions of the same specifications as those of table 2.6, but with log firm age included as an additional control. As expected, firm age is positively and strongly correlated with the number of shareholders, although not with other measures of ownership concentration. However, the inclusion of this variable does not substantially change the estimated effects of the production methods of the corporations on their governance. We can conclude that the results are not driven by firm age.

These results are somewhat speculative, and await confirmation in future work using more detailed data in which production methods can be observed for individual firms, rather than at the industry level. Nonetheless, they suggest that one of the ways in which the corporate form was successfully adapted into different industrial contexts was that ownership structures and governance institutions were varied endogenously. In particular, in corporations that operated in industries that relied heavily on factory production using steam power and a high proportion of unskilled labor, there was more concentrated ownership relative to corporations of similar sizes in industries

---

28. Larger boards of directors have been found to hamper performance across a variety of measures among modern corporations; see Yermack (1996) and the references cited therein.

Table 2.7   Determinants of ownership structures, conditional on firm age

	Dependent variable			
	Log total shareholders (1)	Fraction owned by directors (2)	Board size (3)	Largest stake held (4)
Steam engines per establishment	−0.650*	0.106+	−0.606+	0.0860+
	(0.260)	(0.0540)	(0.313)	(0.0463)
Log paid-in capital	0.416**	−0.0512**	0.244**	−0.0252*
	(0.0815)	(0.0159)	(0.0642)	(0.0100)
Log firm age	0.138**	−0.0142	−0.0706	−0.000689
	(0.0432)	(0.0113)	(0.0587)	(0.00677)
Constant	−1.818+	1.039**	1.610*	0.539**
	(0.904)	(0.183)	(0.624)	(0.116)
Observations	455	457	457	456
R-squared	0.308	0.143	0.097	0.103
Log wage, adult male employees	0.815**	−0.156**	0.482	−0.131**
	(0.283)	(0.0526)	(0.359)	(0.0379)
Log paid-in capital	0.438**	−0.0539**	0.250**	−0.0260*
	(0.0883)	(0.0180)	(0.0699)	(0.0113)
Log firm age	0.132**	−0.0147	−0.0733	−0.00281
	(0.0441)	(0.0107)	(0.0585)	(0.00691)
Constant	−7.533**	2.109**	−1.797	1.426**
	(2.199)	(0.430)	(2.711)	(0.283)
Observations	449	451	451	450
R-squared	0.304	0.140	0.089	0.105
Fraction workforce female	−0.187	0.0972*	−0.202	0.0727+
	(0.251)	(0.0409)	(0.297)	(0.0380)
Log paid-in capital	0.421**	−0.0545**	0.239**	−0.0260*
	(0.0856)	(0.0174)	(0.0722)	(0.0115)
Log firm age	0.120**	−0.0132	−0.0802	−0.00128
	(0.0424)	(0.0103)	(0.0584)	(0.00639)
Constant	−2.120*	1.101**	1.435+	0.573**
	(0.957)	(0.200)	(0.722)	(0.130)
Observations	460	462	462	461
R-squared	0.296	0.138	0.083	0.095

Note: Robust standard errors, adjusted for clustering by firm county, in parentheses. All specifications include county fixed effects.
**Significant at the 1 percent level.
*Significant at the 5 percent level.
+Significant at the 10 percent level.

that relied more on skilled labor and less on steam power. This is consistent with the notion that incorporators and investors responded to the challenges posed by the complex role performed by managers in those firms by ensuring that there was adequate ownership incentives to monitor and supervise management.

2.5   Conclusion and Epilogue

Over the course of the nineteenth century the corporate form was adopted at high rates by manufacturing firms, particularly in Massachusetts. This chapter has analyzed the variation in incorporation rates, and the ways that corporations were owned and configured, across industries in 1875.

One important finding of the chapter is that among the large textile corporations of the state—the so-called Waltham-Lowell mills, whose shares were traded on the Boston Stock Exchange—the degree of ownership by the board was extraordinarily low, and there were very few if any large blockholders. The degree of separation of ownership from control among these firms was in fact typical of widely held modern American firms. However, the data presented in the chapter indicate that these great textile corporations were quite unusual. Most nineteenth-century manufacturing corporations were smaller, had fewer owners, and a high degree of ownership by their managers. Some were indeed extremely small—around 10 percent had four shareholders or fewer. Many of these firms adapted the corporate form to their needs by creating extremely small boards of directors; 10 percent had boards of two or fewer people. Most Massachusetts corporations were in fact controlled and operated by the men who owned them.

Unsurprisingly, the corporate form was adopted more frequently among firms in industries where average establishment size was higher. However, conditional on firm size, industries that made greater use of steam power and unskilled labor were incorporated at higher rates. This implies that the corporate form found heaviest use among those industries in which production was undertaken within factories, rather than artisanal shops. Evidently the corporation was used not only to achieve greater scale, but also to adopt mechanized, factory-based production methods.

The results also indicate that, conditional on firm size, corporations operating in industries that made greater use of steam power and unskilled labor had more concentrated ownership. That is, relative to corporations of similar sizes, those in industries that organized production within factories, rather than artisanal shops, had fewer shareholders, and a greater proportion of the shares were held by the directors. This is consistent with the notion that incorporators and investors responded to the challenges posed by the complex role performed by managers in those firms by ensuring that there was adequate ownership incentives to monitor and supervise management.

What happened after 1875? In the 1890s, several states, beginning with New Jersey, substantially liberalized their corporation laws, permitting businesses located in other states to incorporate within their borders, eliminating many restrictions on capital contributions, and enabling the formation of holding companies (see Larcom 1937; Grandy 1989). For a brief period, Massachusetts's corporation laws, with their detailed annual disclosure requirements and strict limitations on corporate powers, were among the most conservative in the United States.[29] Ultimately in 1903, Massachusetts substantially liberalized its laws to reflect the "modern view that the State owes no duty to investors to look after the solvency of corporations" (Hall 1908). With this change, the detailed data on business corporations utilized for this study ceased to be collected.

Nevertheless, it is possible to follow the evolution of the use of the business corporation in Massachusetts into the early twentieth century using data generated by the imposition and collection of the federal corporate income tax in 1909. In 1909, there were 3,637 operating manufacturing corporations in the state, with $1.013 billion in capital. This was equivalent to 1.08 manufacturing corporations and $598 in capital per 1,000 persons, relative to a national average of 0.97 manufacturing corporations and $234 in capital nationally.[30] Thus Massachusetts remained a prominent center of manufacturing corporations, but it was no longer as unusual in the extent to which the corporate form was utilized as it had been in the mid-nineteenth century. As new industries and new centers of innovation emerged, and as many states revised and liberalized their corporation laws, Massachusetts was eclipsed by other states.

References

Acheson, Graeme, Gareth Campbell, John D. Turner, and Nadia Vanteeva. 2014. "Corporate Ownership and Control in Victorian Britain." QUCEH Working Paper Series no. 14–01. Queen's University Centre for Economic History, Queen's University Belfast.

Atack, Jeremy, Fred Bateman, and Robert A. Margo. 2008. "Steam Power, Establishment Size, and Labor Productivity Growth in Nineteenth-Century American Manufacturing." *Explorations in Economic History* 45:185–98.

Atack, Jeremy, and Peter Rousseau. 1999. "Business Activity and the Boston Stock Market, 1835–69." *Explorations in Economic History* 36:144–79.

Ayer, J. C. 1863. *Some of the Usages and Abuses in the Management of Our Manufacturing Corporations.* Lowell, MA: C. M. Langley & Co.

Becht, Marco, and J. Bradford Delong. 2005. "Why Has There Been So Little Blockholding in America?" In *A History of Corporate Governance around the World,* edited by R. Morck. Chicago: University of Chicago Press.

29. When Theodore Roosevelt became president, his first message to Congress signaled his intention to impose federal corporation laws, but reassure the business community that "supervision of corporations by the National Government need not go so far as is now the case with the supervision exercised over them by so conservative a State as Massachusetts" (Roosevelt 1901).

30. Author's calculations from the US Treasury Department (1910) and the federal census. It is important to note that these data are not directly comparable to those of figure 2.1, which presents the total number of corporations created in all sectors, rather than manufacturing corporations that were actually in operation.

Berle, Adolf, and Gardiner Means. 1932. *The Modern Corporation and Private Property.* New York: Macmillan.

Bodenhorn, Howard. 2012. "Voting Rights, Share Concentration and Leverage in Nineteenth-Century US Banks." NBER Working Paper no. 17808, Cambridge, MA.

———. 2013. "Large Block Shareholders, Institutional Investors, Boards of Directors and Bank Value in the Nineteenth Century." NBER Working Paper no. 18955, Cambridge, MA.

Cantillo Simon, Miguel. 1998. "The Rise and Fall of Bank Control in the United States: 1890–1939." *American Economic Review* 88 (5): 1077–93.

Chandler, Alfred D. 1977. *The Visible Hand.* Cambridge, MA: Harvard University Press.

Cheffins, B. R., D. Chambers, and D. K. Koustas. 2013. "Ownership Dispersion and the London Stock Exchange's 'Two-thirds Rule': An Empirical Test." *Business History* 55 (2013): 670–93.

Coffee, John C. 2001. "The Rise of Dispersed Ownership: The Roles of Law and the State in the Separation of Ownership and Control." *Yale Law Journal* 111 (1): 1–82.

Davis, Joseph S. 1917. *Essays in the Earlier History of Corporations.* Cambridge, MA: Harvard University Press.

Davis, Lance E. 1958. "Stock Ownership in the Early New England Textile Industry." *Business History Review* 32:204–22.

Dodd, Edwin M. 1938. *Lectures on the Growth of Corporate Structure in the United States with Special Reference to Governmental Regulation.* Cleveland, OH: Cleveland Bar Association.

Freeman, Mark, Robin Pearson, and James Taylor. 2011. *Shareholder Democracies? Corporate Governance in Britain and Ireland Before 1850.* Chicago: University of Chicago.

Grandy, Christopher. 1989. "New Jersey Corporate Chartermongering, 1875–1929." *Journal of Economic History* 49 (3): 677–92.

Guinnane, Timothy W., Ron Harris, Naomi Lamoreaux, and Jean-Laurent Rosenthal. 2007. "Putting the Corporation In Its Place." *Enterprise and Society* 8:687–729.

Hall, Prescott F. 1908. *The Massachusetts Business Corporation Law of 1903.* Boston: William J. Nagel.

Handlin, Oscar, and Mary Flug Handlin. 1974. *Commonwealth: A Study of the Rule of Government in the American Economy, Massachusetts, 1774–1861.* Cambridge, MA: Harvard University Press.

Hannah, Leslie. 2007. "The Divorce of Ownership from Control from 1900: Re-Calibrating Imagined Global Historical Trends." *Business History* 49:404–38.

Hilt, Eric. 2008. "When Did Ownership Separate from Control? Corporate Governance in the Early Nineteenth Century." *Journal of Economic History* 68:645–85.

———. 2014. "General Incorporation and the Shift toward Open Access in the Nineteenth-Century United States." Working Paper, Wellesley College.

Hilt, Eric, and Jacqueline Valentine. 2012. "Democratic Dividends: Stockholding, Wealth, and Politics in New York, 1791–1826." *Journal of Economic History* 72 (2): 332–63.

Hovenkamp, Herbert. 1991. *Enterprise and American Law, 1836–1937.* Cambridge, MA: Harvard University Press.

Hurst, James W. 1970. *The Legitimacy of the Business Corporation in the Law of the United States, 1780–1970.* Charlottesville: University of Virginia Press.

Katz, Lawrence, and Robert Margo. 2013. "Technical Change and the Relative Demand for Skilled Labor: The United States in Historical Perspective." NBER Working Paper no. 18752, Cambridge, MA.

Knowlton, Evelyn H. 1948. *Pepperell's Progress: History of A Cotton Textile Company, 1844–1945.* Cambridge, MA: Harvard University Press.

Lamoreaux, Naomi. 2014. "Revisiting American Exceptionalism: Democracy and the Regulation of Corporate Governance in Nineteenth-Century Pennsylvania." NBER Working Paper no. 20231, Cambridge, MA.

La Porta, Rafael, Florencio Lopez-de-Silanes, and Andrei Shleifer. 1999. "Corporate Ownership around the World." *Journal of Finance* 54 (2): 471–517.

Larcom, Russell C. 1937. *The Delaware Corporation.* Baltimore: Johns Hopkins Press.

Majewski, John. 2006. "Toward a Social History of the Corporation: Shareholding in Pennsylvania, 1800–1840." In *The Economy of Early America: Historical Perspectives and New Directions,* edited by C. Matson, 294–316. Philadelphia: University of Pennsylvania.

Martin, Joseph G. 1886. *Martin's Boston Stock Market.* Boston: Published by the author.

McGouldrick, Paul F. 1968. *New England Textiles in the Nineteenth Century.* Cambridge, MA: Harvard University Press.

Porter, Kenneth W. 1937. *The Jackson and the Lees.* Cambridge, MA: Harvard University Press.

Roosevelt, Theodore. 1901. *Message of the President of the United States Communicated to the Two Houses of Congress at the Beginning of the First Session of the Fifty-Seventh Congress.* Washington, DC: Government Printing Office.

Sylla, Richard, and Robert E. Wright. 2013. "Corporation Formation in the Antebellum United States in Comparative Context." *Business History* 55 (4): 653–69.

Temin, Peter. 2000. "The Industrialization of New England, 1830–1880." In *Engines of Enterprise: An Economic History of New England,* edited by P. Temin, 109–52. Cambridge, MA: Harvard University Press.

US Treasury Department. 1910. *Annual Report of the Commissioner of Internal Revenue for the Fiscal Year Ended June 30 1910. House of Representatives, Document 1045.* Washington, DC: Government Printing Office.

Ware, Caroline F. 1931. *The Early New England Cotton Manufacture.* New York: Houghton Mifflin.

Werner, Walter. 1986. "Corporate Law In Search of Its Future." *Columbia Law Review* 81:1610–66.

Wright, Carroll D. 1877. *A Compendium of the Census of Massachusetts: 1875.* Boston: Albert J. Wright.

Wright, Robert E. 1999. "Bank Ownership and Lending Patterns in New York and Pennsylvania, 1781–1831." *Business History Review* 73:40–60.

Yermack, David. 1996. "Higher Market Valuation of Companies with a Small Board of Directors." *Journal of Financial Economics* 40 (2): 185–211.

Comment   Claudia Rei

Eric Hilt's chapter focuses on late nineteenth-century Massachusetts, a state at the forefront of America's industrial revolution. In particular, Hilt writes about the expansion of the corporate form among manufacturing firms that

Claudia Rei is assistant professor of economics and history at Vanderbilt University.
For acknowledgments, sources of research support, and disclosure of the author's material financial relationships, if any, please see http://www.nber.org/chapters/c13352.ack.

went far beyond the well-known cases of the large textile mills in Waltham and Lowell. These mills were at the very start of America's corporate ownership, but whether they were representative or exceptional in the set of firms adopting the corporate form is unclear in the current literature. Also unclear thus far is the organization of other manufacturing firms that adopted the corporate form. This chapter is therefore a welcome addition to the literature on organizational innovation that has lagged behind that on technological innovation.

Corporation data are available for Massachusetts since the early 1870s, when the state required all firms that had ever adopted the corporate form to file corporate certificates listing all managers and owners. Hilt collects information on all corporate certificates for 1875, matching 601 of these firms to business directories (for the business category), and also to the state manufacturing censuses (for firm size and incorporation date). The findings in table 2.1 show that textile firms were not typical among Massachusetts's corporations, due to their unusually large size and dispersed ownership structure. Furthermore, there was a wide range of corporations in a variety of other sectors that adapted the corporate form to their particular needs, maintaining a small number of directors and stockholders with a high degree of manager ownership.

The diverse set of corporations in the Massachusetts manufacturing sector could be illustrated with further analysis of the available information in table 2.1. Incorporation rates are higher in more capital-intensive industries, as seen in figure 2.2, but incorporation rates could also have varied with respect to the degree of competition in a given industry. In a sector with few firms, adopting the corporate form may have been the only way to compete effectively, whereas in the presence of a large number of competitors such strategic behavior may not have paid off.

It is unclear where textiles fit in this picture. Even though the average capital in all textile establishments (as well as textile corporations) was higher than in other sectors, the incorporation rates did not take extreme values and varied between 17 and 56 percent. Nevertheless, these were higher incorporation rates than the nontextile average, which is perhaps telling of how special this sector was. Since one of the main contributions of the chapter is to highlight the importance of Massachusetts's manufacturing firms beyond textiles, it would be useful to evaluate the overall impact of the textile sector. Do the average variables of interest (for example adoption of the corporate form, capital concentration) vary substantially if textiles are included? There certainly is value in the characterization of Massachusetts's manufacturing industry beyond textiles. But the interested reader would also like to know how much the current literature missed of the early industrial revolution in the United States by focusing primarily on textiles.

Other than characterizing Massachusetts's manufacturing firms, the chapter also evaluates two potential challenges of the adoption of the corporate form. The first is managerial opportunism occurring when a firm's ownership is so widespread that managers were virtually unaccountable to shareholders. The second is minority oppression present when managers use their privileged position to pursue their own interest, or that of large shareholders, at the expense of small shareholders.

To investigate the prevalence of these problems Hilt extracts ownership and governance data from the 1875 corporate certificates for the 601 matched firms in table 2.4. These firms show high degrees of ownership concentration relative to modern standards. The standard deviations of total paid-in capital and total shareholders are higher than the corresponding averages, which in turn are higher than the median values. This pattern signals a highly skewed distribution where very large firms distort average and median results, an indicator of minority oppression. Once the analysis is restricted to the very large firms traded on the Boston Stock Exchange (thirty-one in total) ownership concentration was considerably lower. This evidence suggests the prevalence of managerial opportunism for which there is indeed some anecdotal evidence in the large textile corporations (Ayer 1863; Porter 1937).

On this note, it would be useful to explore whether there was a trade-off between managerial opportunism and minority oppression as ownership concentration varied. In theory, higher managerial ownership should lead to minority oppression but there seems to be no anecdotal evidence for this, potentially due to three reasons: (a) higher degrees of ownership tend to occur in smaller firms, which do not make it to the newspapers or pamphlets and, in general, have less information available in the surviving records; (b) even if such information exists, minority oppression may have been easier to hide since it likely referred to small numbers of minority shareholders; and (c) minority oppression may also have been a smaller problem as minority shareholders in smaller corporations could have been more passive, otherwise they would probably be in management. The available data may not allow the analysis of all these issues, but some exploration of the trade-off would be welcome.

Among the thirty-one firms that were publically traded in 1875 it would be good to know the exact contribution of the large textile mills and if there was any considerable portion of those mills out of this restricted sample. Would excluding the other few major industrial firms from this set change in any way the comparison with the full sample? If the contribution of the remaining firms was substantial and that of unincorporated textile firms was negligible, it could be the case that only firms above a certain scale (eventually just in textiles) could take full advantage of the corporate form. Small firm owners (in textiles or not), therefore, could just have experimented with the new organizational form to surpass original resource constraints but not to considerably expand their production and become big firms.

Ultimately, the objective would be to evaluate the backbone of the Massachusetts manufacturing sector and whether the organizational innovation helped it thrive. Were just a few large corporations pulling all the weight, or was this the role of many tiny firms whether or not they had adopted the corporate form? A clear answer to this question would allow for two additional avenues of research: (a) a within-industry comparison of adopters and nonadopters of the new organizational form to possibly identify its differential effect, and (b) Massachusetts's changing role in American industrialization from an organizational perspective.

The epilogue alludes briefly to the stagnant status of corporate law in Massachusetts after 1875 when other states (New Jersey, for example) embarked in a liberalization trend, which made Massachusetts relatively less competitive. The natural question to ask is, therefore, whether Massachusetts was also falling behind in technology in the last quarter of the nineteenth century, or if textiles were no longer contributing much to the country's industrial production. In either case, if the more competitive sectors were underrepresented in the state of Massachusetts there was little scope to compete with more organizationally advanced states.

Regarding the origin of Massachusetts's organizational advantage, figure 2.1 shows a rapid rise of corporation charters in the state, relative to New England and also to the entire United States, until 1850. The data analyzed later in the chapter, however, comes from 1875 when Massachusetts may or may not have been dominant in the adoption of the corporate form. After the Civil War, Massachusetts's organizational advantage could have changed via industry relocation due to the temporary disruption of cotton prices (Hanlon 2013) or the rising availability of cheap labor in the South in the last quarter of the nineteenth century (Carlson 1981; Wright 1979). Both these events were occurring under continuous innovation in the power technology sector, which itself could have affected Massachusetts's competitive edge (Hekman 1980). Were figure 2.1 extended another fifty years we would be able to observe not only the rise of Massachusetts's corporate advantage, but also its erosion. The latter was evident by 1901 when the state was considered one of the most conservative in terms of corporate law.

An ideal figure would provide a direct comparison of Massachusetts's corporate and industrial advantages between 1790 and 1900. There would be two sets of lines corresponding to two different scales: the first would illustrate the number of corporations per 1,000 persons relative to New England and the United States (as already seen in figure 2.1) and the second set of lines would show industrial capacity per 1,000 persons (or any other metric) also relative to New England and the United States. We already know from figure 2.1 that Massachusetts outperformed New England and the United States until 1850 and supposedly the trend in industrial capacity was no different during that time period. We also know that at some time between 1850 and 1901 the state's organizational advantage vanished, but this was a very eventful half-century in United States history so more discussion is needed on this matter.

If the industrial advantage was still favoring Massachusetts in the early twentieth century, then the chapter could potentially say that the organizational edge was a leading indicator of future economic activity. In particular, it would be relevant to investigate whether the textile sector (despite not being representative of Massachusetts's manufactures) was still at the technological forefront once the corporate edge was gone. If, on the contrary, the two types of advantages showed similar progress, organization may be more connected to technology than previously thought and there may be lessons to take from that as well.

In sum, Eric Hilt's chapter sheds much-needed light in the understudied field of organizational change during the industrialization period and raises important questions about the contribution of the corporate form to American enterprise.

References

Ayer, J. C. 1863. *Some of the Usages and Abuses in the Management of Our Manufacturing Corporations.* Lowell, MA: C. M. Langley & Co.

Carlson, Leonard A. 1981. "Labor Supply, the Acquisition of Skills, and the Location of Southern Textile Mills, 1880–1900." *Journal of Economic History* 41 (1): 65–71.

Hanlon, Walker. 2013. "Industry Connections and the Geographic Location of Economic Activity." Unpublished Manuscript, Department of Economics, University of California, Los Angeles.

Hekman, John S. 1980. "The Product Cycle and New England Textiles." *Quarterly Journal of Economics* 94 (4): 697–717.

Porter, Kenneth W. 1937. *The Jacksons and the Lees.* Cambridge, MA: Harvard University Press.

Wright, Gavin. 1979. "Cheap Labor and Southern Textiles before 1880." *Journal of Economic History* 39 (3): 655–80.

3

The Evolution of Bank Boards of Directors in New York, 1840–1950

Howard Bodenhorn and Eugene N. White

In December 1826, the board of the Franklin Bank of New York City asked Samuel Leggett, a former president of the bank, to reassume his previous position. The bank was in trouble and the board was hopeful that his experience and oversight might help in its recovery. By his own account, Leggett accepted the task reluctantly, and his worse fears were soon realized. During his first week back, he pored over the bank's records, which revealed *"mismanagement, improvident* loans, *irregular* transactions, *false* books . . . [the] total disregard to the fundamental rules of Banking . . . was frightfully apparent every where [sic]" (Leggett 1831, 10). When he pieced the puzzle together, Leggett found a bank undercapitalized by directors having borrowed against surrendered shareholdings, insufficient specie reserves due to an ill-advised banknote redemption agreement with the New Jersey Manufacturing and Banking Company, and a massively overdrawn account of the Hoboken Bank. Leggett proposed a restructuring of the board, a recapitalization effort, and closing the accounts of the New Jersey banks. The board refused to adopt any of his recommendations. Shortly thereafter New York's other banks refused to accept and redeem the Franklin Bank's notes.

Howard Bodenhorn is professor of economics at Clemson University and a research associate of the National Bureau of Economic Research. Eugene N. White is professor of economics at Rutgers University and a research associate of the National Bureau of Economic Research.

The authors would like to thank Pam Bodenhorn, Juliana Carattini, and Ghanshyam Sharma for exceptional research assistance. We extend special thanks to the archivists at the New York State Archives for their assistance. We also thank Jeremy Atack, William Collins, Brad Hansen, Matt Jaremski, Robert Margo, Larry Neal, and the participants at the December 14, 2013, "Enterprising America: Businesses, Banks and Credit Markets in Historical Perspective" conference held at Vanderbilt University for their comments on earlier drafts. For acknowledgments, sources of research support, and disclosure of the authors' material financial relationships, if any, please see http://www.nber.org/chapters/c13135.ack.

When he was told that local merchants no longer accepted the bank's notes, Leggett personally appeared before Chancellor Kent, requested an injunction closing the bank, and handed the chancellor the keys to the bank.[1]

The magnitude of the losses following from the failure of the Franklin Bank pale in comparison to the losses incurred in the 2008 crisis, but the basic features are much the same. A speculative period in the mid-1820s was followed by the Wall Street crash of 1826. The resulting liquidity scramble revealed uncovered counterparty risks, financial innovations undertaken without a full understanding of the downside risks, tunneling, fraud, interlocking directorates, and a near complete breakdown of effective corporate governance. Hilt (2009) documents populist anger at the "swindles" perpetrated by "scoundrels," and the press's characterization of the episode as a "bold, well-combined, and far reaching system of deception." Criminal indictments were brought against directors and shareholders brought civil suits, but current law provided little relief.

In the next session the legislature enacted a number of reforms designed to improve corporate governance. The new law introduced financial reporting rules and requirements, changed the rules governing the election of directors, regulated capital contributions, and created new legal responsibilities for directors (Hilt 2008). Although the 1828 revisions were amended and modified over time, they laid out a set of basic rules for corporate governance over the long term. Banks chartered under New York's Safety Fund System (1829–1837) were subject to it, as were banks organized during the Free Banking era (1838–1863).

Despite the centrality of corporate governance in capitalist finance and the growth of enterprise in America, relatively little is known about the development of corporate governance in the early stages of economic modernity despite the fundamental contributions of several recent studies (Lamoreaux and Rosenthal 2006; Lamoreaux 2009; Hilt 2008; Hilt [chapter 2, this volume]). In this chapter, we examine several aspects of the development of corporate governance in the century following New York's establishment of a new regime in 1828. We situate our discussion of the evolution of banking law within the context of the modern economic literature on corporate governance. Much of our attention is focused on New York State, given its long history as a financial center and wealth of archival materials and published records. Using newly collected data, we provide a sketch of how the banks' boards of directors changed over time and analyze how those changes may have affected bank performance. We find that from the early charters of

---

1. There is some confusion in Leggett's discussion. The text claims that he appeared before Chancellor William Kent, but William Kent was never chancellor, and his father retired from that position in 1823. William Kent was James Kent's son and a New York circuit court judge. Under colonial law New York established both courts of law and courts of equity (or chancery). The chancellor was the highest judicial officer of equity and would be (roughly) equivalent to the state's chief justice.

the nineteenth century to the first decades of the twentieth century, there was considerable continuity in the corporate governance of banks. At the outset the basic rules were set down and over the course of a century they were refined and detailed, but the key features constraining risk taking and expropriation of returns by management were largely retained. Only after the New Deal did state legislation begin to change and alter the set of rules that had long governed state banking institutions.

There are a multitude of issues discussed in the modern corporate governance literature that would benefit from historical perspective, but we focus on two issues specific to boards of directors: (a) the separation of ownership and control, and (b) the number of directors on bank boards. Consistent with discussions in Hilt (2008), Freeman, Pearson, and Taylor (2012), and Hansmann and Parglender (2012), New York bank directors were heavily invested in the firms they managed. On average, the combined shareholdings of board members represented more than one-half the total outstanding shares of early banks. The fraction of shares held by the directors was smaller in larger banks, but it was rarely a trivial fraction. Our finding is consistent with Hilt's (chapter 2) finding reported in this volume. He, too, finds that corporate ownership was highly concentrated in the nineteenth century and that managerial ownership declined in manufacturing firm size. Our chapter, like his, reveals a general pattern of corporate ownership and control in the early stages of development.

Our second notable finding is that the size of bank boards changed over time as regulatory regimes changed. Prior to the 1860s, the average bank board had twelve to thirteen members. Although it only directly affected the federally chartered national banks, the passage of the National Bank Act of 1864 altered the rules of the game by setting a new regulatory standard, with national banks competing with state-chartered banks. During the so-called National Banking era (1864–1913), the average bank board for state-chartered banks declined in size by about two members. From the establishment of the Federal Reserve System in 1914 through the New Deal era, beginning in 1934, the average bank board declined by a further two members. Thus, the average board of directors at a New York bank in the mid-twentieth century had about half as many members as a century earlier. It remains unclear how much of the decline was an endogenous response to the changing nature of banking practice and governance and how much was a response to regulatory regime change. It also remains unclear whether declining board size was an endogenous movement toward more effective governance. If large boards slowed decision making and encouraged shirking among board members, smaller boards many have streamlined internal governance. If, on the other hand, larger boards brought more diverse points of view and improved the capacity of the board to oversee management, the decline in board size may have had detrimental consequences for governance. Our exploration does not directly address this issue, which remains a fundamental issue for future research. But our findings on New York board sizes reflect on Lamoreaux's (chapter 1) discussion in this volume about understanding local variations in the corporation. We find that bank board size in New York responded endogenously to evolving practice and changing regulatory regimes. This result may not generalize. In Pennsylvania, for example, bank board size was established by charter and statute. Prior to adopting a national charter all Philadelphia banks were required to have exactly thirteen directors. Deviations from that value occurred only when a board seat was vacated by death or resignation, and then only briefly. Such an exploration is well beyond the scope of this chapter, but it would be valuable to know whether the long-term fixity of board size tied the hands of Pennsylvania's banks in a meaningful, observable way.

3.1   Corporate Governance and New York State Banking Law

In contemporary analysis, corporate governance is treated as an agency problem arising from the separation of ownership and control of the firm.[2] The problem facing owners who provide the capital for the firm is that they cannot write a complete contract to specify how managers will behave in all circumstances. Consequently, managers have substantial residual control rights, which they may use to expropriate returns that would otherwise be received by the owners. Because managers exercise some control over the firm, investment decisions and the consequent long-term risk-return profile may differ from that desired by shareholders.

Agency problems would be less severe if the markets for the firm's inputs and outputs were perfectly competitive. Managers would be forced to rent labor and capital in spot markets at competitive prices. But, if firm capital is highly specific and sunk, it will become difficult to prevent managers from expropriating part of the return from the sunk capital. This simple insight is important for understanding the nature of the agency problem for the beginnings of banking in the United States. While one might imagine that many industries in nineteenth-century America were highly competitive with little sunk capital, banking was different. For firms wishing to make loans, take deposits, and issue banknotes, state legislatures controlled the process of chartering limited liability corporations, first by requiring prospective bankers to obtain a charter by special legislative act and then later in most states to meet the requirements of a general incorporation act for banks. This process controlled the location of the bank and a bank's initial capital—the geography and minimum size of banks was thus determined. Various studies have shown that although financial markets might have been integrated early, banks often had some local monopolistic power for a good portion of the

---

2. We draw heavily on Shleifer and Vishny's (1997) survey of the literature on corporate governance.

nineteenth century (Davis 1965; James 1976; Bodenhorn 1992). The potential for economic profits increased the potential for expropriation by managers.

3.1.1   Pre-1838 Chartering Acts

In New York State, from Independence until the Free Banking Act of 1838, the state legislature controlled the issue of banking charters.[3] Bodenhorn (2006) chronicles the struggles of hopeful bankers to secure a charter. Of the hundreds of legislative petitions asking for a charter, only a few successfully wended their way through the committee process to be reported out as bills, and then only a small fraction of the reported bills resulted in chartering acts. The extent of bribery during the chartering process suggests not only considerable unsatisfied demand for banking services but also, once a charter was received, an ability for the new institution to earn inframarginal rents. Bribery provided legislators with their share.

Although the charters presented before the legislature could be individually crafted, they shared many features that became standard in nineteenth-century American banking law. To take a typical example, the 1828 act incorporating the Canal Bank of Albany established a one share-one vote regime (New York 1828, ch.353). A prominent feature of this and other charters was the regulations governing the board of directors who were expected to oversee the operation of the bank on behalf of the shareholders between annual meetings when their election was specified. The "stock, property, affairs, and concerns" of the bank fell under the management of fifteen directors, each of whom was required to own at least fifty shares and be a citizen of the state of New York. Alert to the potential for manipulation of elections, the charter required the appointment of independent inspectors to administer the elections on the second Tuesday of each July, thus strengthening the legal protection given by the voting rights to shareholders.[4] To ensure that the directors continued to have a significant financial interest, Article 17 of the charter noted that if a director reduced his holdings below fifty shares or moved out of the state, his seat would be declared vacant and a replacement elected by the board for the remainder of his term. In a feature that would become common in American banking law, Article 18 required that a president be elected from among the board of directors, and it empowered the board to appoint the cashier and any other officers. It further ceded to the board the power to draft bylaws and other rules "as shall be needful."

In terms of the theory of modern corporate governance, the charter for the Canal Bank had many features that reduced agency problems. By requir-

---

3. For the development of chartered banking in Philadelphia, another financial center, see Schwartz (1947).

4. This concern continues today. During the proxy vote on whether the CEO of JPMorgan Chase should give up the chairmanship of the board of directors, the shareholders proposing the change complained that the independent firm handling the vote count was only reporting tallies to the management (Craig and Silver-Greenberg 2013).

ing the president to be a member of the board, there was little separation of ownership and management. Directors who were delegated to oversee the operations of the bank on behalf of the shareholders were required to be at least modest minority shareholders. A share capital of $300,000 was set, divided into 15,000 shares of $20 denomination. At fifty shares, each director was required to invest $1,000 in the bank and collectively they held a minimum of $15,000 or 5 percent of the bank's capital.[5] As Shleifer and Vishny (1997) note, this concentration mitigates the free rider problem with many small shareholders, and provides directors with incentives to closely monitor the president and other officers. The power granted to the board to draw up bylaws provided directors with authority to amend their contracts with the officers of the banks. Given that directors met frequently, they could respond to most any contingency and closely monitor the president, cashier, and others. The danger, of course, was that larger shareholder-directors might use their position of privileged information, perhaps in collusion with the president-director, to expropriate the resources of the firm at the expense of the smaller shareholders. On these possibilities, the Canal Bank charter was silent.[6]

It is important to note that bank directors from the beginning well into the twentieth century were much more deeply engaged in the firm's daily operations than many modern directors. Board meetings to consider loan requests were sometimes held several times each week. It was not until 1904, for example, that the board of the Philadelphia National Bank reduced the frequency of its meetings from twice to once each week (Wainwright 1953, 168). Board meetings were usually weekly affairs at smaller banks. At the typical board meeting the cashier provided a list of loan applicants, the amounts requested, and whether the applicant "kept a good, middling, or small account" at the bank (Wainwright 1953, 19). Boards might ration credit based on each applicant's account balances and reputation, as well as macroeconomic considerations. Some bank bylaws required unanimous consent of a quorum of the board; some instituted black ball systems to preserve anonymity in loan approvals; some allowed the cashier to make small,

5. According the conversions available on EH.net, the $1,000 minimum director investment in 1828 is the equivalent of $25,000 in "real price" terms in 2012. It is the equivalent of $700,000 in "economic status" value. By either metric, it was a nontrivial investment for all but the very wealthiest families in 1828.

6. Early American legislators and investors were aware of the potential for majority shareholder expropriation and they devised methods to limit its extent. The 1784 articles of association written by Alexander Hamilton for the Bank of New York, for example, attempted to limit majority shareholder domination by limiting the number of votes that they could cast at shareholder meetings. These so-called "graduated voting" rules appear to have allayed at least some fears, as banks in states that imposed these rules had many more shareholders than banks in one share-one vote regimes. Why New York chose to abandon graduated voting in favor of one share-one vote rules remains an unresolved issue. On the economics of majority shareholder expropriation see Shleifer and Vishny (1997), and on the economics of graduated voting see Hilt (2008) and Bodenhorn (2014).

run-of-the-mill loans and reserved for themselves prior approval of large loans or loans to unfamiliar applicants, a procedure that became more common over time. In addition to their regular duties, board committees were regularly appointed to inspect the books, count the money in the vault, and meet with representatives from other banks to discuss such wide-ranging topics as the value at which foreign coins and banknotes would be accepted, how to prosecute counterfeiting, and the terms under which new entrants would be invited to enter into joint clearing arrangements. Bank directors actively participated in the development and implementation of short- and long-term corporate policy and strategy.

Given the responsibilities of shareholders to other stakeholders—banknote holders, deposits, and other creditors—the act of incorporation put them under the public gaze. Stakeholders knew (or could know) who the shareholders were and if any notable changes in ownership had occurred. The law required that a register of stock transfers be kept by the directors, which "shall at all reasonable hours of transacting business, be open to the examination of any person having in his possession any note, bill, or other evidence of debt issued by such corporation, the payment of which shall have been refused"(New York State 1829). If an employee or officer refused to produce the book, they were fined $250, which would be paid to the person refused.[7]

If a regulatory regime is judged by how well it protected the banks' minority shareholders and other stakeholders, the verdict on New York's chartering regime is unclear. On one hand, a majority of the banks chartered between 1790 and 1828 survived into the late antebellum period and beyond—many reorganized as free banks after 1838 and then again as national banks after 1864. But there were notable failures that imposed large losses on depositors, noteholders, and the state's taxpayers. The failure of the Safety Fund System, New York's first attempt at bank liability insurance, is well documented (Calomiris 1990; Bodenhorn 2003), but was attributable more to the regulatory authority's failure to mitigate moral hazard than to poor corporate governance systems. Most of the banks that failed, in fact, were very close corporations in which the owners-managers exploited the subsidy to risk taking at the taxpayers' expense more than at the minority shareholders' expense.

Still, the period was not without its corporate governance failures. The 1848 collapse of the aforementioned Canal Bank of Albany brought to light the potential for insider self-dealing. New York's comptroller, Millard Fillmore, appointed two receivers to take control of the bank and report on its activities. The receivers, Andrew White and Thomas McMullen, returned a

---

7. Although New York did not enact such a law, some states required banks to provide an annual list of current shareholders and their shareholdings to the clerk of the county court in which the bank was situated. The clerk was then charged with entering this information into the public record for easy inspection. New Hampshire's bank commissioners, for example, sometimes noted in their annual reports when a bank had failed to submit the required list to the clerk of the court.

scathing report. In the report's opening paragraphs, the receivers stated that "the funds of the bank for a period of time, have been used for speculating purposes, and that abuses of a criminal and aggravated nature have been perpetrated for a number of years upon the stockholders and creditors of the institution" (New York State Comptroller's Office 1848, 1). The receivers uncovered several abuses by the directors, the cashier, and other bank employees, but what brought the bank to failure was the directors' practice of allowing each other to discount notes far in excess of the limits prescribed in the bank's bylaws. The bank's charter and its bylaws included provisions for good corporate governance, but there was apparently no effective supervisory mechanism capable of enforcing good practice, absent effective shareholder oversight.

3.1.2   The New York Free Banking Act of 1838

After the legislature had provided relatively detailed special charters, the New York Free Banking Act of 1838—a model for other states and the National Bank Act of 1864—provided very little guidance in terms of corporate governance.[8] The only mention of directors in the 1838 act was that individuals associating in a bank were obliged "to choose one of their number as president of such association, and to appoint a cashier, and such other officers and agents as their business may require" (Barnard 1838). The only rule imposed on directors was set by an amendment in the act of March 4, 1863, which set a quorum of five for directors meetings if the articles of association did not define a quorum. Neither the free banking act, nor any other statute we found, established board-size minima or maxima. The choice appears to have been left to the discretion of the bank's organizers to be included in the articles of association. The minimalist nature of this act may have reflected continued satisfaction with the rules imposed in the 1828 revised statutes and a political desire to leave the rules of the bank to the organizers and shareholders. Nevertheless, in all cases that we have examined, the articles of association of the banks bore an uncanny resemblance to the pre-1838 charters of incorporation, perhaps reflecting the advice given by the attorneys drafting the articles, who used charter conditions as models for articles. For example, the articles of association for the Oneida Valley Bank, organized in 1852, included in Article 3, Section 1, a statement that "all the powers and privileges of the associates [shareholders] . . . shall be exercised by a board of directors," which was to consist of between two and ten persons.[9] In addition, there was one share-one vote by ballot or proxy. Annual election of directors was prescribed for the first Tuesday in June and managed by independent inspectors, minimum share ownership for direc-

---

8. The law required a minimum capital of $100,000, but was later amended to allow five or fewer owners to associate and form banks with just $25,000 in paid-in capital.

9. New York State Archives, Series 14272, Box 43, Number 85.

tors, the power to fill director vacancies, a quorum for meetings of the board of directors, and the power for directors to appoint officers.

Of course, a key feature of the New York free banks was that they had a bond-secured issue of banknotes, and loans by a bank were made out of a mix of capital, note issue, and deposits. As Shleifer and Vishny (1997) note, the use of debt (banknotes and/or deposits for banks) to finance a firm presents another dimension to the agency problem when a firm is financed by more than capital alone. Debt represents a contract with a specific repayment promise, and if the firm defaults, the creditor has certain rights to its assets. Given that holders of banknotes and deposits are likely not to be concentrated, there is a strong free rider problem. Depositors, holders of banknotes, and other creditors also have limited information relative to that of large shareholders, as well as directors, presidents, and other managers with an ownership stake who may have incentives to take on risk since they share in the upside while other investors and creditors bear the costs of failure (Shliefer and Vishny 1997; Jensen and Meckling 1976). In this situation, creditors might be enticed to provide funds if the bank invests in reputation (Gorton 1996). Of course, reputation is fragile in banking where banknotes and deposits are convertible into coin on demand. Bad news concerning a bank may lead to a run and perhaps its failure.

The problem was that unless a shareholder, banknote holder, or depositor was also a director they faced a sizable information asymmetry compared to the board and president. The directors or a subset of the board might expropriate the other stakeholders by a variety of means. They could increase salaries and other perks, they could take advantage of announcements to make strategic purchases or sales of stock, or, as at the Canal Bank, they could arrange for advantageous loans for themselves or other firms in which they had an interest. By the time such practices were uncovered, the malefactors could have effectively looted the bank.

The free banking act, however, provided a strong legal protection for banknote holders. Before issuing banknotes, banks were required to buy specified bonds and deposit them with the state. In the event of a failure, the bonds would be sold and the banknote holders made whole. Rules governing the selection and conservation of bonds were detailed. The other creditors—primarily depositors—had no such protection until the 1838 act was amended by the act of April 5, 1849, which specified that if there was a default in the payment of any debt after January 1, 1850, by any bank issuing bank notes, the shareholders would be individually responsible, equally and ratably, to the extent of their shares (Cleaveland and Huchinson 1864).[10]

---

10. The language of the act does not make it clear whether this is double liability or a more extended liability, though later legal scholars considered it to be a double liability, or possible assessments by a receiver up to the original par value of the shares (Cleaveland and Huchinson 1864; Leonard 1940). It should be noted that this only applies to banks of issue.

Beyond the assets of the bank, depositors now had a limited legal claim on the personal wealth of shareholders. This extended liability would presumably provide an incentive for the shareholders and directors to control risk taking. As this protection depended on the shareholders being available and having sufficient wealth, a further amendment to the 1838 act, the act of April 15, 1859, required that a book of shareholders with names, addresses, and holdings be available and open for inspection during the business hours of the bank. Failure to do so would lead to a fine of $100 in first instance, for subsequent failures a fine plus imprisonment for a term not exceeding six months for the responsible officer was imposed. For this time period, the law allowed shareholders to be monitored relatively carefully.

Given the incentives provided by the law, it is perhaps not surprising that free banking in New York was reasonably safe and sound. Rockoff (1974) effectively debunks the myth of the wildcat bank and Rolnick and Weber (1983) find that failure rates among New York's free banks were relatively low, just 34 of 449 free banks failed between 1838 and 1863. King (1983) also shows that banknote losses were low. After 1843 the expected redemption value of a typical New York banknote approached ninety-nine cents on the dollar. Clearly, the success of New York free banking was not entirely attributable to the quality of corporate governance imposed by statute; effectively, there were no corporate governance standards imposed by statute. However, it is not unreasonable to speculate that the era was one in which bank promoters and bank shareholders negotiated contractual agreements, as outlined in each bank's articles of association, and developed oversight mechanisms capable of limiting managerial self-dealing and poor corporate governance.

3.1.3   The National Bank Act of 1864

The National Bank Act of 1864 introduced an abrupt shift in the American banking regime. By creating a federal free banking system and imposing a 10 percent tax on state banknotes, most state banks shifted to federal charters, leaving few under the supervision of Albany's superintendent of banks. The new federal law, which established the Office of the Comptroller of the Currency, headed by the comptroller and staffed with bank examiners, as the supervisory agency, also set a standard for the future, either to be imitated or undermined by the state legislatures.

While later legal writers would claim that the New York Act of 1838 provided the basis for the National Bank Act of 1864, the latter provided much more detailed rules concerning the governance and management of national banks compared to their New York free bank precursors, although what it prescribed reflected much of the standard practice as embodied in the New York banks' articles of association (National Banks of the United States 1864). The protections afforded shareholders and the constraints imposed on management were thus very similar. While the 1838 New York

Act did not set a minimum number of initial shareholders, the 1864 act set a minimum of five. Each shareholder had one vote per share in the elections for directors and, though they were permitted to have proxies, no officer or employee of the bank could act as a proxy.

The 1864 act specified that the affairs of the bank should be managed by not less than five directors, one of whom should be the president, selected by the board. All directors had to be citizens of the United States and three-fourths of them had to be residents of the state or territory in which the bank was located at least one year prior to election. One year was set for a director's term, with a specific day in January established for the election in each bank's bylaws.

One innovation was the oath that directors, including the president, were required to take. Every national bank director was required to take an oath that he would "diligently and honestly administer the affairs of such Association, and will not knowingly violate or willingly permit to be violated, any of the provisions of the this Act, and that he is the *bona fide* owner in his own right, of the number of shares of stock required by this Act, subscribed by him, or standing in his name on the books of the Association, and that the same is not hypothecated or in any way pledged, as security for any loan or debt" (Pratt 1887, 20). If any of the provisions of the act are violated and the Comptroller of the Currency brought a suit in federal court, the directors were personally and individually liable for damages. In the literature on corporate governance, oaths are considered one of the legal protections offered to shareholders; however, Shleifer and Vishny (1997, 743) are somewhat skeptical about oaths: "it is difficult to describe exactly what this duty obligates managers to do."[11]

The incentives for directors were influenced by the rules for capital and their stock ownership. Every national bank director was required to own at least ten shares of stock in the bank. A minimum capital for national banks of $50,000 was set for towns with a population of under 6,000, $100,000 for towns between 6,000 and 50,000, and $200,000 for larger towns.[12] If there were the minimum of five directors for a bank with an initial capital of $50,000 and each had to hold ten shares with a par value of $100, the five directors would hold $5,000 or 10 percent of the bank's capital with potential extended liability of another $5,000. For the largest banks with a capital of $200,000, each of five directors would have had smaller proportionate voting power and a smaller proportionate liability with the minimum $5,000 initial investment, which here represented only 2.5 percent of the bank's capital. Directors and the director-president may well have held more

---

11. One possibility is that the oath prevents ex post bargaining, whereby managers are bribed by owners to give up some of their expropriation. On the other hand, it may be simply removing the possibility of constant threats by management.

12. The Act of 1864 required that half of the capital be paid in before the bank opened for operations and the remainder could be paid in installments of at least 10 percent a year.

than the minimum number of shares, but modern empirical studies find that firm value increases when large shareholders increase their holdings up to 5 percent of the total, though value decreases thereafter (Morck, Shleifer, and Vishny 1988). Such a nonlinear relationship in board ownership and firm value points to the trade-off between directors holding a sufficiently large stake to encourage monitoring and holding a stake sufficient to take control and direct the firm's resources to their own use.

The large shareholders, as represented by the board, had control and monitored the bank's officers. Boards had power to appoint the vice president, cashier, and other officers, define their duties, and require bonds and fix penalties. Requiring surety bonds may well have been another federal innovation. Based upon our brief inspection of late nineteenth-century national bank examiner reports, the device of using a security bond was fairly common.[13] Some banks forced every employee, except the president and manual laborers, to have a bond; the amounts were typically some multiple of their annual salary. The effect of these bonds was to add some downside risk to bank officer defalcations. The surety bond requirement may have been designed to reduce the incentive for risk taking that would increase returns that could be expropriated.

Banknote holders and depositors were given protections similar to those provided by state law in the new federal legislation. Like the 1838 New York act, the act of 1864 permitted banks to issue a bond-backed currency, but the use of US government bonds, valuation, and tight controls prevented any expropriation and yielded a safe and stable currency. Depositors who were most exposed benefited most from the law's provision for double liability; if the bank were insolvent, shareholders would be liable for up to the

---

13. There is little systematic evidence on officers tendering performance bonds prior to the National Banking Act, but it appears to have been common practice. Bank charters allowed directors to ask for a bond from cashiers, but did not require it. Most New York bank charters between 1805 and 1836 contained a clause similar to that appearing in the charter of the Merchants' Bank of New York City: "directors . . . have power to appoint so many officers, clerks, and servants for carrying on the said business, and with such salaries and allowances as to them shall seem meet" (New York State 1806, ch. XLIII, 64). The 1833 charter of the Chemung Canal Bank included the following paragraph, which was typical: "The directors of the said corporation shall have power, from time to time, to appoint so many officers, clerks and servants, for carrying on the business of the corporation, and with such compensation as to them shall seem meet" (Laws of New York 1833, ch.132, 150). Compare this to the charter of the Farmers' and Mechanics' Bank of Philadelphia (1809), which stated: "it shall be the duty of said board to take of bond of the cashier, with two or more sufficient sureties . . . for sum not less than forty thousand dollars" (Farmers' and Mechanics Bank 1849, 20). In 1824 Pennsylvania passed an act applicable to all banks, which included the same language less the specific dollar amount. Few state bank commissioners consistently reported information about surety bonds in their annual reports. One known exception is New Hampshire. In 1845, 60 percent of New Hampshire's fifteen reporting banks provided the value of the cashier's surety bond. The average value was $21,667 (New Hampshire 1845). In 1865, the bank commissioners reported an average $24,000 surety bond at 88 percent of the state's forty-nine banks (New Hampshire 1865). In a study of 200 national banks' examination reports from the early 1890s, Calomiris and Carlson (2013) find that 57 percent of bank cashiers were bonded.

par value of their stock. The bank was charged with maintaining a list of the shareholders, their addresses and shareholdings, which were open to inspection and would facilitate the assessment of double liability if needed.

In sum, the federal act of 1864 may be viewed as a tougher version of the state act of 1838. It ensured that there were some substantial shareholders on the board of directors and strengthened a variety of protections for all who had supplied funding—shareholders, banknote holders, and depositors. Although there are no studies that have examined whether these changes improved bank performance, if one simply considers small losses to various stakeholders from national bank insolvencies, the law appears to have prevented excessive risk taking. Between 1865 and 1913, there were 501 national bank insolvencies, their share capital totaled $86.8 million, or an average of $160,000 (White 2013). This was a small fraction of total national bank share capital, which stood in August 1913 at $1,056.3 million, and for the 10,457 banks organized since 1863 (Comptroller of the Currency 1913, 6, 104). The 7,488 banks in operation in August 1913 also had $5,761.8 million in individual deposits. Proven claims of the insolvent 501 banks totaled $191.0 million. Receivers recouped $146.9 million, including $22.5 million in assessments from shareholders. After expenses, the total losses to depositors and creditors were $44 million or a payout of 76.9 percent for this fifty-year period. At under $1 million in losses per year (a few cents per capita), it appears that regulations that set the incentives for corporate governance and the behavior of management constrained them from taking large risks to increase the appropriable returns.

3.1.4   The Revival of State-Chartered Banking and the Rise of the Trust Companies

There appears to have been little state bank legislation of any importance in New York until a comprehensive revision of the law was undertaken in the Act of 1882 (New York State 1882; Hilt 2009). The intent of the law was to enable state banks to compete with national banks. Its provisions were a blend of the act of 1838 and the National Bank Act of 1864. Once again, any number of persons could associate to form a bank, but minimum capital rules were set lower than for national banks and graded according to population. A minimum of $100,000 was set unless the town where the bank would be opened had a population under 30,000, in which case, a minimum of $50,000 was required. If the population of the town was under 6,000, then only $25,000 of capital was required to open a bank. A true and correct public list of shareholders had to be maintained; shareholders of note-issuing banks faced the same double liability. The members of the association were to choose one of their number as president.

A more complete revision was attempted in 1891. The Commissioners of Statutory Revision submitted the new legislation to the state legislature, which became law on May 18, 1892 (Groesbeck and Dickinson 1892; Hall

1895). A minimum of five individuals was required to organize a bank and five was set as the minimum number of directors. For banks with a capital of $50,000 or more, a director had to own shares worth at least $1,000 (market value) in his own right or if the bank has a capital less than $50,000, directors must hold stock worth a minimum of $500. Directors were required to be citizens of the United States and three-quarters of the directors were required to be residents of the state of New York. One of the directors was to be chosen by the board to serve as president. If the certificate of incorporation or bylaws did not prescribe the number of directors for a quorum, the directors were allowed to fix a number necessary for transaction of business, with a minimum of five. Directors were required to take an oath that they would "diligently and honestly administer the affairs of such corporation, and will not knowingly violate or willingly permit to be violated, any of the provisions of the law applicable to such corporation, and that he is the owner in good faith and in his own right, of the number of shares of stock required by this chapter, subscribed by him or standing in his name on the books of the corporation and that the same is not hypothecated, or in any way pledged as security for any loan or debt" (Hall 1895, 420). The act of 1892 required some rotation of directors with an annual election of at least one of its directors. The number of directors could be changed by first securing the permission of the New York superintendent of banking and then by gaining a majority of shareholders votes. Directors were forbidden to declare dividends except from profits; if dividends impaired capital, the directors were jointly and severally liable. Formerly, only shareholders of banks issuing circulating notes were ratably responsible for the debts (liabilities) of the bank, but in recognition that this was a dead letter, as only national banks issued banknotes, this liability was now extended to all banks' stockholders so that they now had the same liability as the shareholders of national banks.

In most respects, the New York code governing state banks appears to be very similar to the federal laws governing national banks. But state banking law was then extended to a new financial intermediary. The act of 1892 also included regulation of trust companies, which began to compete with national banks and the remaining state banks. The rules for directors of trusts differed significantly. A minimum of thirteen could form a trust company and the board of directors was to have not less than thirteen or more than twenty-four members, one of whom would be selected as president. The directors were divided into three classes for a three-year rotation of elections. Directors were required to hold at least ten shares in the trust company. To begin a trust company a minimum capital of $500,000 was required if the town in which it had its office had a population above 250,000; $200,000 if the population was between 100,000 and 250,000; $150,000 if the population was between 100,000 and 25,000; and $100,000 if was under 25,000. Shareholders were subject to the same extended liability as state banks.

3.1.5 The Era of the Federal Reserve

State banking law changed little following the Federal Reserve Act of 1913. The rules set in 1892 were largely retained, but directors' obligations had become much more explicit. With an apparent awareness that not all directors would be intimately involved or knowledgeable about a bank's operations, the law allowed for the creation of an executive committee of the board (Morgan and Parker 1914). The board of directors was required to meet once a month, where an officer would present a written statement of all purchases and sales of securities and of every discount, loan, or advance including overdrafts and renewals since the last meeting, describing the collateral, excluding items under $1,000. Twice a year, March–April and September–October, the board of directors or a committee of at least three members, with assistants if needed, was obligated to conduct a thorough and complete examination of the books, papers, and affairs of the bank.

Any loans or discounts made to officers or directors or to any corporations of which such officers or directors were also officers or directors and had a beneficial interest merited particular scrutiny and had to be identified. Although insider loans had been an issue throughout the nineteenth century, it is striking that regulation did not formally address this issue until the era of the "Money Trust." The law now explicitly acknowledged that those controlling the bank might use it to their particular benefit. This information would be passed on to the New York Superintendent of Banks. If the bank was a member of the Federal Reserve or the New York Clearing House and was subject to at least one examination per year by either, the bank "on account of such liability to such examination . . . may omit the latter of the two examinations." Still, the bank was required to tender the Federal Reserve or New York Clearing House report to the superintendent of banks.

3.1.6 State Law and the New Deal

Small banks in the Midwest and other rural parts of the country had long been keen enthusiasts about deposit insurance as a means to protect them again customer-driven panics. (Calomiris and White 1994). Although the seven state-sponsored deposit insurance adopted after the panic of 1907 collapsed from bad design, the panics of the 1930s gave its proponents the opportunity to pressure for it at the federal level. Once the Federal Deposit Insurance Corporation was established in 1934, bankers and bank shareholders across the country began to lobby to eliminate double liability (Macey and Miller 1992). In New York State double liability was removed by a change in state law that permitted individual banks to remove double liability by giving public notice of termination. More generally for all banks insured by the FDIC since 1938, once the agency has paid off insured deposits to the depositors, it has the authority to waive their claims against shareholders, thus rendering double liability inoperative, changing a key feature of corporate governance that had been in place for over a century (Vincens 1957).

For purposes of this study, we consider New York State to have had the following regulatory/supervisory regimes: (a) chartered banking 1789–1837; (b) Free Banking 1838–1863; (c) the National Banking System, 1864–1913; (d) the Early Federal Reserve, 1914–1933; and (e) New Deal Banking, 1934–1970s. A central question is whether these regulatory regimes changed the character and incentives for boards of directors or whether banking followed its own internal technological dynamic.

3.2   The "Optimum" Board of Directors

Given the essential role of the board of directors in serving as the agent of shareholders' interests, its composition and structure are keys to enhancing its performance. In this chapter, we focus on two key dimensions of the board—the ownership stakes of board members and the number of board members. Boards are presumed to monitor management and act on behalf of shareholders who cannot do so directly because of the collective action problem. But, because of their very modest ownership stakes, directors have weak incentives to exert themselves to exercise effective control and ensure that management pursues policies that maximize firm value. Shareholders, wrote Berle and Means (1932, 114), are "most emphatically . . . not served by a profit seeking controlling group."

The diminished incentives to control managers may lead to agency problems of two types: *managerialism* and *debt-agency* (John and Senbet 1998). Managerialism refers to the potential for managers to act in a self-serving fashion at the expense of shareholders (Jensen and Meckling 1976). Managers consume perks rather than maximize firm value, perhaps augmenting leverage to take more risks to increase the potential returns that they can expropriate. On the other hand, when there is a debt-agency problem for managers, they may take too few risks in order to protect their investments in firm-specific human capital. In this scenario, the management-controlled firm operates on lower leverage ratios than value maximization to avoid bankruptcy. While the second case is a possibility, the concern for most of American banking history has been about excessive risk taking and managerialism, perhaps because banking skills are transferable from one bank to another.

To master these agency problems the structure and composition of the board matters, and there may be some optimum mix of concentration of ownership and the number of directors. In terms of concentration of ownership, if one moves from inattentive directors who own insignificant shares of firm equity to a single controlling shareholder, that shareholder will have a greater incentive to monitor management. However, the presence of one or even a few controlling shareholders creates an alternative agency problem; the controlling shareholder(s) may exercise his (their) voting power to install a board committed to maximizing the value of the firm to the controlling shareholder(s) (Easterbrook and Fischel 1983; Shleifer and Vishny 1997; Freeman, Pearson, and Taylor 2012; Hansmann and Parglender 2012). Determining the optimum concentration is an empirical issue. One study (Morck, Shleifer, and Vishny 1988) found that as directors' ownership rises from 0 to 5 percent firm value increases, but value declines beyond the 5 percent threshold. Further studies confirm that at high levels of concentrated director ownership, firm values are lower, suggesting that directors may engage in behavior detrimental to small shareholders (Morck, Shleifer, and Vishny 1988; Liu and Tian 2012; Bae et al. 2012; Bodenhorn 2013).

The agency problem is also affected by the size of a bank's board of directors: too many directors may lead to a free rider problem on the board, while too few may open the door for the few directors to expropriate. There is no general model of equilibrium board size, but there is consensus in the literature that its optimal size is based on the costs and benefits of the board's monitoring and advising roles (Pathan and Skully 2010). Given the many duties expected of its members, a larger board might divide its members' labor in a way that leads to greater specialization and effectiveness (Klein 1998). Yet, following Yermack (1996), a host of studies find that, ceteris paribus, larger boards are less effective than smaller ones, an insight offered a century ago by Conyngton (1913), who was concerned mostly with how promptly a large board might act.[14] Modern scholars contend that, compared to smaller ones, large boards may be subject to more shirking, face greater coordination costs, provide less timely advice, monitor less effectively, or become dysfunctional in other dimensions. But smaller is not always better. Complex firms, large firms, and those with greater debt-equity ratios place greater advising demands on directors and may be better served by larger, more diverse boards. Coles, Daniel, and Naveen (2008) find that smaller boards are associated with higher firm value for small, simple firms, but larger boards enhance value for large, complex firms.[15]

This chapter is part of a larger research agenda on the connection between board composition, board diversity, board size, and firm performance. The task at hand is basic, namely to establish some facts about bank boards. Very little is currently known about the historical corporate board and we begin by exploring two basic features: the separation of ownership and control and trends in the number of directors. One important question is whether changes in the bank regulatory/supervisory regime altered the structure and composition of the board of directors and hence corporate governance.

---

14. Conyngton (1913, 81) wrote: "For all ordinary corporations a small board is most convenient, and, as a rule, most effective."

15. Adams, Hermalin, and Weisbach (2010) provide a parsimonious model, which shows that the Coles, Daniel, and Naveen (2008) result emerges under fairly general conditions.

We offer some preliminary evidence that board size responded to different regimes.

3.3   Data

Sources of the data are provided in the appendix, but fall into one of three broad types. The principal sources of information were annual reports of the New York Bank Superintendent. The office of the superintendent, or its predecessor, collected quarterly bank balance sheets after passage of the state's 1838 free banking act. Details about the boards of the reporting banks do not appear until the mid-1880s, after which the annual reports provide a list of each bank's directors. Our study makes use of the 1887, 1900, 1920, 1935, 1940, and 1950 annual reports. With the exception of 1940 and 1950, all data appearing in the annual reports for each bank with a name beginning with letters A through H (including all banks with a name starting with "Bank of . . .") were transcribed into machine-readable form.[16] Because the number of state-chartered banks declined after the Great Depression, all banks appearing in the 1940 and 1950 annual reports are included. The annual reports provide quarterly balance sheets, but only the late September or early October reports of condition are transcribed.

These post-1887 data constitute an unbalanced panel: some banks appear in as many as five years; some banks, especially in the later years, appear only once. In the subsequent analysis, we mostly estimate pooled cross-section specifications, but exploit the panel nature of the data to empirically estimate fixed-effects specifications of board size.[17] Although this approach is sometimes used in the modern literature (e.g., Lehn, Patro, and Zhao 2009), it is important to note that fixed-effects estimates rely on time-series (more than cross-section) variation for identification of causal effects. Fixed-effects estimates are also problematic if the fixed effects themselves account for most of the variation in the dependent variable. Although board size, as we demonstrate below, evolves slowly over time, our results generate reasonable results. Still it is important not to read too much into these preliminary results: neither the ordinary least squares (OLS) nor the fixed-effects estimates are likely to reveal true causal effects. Thus, we approach our results cautiously and consider them preliminary explorations of interesting correlations.

A second important source of information on bank directors for the earlier era is the New York State Archives, which holds the records of the New York State Banking Department between 1838 and 1967. The archive con-

---

16. The A through H selection rule includes more than one-half of all banks operating at each date.

17. Hausman and Taylor (1981) show that fixed-effects estimates control for omitted variable bias in panel data sets, but Angrist and Pischke (2009) show that instrumental variables estimates are more likely to produce causal estimates when a good instrument can be identified. We have not been able to identify a valid instrument.

sists of 125 boxes, and each bank is allotted a separate folder in one of the boxes. All surviving correspondence between the bank and state regulators are included in each folder. Up to 1,851 banks organized under the 1838 free banking act filed their articles of association with the secretary of state, along with a list of bonds and mortgages to secure their circulation with the state's comptroller. Articles of association defined shareholder voting rights, board size, residency and shareholding requirements for directors, the time and place of shareholder meetings, and other governance features of the bank, in addition to a complete list of subscribing shareholders and the names of the original directors. During a three-day visit to the archives in June 2013, 127 bank files were randomly chosen and photographed. These records were used to construct board size and director share ownership. Autumn or early winter balance sheet information for the pre–Civil War banks included in the sample was matched, when possible, to bank balance sheets available at an online archive maintained by Weber (2011).

Post–Civil War files at the archive tended to include a certificate of organization rather than the more detailed articles; certificates only provided information on a bank's corporate name, the city in which its business was to be located, its capital, and its subscribing shareholders. Directors were not regularly identified in the certificates, though director lists could sometimes be recovered from other correspondence between a bank and the superintendent. Petitions to the superintendent for permission to increase a bank's capital, to move to a new banking office, or to change the number of members of the board, among other actions, often included the names of the directors and this information was used to construct board size at dates other than the bank's organization. September balance sheet information was matched to the banks when a superintendent's report for the relevant year could be located.

The third broad source of information on bank boards was city directories published in New York City, Albany, Buffalo, and Rochester. The directories often included a list of banks and a complete roster of their directors. Detailed director lists regularly appeared in the 1850s, and we transcribe four years of lists for New York City (1851, 1857, 1859, and 1860) and three years of lists for Albany (1844, 1850, and 1853). Banks with director lists were then matched to bank balance sheets for the autumn of the year preceding publication of the list. Publication lags imply that a list published in, say, May 1851, was likely collected in late 1850 and the data matching accounts for those lags.

Drawing data from so many and such different sources sometimes makes comparisons across regimes problematic. Our greatest concern is with the changing nature of the bank balance sheet information. In the Free Banking era, accounting standards were rudimentary and auditing nonexistent. The balance sheets provided in Weber (2011) were originally reported in annual legislative documents and were voluntarily tendered by the banks, though each bank's cashier and/or president attested to their accuracy and the statements were notarized. One reason for concern is that a few balance sheets did not balance (assets do not equal liabilities), which may have been due to failure to report some otherwise important aspect of bank activity, though a more likely explanation is omission. With the professionalization of accounting and improved reporting practice, it is likely that the accuracy of the data improved over time. But, so far as we can determine, none of the balance sheets were audited. Balance sheets were produced in-house, notarized, and submitted to the state bank commissioners with an oath sworn by the bank president and cashier that they were accurate. There is no reason to think that the quality of information on the number of directors improved over time because board sizes were determined by simply counting the names of the directors serving at the time the statements were forwarded to the bank commissioners.

The balance sheets between the late 1830s and circa 1900 demonstrate a great deal of reporting continuity. The basic balance sheet categories did not change dramatically until after 1920. In the New Deal era, new categories were included in the balance sheets, most notably in reporting deposits. Up to 1920, balance sheets tended to report "Deposits" and "Deposits of Other Banks," which sometimes included deposits by local savings banks. After 1920, deposits were separated into demand deposits, time deposits, deposits by governmental agencies, and deposits of other banks. For this project, we combined the many post-1920 deposit categories into the pre-1920 categories, namely "Deposits" and "Deposits of Other Banks." In the regression analysis, the only relevant categories are Capital and Total (real) Assets. While reporting surely improved over the century considered here, our reliance on the two most easily measured features—capital (= shares outstanding * par value) and total assets—provides us with some assurance that the results do not turn on changing reporting procedures.

The changing nature of banking, too, might give pause. While banks' adherence to its strictures was a source of constant comment, the foundational principal from the Free Banking through the Early Fed regimes was the "real-bills" doctrine (Bodenhorn 2003; Lamoreaux 1996; Meltzer 2004). Strict adherence to real bills placed severe limits on bank lending: advances on short-term, self-liquidating commercial paper. The two sources of real bills were mercantile activities (borrowing to move goods, such as cotton, across space with the loan collateralized with the goods in transit) or goods in process (borrowing working capital to finance inventories). Statistics reported in table 3.1 reveal that the real-bills convention was relaxed over time. Mortgage lending, which represented about 5 percent of reported assets in the Free Banking, National Banking, and Early Fed eras increased to more than 11 percent during the New Deal. It was not uncommon for banks to maintain the real-bills fiction by hiding mortgage and other long-

Table 3.1   **Bank operating ratios in four eras**

	Free Banking	National Banking	Early Fed	New Deal
Loan/assets	0.685	0.668	0.439	0.362
	(0.182)	(0.138)	(0.165)	(0.174)
Mortgages/assets	0.049	0.046	0.054	0.113
	(0.109)	(0.268)	(0.048)	(0.093)
Securities/assets	n/a	0.028	0.314	0.308
		(0.053)	(0.156)	(0.259)
Capital/liabilities	0.414	0.191	.055	0.075
	(0.158)	(0.153)	(0.039)	(0.087)
Surplus/liabilities	n/a	0.064	n/a	0.054
		(0.056)		(0.031)
Circulation/liabilities	0.128	n/a	n/a	n/a
	(0.107)			
Deposits/liabilities	0.323	0.696	n/a	0.305
	(0.162)	(0.163)		(0.173)
Real assets ($m 1900)	2.325	2.236	3.271	2.125
	(2.895)	(3.455)	(10.292)	(17.563)
Observations	84	62	129	235

Sources: See appendix and text.

term lending as short-term loans constantly renewed, but the reported values reveal a certain constancy of practice over time.

Although securities holdings appear to increase over time, the actual change was much smaller than the statistics in table 3.1 suggest. During the Free Banking era, banks were required to buy state bonds, tender them to the state comptroller, and receive banknotes in return. Banks rarely reported these bond holdings, but most banks' securities holdings were approximately equal to their paid-in capital. Securities holdings, thus, were markedly lower in the National Banking era than in other eras. The tax on state bank notes made circulation unprofitable, which freed state banks from holding collateral securities. In the twentieth century, securities holdings may have increased as increased liquidity in securities markets reduced the risks of holding corporate and government-issued debt.

The most significant changes in banking over the century occurred on the liability side of the balance sheet. Bank leverage, measured as the inverse of the ratio of capital to total assets, increased dramatically. In the Free Banking era, the average bank's capital represented more than 40 percent of its total liabilities (assets). In the National Banking era the ratio declined by half, and it declined by a further three-quarters in the Early Fed era. Leverage matters because it provides one measure of a bank's capacity to absorb losses before becoming bankrupt. Banks might have countered the bankruptcy risk by accumulating retained earnings (surplus) to further insulate themselves from bankruptcy, but the available evidence does not provide

Table 3.2   Bank director share ownership in two eras

	Free Banking 1838–1864	National Banking 1865–1908
Number of directors	11.39	10.23
	(3.58)	(5.06)
	[38]	[83]
Shares required to serve	18.04	15.00
	(19.64)	(14.14)
	[23]	[8]
Average director shareholding	75.34	70.71
	(55.74)	(58.21)
	[22]	[17]
Fraction of shares owned by directors	0.58	0.53
	(0.30)	(0.36)
	[24]	[15]
Number of shareholders	83.15	48.22
	(102.84)	(59.16)
	[61]	[41]
Capital ($000)	278.14	376.61
	(450.29)	(929.01)
	[66]	[91]

Source: New York State Archives, Record Group 14272.
Note: Bank-year observations. Standard deviation in parentheses; observations in brackets.

any evidence that banks did so. Over the century considered here, banks worked on thinner capital margins, which increased their bankruptcy risk.

3.4   Evidence on Bank Boards

3.4.1   The Separation of Ownership and Control and Ownership Concentration

Ownership statistics that come from data collected at the New York State bank superintendent's archives are presented in table 3.2. The data span only two of the regulatory eras discussed above, namely, the Free Banking (1838–1864) and National Banking (1865–1913) eras. Because the files are not complete, there are a different number of observations in each cell, which represents bank-year averages. Bank boards were about one member larger during free than national banking, though the difference is statistically significant only at the 10 percent level.

The value of the archival data is that it shows, consistent with the findings of Freeman, Pearson, and Taylor (2012) and Hansmann and Parglender (2012), that ownership and control were not separated in early incorporated banks. Articles of association for the sample of free banks included here mandated that directors own, at a minimum, between five and one hundred shares. Free bank directors, on average, owned eighteen shares with an average par value of $85, for an average value of $1,530 ($47,900 in 2012 dollars in "real price" terms or $838,000 in "economic status" value).[18] Directors' actual shareholdings exceeded the minimum by a wide margin. The typical bank director owned more than seventy-five shares, for a total investment of $6,375 (2012 "real price" equivalent of $200,000). Directors were heavily invested in their banks; they collectively owned nearly 60 percent of their banks' outstanding shares.

The national era did not bring great changes in director ownership. Articles of association required potential directors to own between ten and fifty shares before they could serve, but they owned, on average, nearly seventy-one shares with an average par value of $84. In the National Banking era, directors continued to own more than one-half of their bank's shares. Evidence on share ownership is consistent with recent interpretations of the historical corporation: it was not owned by atomistic, fully diversified investors; it was not managed by individuals with, at most, a trivial ownership stake; rather, it was a close corporation with owner-managers whose investments most likely represented a substantial fraction of their overall portfolios.

Archival data found in the New York State bank superintendent's archives also affords a rare opportunity to investigate the distribution of shareholdings among directors with a sample of twenty-three New York State banks observed between 1839 and 1908. In certain communications with the superintendent, banks provided complete lists of directors and shareholders and those data are tabulated to better understand director shareholdings. Table 3.3 reports the fraction of shares owned by the five directors with the largest shareholdings among the directors. The data are informative because they span much of the period of interest and include small and large banks, as well as city and country banks. The mean board in the sample had 12.2 directors and the largest proportional director shareholding ranged from 0.9 percent to 50.0 percent of all outstanding shares with a mean of 13.8 percent, and the fifth largest director holdings varied from 0.0 percent to 12.5 percent with a mean of 4.0 percent.

Concerns with separation of ownership and control do not appear to be particularly relevant to early banks. Not only did many bank bylaws or articles of association impose minimum shareholdings for men and women standing for election to the board, but actual shareholdings tended to exceed the mandated minima and represented not insignificant investments for most households. At New York City's Park Bank, for example, the largest fractional director shareholding represented just 0.9 percent of the bank's existing shares, or 200 shares. With a par value of $100, William P. Earle's

18. Economic status measures the relative prestige of a value between the two periods using annual income index values of per capita gross domestic product. For further details see Williamson (2014).

Table 3.3   Ownership share by five largest shareholding directors

Bank name	Place	Year	Shareholders (no.)	Directors (no.)	Largest director (%)	Second-largest director (%)	Third-largest director (%)	Fourth-largest director (%)	Fifth-largest director (%)
Agricultural Bank	Herkimer	1839	58	13	9.8	7.8	4.9	4.9	2.9
Bank of Brockport	Brockport	1838	57	15	16.7	13.3	4.4	2.0	1.7
Farmers & Mechanics Bank	Batavia	1838	8	8	12.5	12.5	12.5	12.5	12.5
Commercial Bank	Albany	1847	148	12	6.0	5.1	4.9	1.4	1.3
Buffalo City Bank	Buffalo	1853	11	7	15.0	15.0	10.0	10.0	5.0
Spraker Bank	Canajoharie	1853	21	15	15.2	15.2	15.2	12.7	5.1
Bank of Albany	Albany	1854	161	12	8.2	3.5	2.9	1.9	1.4
Onondaga Bank	Syracuse	1854	20	11	23.3	8.6	8.6	8.6	8.6
Park Bank	New York City	1856	451	22	0.9	0.9	0.7	0.7	0.7
Market Bank	Troy	1859	107	14	3.2	2.9	2.9	2.9	2.5
Bank of Otego	Ostego	1861	4	5	50.0	40.0	7.0	3.0	0.0
Ulster County Bank	Kingston	1861	63	11	5.0	4.7	2.2	1.0	0.7
Central Bank	Rome	1865	119	16	3.2	3.0	2.2	1.9	1.6
Cuba Bank	Cuba	1865	36	13	29.3	13.2	6.0	5.4	5.2
Genesee River Bank	Mount Morris	1865	12	8	26.5	25.1	20.8	6.3	5.0
Fulton County Bank	Gloversville	1865	32	15	12.3	11.2	9.4	9.2	6.3
Ulster County Bank	Kingston	1865	69	11	5.6	5.0	2.5	1.4	1.0
Dry Goods Bank	New York City	1871	174	20	1.0	1.0	1.0	1.0	1.0
Brewers & Grocers Bank	New York City	1876	13	10	14.6	14.6	14.6	9.8	9.8
Bank of Long Island	Jamaica	1902	8	8	20.0	20.0	20.0	10.0	10.0
Bank of Metropolis	New York City	1903	22	15	11.1	7.4	3.9	3.4	3.4
Bank of Angola	Angola	1905	61	9	5.4	5.4	4.3	3.3	2.7
Bank of Corfu	Corfu	1908	11	10	22.0	20.0	20.0	4.0	4.0
Free banking (1838–184) average			92.4	12.1	13.8	10.8	6.4	5.1	3.5
National banking (1865–1908) average			50.6	12.3	13.7	11.4	9.5	5.1	4.5

Source: See table 3.1.

and R. W. Howe's $20,000 investments in the bank were surely sizable personal investments. Besides being the Park Bank's president, Howe was a wholesale shoe dealer; Earle owned a hotel at the corner of Park Row and Sixth Avenue (*Trow's* 1856).

Except at the smallest banks, which were very close corporations, the directors' fractional shareholdings also allay concerns with majority shareholder tunneling or other behaviors that might expropriate from minority shareholders. Holding less than 14 percent, on average, of these bank's shares, the largest shareholder generally did not own enough shares to unilaterally impose his will. He might, of course, form a coalition with other directors, but in most cases even the five largest shareholding directors failed to command a majority of a bank's shares. Without detailed information about a bank's lending practices and its customers, it is impossible to offer definitive statements about large shareholder control, but the statistics reported in table 3.3 are not consistent with large shareholders controlling the firm.

3.4.2   Evidence on the Size of Bank Boards

Table 3.4 reports board size by year and location. The top row reports averages for New York banks taken from all sources that reported board size. Due to the small number of banks reporting in the early years, averages are calculated for banks reporting in several years surrounding the report date: circa 1840 includes all banks reporting between 1835 and 1845; circa 1860 includes 1855 to 1865, except New York City, which reports values only for 1859; circa 1885 reports values for 1887, which was the first year the superintendent's annual reports include a director list; and the values for 1900 through 1950 include data drawn from only those years' annual reports.

There is a discernible decrease in the average number of directors over time and across the evolving regulatory and supervisory regimes. For the entire sample, the average number of directors declines from approximately thirteen in the pre–Civil War era, to about ten between the 1880s and the 1920s. The average number further declines to approximately eight in the period after 1935. The regulatory regimes may be represented by the following groupings: the Free Banking era, columns (1) and (2); the National Banking era, columns (3) and (4); the Early Federal Reserve, column (5); and the New Deal era, columns (6), (7), and (8). Given the standard deviations, the Free Banking and National Banking eras may not be distinguishable, nor the National Banking, Early Fed, and New Deal eras. The trend, however, is unmistakable; the Free Banking and New Deal eras are strikingly different.

The downward trend in average board size for the entire sample is also evident in subsamples of New York City banks, at which the average board size declines from thirteen to nine; at country banks average board size declines from approximately twelve to seven directors. Few observations at banks in other cities—Albany, Binghamton, Buffalo, Rochester, and Syracuse—make inference problematic, but it appears that board size declined at these banks as well.

Table 3.4   Mean number of bank directors by era and bank location

	Free Banking		National Banking		Early Fed		New Deal	
	ca.1840 (1)	ca.1860 (2)	ca.1885 (3)	1900 (4)	1920 (5)	1935 (6)	1940 (7)	1950 (8)
All banks	13.15 (5.08) [20]	12.53 (3.41) [64]	10.65 (3.84) [60]	10.46 (3.89) [145]	10.73 (4.22) [146]	8.47 (2.80) [107]	7.41 (2.12) [127]	7.40 (2.24) [67]
New York City banks	17.00 (n/a) [1]	13.11 (3.07) [51]	12.03 (3.60) [36]	12.51 (4.26) [54]	12.94 (4.65) [31]	11.90 (2.77) [10]	10.29 (3.59) [7]	8.75 (3.92) [8]
Other city banks	13.55 (6.07) [11]	9.17 (3.97) [6]	8.63 (2.26) [8]	10.56 (2.82) [27]	15.78 (5.85) [9]	5.00 (n/a) [1]	5.00 (n/a) [1]	5.00 (n/a) [1]
Country banks	12.13 (3.68) [8]	11.14 (3.72) [7]	8.56 (3.76) [16]	8.69 (3.01) [64]	9.66 (3.35) [106]	8.16 (2.56) [96]	7.26 (1.89) [119]	7.26 (1.88) [58]

Source: See appendix.

Notes: New York City includes the boroughs of Manhattan, Brooklyn, and the Bronx. Other cities include Albany, Binghamton, Buffalo, and Rochester; (standard deviation), [observations].

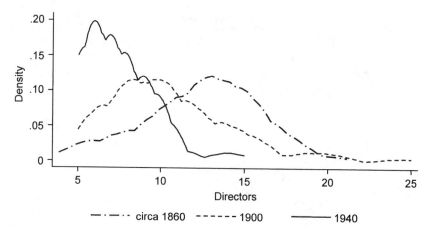

Fig. 3.1 Board size distribution by year
Source: See appendix and text for discussion.

Figure 3.1 presents a kernel density plot of board size for three regimes (Free Banking, National Banking, and New Deal) to further investigate changes in board size over time. Like the averages reported in table 3.4, the diagram reveals the decline in mean board size. More importantly, however, the density plots reveal that the entire distributions of board size changed over the century. Not only do the mean values decline, the distributions themselves become more peaked, especially after 1900. Two-way Kolmogorov-Smirnov (KS) tests for equality of distributions, a nonparametric test that is sensitive to both the center and shape of distributions, reject the null of equality; the two-way p-values in all cases are 0.00. Regardless of how it is parsed, the data point toward markedly declining board size over time.

Table 3.5 parses the data by bank age and regulatory regime. Board size declines from twelve or thirteen members for new banks at birth (zero years of age) in the pre–New Deal era to seven members for the one bank in our sample that opened in the New Deal era. The sample sizes for more seasoned banks (six years and older) all point toward a distinct change in board size in the New Deal era. National and Early Fed-era banks in their second decade had boards with about eleven directors; equally seasoned banks in the New Deal era had just over eight directors. A comparable decline in board size occurs for banks twenty-one years of age and older.

Although the conjecture deserves a larger study, the evidence is consistent with Gorton's (1996) study of free banking in which he demonstrates that it requires several years for new banks to develop reputations for safety and soundness. New banks might accelerate the reputation-formation process by electing a relatively large board of well-known men and women. As the bank ages and its reputation establishes, board sizes decline. At the same time, it

Table 3.5   **Mean number of directors by bank age and era**

	Free Banking (1)	National Banking (2)	Early Fed (3)	New Deal (4)
New banks	12.86	11.5	12.00	7.00
	(6.14)	(4.64)	(1.73)	(n/a)
	[14]	[6]	[3]	[1]
1–5 years	11.2	10.13	11.20	9.00
	(4.85)	(3.73)	(5.20)	(5.29)
	[10]	[32]	[25]	[3]
6–10 years	13.44	11.53	9.76	10.40
	(3.19)	(4.18)	(2.63)	(3.44)
	[27]	[45]	[17]	[15]
11–20 years	13.25	10.61	11.03	8.18
	(2.63)	(4.08)	(3.81)	(2.60)
	[4]	[77]	[31]	[76]
21+ years	12.07	9.49	10.61	7.42
	(2.46)	(2.90)	(4.42)	(2.12)
	[27]	[45]	[70]	[213]

Source: See table 3.3.
Notes: See table 3.3.

may be that founding shareholders are more involved in the daily management of young banks than later, passive investors. There is evidence among modern nonfinancial firms that the market value of young, post-IPO firms is higher for founder-controlled than professional manager-controlled firms (Nelson 2003). It is not clear how this result would translate to the historical financial firm, but it points toward an important role for founders as board members. The existing literature specifically on bank board size is largely silent on the association between bank age and board size. Pathan and Skully (2010) and Adusei (2012) include bank size as a proxy measure of "scope of operations," or that banks engage in more and more complex functions over time and will endogenously respond with larger boards populated by members more capable of monitoring complex activities. In neither case does the data bear out the hypothesis. Board size tends to increase in firm size among modern firms, and the same is true for historical banks.

It is widely believed that board size responds endogenously to features of the firm and the market in which it operates (Hermalin and Weisbach 1998, 2003). Evidence for banks operating in New York between the mid-nineteenth and mid-twentieth century are consistent with that belief. Not only did mean board size respond predictably to bank age, bank location, and bank size, but distributions of board size also varied.

3.4.3   Multivariate Analysis of Bank Board Size

In this section, we use regression analysis to investigate the relative magnitudes of the several features of the firm and its market thought to influence board size. The regressions account for firm size, firm age, and market size, in addition to other features that firms are believed to endogenously respond to. Thus, the regressions do not identify causal effects; rather, they are provided to offer insights into how bank boards responded to its other strategic choices and other features of the banks' environments.

Modern studies of board size and structure have generated three hypotheses to explain board size: (a) the scope of operations hypothesis, (b) the monitoring hypothesis, and (c) the negotiation hypothesis (Boone et al. 2007). The scope of operations hypothesis treats firm size and complexity as the principal determinants of board size. Larger and more complex firms tend to have larger boards, which affords the opportunity to include directors with specialist knowledge of certain features of the firm's activities. The monitoring hypothesis holds that board size and structure are driven by the corporation's competitive and informational environment. High-growth and/or innovative firms will have smaller boards because the cost of monitoring is high and outside board members are typically poorly positioned to offer meaningful advice (Lehn, Patro, and Zhao 2009; Coles, Daniel, and Naveen 2008). The monitoring hypothesis does not directly relate board size and firm performance; rather, it implies that the net benefits of alternative board sizes are dependent on a firm's competitive position, which is commonly measured by a market concentration measure and research and development expenditures, among other firm and market features. The negotiation hypothesis proposes that board size and structure results from negotiations between an influential chief executive officer (CEO) and outside directors. The CEOs capable of generating firm value use their influence with outside board members to capture some fraction of the incremental product for themselves (Hermalin and Weisbach 1998). Because we cannot account for the number of outside directors on bank boards, we cannot analyze if the negotiation approach applies to banks in our sample.

The choice of independent variables to include in the regressions is informed by the "scope" and "monitoring" hypotheses. A polynomial in age is included to account for the observation that board size decreases in age. We also include a polynomial in total assets to investigate how board size changes with bank size. Unless managerial capacity is subject to increasing returns, board size is expected to increase in firm size. Larger firms simply require more oversight, which demands more directors. Two measures are constructed to control for bank "scope" effects. First, *leverage* is measured as the ratio of total assets to capital and is included to capture a bank's overall riskiness. Capital provides a buffer against loan losses or the decline in the market value of other assets in a bank's portfolio. The greater the leverage the smaller the buffer relative to its at-risk portfolio, and the more likely a bank is to becoming bankrupt. Second, *correspondent* is a dummy variable equal to one if the bank's "due to other banks" account in the balance sheet exceeds 15 percent of its total assets.[19] As is well known, New York City served as central reserve city during the National Bank era, a role begun before the Civil War. Some Albany banks, too, provided correspondent services to country banks, especially in the antebellum era. Acting as a correspondent increased the demands on a bank's board because correspondents held large interbank balances. Banks paid interest on these accounts and funneled them into profitable investments. It is also well known that correspondent accounts were subject to unanticipated withdrawals and exposed banks to short-term liquidity problems, particularly during seasonal peak demands for credit and credit crunches during cyclical downturns (Calomiris and Gorton 1991). Providing correspondent services complicated a bank's operations and may have required additional director oversight, which may then have prompted banks to employ larger boards of directors.

Lacking information on national banks in New York, we cannot directly account for the banks' competitive environment. City and year fixed effects are used to (imperfectly) account for each bank's local competitive environment. Davis (1966), Sylla (1969), and James (1976) characterize urban banking markets as monopolistically competitive and rural markets as (near) monopolies. Thus, we include dummy variables for New York City and the state's other cities with several state banks. The excluded category is smaller towns and rural places, where a lone state bank is typical.

Table 3.6 reports summary statistics of the dependent and independent variables (column [1]), as well as four regression specifications. For the first four regressions, we use OLS and for the last specification we use a negative binomial regression that takes into account the fact that the dependent variable consists of positive integers.[20] Only two coefficients do not have the expected signs—those for leverage and correspondent banking. These are difficult to explain as it might be thought that a highly leveraged bank or one engaged in correspondent banking would require more directors because they are more complex. However, without further information on the structure of their portfolios, complexity is difficult to judge and a highly leveraged bank might be focusing carefully on a very few activities, as might a correspondent bank.

For the remainder of the variables, the coefficients conform fairly closely with the hypotheses. Coefficients on age and its square in the baseline regression (column [1]) imply that, in the reference year (1900), board size is minimized at eighty-five years, which is well out on the right tail of the age distribution.

---

19. The variable was alternatively specified as 10 percent and 20 percent. The results are not substantially different and, since we have no strong prior concerning the true percentage for city banks that acted as country bank correspondents, we report results for the intermediate value.

20. Mroz (2012) offers a set of flexible tests for regressions with count data dependent variables. After some experimentation with alternative specifications, we use the negative binomial specification because it is easily interpreted and accounts for over- or underdispersion in the dependent variable, relative to a Poisson specification.

Table 3.6   Determinants of bank board size

	Mean (std. dev.) (1)	OLS(2) (2)	OLS (3)	OLS (4)	Negative binomial (5)	Fixed effects (6)
Age	24.3 [17.83]	-0.06 [0.022]**	-0.089 [0.025]**	-0.11 [0.029]**	-0.01 [0.003]**	-0.029 [0.123]
Age squared	907.95 [1389.55]	0 [0.000]	0 [0.000]	0 [0.000]	0 [0.000]	-0.001 [0.007]
Assets ($mil)	2.43 [12.55]	0.154 [0.042]**	0.183 [0.053]**	0.262 [0.089]**	0.023 [0.007]**	0.31 [0.074]**
Assets squared	163.24 [3493.06]	0 [0.000]	-0.001 [0.000]	-0.001 [0.001]	0 [0.000]	0 [0.000]
Leverage	16.03 [13.28]	-0.013 [0.012]	-0.015 [0.012]	-0.022 [0.012]	-0.002 [0.001]	-0.044 [0.015]**
Correspondent	0.048 [0.21]	-1.824 [0.783]*	-1.661 [0.788]*	-2.215 [0.791]**	-0.175 [0.068]*	0.309 [1.121]
New York City	0.27 [0.45]	2.992 [0.471]**	3.128 [0.475]**	3.024 [0.500]**	0.285 [0.045]**	
Albany	0.02 [0.13]	1.795 [1.464]	1.913 [1.327]	1.782 [1.428]	0.173 [0.125]	
Buffalo	0.04 [0.19]	0.766 [0.820]	1.01 [0.805]	1.023 [0.826]	0.104 [0.081]	
Rochester	0.02 [0.13]	3.521 [1.584]*	3.581 [1.521]*	3.548 [1.504]*	0.316 [0.111]**	
Binghamton	0 [0.07]	4.586 [0.569]**	4.429 [0.623]**	4.375 [0.659]**	0.372 [0.051]**	
Syracuse	0.01 [0.07]	-1.055 [1.743]	-0.851 [1.690]	-0.697 [1.624]	-0.087 [0.189]	
1840	0.02 [0.14]	2.967 [1.924]	2.369 [2.210]	1.959 [2.317]	0.156 [0.171]	

Table 3.6   (continued)

	Mean (std. dev.) (1)	OLS(2) (2)	OLS (3)	OLS (4)	Negative binomial (5)	Fixed effects (6)
1860	0.08 [0.28]	1.235 [0.584]*	0.517 [0.788]	-0.141 [0.839]	-0.02 [0.070]	
1885	0.08 [0.28]	-0.519 [0.512]	-0.773 [0.780]	-0.822 [0.810]	-0.082 [0.073]	0.443 [1.250]
1900			*Reference year*			
1920	0.18 [0.39]	1.015 [0.441]*	0.299 [0.691]	0.007 [0.692]	0.005 [0.063]	-2.11 [4.835]
1935	0.14 [0.35]	-0.318 [0.443]	-1.225 [0.720]	-1.228 [0.746]	-0.113 [0.074]	-8.084 [12.275]
1940	0.18 [0.38]	-1.022 [0.449]*	-2.144 [0.688]**	-2.725 [0.707]**	-0.303 [0.079]**	-10.171 [15.392]
1950	0.1 [0.30]	-0.722 [0.582]	-3.209 [1.053]**	-3.16 [1.101]**	-0.385 [0.129]**	-12.671 [23.043]
Age * 1840			0.037 [0.046]	0.037 [0.050]	0.004 [0.004]	
Age * 1860			0.038 [0.027]	0.031 [0.032]	0.004 [0.003]	
Age * 1885			0.011 [0.027]	0.021 [0.035]	0.002 [0.003]	-0.084 [0.202]
Age * 1920			0.045 [0.026]	0.077 [0.030]*	0.007 [0.003]**	0.139 [0.291]
Age * 1935			0.054 [0.025]*	0.059 [0.029]*	0.004 [0.003]	0.229 [0.506]

	(1)	(2)	(3)	(4)	(5)
Age * 1940		0.06 [0.024]*	0.072 [0.027]**	0.006 [0.003]*	0.25 [0.578]
Age * 1950		0.091 [0.030]**	0.099 [0.032]**	0.01 [0.003]**	0.291 [0.722]
Assets * 1840			0.828 [1.202]	0.057 [0.093]	
Assets * 1860			0.265 [0.161]	0.013 [0.012]	
Assets * 1885			-0.064 [0.110]	-0.006 [0.009]	0.452 [0.125]**
Assets * 1920			-0.11 [0.096]	-0.011 [0.008]	-0.203 [0.077]**
Assets * 1935			0.068 [0.189]	0.007 [0.013]	-0.212 [0.084]*
Assets * 1940			0.588 [0.208]**	0.069 [0.019]**	-0.145 [0.202]
Assets * 1950			0.052 [0.136]	0.014 [0.012]	-0.203 [0.151]
Constant	9.749 [0.403]**	10.224 [0.494]**	10.462 [0.520]**	2.339 [0.049]**	11.738 [2.672]**
Observations	711	711	711	711	637
R-squared	0.38	0.39	0.4		0.29
F statistic/Wald chi sq.	33.87	24.48	31.54	967.3	

Note: Robust standard errors in brackets.
**Significant at the 1 percent level.
*Significant at the 5 percent level.

The maximum age observed in the sample is 136 years (Manhattan Bank in 1935). The coefficients on assets and its square imply that board size was maximized for banks with total real assets between $131 million and $171 million, which are larger values than for all but the Manhattan Bank. Older banks have smaller boards and larger banks have larger boards, which is consistent with findings for modern boards for financial and nonfinancial firms. It is not evident, as least by our observable measures, that banks that took on more risk or interacted with other banks relied on larger boards of directors. Coefficients on the city variables are consistent with a monitoring hypothesis. New York and other cities were notably more competitive markets than small towns, and banks adopted larger boards in response.

One feature of note is that early bank board size declined over time. Using the estimates in the baseline regression (column [2]), for example, bank boards, circa 1840, had nearly three more members than in the reference year of 1900. When we control for Age X Era effects (column [3]), boards circa 1840 were larger by 3.3 members and when controlling for Age X Era and Real Assets X Era effects (column [4]), boards circa 1840 were nearly five members larger than in 1900. Relative to 1900, boards in 1950 were between one-half and one member smaller. With estimated averages around ten members, the estimated era effects are notable. Early in the Free Banking era, bank boards were about 40 percent larger than national banks; late in the New Deal era, bank boards were about 10 percent smaller. In column (6) of table 3.6, we take advantage of the panel nature of the post-1860 data and estimate the model using bank fixed effects. It is an unbalanced panel in which banks appear between one and six times. The results are consistent with our pooled cross-sectional results. The so-called within estimates imply that board size increased in bank size, decreased in age and bank leverage, and declined in size after 1900.

Boards, as the modern literature suggests, serve several functions, principally the monitoring of and advice to management. By 1950, bank managers were trained professionals—there were university programs, such as the one at Rutgers that specialized in training bankers—and directors, who remained substantial investors, mostly monitored and advised. In the 1840s, bankers were not trained professionals; they tended to be merchants who brought their general human capital to the enterprise. Given the lack of professionalism, bank boards provided a vital monitoring and advising role and were, by all accounts, much more involved in the day-to-day operations of the banks they directed. It is also important to recall that finance is about reputation and it took time for a bank to establish a reputation for soundness and stability. Gorton (1996) shows that reputation was established slowly. One way to accelerate the process was for a bank to have a large board of local notables. There is evidence that such was the case, but a systematic investigation of board members is the subject of future research.

3.5   Conclusions

Our survey of New York banking law suggests that directors were closely bound to the rest of the owners and stakeholders in a bank, being given incentives to closer monitor management to push for maximizing firm value. From the early years of the nineteenth century through the early years of the Fed, legislation did not change in essence but appears to have tightened the rules. Only with the onset of the New Deal did some of the incentives for directors weaken. From the limited empirical evidence on stock ownership of directors—who for the first century of banking were often directly involved in management—it appears that management and ownership were hardly separable. The ownership stakes of directors bound them closely to the interests of their fellow shareholders. Older banks may have shed inexperienced directors and kept a competent core of directors, but larger banks tended to retain larger boards. In addition, over time boards tended to shrink in size. Whether the last features were due to increasing bank sophistication from experience individually or in terms of the experience of the whole banking system or from movement to a regulatory/supervisory regime that allowed a small number of directors to capture a bank with management for their benefit are subjects of further research.

Appendix

Albany Argus. 1851. August 22.

Belden, E. Porter. 1851. *New York: Past, Present, and Future; Comprising a History of the City of New York, A Description of its Present Condition and an Estimate of its Future Increase*, 5th ed. New York: Prall, Lewis & Co.

Buffalo Business Directory, with Alphabetical and Classified Index, vol. 1. 1855. Buffalo, NY: Hunter & Ostrander.

Charter and Directory of the City of Rochester. 1834. Rochester, NY: C. & M. Morse.

A Directory for the City of Buffalo; Containing the Names and Residence of the Heads of Families and Householders. 1832. Buffalo, NY: I. P. Clary.

Munsell, Joel. 1850. *Albany Annual Register for 1850: Containing a Directory to the Places of Business and Public Institutions*. Albany, NY: E. H. Pease & Co.

———. 1853. *Munsell's Albany Directory and City Register for 1853–54*. Albany, NY: J. Munsell.

———. 1858. *Annals of Albany*, vol. 9. Albany, NY: Munsell & Rowland.

New York (State). Banking Department. Inactive Institution Files, 1838–1967. Series (N-Ar)14272. Albany, NY: New York State Archives.

———. 1888. Superintendent of Banks. *Annual Report of the Superintendent of Banks of the State of New York*. Albany, NY: New York State Banking Dept.

———. 1901. Superintendent of Banks. *Annual Report of the Superintendent of Banks of the State of New York*. Albany, NY: James B. Lyon.

———. 1902. Superintendent of Banks. *Annual Report of the Superintendent of Banks of the State of New York*. Albany, NY: J. B. Lyon.

————. 1921. Superintendent of Banks. *Annual Report of the Superintendent of Banks for the Year Ending December 31, 1920*. Legislative Document no. 4. Albany, NY: J. B. Lyon.

————.1951. Superintendent of Banks. *One Hundredth Annual Report of the Superintendent of Bank State of New York for the Year Ending December 31, 1950*. Legislative Document no. 22. Albany, NY.

Peck, William F. 1884. *Semi-Centennial History of the City of Rochester*. Syracuse, NY: D. Mason & Co.

Wilson, H. (compiler). 1857. *Trow's New York City Directory*. New York: John F. Trow.

————. 1859. *Trow's New York City Directory*. New York: John F. Trow.

Weber, Warren E. 2011. Balance Sheets for US Antebellum State Banks. Research Department, Federal Reserve Bank of Minneapolis.

References

Adams, Renée B., Benjamin E. Hermalin, and Michael S. Wesibach. 2010. "The Role of Boards of Directors in Corporate Governance: A Conceptual Framework and Survey." *Journal of Economic Literature* 48 (1): 58–107.

Adusei, Michael. 2012. "Determinants of Bank Board Structure in Ghana." *International Journal of Business and Finance Research* 6 (1): 15–23.

Angrist, Joshua D., and Jörn-Steffen Pischke. 2009. *Mostly Harmless Econometrics: An Empiricist's Companion*. Princeton, NJ: Princeton University Press.

Bae, Kee-Hong, Jae-Seung Baek, Jun-Koo Kang, and Wei-Lin Liu. 2012. "Do Controlling Shareholders' Expropriation Incentives Imply a Link between Corporate Governance and Firm Value? Theory and Evidence." *Journal of Financial Economics* 105 (2): 412–35.

Barnard, Daniel Dewey. 1838. "An Act to Authorize the Business of Banking Passed April 18, 1838." In *Speeches and Reports in the Assembly of New York, at the Annual Session of 1838*. Albany, NY: Oliver Steele.

Berle, Adolph A., and Gardiner C. Means. 1932. *The Modern Corporation and Private Property*. New York: Macmillian.

Bodenhorn, Howard. 1992. "Capital Mobility and Financial Integration in Antebellum America." *Journal of Economic History* 52 (3): 585–610.

————. 2003. *State Banking in Early America: A New Economic History*. New York: Oxford University Press.

————. 2006. "Bank Chartering and Political Corruption in Antebellum New York: Free Banking as Reform." In *Corruption and Reform: Lessons from America's History*, edited by Edward Glaeser and Claudia Goldin, 231–57. Chicago: University of Chicago Press.

————. 2013. "Large Block Shareholders, Institutional Investors, Boards of Directors and Bank Value in the Nineteenth Century." NBER Working Paper no. 18955, Cambridge, MA.

————. 2014. "Voting Rights, Share Concentration, and Leverage in Nineteenth-Century US Banks." *Journal of Law and Economics* 57 (2): 431–58.

Boone, Audra L., Laura Casares Field, Jonathan M. Karpoff, and Charu G. Raheja. 2007. "The Determination of Corporate Board Size and Composition: An Empirical Analysis." *Journal of Financial Economics* 85 (1): 66–101.

Calomiris, Charles W. 1990. "Is Deposit Insurance Necessary? A Historical Perspective." *Journal of Economic History* 50 (2): 283–95.

Calomiris, Charles W., and Mark Carlson. 2013. "National Bank Examinations and Operations in the Early 1890s." Working Paper.

Calomiris, Charles W., and Gary Gorton. 1991. "The Origins of Banking Panics: Models, Fact, and Bank Regulation." In *Financial Markets and Financial Crises*, edited by R. Glenn Hubbard, 109–73. Chicago: University of Chicago Press.

Calomiris, Charles W., and Eugene N. White. 1994. "The Origins of Federal Deposit Insurance." In *The Regulated Economy: A Historical Approach to Political Economy*, edited by Claudia Goldin and Gary D. Libecap, 145–88. Chicago: University of Chicago Press.

Cleaveland, John, and G. S. Huchinson. 1864. *The Banking System of the State of New York*. New York: John S. Voorhies.

Coles, Jeffrey L., Naveen D. Daniel, and Lalitha Naveen. 2008. "Boards: Does One Size Fit All?" *Journal of Financial Economics* 87 (2): 329–56.

Comptroller of the Currency. 1913. *Annual Report*. Washington, DC: US Government Printing Office.

Conyngton, Thomas. 1913. *The Modern Corporation: Its Mechanism, Methods, Formation and Management*, 4th ed. New York: Ronald Press.

Craig, Susan, and Jessica Silver-Greenberg. 2013. "Shareholders Denied Access to JP Morgan Vote Results." *New York Times*, May 15.

Davis, Lance E. 1965. "The Investment Market, 1870–1914: The Evolution of a National Market." Journal of Economic History 25 (3): 355–99.

Easterbrook, Frank H., and Daniel R. Fischel. 1983. "Voting in Corporate Law." *Journal of Law and Economics* 26 (2): 395–427.

Farmers' and Mechanics' Bank. 1849. *The Charter and By-Laws of the Farmers' and Mechanics' Bank, to Which Are Added the Several Acts of the Assembly, Relative to Banks, Prepared for the Bank, By Order of the Directors*. Philadelphia: J. B. Lippincott & Co.

Freeman, Mark, Robin Pearson, and James Taylor. 2012. *Shareholder Democracies? Corporate Governance in Britain and Ireland before 1850*. Chicago: University of Chicago Press.

Gorton, Gary. 1996. "Reputation Formation in Early Bank Note Markets." *Journal of Political Economy* 104 (2): 346–97.

Groesbeck, Edward A., and Charles C. Dickinson. 1892. *The General Banking Laws of the State of New York*. Albany, NY: James B. Lyon.

Hall, Charles Roswell. 1895. *Hall's Bank Laws, Containing the Banking Law of the State of New York*. Albany, NY: Matthew Bender Law Publisher.

Hansmann, Henry, and Mariana Parglender. 2012. "The Evolution of Shareholder Voting Rights: Separation of Ownership and Consumption." *Yale Law Journal* 123:100-65.

Hausman, Jerry A., and William E. Taylor. 1981. "Panel Data and Unobservable Individual Effects." *Econometrica* 49 (6): 1377–98.

Hermalin, Benjamin E., and Michael S. Weisbach. 1998. "Endogenously Chosen Boards of Directors and Their Monitoring of the CEO." *American Economic Review* 88 (1): 96–118.

———. 2003. "Boards of Directors as an Endogenously Determined Institution: A Survey of the Economic Literature." FRB-NY *Economic Policy Review* 2003 (April): 7–26.

Hilt, Eric. 2008. "When Did Ownership Separate from Control? Corporate Governance in the Early Nineteenth Century." *Journal of Economic History* 68 (3): 645–85.

———. 2009. "Wall Street's First Corporate Governance Crisis: The Panic of 1826" NBER Working Paper no. 14892, Cambridge, MA.

James, John A. 1976. "The Development of a National Money Market, 1893–1911." *Journal of Economic History* 36 (4): 878–97.

Jensen, Michael C., and William H. Meckling. 1976. "Theory of the Firm: Managerial Behavior, Agency Costs and Ownership Structure." *Journal of Financial Economics* 3 (4): 305–60.

John, Kose, and Lemma W. Senbet. 1998. "Corporate Governance and Board Effectiveness." *Journal of Banking & Finance* 22:371–403.

King, Robert G. 1983. "On the Economics of Private Money." *Journal of Monetary Economics* 12 (1): 127–58.

Klein, April. 1998. "Firm Performance and Board Committee Structure." *Journal of Law & Economics* 41 (1): 275–304.

Lamoreaux, Naomi R. 1996. *Insider Lending: Banks, Personal Connections, and Economic Development in Industrial New England*. New York: Cambridge University Press.

———. 2009. "Scylla or Charybdis? Historical Reflections on Two Basic Problems of Corporate Governance." *Business History Review* 83 (1): 9–34.

Lamoreaux, Naomi, and Jean-Laurent Rosenthal. 2006. "Corporate Governance and Minority Shareholders in the United States before the Great Depression." In *Corruption and Reform: Lessons from America's Economic History*, edited by Edward Glaeser and Claudia Goldin, 125–52. Chicago: University of Chicago Press.

Leggett, Samuel. 1831. *The Explanation and Vindication of Samuel Leggett, Late President of the Franklin Bank of the City of New York*. New York: E. Conrad.

Lehn, Kenneth M., Sukesh Patro, and Mengxin Zhao. 2009. "Determinants of the Size and Composition of US Corporate Boards, 1935–2000." *Financial Management* 38 (4): 474–780.

Leonard, Joseph M. 1940. Superadded Liability of Bank Stockholders." *Temple Law Review* 14:522–24.

Liu, Qiqui, and Gary Tian. 2012. "Controlling Shareholders, Expropriation, and the Firm's Leverage Decisions: Evidence from Chinese Non-Tradable Share Reform." *Journal of Corporate Finance* 18 (4): 782–803.

Macey, Jonathan R., and Geoffrey P. Miller. 1992. "Double Liability of Bank Shareholders: History and Implications. *Wake Forest Law Review* 27 (1): 31–62.

Meltzer, Allan H. 2004. *A History of the Federal Reserve, Vol. 1: 1913–1951*. Chicago: University of Chicago Press.

Morck, Randall, Andrei Shleifer, and Robert W. Vishny. 1988. "Management Ownership and Market Valuation." *Journal of Financial Economics* 20 (1): 293–315.

Morgan, George Wilson, and Amasa J. Parker, Jr. 1914. *Banking Law of New York*, 7th ed. New York: Bank Law Publishing Company.

Mroz, Thomas A. 2012. "A Simple, Flexible Estimator for Count and Other Ordered Discrete Data." *Journal of Applied Econometrics* 27 (4): 646–65.

The National Banks of the United States. 1864. "An Act to Provide a National Currency, Secured by a Pledge of United States Bonds, and to Provide for the Circulation and Redemption Thereof, Approved, June 3, 1864." New York: Office of the *Bankers' Magazine*.

Nelson, Teresa. 2003. "The Persistence of Founder Influence: Management, Ownership, and Performance Effects at Initial Public Offering." *Strategic Management Journal* 24 (8): 707–24.

New Hampshire Bank Commissioners. 1845. "Bank Commissioners' Reports." *Journal of the House of Representatives of the State of New Hampshire*. Concord: Carroll & Baker.

————. 1865. *Annual Report of the Bank Commissioners of the State of New Hampshire*. Concord: Amos Hadley.

New York State. 1806. "An Act to Incorporate the Stockholders of the Merchants' Bank, in the City of New-York." *Laws of the State of New York*, 62–66. Albany, NY: Websters and Skinner.

————. 1829. "An Act to Incorporate the President, Directors and Company of the Canal Bank, of Albany, Passed May 2, 1829." *Laws of the State of New York*, 531–38. Albany, NY: F. Croswell.

————. 1833. "An Act to Incorporate the President, Directors and Company of the Chemung Canal Bank, Passed." *Laws of the State of New York*, 146–53. Albany, NY: F. Croswell.

————. 1882. *Banking Laws: An Act to Revise the Statutes of the States of New York Relating to Banks, Banking and Trust Companies*. Albany, NY: Weed, Parsons and Company.

New York State Comptroller's Office. 1848. *Special Agent's Report to the Comptroller, in Relation to the Affairs of the Canal Bank*. Albany, NY: Comptroller's Office.

Pathan, and Skully. 2010. "Endogenously Structured Board of Directors." *Journal of Banking & Finance* 34:1590–606.

Pratt, A. S. 1887. *Pratt's Digest of the National Bank Act and Other Laws Relating to National Banks for the Revised Statutes of the United States*, rev. ed. Washington, DC: Pratt and Sons.

Rockoff, Hugh. 1974. "The Free Banking Era: A Reexamination." *Journal of Money, Credit, and Banking* 6 (2): 141–67.

Rolnick, Arthur J., and Warren E. Weber. 1983. "New Evidence on the Free Banking Era." *American Economic Review* 73 (5): 1080–91.

Schwartz, Anna Jacobson. 1947. "The Beginning of Competitive Banking in Philadelphia, 1782–1809." Journal of Political Economy 55 (5): 417–31.

Shleifer, Andrei, and Robert W. Vishney. 1997. "A Survey of Corporate Governance." *Journal of Finance* 52 (2): 737–83.

Sylla, Richard. 1969. "Federal Policy, Banking Market Structure, and Capital Mobilization in the United States, 1863–1913." *Journal of Economic History* 29 (4): 657–86.

Vincens, John R. 1957. "On the Demise of Double Liability of Bank Shareholders." *Business Lawyer* 12:275–79.

Wainwright, Nicholas B. 1953. *History of the Philadelphia National Bank: A Century and a Half of Philadelphia Banking, 1803–1953*. Philadelphia: William F. Fell.

White, Eugene. 2013. "To Establish More Effective Supervision of Banking: How the Birth of the Fed Altered Bank Supervision." In *A Return to Jekyll Island: The Origins, History, and Future of the Federal Reserve*, edited by Michael D. Bordo and William Roberds, 7–55. New York: Cambridge University Press.

Williamson, Samuel H. 2014. "Seven Ways to Compute the Value of a US Dollar Amount, 1774 to Present." MeasuringWorth. www.measuringworth.com/uscompare/.

Yermack, David. 1996. "Higher Market Valuation of Companies with a Small Board of Directors." *Journal of Financial Economics* 40 (2): 185–211.

II

Bank Behavior and Credit Markets

Did Railroads Make Antebellum US Banks More Sound?

Jeremy Atack, Matthew S. Jaremski,
and Peter L. Rousseau

4.1 Introduction

Before the Civil War and the passage of the National Banking Acts, banks in the United States operated under state laws. These laws varied across states and over time, but for the most part shared the common characteristic that bank note issues, where permitted, were not statutorily limited. Prior to the Bank War that ended the federally chartered Second Bank of the United States in 1836, however, the Second Bank could and did indirectly limit money creation by individual banks through its policy of returning notes to the cashiers of the banks of issue for redemption in gold and silver coins. This policy alone was insufficient to ensure universally sound banking practices and the condition of banks and bank money only worsened after the Second Bank's demise. Indeed, the term "wildcat banking" is often used to describe the operation of some US banks during the period that followed until the passage of the National Banking Acts in 1863 and 1864 reformed and reshaped the system. The very idea of wildcat banking is premised on the notion that irresponsible banks would tend to locate away from population centers—"where the wildcats throve" (quoting Luckett 1980; Quinn and Samad 1991)—so they could issue notes that would circulate in more

Jeremy Atack is research professor of economics and professor emeritus in economics at Vanderbilt University and a research associate of the National Bureau of Economic Research. Matthew S. Jaremski is assistant professor of economics at Colgate University and a faculty research fellow of the National Bureau of Economic Research. Peter L. Rousseau is professor of economics and of history at Vanderbilt University and a member of the board of directors of the National Bureau of Economic Research.

We thank William Collins, Robert Margo, Paul Rhode, David Wheelock, and participants in the "Enterprising America" NBER-Vanderbilt University conference, December 14, 2013. For acknowledgments, sources of research support, and disclosure of the authors' material financial relationships, if any, please see http://www.nber.org/chapters/c13136.ack.

populated areas yet be difficult to redeem because of the issuing bank's remoteness. By the time such notes might appear for redemption at the bank of issue, so the legend goes, the wildcat bankers themselves had disappeared.

While there are colorful stories of such instances in antebellum banking history, accounts of this form of wildcatting are surely overstated (Rockoff 1974; Rolnick and Weber 1983). Nevertheless, the American frontier was still quite vast and sparsely populated throughout the antebellum period, and it is in this sense that many (or most) banks outside of the eastern cities and a few population centers elsewhere, such as Cincinnati and St. Louis, could be considered remote. They might thus have been tempted to take advantage of their remoteness to act in ways that compromised the positions of their liability holders. Even so, this type of "quasi-wildcatting" (for want of a better term) would have suffered a serious setback as improved means of transportation and communications, especially the railroads, diffused through the nation's interior, connecting communities—and their banks—with faster means of communication that allowed for more direct oversight while also improving opportunities for trade. Railroads therefore would have made it increasingly difficult for bankers to seek private gain through excessive risk taking. In this chapter, we offer evidence that is consistent with and supportive of this hypothesis.

In the decades before the Civil War, the United States economy was transformed from an outpost of the European Atlantic economy perched on the eastern seaboard to a rapidly growing, dynamic domestic economy and continental power. Improvements in transportation were a critical factor in this transformation, and made it possible for large segments of the population to live at ever-increasing distances from natural waterways. Improvements in finance over the period also provided a means of payment that promoted increasingly impersonal trade. To the extent that the railroads drew new banks closer to the centers of economic activity and allowed existing banks to participate in the growth opportunities afforded by efficient connections to major population centers, railroads provided incentives for banks to serve their communities while pursuing private profits. It is in this sense that railroads may also have helped to align the interests of bankers with their liability holders, providing bankers with a reason to acquiesce to monitoring and to persist as ongoing businesses rather than settle for one-time gains.

The links between transportation improvements and banking were, in some cases, quite explicit and direct. For example, in 1837 the Illinois legislature passed "an act to increase the capital stock of certain banks, and to provide means to pay the interest on a loan authorized by an act entitled 'an act to establish and maintain a general system of internal improvements'" (quoted in Callender 1902).[1] However, as we will show, the positive interaction between transportation improvements and banking was more

---

1. Indiana and Tennessee also passed similar laws.

general and pervasive even where state legislatures did not intervene directly. Specifically, in this chapter we examine the relationship between internal improvements, particularly the railroad, and the survival rates and operating characteristics of banks.

How could railroads have affected the operation of banks? Hitherto, answers to this question have been limited to the *suggestion* that proximity to transportation routes limited bank opportunities to engage in irresponsible and private rent seeking (see, for example, Bullock 1900; Dwyer 1996; Economopoulos 1988). We, on the other hand, show in a series of probability models that proximity to a railroad was associated with lower failure rates and better balance sheet management. Moreover, these findings are more wide reaching than the few documented cases of traditional "wildcatting."

Others have shown that the coming of the railroad was associated with a wide variety of changes associated with economic growth and development. These range from increases in urbanization, higher farmland values, and greater agricultural productivity to the growth of large-scale manufacturing plants and more investment in education (Atack et al. 2010; Atack, Haines, and Margo 2011; Atack and Margo 2011; Atack, Margo, and Perlman 2012). Each of these changes separately and collectively should have increased the attractiveness of an area to banks. Moreover, elsewhere, we have shown that nearly half of new Midwest banks established after 1840 opened within a few years of a railroad's arrival in their county (Atack, Jaremski, and Rousseau 2014).

Here, we describe a mechanism by which railroads not only affected finance on the extensive margin, but also led to efficiency changes that enhanced the intensity of financial intermediation. And, of course, it is the interaction of the intensity of intermediation with its quantity that seems most important for long-run growth (Rousseau and Wachtel 1998, 2011). This relationship proves to be one that does not generalize to all types of transportation; rather, railroads seem to have been the only transportation method that affected banks in this way.

Our chapter is organized as follows. In section 4.2 we offer some background on the nature of antebellum banking. Section 4.3 describes our data. These make extensive use of geographic information systems (GIS) technology for transportation and bank locations. Section 4.4 contains estimates from a series of multivariate proportional hazard models that relate proximity to transportation with lower bank failure rates and sounder balance sheet characteristics. Section 4.5 concludes.

4.2   Antebellum Bank Failures

The key to understanding the operation of antebellum banks is to recognize their reliance on bank notes rather than deposits as the dominant means of financing their operations. Unlike today, deposits during the period were not demandable or subject to check writing, nor were they a high priority debt. Therefore, to obtain liquidity and make investments, states gave banks the right to issue bank notes. These notes functioned as a medium of exchange in the marketplace, but they were also dollar-denominated liabilities that promised to pay the equivalent in specie when demanded by the note holder at the bank of issue. Thus, they also served as a store of value. Due to the importance of bank notes in the payments system, states generally mandated that each note be fully backed by some form of collateral. Moreover, the state representative could close and liquidate the bank to redeem all outstanding notes if so much as a single request for note redemption went unmet.

Prior to 1837 each potential bank petitioned its state legislature for a unique charter, and approval thereof depended as much on political influence as on need.[2] The terms of these charters varied according to the whims of particular legislatures, but most states allowed almost any asset to be used as collateral for a bank's notes and even allowed the bank itself to hold the collateral on site.[3] But beginning in 1837 and gaining momentum in the early 1850s, a series of "free banking" laws in some states replaced the need for legislative approval of each individual bank with general enabling legislation that established instead a well-defined set of capital, reserve, and note requirements.[4] While reserve requirements and the like still varied by state, the new laws generally mandated that free banks purchase specific types of assets, often that state's (or federal) debt as collateral for each note.[5] Moreover, this collateral was to be held by the state in trust and only relinquished when the bank returned an equal amount in notes.

Despite this backing requirement, the assets of closed banks were not always sufficient to cover their note circulations due to adverse market fluctuations in the price of the collateral assets. In such cases, bank notes were redeemed at cents on the dollar, as would be the usual case in bankruptcy actions. Rockoff (1974) and Rolnick and Weber (1983) show that some of the losses were minimal (most Indiana banks, for example, redeemed at ninety-five cents on the dollar), but in other cases losses were nearly total (e.g., Minnesota "railroad" banks repaid less than thirty-five cents of each dollar issued).

Following Rolnick and Weber (1984), we consider "failed banks" to be those institutions that did not redeem their notes at full value. "Closed

---

2. For convenience, we define "charter banks" to be any institution established by a specific law of a state legislature. This distinction is necessary because charter banks continued to operate even after free bank laws were passed.

3. Most banks' notes described the type of assets used as collateral somewhere on the note.

4. Three states adopted free banking in the late 1830s. One other, Alabama, would do so in the (very late) 1840s. Eleven states, however, passed free banking laws between 1850 and 1853 with two others (Iowa and Minnesota) passing laws in 1858. See Rockoff (1975) and Rolnick and Weber (1983).

5. Other assets were occasionally allowed to back notes, such as real estate in Michigan and slaves in Georgia.

Table 4.1   **Proximity to transportation and bank outcomes**

	Number of banks	Fail (%)	Close (%)
Charter banks			
On rail	1,014	7.2	11.0
Not on rail	203	34.5	39.9
On canal	517	10.7	12.6
Not on canal	700	12.6	18.1
Free banks			
On rail	493	15.8	21.9
Not on rail	108	60.2	27.8
On canal	279	11.8	25.8
Not on canal	322	34.2	20.5

Notes: Banks are denoted as being on a rail or canal if they were within ten miles of one at any time between 1830 and 1862.

banks," on the other hand, simply ceased operations but repaid their notes at par. Based on this distinction, 30 percent of the 861 free banks that ever existed ended in failure. In comparison, only 19 percent of the 1,828 charter banks failed, even though charter banks could back their notes with almost any type of asset.

Based on an examination of bank balance sheets over time, Jaremski (2013) reached two conclusions about free bank failures. First, the highly specific backing requirements for note issues mandated in the various free banking laws seem to be the underlying cause of the free banking system's high failure rate relative to the charter banking system. Moreover, this statistical relationship was not the result of general declines in bond prices. Rather, banks were sensitive only to the prices of those bonds used as collateral. Second, solvent free banks seem to have diversified their assets away from bonds (to loans, for example) and their liabilities away from note circulation (to equity or debt), and these actions seem to have at least partially shielded those banks from bond price declines.

From both theoretical and empirical standpoints, however, other factors might also play an important role in the success or failure of financial intermediaries, especially factors related to the community and the environs that these banks served. Here, we examine the effects of transportation and communications improvements on bank operations and survival. Such an analysis was hitherto nearly impossible due to a lack of comprehensive data on bank locations relative to means of transportation and communication, yet recent advances in the development of historical geographic information systems databases have now removed this impediment.

As table 4.1 shows, the distance of a bank from the nearest railroad was positively correlated with the probability of bank failure for both charter and free banks—that is to say, the further away that a bank was from a railroad, the more likely the bank would fail. Only 7.2 percent of charter banks within ten miles of a railroad failed compared to 34.5 percent of those located further away.[6] Failure rates among free banks are higher, but show the same pattern. Whereas 15.8 percent of free banks within ten miles of a railroad failed, the rate among those located at a greater distance was 60.2 percent. Plausible variations in the distance cut-off show the same pattern: banks located closer to railroads were less likely to fail than those located further away. This pattern is consistent with a central role for market forces in bank survival.

Canals, however, did not have the same stabilizing effect across either bank type. The probability of failure is roughly the same for charter banks on and off a canal, whereas free banks on a canal were more than 20 percentage points *less* likely to fail. One possible explanation for the difference in pattern between charter and free banks with respect to canal proximity is that free banks only began to be chartered after 1837, by which time most canals had already been built or were under construction, thereby removing some of the uncertainties about local development prospects and progress.

There are several possible explanations for why proximity to a railroad might have affected the probability of bank failure for both free and charter banks. First, railroads brought population and increased economic activity to an area (Atack et al. 2010; Atack, Haines, and Margo 2011). These additions would have increased a bank's access to liquidity and increased its return on loans. Moreover, since railroads often encouraged the development of larger scale manufacturing, they might have allowed banks to diversify their loan portfolios more fully and lower their exposure to agricultural shocks. Indeed, Bodenhorn (2003) shows that banks often held loan portfolios matching the distribution of firms in the surrounding area.

Second, the arrival of a railroad would have increased the acceptability of bank notes by enabling note holders to reach the bank more quickly and cheaply while simultaneously increasing local demand for the means of payment as trade and commerce expanded. Notes from trusted banks would be discounted less and travel further from the bank, but note holders and exchange centers in large cities could more easily return notes en masse if they thought the bank was operating riskily. Indeed, Gorton (1999) and Jaremski (2011) show that the discount from face value at which a bank's note traded at in New York City and Philadelphia was tied to the transportation "costs" of returning the note as well as the bank's riskiness.[7] In particular, Bodenhorn (1998) shows that bank discounts increased several quarters

6. This is not to imply that those banks at a greater distance that failed should be considered "wildcat banks." Our choice of ten miles is arbitrary but represents a distance that someone might plausibly cover on foot to tend to important business and could easily and routinely be covered on horseback.

7. While Gorton uses distance between cities, Jaremski calculated the specific travel cost using travel guides that provided the specific cost of each railroad trip in 1836, 1851, 1856, and 1861.

before banks actually failed, suggesting that bank-specific information was an important determinant of note values.[8] Therefore, a railroad's arrival may have encouraged banks to hold less risky portfolios and adjust their operations to reflect the new degree of community and note holder oversight as banks took advantage of the increased acceptability of their notes.

Third, locations with a railroad might have simply attracted more stable bankers. Certainly, statements by contemporaries suggested that wildcat banks tended to form in wilderness areas where they could issue notes that they never intended to redeem. While such accounts surely overstate the case, banks that wanted to take greater risks and avoid firsthand oversight by regulators should have been less likely to locate along a transportation route.

As suggested by table 4.1, however, the benefits of railroads would not necessarily have translated to all forms of transportation. Access to the coastline would have expanded an area's ability to trade, but most of that trade tended to be centered in major ports (e.g., New York City, Boston, and New Orleans, or Detroit and Buffalo on the Great Lakes). Rivers and canals were more geographically specific, but they were slow and indirect, making them better suited to transporting bulky, heavy goods rather than passengers and time-sensitive goods (including financial instruments). Moreover, other than the Erie Canal, most canals did not have much long-term financial success and were quickly displaced by railroads. Consequently, canals would not have had the same effect on a location's urbanization and manufacturing activities as the railroad, and certainly would not have enabled quick redemption of bank notes or increased the opportunity for bank supervision and oversight.

4.3   Data

We restrict our analysis to those areas of the country that were a part of the United States from 1840 onward[9] and to those parts of the United States for which it is possible to get consistent geographic boundaries that map into political units, since we also use various census county data as controls in

8. Like the railroad, the telegraph also improved and accelerated communications and information flows. Indeed, the speed of transmission by telegraph was orders of magnitude faster than the railroad, even allowing for delays in relaying messages. However, bank notes still had to be physically presented to the cashier at the bank of issue for redemption in specie. Moreover, the telegraph system was not coextensive with the railroad (although telegraph lines did frequently use railroad rights of way). For example, Williams's (1854) map of telegraph lines and railroads in New England shows a direct telegraph line between New London and Middletown, Connecticut, but no direct rail link between these two towns so that travelers had to get there by way of New Haven to the east or via Windham and Hartford to the north. On the other hand, a Morse Telegraph line followed the Western Railroad track from Springfield to Boston. None of our databases currently include telegraph lines.

9. Thus, for example, Texas, which was not annexed by the United States until 1845, and California, which was ceded to the United States by Mexico in 1848 are excluded from the analysis.

our estimations.[10] The county-level information is from the Haines (2010) update of the original Inter-university Consortium for Political and Social Research (ICPSR) (1979) decennial census county database.

Using two antebellum bank databases originally assembled by Warren Weber (Weber 2005, 2008), we construct a data set that provides financial and biographical information for almost every bank in operation in the United States between 1830 and 1862. Weber's data end in 1860, but Jaremski (2010) extends the bank census to the outbreak of the Civil War using annual editions of the *Merchants and Bankers' Almanac* (Merchant and Bankers' Almanac n.d.). These provide comprehensive lists of US banks in each year. This extension is important for two reasons. First, over 120 banks failed in 1861 and 1862, and excluding these failures halves the failure rate of free banks, thereby making them appear much more stable than they were. Second, because our empirics examine the failure of banks in subsequent years, we would either have to assume implicitly that all banks in operation in 1860 survived (when they did not), or end our analysis before then. Either choice would bias the findings. In the process of extending Weber's databases, we have also taken the opportunity to make a few other changes based upon the directory listings and other contemporaneous information.[11]

The augmented database contains information on 2,689 banks, of which 2,582 were located within the geographic bounds for which we can define consistent political borders. Of these, 156 banks were excluded from our analysis since they closed their doors before 1830. Furthermore, we excluded banks with missing data, particularly balance sheet data.[12] The final bank database contains information on 1,818 banks. Collectively, these exclusions slightly bias our sample toward more stable (possibly nonfraudulent) banks.

---

10. This restriction excludes much of Iowa and the northern part of Wisconsin and all points north and west thereof but retains all of Arkansas, Louisiana, and Missouri. Our procedure differs from the "border fix" solution proposed by Hornbeck (2010), who essentially redistributes population and economic production proportionately among counties based upon their loss or gain of territory from adjacent counties. Instead, we adopt the GIS-based procedure used by Atack, Jaremski, and Rousseau (2014), but broadened to encompass the entire settled area of the United States by combining non-GIS identical counties *within a state* into contiguous areas made up of variable numbers of individual counties in each year sharing a common external boundary.

We limited this linkage procedure to the period from 1840 onward because extending it back to 1830 would necessitate the combination of nearly all midwest and southern counties into "super-counties." Moreover, since the few banks existing in 1830 and 1835 were almost solely in northeast counties that did not change borders, it was more efficient to exclude those few counties that changed boundaries in this period and then pick them back up in 1840. Our results are similar if we eliminate observations from 1830 and 1835 or if we do not include census variables but include all banks.

11. The changes involved merging banks that "closed" within one year with those that "opened" almost immediately thereafter under the same name. We believe that these reflect charter renewals or mergers so that the "new" bank was not necessarily an entering bank. We also dropped those banks with undefined start and end dates.

12. We also excluded, for example, banks that were opened *and* closed within one of the five-year intervals, since these are our basic intervals of analysis as described below.

The transportation data come from a number of different GIS databases, including three covering transportation for the antebellum period developed by Atack (2013) from a variety of contemporary and retrospective sources. These include historic digitized maps, modern topographical maps produced by the US Geological Survey showing "old railroad grade" and other features of the landscape (like the remains of a canal bed or a lock), reports by various government agencies, compilations from travel guides, and the like. The databases provide information on the location and operational dates for canals, steamboats on rivers, and railroads.

The canal mapping was initially derived from those produced by Poor (1970) and by Goodrich (1961) for 1860 but modified with respect to exact locations based upon USGS topographical maps and histories of the various canals.[13] These histories also provide a dating as to when specific sections of each canal were first opened (and closed) to traffic. For rivers, we defined navigability in terms of the river's use by steamboats, ignoring earlier as well as concomitant use of the waterway by other craft such as rafts, canoes, and bateaux because only steamboats provided speedy and reliable service both upstream as well as down (Haites, Mak, and Walton 1975; Hunter 1949). The dating and details of which communities were served by steamboats is based upon sources such as Hunter (1949), contemporary gazetteers (Rowell 1873), newspaper accounts, and reports by the US Army Corps of Engineers who eventually assumed responsibility for maintaining and promoting navigation of the nation's rivers (US Congress House et al. 1871). We also generated coastlines for the Great Lakes, the Atlantic, and the Gulf of Mexico from the NHGIS shape files.[14]

Whereas the river and canal GIS databases provide annual information on the extent of navigation, our railroad databases only provide snapshots at five-year intervals because of the difficulty of assembling a reliable annual series from the sources we have consulted.[15] The railroad GIS files also differ from those for water transportation in so far as they are (currently) less

13. See especially Whitford's (1906) history of the Erie Canal. Briefer discussions of other canals have been produced by various historical societies. For example, http://www.indcanal .org/ regarding canals in Indiana and http://www.middlesexcanal.org/ or http://www .winchestermass.org/canal.html on the Middlesex Canal.

14. This proved more complicated than the simple description suggests because of the extremely high resolution of the TIGER files that underlie the NHGIS shape files and the complexity of coastal features that include bays, headlands, inlets, and estuaries as well as small islands.

15. Unfortunately, the most obvious source from which to produce a mapping—maps—cannot be used to produce an accurate *annual* mapping because of uncertainty regarding dating (copyright v. map titling v. underlying data) and imprecision arising from factors such as the map scale, imperfect surveying, and care with which the engraving was made. The work of Paxson (1914) for the five midwestern states of the Old Northwest before the Civil War, however, shows that such a goal may ultimately be attainable given sufficient time to cull through literary sources such as the *American Railroad Journal* (1832–1887), annual reports of various railroads, and the American Railway Guide (see, for example, Cobb 1945; Dinsmore 1850).

precisely located. Today, we can map exact locations using satellite imagery and GPS. Historically, however, the railroad network was much more extensive than that which we have today, but much of the old roadbed has been recycled and reused (for example, by highways), obscuring its earlier use. For example, according to *Historical Statistics,* miles of main railroad track essentially plateaus between 1916 and 1930 at around 260,000 miles, but had declined to under 183,000 miles by 1980 (a decline of about 30 percent), and there are substantially fewer miles today (Carter et al. 2006, series Df932). Track has also been realigned and straightened due to improvements in civil engineering and the advent of higher speed trains on some routes, thereby changing the historical railroad route.

Atack's mappings of historical railroads are, instead, based on small scale, state-level maps of the rail system in 1911 by Matthews Northrup Co. for the "New Century Atlas" (Whitney and Smith 1911). Where railroad lines are still in operation today or appear on USGS topographical maps, these 1911 maps have proved to be very accurately and carefully drawn, especially taking into account the limitations created by their small scale. These maps were georeferenced against NHGIS state boundary shape files using the ArcGIS 10 software, and the rail lines shown were then traced into their own shape files. These shape files thus define the location and extent of railroads in 1911. Mappings for earlier years were created by working backward in time, based upon what Atack thought to be the "best" mapping of the rail system in a particular year and then deleting lines from the later shape file that did not appear on the earlier map.[16] For our purposes, the map for year t is based upon the map for year $(t + 5)$ working backward from Atack's (2013) 1860 mapping of the rail system, generated by the procedure described above.[17]

Using these various GIS and geocoded databases, we are able to measure the distance between each bank and its nearest railroad, canal, steam-navigable river, ocean, and Great Lake every five years starting in 1830.[18]

Our analysis includes a number of controls. In particular, we add a bond price index to control for the value of a bank's collateral against notes from Jaremski (2010). For each bank, this index is the average fraction of par value for those bonds eligible as note collateral. While most states allowed any state or federal bonds paying full interest to be used in this way, some— Alabama, New Jersey, New York, and Ohio—only allowed their banks to use specific bonds. The bond price index in states not subject to a specific

---

16. The specific maps underlying each shape file are generally those drawn by the most respected mapmakers of the time including Colton and Rand McNally, both of whom published topical and frequently updated travel guides. See reader guides from the Library of Congress (Modelski 1984, 1975).

17. The "base" map for the 1860 mapping (subject to the procedures detailed in the text) was by J. H. Colton (Colton 1860).

18. Distances are measured by ArcGIS using the Toolbox function, "Near" from the Analysis/Proximity toolbox for use in our panel. These are "as the crow flies" distances and the GIS mappings are projected in Albers equal area.

bond constraint consists of the average for the fourteen available state bonds. However, per state law, the index for Alabama and New Jersey banks contains only the US Treasury bonds, while Ohio banks were limited to holding only Ohio state bonds.[19] The situation in New York was more complex. Prior to the 1842 change in its free banking law, the price index for New York banks is the average of the fourteen state bonds as for most other states, but the index thereafter contains only New York state bonds per the law.

Figure 4.1 shows the decennial coevolution of banks and railroads between 1830 and 1860. It also shows the geographical bounds of our analysis. In 1830, banks tended to be concentrated in the Northeast and along the eastern seaboard. The few railroads then in existence were generally short, such as the Baltimore and Ohio, which had fourteen miles of track stretching toward Washington, DC, or the Tuscumbia Railway Company in Alabama, which operated about two miles of track reaching to the Tennessee River.[20] Consequently, in 1830, relatively few banks–thirty-three by our count—were "on a railroad," that is, operated within ten miles of one. This is fewer than 10 percent of all banks (table 4.2). During the ensuing decades, banks—and railroads—spread into the Midwest, but spread much more slowly in the South, especially during the 1850s. During the 1830s, however, the railroad system expanded rapidly, primarily east of the Appalachians. Consequently, by 1840, the fraction of banks within ten miles of a railroad had grown sevenfold to almost two-thirds of all banks. By 1850, more than 80 percent of banks were within ten miles of a railroad.

There was also a marked increase in the percentage of banks within ten miles of a canal as Pennsylvania and New York built out their state canal systems and Ohio began to follow suit. As a result, the fraction of banks located close to canals peaked around 1850. For navigable rivers, the peak was in 1840 and a majority of banks were never located in close proximity to either canals or navigable rivers. However, the geographic association between banks and other modes of transportation was much weaker than it was for railroads, despite antebellum improvements in these means of transportation. Moreover, the declining fraction of banks located within ten miles of the coast (and changes with respect to proximity to the Great Lakes) reflects shifts in the locus of economic activity and population as US economic development pushed westward.

4.4 Empirical Analysis

The empirical analysis uses the multivariate proportional-hazard model with time-varying covariates proposed by Cox (1972; Cox and Oakes 1984), and models the probability of failure of bank i given survival to the period t as:

---

19. States that did not pass a free banking law are assumed to face no bond constraint.
20. See, for example, the database (and related notes) for 1830 at http://oldrailhistory.com.

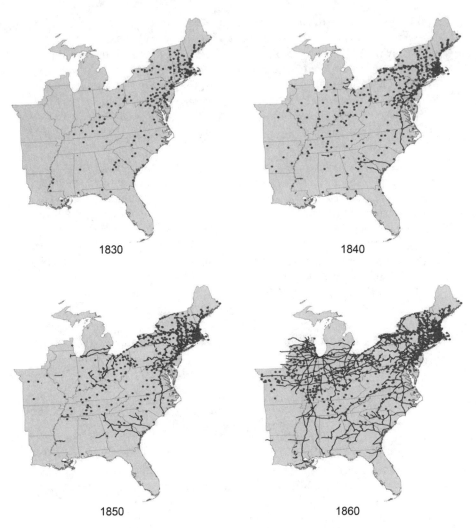

Fig. 4.1 The spread of railroads and banks, 1830–1860, by decade
Notes: Figures display the location of railroads and banks in each year.

(1) $\lambda\left(t, X_i, \beta, \lambda_0\right) = \lim_{h \to 0} \dfrac{P(t \leq T < t + h \mid T \geq t)}{h} = \lambda_0 \exp\left(X_i\left(t\right)\beta\right),$

where T is the failure date, λ_0 is the baseline hazard function common to all banks, and the exponential function captures the effects of the explanatory variables, X_i. Cox's method estimates the equation using a semiparametric "partial likelihood" approach that requires the specification of the scale function, but not the baseline hazard. Moreover, and of particular relevance for our use here, the model takes account of a bank's specific entry and exit

Table 4.2   **The expanding transportation web and percentage of banks located near specific forms of communication and transportation**

Year	Number of banks	Within ten miles of a railroad (%)	Within ten miles of a canal (%)	Within ten miles of a navigable river (%)	Within ten miles of the Great Lakes (%)	Within ten miles of the coast (%)
1830	343	9.6	34.1	31.2	1.7	58.9
1835	557	38.6	45.4	35.2	2.9	53.0
1840	711	62.3	47.7	36.1	5.2	47.1
1845	611	71.4	48.9	31.3	5.2	47.8
1850	738	82.2	49.7	29.3	6.4	43.5
1855	1,226	88.1	47.1	32.0	6.5	38.1
1860	1,353	91.4	44.3	33.3	5.5	36.7

Note: Percentages in any year add to more than 100 because a bank could be in close proximity to two or more different modes of transportation.

dates even though we might only observe the bank at a few specific moments, identifying the βs from variation across starting and failure dates.[21] Because our railroad data are only observed at five-year intervals, each observation covers a five-year period and the β coefficients should be interpreted as effects of the variables on the probability of failure over the *following* five years.

Like a panel probit or logit model, the hazard function treats each period that a bank was open (t) as a unique observation linked to the individual bank (hence the 5,636 observations, although our data set contains only 1,818 individual banks for which we have all the necessary information). However, it gains efficiency over other binary choice models by explicitly taking into account survival through that period. The hazard model also explicitly accounts for bank age. Therefore, even if we do not observe a bank early in its operation, the hazard model does not mistakenly consider it as a new bank.

On the other hand, a drawback of the model is the need to make additional assumptions regarding the initial hazard function in order to calculate the marginal effect of each variable. Absent good information, we are reluctant to make assumptions regarding those initial conditions, and instead report the raw coefficients. These provide information on the direction and relative size of an explanatory variable's effect on the probability of failure, but not on its marginal effect.

We measure the impact of transportation using a series of dummy variables that indicate whether a particular transportation method (i.e., railroad,

21. The model treats banks that were solvent at the end of 1862 or closed during the period as censored observations.

canal, ocean, river, or Great Lakes coastline) was within ten miles of the bank, which we think of as close enough to enter a user's choice set. We will show later that the results are not sensitive to reasonable variations in this distance.

Our choice of other explanatory variables is motivated by modern bank regulatory practice that was implemented in 1979 under the Uniform Financial Institutions Rating System (Federal Deposit Insurance Corporation 1997) and the information available on each bank from nineteenth-century balance sheets. In particular, we lack information on a bank's income or the quality of its assets and management, and thus are unable to estimate the full set of CAMELS measures that modern regulators use to assess a bank's soundness. Instead, we follow Jaremski (2010) and construct as many CAMELS metrics as possible.[22] Specifically,

- the average value of the state's allowable fraction of par or market value on bonds used as collateral measures the bank's "sensitivity to market risk";
- *log(assets)* measures size differences among banks but is not a metric that modern regulators consider in their CAMELS rating;
- *capital* (defined as the ratio of capital to total assets) measures "capital adequacy";
- *specie* (defined as specie divided by total assets) is an index of bank "liquidity," measuring the bank's capacity to meet bank runs in specie;
- *deposits* (defined as the ratio of deposits to total assets) measure the bank's liability diversity;
- *loans* (defined as the ratio of loans and discounts to total assets) and *bonds* (defined as the ratio of state and US government assets on the bank's balance sheet to total assets) measure asset diversity and quality;[23] and
- *circulation* (defined as the ratio of circulation to total assets) measures the level of potential future redemptions.

Moreover, we include fixed effects for states to account for heterogeneity across them such as regulatory enforcement, and for individual years to account for the periodic financial panics and specie suspensions during the period from 1830 to 1860.[24]

22. The CAMELS ratings are a modern measure of a bank's quality. Each letter stands for a factor in the rating: C for capital adequacy, A for asset quality, M for management quality, E for earnings, L for liquidity, and S for sensitivity to market risk.

23. Unlike modern studies where government debt is generally considered safe, *loans* can also be thought of as a crude measure of "asset quality" due to their relatively high return and short maturity compared to bonds of the period.

24. Given the small number of banks in most counties, county-fixed effects would degrade the model into a bank-fixed effect and limit us from comparing stable banks that did not fail to those that did.

4.4.1   The Effects of Proximity to Railroads on Bank Failure Rates

The first column in table 4.3 presents estimates of equation (1) with only the transportation variables, a dummy variable for free banks,[25] year fixed effects, and state fixed effects. The second column then adds bank balance sheet variables and the average bond price to that specification. As access to transportation could have altered the composition of a bank's balance sheet, the first column provides the full effect of transportation on bank stability, whereas to measure the full effect of transportation in the second column we must include something about how balance sheets changed in response to transportation.

The results show a tendency for free banks to be less stable than chartered banks over the five-year intervals we examine. However, once we control for balance sheet variables, the positive coefficient loses its statistical significance and even becomes negative.

Railroads are the only transportation mode that has a negative impact on bank failure.[26] Moreover, that effect is statistically significant. While the coefficients we report do not represent marginal effects, the underlying hazard ratios indicate the effect of having a railroad nearby was quite large. This effect becomes smaller when we add balance sheet variables to the specification but remains statistically and economically significant, suggesting that railroads may have pushed bankers to reduce the riskiness of their portfolios. Alternatively, banks that were close to rivers and the Great Lakes actually seem more likely to fail. The fact that the other transportation methods do not stabilize banks indicates that railroads were special. Not only did they bring greater economic diversity and population to the area, but they also would have enabled sudden note redemption and greater note-holder oversight.

Several of the other variables also have statistically significant effects on bank failure. The value of bond collateral is negatively and significantly related to the probability of failure. While the size of the coefficient is biased by the large declines in bond prices during the early parts of the Civil War, the coefficient remains significant for other periods due to the declines in bonds just prior to the Panics of 1837, 1839, and 1857. Larger banks with more reserves, loans, and deposits and fewer bank notes were less likely to fail. These results are consistent with Jaremski (2010) despite our inclusion of the transportation variables.

---

25. When we estimate the hazard functions separately for free and charter banks, the railroad coefficient is significantly negative for free banks and insignificantly negative for charter banks. The insignificance for charter banks, however, seems to be the result of banks that entered after a railroad. Once these late-entering charter banks are dropped from the sample, the coefficient regains its significance and grows in magnitude.

26. The results for railroads are similar when we include banks outside the consistent and constant 1840 boundaries. The only change is that the coefficient on the Great Lakes dummy is no longer statistically significant.

Table 4.3   Determinants of bank failure (1830–1860)

Free bank dummy	0.729**	−0.148	0.662**	−0.158
	[0.295]	[0.339]	[0.295]	[0.340]
Within ten miles	−0.598***	−0.279**	−0.354***	−0.227*
of railroad	[0.130]	[0.128]	[0.137]	[0.137]
Within ten miles	0.050	0.187	0.287*	0.243
of canal	[0.155]	[0.155]	[0.160]	[0.160]
Within ten miles	0.057	0.246*	0.220	0.289**
of river	[0.130]	[0.128]	[0.135]	[0.128]
Within ten miles	0.198	0.614***	0.535**	0.731***
of Great Lakes	[0.245]	[0.217]	[0.244]	[0.224]
Within ten miles	−0.221	0.234	0.231	0.337
of Atlantic coast	[0.228]	[0.246]	[0.277]	[0.261]
Ln(population)			−0.039	0.047
			[0.068]	[0.072]
Fraction urban			−1.673***	−0.629
			[0.460]	[0.465]
Bond value		−0.022***		−0.021***
		[0.008]		[0.008]
Bonds/assets		−0.398		−0.281
		[0.657]		[0.667]
Circulation/assets		2.704***		2.517***
		[0.872]		[0.888]
ln(assets)		−0.358***		−0.334***
		[0.080]		[0.082]
Capital/assets		1.720**		1.671**
		[0.836]		[0.831]
Specie/assets		−10.426***		−10.144***
		[2.429]		[2.472]
Loans/assets		−1.038**		−1.081**
		[0.436]		[0.438]
Deposits/assets		−2.705**		−2.704**
		[1.242]		[1.245]
Observations	5,539	5,539	5,539	5,539
Pseudo R-squared	0.140	0.178	0.145	0.178

Notes: The model is proportional-hazard partial likelihood. The dependent variable is whether the bank failed during the following five-year period. The model treats each five-year period a bank was open as a unique observation, but links them under the individual bank. Fixed effects for state and each five-year period have been added to all specifications. Robust standard errors are listed below the coefficients in brackets.

***Significant at the 1 percent level.
**Significant at the 5 percent level.
*Significant at the 10 percent level.

While railroads seem associated with bank stability, this raises the obvious question of *how* they might have affected bank operations. The most obvious answer is that the railroads brought about greater urbanization (Atack et al. 2010) and other changes associated with economic development, thus generating more bank deposits and greater customer scrutiny. To capture this, we add the log of population and the fraction of population living in an urban area to the hazard model to the final two columns of table 4.3.[27] While the additions slightly reduce the size of the railroad coefficient, it remains both statistically and economically significant. To the extent that railroads were exogenous to existing bank stability, they made banks less likely to fail through changes in balance sheet variables and urbanization as well as through other channels.[28]

While urbanization tends to reduce the probability of bank failure, this factor is not statistically significant when we include the balance sheet variables—probably because the size of the bank was in part dependent on the size of its customer base. While the inclusion of the census variables lowers the effect of railroads, it actually increases the effect of being on a navigable river and on the Atlantic coast. The smaller positive coefficients on these variables when we do not control for urbanization thus might be due to the tendency for most urban areas before 1830 to be located along water routes, and especially those close to the coast. Once the stabilizing effect of urbanization is removed, water transportation is associated with a higher probability of bank failure.

4.4.2   Controls for Potential Endogeneity of Railroad Entry

To interpret the coefficient on railroads as causal, the timing and the location of the railroad must be exogenous, and there are reasons why the route chosen by railroads (especially in the Northeast) would not have been related to the *stability* of banking.[29] While we cannot fully control for this type of endogeneity, we can control for two other possible sources. First, railroads were attracted to populated areas and sources of economic activity because these conditions generated people and cargo to carry. This economic

---

27. We implicitly assume that population and urbanization grew at constant rates between successive decennial censuses. While we would like to include measures of manufacturing and agriculture, these are not included in the census until after 1830 (see Wright 1900).

28. Some banks were clearly endogenous to internal improvements such as railroads. For example, the 1837 Illinois law "to increase the capital stock of certain banks, and to provide means to pay the interest on a loan authorized by an act entitled 'an act to establish and maintain a general system of internal improvements'" (quoted in Callender 1902). Even more directly, some banks and railroads were chartered jointly, such as the Erie and Kalamazoo Railroad Bank and the Benton and Manchester Railroad and Banking Co. in Mississippi. To the extent that bank officers held wealth and influence in the local community, it is likely that they also acted as "boosters." As such, they would have been actively solicited as investors in any railroad promotion. We discuss these and other endogeneity issues in section 4.4.2.

29. We have also estimated two-stage least squares models using the number of miles that a bank was away from the nearest straight line linking the nation's fifteen largest cities as an instrument. As railroads were costly to build, a straight line between cities was the most likely ex ante path regardless of banks. In the 2SLS models, the coefficient on the railroad dummy loses its statistical significance but remains negative. When banks that entered after a railroad are dropped from the sample, the 2SLS estimate for the railroad dummy becomes more negative and statistically significant. Consequently, we believe the results are not driven by endogeneity of existing stable banks and might be slightly biased downward banks that followed railroads (a result that is confirmed in table 4.5).

opportunity also attracted banks. Many of these attractions are captured by the other transportation media and by the county population variables, but other economically meaningful metrics such as production data are not available before 1840 for the entire country.[30]

In table 4.4, we truncate the earlier years of our sample period so that we can control for manufacturing capital (1840–1860) and agricultural capital per person (1850–1860). This approach not only captures the endogeneity of railroads, but also captures the effect of railroads on economic activity. Even when we include these variables, the coefficient on the railroad variable remains negative and statistically significant. This is consistent with railroads affecting banks through note redemptions, population, economic activity, and possibly other factors. It also should be noted that the stabilizing effect of railroads seems to grow over time as the coefficient is larger for the 1840s and 1850s than for the longer period. This is likely due to the spread of banks and rails into the undeveloped Midwest and the emergence of a more interconnected and extensive transportation system.

Second, it is possible that only stable banks entered an area after the arrival of railroad transportation because only relatively conservative, conventional banks could survive in the more transparent, connected environment associated with the railroad. Thus, the results in the previous tables could partially reflect this reverse causation because the railroad forced structural changes in the way that existing banks operated. However, this type of behavior does not detract from our story. In fact, it might even be the more important aspect of railroads' effects on bank survival and performance given the charges of wildcat banking. To check on this, we examine whether railroads had the same effect on existing banks as on new entrants. In table 4.5, we present two additional types of specifications: (a) eliminating observations for banks that entered after a railroad was in operation in the local area, and (b) removing banks that were present before and after a railroad came within ten miles. In all cases, the coefficient on the railroad dummy is negative and significant, showing that railroads seem to have stabilized both existing banks and new banks. Comparing the two sets of coefficients, the largest (and seemingly more consistent) effect seems to come from banks that were present before a railroad entered—that is to say, we believe that banks changed their behavior when the railroad came close.

4.4.3   Sensitivity to Different Mileage Cutoffs

Thus far we have treated "close to a railroad" as being within ten ("as the crow flies") miles of a railroad. Our choice of cutoff reflects our view

---

30. There was a census of manufactures in 1820 but virtually nothing is recorded for the midwest or south despite the fact that we know there were flour mills everywhere and quite sophisticated machine shops and foundries in Cincinnati and Louisville. Moreover, the county level tabulations are seriously flawed (See US Census Office 1990).

that this was a reasonable distance that contemporaries routinely covered by horseback or wagon. It can also be traversed on foot, albeit with more effort. Our results, however, are not particularly sensitive to reasonable and plausible variations in this cutoff. Specifically, we have reestimated the model specifications including the balance sheet variables from table 4.3 for even mileage cutoffs between four and twenty miles. The resulting coefficients and standard error bands for the railroad dummy both with and without the county variables are shown in figure 4.2. This shows that banks within fourteen miles of a railroad, absent county controls, are significantly less likely to fail. Such a distance is at the limit of a day's (laden) wagon ride and generally beyond what one might consider walking, except in unusual circumstances. Accounting for county-to-county differences narrows the band to between six and ten miles of a railroad. Outside of these ranges, railroads have no statistically significant effect on bank failure. Moreover, it is worth noting the coefficient on the railroad dummy variable was largest for a cutoff of six miles, meaning our use of a ten-mile cutoff slightly biases the results toward zero.

4.4.4   The Effects of Proximity to Railroads on Bank Balance Sheets

The introduction of the balance sheet variables into the model consistently reduces the size of the railroad coefficient. We take this to suggest that banks altered the composition of their assets in response to proximity of the railroad and this made them financially stronger and less likely to fail. We test this possible explanation using the following model:

$$(2)\qquad Y_{i,t} = a + \beta_1 Ln\,(\text{Age})_{i,t} + \beta_2 \text{Free}_{i,t} + \beta_3 X_{i,t} + t_t + u_i + e_{i,t},$$

where the dependent variable $Y_{i,t}$ represents the several balance sheet variables discussed above, $Ln\,(\text{Age})_{i,t}$ is the logarithm of a bank's age, $\text{Free}_{i,t}$ is a free bank dummy, t_t is a time fixed effect, and u_i is either a bank fixed effect or a state fixed effect. Depending on which fixed effects are included, the translation of the railroad coefficient changes. When the fixed effects are not included, the coefficient would at least be partially identified relative to other banks, whereas when it is included, it will only be identified relative to the bank's own time series.

It is important to note that this analysis also provides insight into how railroads were affecting banks. As previously argued, population growth along the rails might have increased the liquid funds to which a bank would have access, manufacturing growth might have increased the profitability of loans, or the threat of sudden note redemptions might have pushed banks to decrease their circulations. Therefore, by seeing which aspects of a bank's balance sheet change, we can gain some understanding of how railroads influenced bank behavior.

The results in table 4.6 show that the arrival of a railroad made for larger banks relative to other banks. This is consistent with the findings of others regarding the economic impact of railroads on urbanization and various kinds of economic activity (Atack et al. 2010; Atack, Haines, and Margo

Table 4.4   Tests of the effect of railroads on bank failure including additional county controls

	1840–1860				1850–1860			
Free bank dummy	0.621** [0.298]	0.529* [0.298]	-0.239 [0.338]	-0.251 [0.339]	-0.444 [0.554]	-0.614 [0.601]	-1.755*** [0.650]	-1.826*** [0.669]
Within ten miles of railroad	-0.646*** [0.132]	-0.369*** [0.140]	-0.321** [0.130]	-0.268* [0.139]	-0.789*** [0.149]	-0.437** [0.180]	-0.390** [0.163]	-0.406** [0.198]
Within ten miles of canal	0.029 [0.158]	0.285* [0.162]	0.131 [0.156]	0.187 [0.161]	-0.262 [0.235]	0.031 [0.235]	-0.023 [0.239]	0.082 [0.248]
Within ten miles of river	0.073 [0.131]	0.232* [0.138]	0.282** [0.129]	0.318** [0.131]	0.127 [0.161]	0.279* [0.162]	0.216 [0.159]	0.300* [0.157]
Within ten miles of Great Lakes	0.243 [0.240]	0.561** [0.239]	0.655*** [0.211]	0.739*** [0.221]	-0.926* [0.501]	-0.181 [0.491]	-0.384 [0.535]	0.130 [0.534]
Within ten miles of Atlantic coast	-0.350 [0.246]	0.050 [0.301]	0.095 [0.262]	0.164 [0.277]	-0.436 [0.376]	0.097 [0.444]	0.174 [0.388]	0.301 [0.419]
Ln(population)		-0.009 [0.069]		0.063 [0.075]		0.036 [0.087]		0.126 [0.097]
Fraction urban		-1.312** [0.523]		-0.387 [0.527]		-3.034*** [0.721]		-1.624** [0.673]
Ln(mfg. capital p.c.)		-0.225** [0.104]		-0.100 [0.105]		-0.010 [0.115]		0.146 [0.122]
Ln(farm capital p.c.)						-0.127 [0.226]		0.224 [0.259]
Bond value		-0.030*** [0.008]		-0.030*** [0.008]		0.011 [0.020]		0.011 [0.020]
Bonds/assets		-0.671 [0.677]		-0.620 [0.690]		-0.196 [1.065]		0.297 [1.069]
Circulation/assets		3.031*** [0.914]		2.811*** [0.934]		2.509** [1.137]		2.286** [1.147]

	(1)	(2)	(3)	(4)	(5)	(6)	(7)	(8)
ln(assets)			-0.358***	-0.337***			-0.713***	-0.662***
			[0.080]	[0.082]			[0.124]	[0.128]
Capital/assets			1.839**	1.785**			1.187	1.169
			[0.886]	[0.880]			[1.153]	[1.169]
Specie/assets			-10.099***	-9.736***			-15.128***	-14.991***
			[2.505]	[2.551]			[4.216]	[4.338]
Loans/assets			-1.030**	-1.076**			-0.421	-0.507
			[0.441]	[0.442]			[0.614]	[0.622]
Deposits/assets			-2.894**	-2.926**			-2.345	-2.326
			[1.318]	[1.320]			[1.489]	[1.513]
Pseudo R-squared	0.120	0.126	0.163	0.164	0.170	0.181	0.215	0.219
Observations	4,639	4,639	4,639	4,639	3,317	3,317	3,317	3,317

Notes: The model is proportional-hazard partial likelihood. The dependent variable is whether the bank failed during the following five-year period. The model treats each five-year period a bank was open as a unique observation, but links them under the individual bank. Fixed effects for state and each five-year period have been added to all specifications. Robust standard errors are listed below the coefficients in brackets.

***Significant at the 1 percent level.

**Significant at the 5 percent level.

*Significant at the 10 percent level.

Table 4.5   Additional tests of the effect of railroads on bank failure (1830–1860)

	Dropping banks that entered after railroad				Dropping banks that were present when railroads entered			
Free bank dummy	1.103***	1.121***	0.368	0.390	0.872**	0.786**	−0.381	−0.421
	[0.412]	[0.412]	[0.565]	[0.563]	[0.364]	[0.369]	[0.364]	[0.368]
Within ten miles of railroad	−1.258***	−1.131***	−0.868***	−0.881***	−0.805***	−0.538***	−0.445***	−0.388**
	[0.293]	[0.302]	[0.280]	[0.300]	[0.141]	[0.153]	[0.145]	[0.157]
Within ten miles of canal	0.276	0.314	0.356	0.345	−0.013	0.197	0.161	0.208
	[0.231]	[0.280]	[0.223]	[0.227]	[0.175]	[0.174]	[0.181]	[0.179]
Within ten miles of river	−0.158	−0.093	−0.015	−0.007	0.014	0.143	0.180	0.223
	[0.162]	[0.167]	[0.165]	[0.166]	[0.139]	[0.147]	[0.135]	[0.137]
Within ten miles of Great Lakes	0.544	0.578	0.537	0.572	0.136	0.439*	0.455**	0.586**
	[0.423]	[0.437]	[0.405]	[0.414]	[0.241]	[0.249]	[0.217]	[0.228]
Within ten miles of Atlantic coast	−0.114	0.066	0.203	0.230	−0.340	0.180	0.090	0.242
	[0.357]	[0.389]	[0.356]	[0.370]	[0.291]	[0.347]	[0.307]	[0.327]
Ln(population)		0.029		0.069		−0.050		0.057
		[0.091]		[0.100]		[0.073]		[0.077]
Fraction urban		−0.975		0.051		−1.644***		−0.718
		[0.729]		[0.776]		[0.547]		[0.518]
Bond value			−0.001	−0.001			−0.034***	−0.033***
			[0.009]	[0.009]			[0.009]	[0.009]
Bonds/assets			−0.443	−0.415			−0.556	−0.394
			[0.907]	[0.914]			[0.683]	[0.696]
Circulation/assets			0.752	0.842			2.913***	2.674***
			[1.370]	[1.411]			[0.880]	[0.895]
ln(assets)			−0.420***	−0.420***			−0.431***	−0.413***
			[0.125]	[0.131]			[0.080]	[0.081]

Capital/assets		0.877	0.884			1.813**	1.746**
		[1.242]	[1.252]			[0.818]	[0.814]
Specie/assets		−3.610	−3.754			−9.376***	−9.159***
		[3.255]	[3.265]			[2.592]	[2.656]
Loans/assets		−0.417	−0.404			−1.442***	−1.483***
		[0.599]	[0.607]			[0.475]	[0.481]
Deposits/assets		−5.477***	−5.484***			−1.905	−1.937
		[2.086]	[2.057]			[1.201]	[1.211]
Pseudo R-squared	0.218	0.219	0.238	0.238	0.139	0.143	0.178	0.179
Observations	3,161	3,161	3,161	2,981	2,981	2,981	2,981	2,981

Notes: The model is proportional-hazard partial likelihood. The dependent variable is whether the bank failed during the following five-year period. The model treats each five-year period a bank was open as a unique observation, but links them under the individual bank. Fixed effects for state and each five-year period have been added to all specifications. Robust standard errors are listed below the coefficients in brackets.

***Significant at the 1 percent level.

**Significant at the 5 percent level.

*Significant at the 10 percent level.

A: Without County Variables

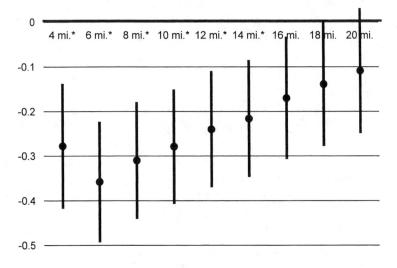

B: With County Variables

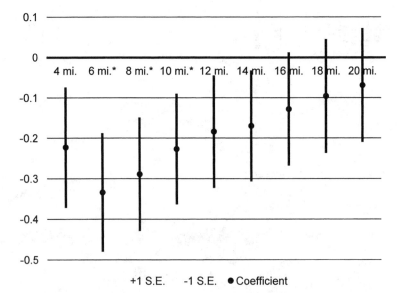

+1 S.E.   -1 S.E.   ● Coefficient

Fig. 4.2 Coefficient on railroad dummy using other mileage cutoffs

Notes: The figure presents the coefficient on the railroad dummy for various mileage cutoffs, as shown. Each coefficient comes from an equation similar to those in columns (1) and (3) of table 4.3. The stated mileage cutoffs denote coefficients that are statistically significant at the 10 percent level or greater.

Table 4.6   Effect of transportation on level of bank balance sheets—five-year periods (1830–1860)

	Ln(assets)		Capital/assets		Deposits/assets		Circulation/assets		Loans/assets		Bonds/assets		Specie/assets	
Ln(bank age)	0.027*** [0.002]	0.019*** [0.001]	0.001 [0.001]	-0.002*** [0.001]	0.001*** [0.001]	0.003*** [0.001]	-0.003*** [0.001]	-0.003*** [0.001]	0.001*** [0.001]	0.003*** [0.001]	-0.001*** [0.001]	-0.001 [0.001]	-0.001 [0.001]	-0.001** [0.001]
Free bank dummy	-0.325*** [0.076]		0.041*** [0.010]		0.026 [0.016]		-0.040*** [0.012]		-0.170*** [0.015]		0.038*** [0.010]		-0.022*** [0.003]	
Within ten miles of railroad	0.028* [0.015]	0.004 [0.019]	-0.006 [0.004]	-0.008 [0.006]	-0.002 [0.003]	-0.012*** [0.004]	-0.016*** [0.004]	0.005 [0.005]	0.018*** [0.005]	0.014* [0.008]	-0.003** [0.001]	-0.001 [0.001]	-0.004*** [0.001]	-0.006*** [0.002]
Within ten miles of canal	0.252*** [0.030]	0.026 [0.058]	0.005 [0.006]	-0.047** [0.021]	0.037*** [0.008]	0.036* [0.019]	-0.061*** [0.006]	-0.025 [0.016]	0.027*** [0.007]	0.030 [0.026]	0.002 [0.004]	0.008 [0.009]	0.007*** [0.002]	0.018*** [0.007]
Within ten miles of river	0.249*** [0.039]		0.013** [0.006]		0.025*** [0.008]		-0.052*** [0.007]		0.040*** [0.008]		-0.005 [0.007]		0.001 [0.002]	
Within ten miles of Great Lakes	0.045 [0.068]		-0.008 [0.011]		0.028* [0.015]		-0.064*** [0.013]		0.040** [0.016]		-0.030** [0.013]		0.002 [0.004]	
Within ten miles of Atl. coast	0.565*** [0.044]		0.001 [0.006]		0.083*** [0.008]		-0.094*** [0.007]		0.005 [0.008]		0.002 [0.003]		0.015*** [0.002]	
Fixed effect	State	Bank	State	Bank	State	Bank	State	Bank	State	Bank	State	Bank	State	Bank
Observations	5,636	5,636	5,636	5,636	5,636	5,636	5,636	5,636	5,636	5,636	5,636	5,636	5,636	5,636
R-squared	0.305	0.312	0.218	0.223	0.165	0.167	0.193	0.202	0.070	0.071	0.014	0.014	0.019	0.022

Notes: Table presents the results of an OLS regression. The dependent variable is described in the column heading. Each observation is a bank-half decade. Dollar values are deflated to 1860 using the US GDP deflator from Officer (2008). Fixed effects for each five-year period have been added to all specifications. Robust standard errors are listed below the coefficients in brackets.

***Significant at the 1 percent level.

**Significant at the 5 percent level.

*Significant at the 10 percent level.

2011; Callender 1902). The railroad dummy coefficient is only statistically significant for assets when not including bank fixed effects.

When looking at the balance sheet ratios, banks decreased the amount of their excess reserves and made more loans after the arrival of a railroad, possibly because more profitable opportunities now existed for these potentially loanable assets. These are the only two variables for which the railroad coefficient is statistically significant in both columns. On the other hand, a bank seems to have decreased its circulation and bond holdings relative to surrounding banks and decreased its deposits after the arrival of a railroad.[31] Decreased note circulation is consistent with a presumed increase in the ease and likelihood that notes would be presented for payment when the railroad made travel easier and faster. The overall pattern of results indicates that one of the key effects of railroads on banks was through the increased economic impact rather than through population or increased monitoring.

Putting these results in the context of bank failure, railroads seem to have lowered failure rates by encouraging banks to operate more safely through more loans as well as lowered bond holdings and circulations, yet also relate to lower holdings of reserves. The latter could simply reflect a greater sense of confidence in banks among the public when located near a railroad, and this allowed them to reduce primary and secondary reserves because of the repeat trades in which they engaged.[32]

4.5   Conclusion

The decades before the Civil War witnessed the transformation of the United States economy into a rapidly growing, dynamic domestic economy and continental power. The nation's bourgeoning financial system was one of the factors at the heart of this transformation (Rousseau and Sylla 2005). However, it was not a smooth development. The financial system was subject to periodic panics and crises, and as a result, nearly one-third of all banks created before 1862 closed with their note holders sustaining losses. Some important changes taking place contemporaneously in the economy may have mitigated these losses. By linking detailed bank and transportation data, we show that the arrival of railroads may have helped stabilize the system despite the association of financial crises with investment cycles and the speculative internal improvements that came with them.

The data indicate the railroads were positively correlated with bank stability even after controlling for local economic activity and population, whereas

---

31. The combined decline in deposits and circulation suggests that either profit or interbank deposits rose after a railroad entered, as these were the remaining two large liability items.

32. This seems reasonable given that findings of Gorton (1999) and Jaremski (2011) as banks that could be more quickly reached had lower bank note discounts.

other means of transportation were either uncorrelated or negatively correlated with bank stability. The effect is apparent not only for banks existing before the railroads went through, but also for new banks that opened up after the rails. Moreover, the arrival of a railroad seems to have encouraged banks to hold safer portfolios consisting of fewer bonds and banknotes and more loans. These changes would well have driven local investment in the local economy, which implies that railroads could have had important indirect effects on local economic growth through the longevity of banks and the stability of longer-term finance. These effects reach beyond the traditional arguments about agglomeration of economic activity usually associated with the arrival of the railroad.

References

American Railroad Journal. 1832–1887. *American Railroad Journal and Advocate of Internal Improvements*. New York: n.p.

Atack, Jeremy. 2013. "On the Use of Geographic Information Systems in Economic History: The American Transportation Revolution Revisited." *Journal of Economic History* 73 (2): 313–38.

Atack, Jeremy, Fred Bateman, Michael Haines, and Robert A Margo. 2010. "Did Railroads Induce or Follow Economic Growth? Urbanization and Population Growth in the American Midwest, 1850–1860." *Social Science History* 34 (2): 171–97.

Atack, Jeremy, Michael Haines, and Robert A Margo. 2011. "Railroads and the Rise of the Factory: Evidence for the United States, 1850–1870." In *Economic Evolution and Revolutions in Historical Time*, edited by Paul Rhode, Joshua Rosenbloom, and David Weiman, 162–79. Palo Alto, CA: Stanford University Press.

Atack, Jeremy, Matthew Jaremski, and Peter L. Rousseau. 2014. "American Banking and the Transportation Revolution Before the Civil War." *Journal of Economic History* 74 (4): 943–86. doi: 10.1017/S0022050714000825

Atack, Jeremy, and Robert A. Margo. 2011. "The Impact of Access to Rail Transportation on Agricultural Improvement: The American Midwest as a Test Case, 1850–1860." *Journal of Transportation and Land Use* 4 (2). https://www.jtlu.org/index.php/jtlu/article/view/188.

Atack, Jeremy, Robert A. Margo, and Elizabeth Perlman. 2012. "The Impact of Railroads on School Enrollment in Nineteenth Century America." Unpublished Manuscript, Boston University.

Bodenhorn, Howard. 1998. "Quis Custodiet Ipsos Custodes." *Eastern Economic Journal* 24 (1): 7–24.

———. 2003. *State Banking in Early America: A New Economic History*. New York: Oxford University Press.

Bullock, Charles Jesse. 1900. *Essays on the Monetary History of the United States, The Citizen's Library of Economics, Politics, and Sociology*. New York: Macmillan and Co.

Callender, G. S. 1902. "The Early Transportation and Banking Enterprises of the States in Relation to the Growth of Corporations." *Quarterly Journal of Economics* 17 (1): 111–62.

Carter, Susan B., Scott Sigmund Gartner, Michael R. Haines, Alan L. Olmstead, Richard Sutch, Gavin Wright, and Louis P. Cain. 2006. *Historical Statistics of the United States Millennial Edition Online*. New York: Cambridge University Press. http://hsus.cambridge.org/HSUSWeb/HSUSEntryServlet.

Cobb, Charles. 1945. *American Railway Guide and Pocket Companion for the United States: Containing Correct Tables for Time of Starting from All Stations, Distances, Fares, etc. on All the Railway Lines in the United States: Together with a Complete Railway Map: Also Many Principal Steamboat and Stage Lines Running in Connection with Railroads*. Milwaukee, WI: Kalmbach Pub. Co.

Colton, J. H. 1860. *Colton's New Railroad & County Map of the United States and the Canadas &c.* New York: Joseph Hutchins Colton.

Cox, D. R. 1972. "Regression Models and Life-Tables." *Journal of the Royal Statistical Society Series B (Methodological)* 34 (2): 187–220. doi: 10.2307/2985181.

Cox, D. R., and David Oakes. 1984. *Analysis of Survival Data, Monographs on Statistics and Applied Probability*. New York: Chapman and Hall.

Dinsmore, Curran. 1850. "American Railway Guide, and Pocket Companion for the United States . . . Together with a Complete Railway Map." In. S.l.: C. Dinsmore. http://proxy.library.umkc.edu/login?url=http://infotrac.galegroup.com/itweb/univmomiller?db=SABN.

Dwyer, Gerald. 1996. "Wildcat Banking, Banking Panics and Free Banking in the United States." *Federal Reserve Bank of Atlanta Economic Review* 81:1–20.

Economopoulos, Andrew J. 1988. "Illinois Free Banking Experience." *Journal of Money, Credit and Banking* 20 (2): 249–64.

Federal Deposit Insurance Corporation. 1997. *FDIC Law, Regulations, Related Acts*. 62 Fed. Reg. 752, January 6, 1997, effective January 1, 1997, September 16, 2013 1997. http://www.fdic.gov/regulations/laws/rules/5000–900.html.

Goodrich, Carter, ed. 1961. *Canals and American Economic Development*. New York: Columbia University Press.

Gorton, Gary. 1999. "The Pricing of Free Bank Notes." *Journal of Monetary Economics* 44 (1999): 33–64.

Haines, Michael R. 2010. *Historical, Demographic, Economic, and Social Data: The United States, 1790–2002*. Ann Arbor, MI: Inter-university Consortium for Political and Social Research (ICPSR).

Haites, Erik F., James Mak, and Gary M. Walton. 1975. *Western River Transportation: The Era of Early Internal Development, 1810–1860, The Johns Hopkins University Studies in Historical and Political Science*. Baltimore: Johns Hopkins University Press.

Hornbeck, Richard. 2010. "Barbed Wire: Property Rights and Agricultural Development." *Quarterly Journal of Economics* 125 (2): 767–810.

Hunter, Louis C. 1949. *Steamboats on the Western Rivers: An Economic and Technological History, Studies in Economic History*. Cambridge, MA: Harvard University Press.

Inter-university Consortium for Political and Social Research. 1979. *Historical, Demographic, Economic, and Social Data: The United States, 1790–1970*. Ann Arbor, MI: ICPSR.

Jaremski, Matthew. 2010. "Free Bank Failures: Risky Bonds versus Undiversified Portfolios." *Journal of Money, Credit and Banking* 42 (8): 1565–87. doi: 10.1111/j.1538–4616.2010.00354.x.

———. 2011. "Bank-Specific Default Risk in the Pricing of Bank Note Discounts." *Journal of Economic History* 70 (2011): 950–75.

———. 2013. "State Banks and the National Banking Acts: Measuring the Response to Increased Financial Regulation, 1860–1870." *Journal of Money, Credit and Banking* 45 (2–3): 379–99. doi: 10.1111/jmcb.12006.

Modelski, Andrew M. 1975. *Railroad Maps of the United States: A Selective Annotated Bibliography of Original 19th-Century Maps in the Geography and Map Division of the Library of Congress*. Washington, DC: Library of Congress.

————. 1984. *Railroad Maps of North America: The First Hundred Years*. Washington, DC: Library of Congress.

Luckett, Dudley G. 1980. *Money and Banking*, 2nd ed. New York: McGraw-Hill.

Merchant and Bankers' Almanac. n.d. *The Merchants and Bankers' Almanac*. New York: J. S. Homans.

Officer, Lawrence. 2008. "What Was the Value of the US Consumer Bundle Then?" MeasuringWorth. http://www.measuringworth.com/consumer/.

Paxson, Frederic L. 1914. "The Railroads of the 'Old Northwest' before the Civil War." *Transactions of the Wisconsin Academy of Sciences, Arts, and Letters* 17 (Part 1): 247–74.

Poor, Henry Varnum. 1970. *History of the Railroads and Canals of the United States of America, Library of Early American Business & Industry, 34*. New York: A. M. Kelley.

Quinn, Stephen F., and A. Samad. 1991. "Wildcat Banking in Illinois: A Look into Our Financial History." *Illinois Business Review* 48 (4): 16–17.

Rockoff, Hugh. 1974. "The Free Banking Era: A Reexamination." *Journal of Money, Credit, and Banking* 6:141–67.

————. 1975. *The Free Banking Era: A Re-Examination, Dissertations in American Economic History*. New York: Arno Press.

Rolnick, Arthur J., and Warren E. Weber. 1983. "New Evidence on the Free Banking Era." *American Economic Review* 73 (5): 1080–91.

————. 1984. "The Causes of Free Bank Failures: A Detailed Examination." *Journal of Monetary Economics* 14:269–91.

Rousseau, Peter L., and Richard Sylla. 2005. "Emerging Financial Markets and Early US Growth." *Explorations in Economic History* 42 (1): 1–26.

Rousseau, Peter L., and Paul Wachtel. 1998. "Financial Intermediation and Economic Performance: Historical Evidence from Five Industrialized Countries." *Journal of Money, Credit and Banking* 30:657–78.

————. 2011. "What is Happening to the Impact of Financial Deepening on Economic Growth." *Economic Inquiry* 49 (1): 276–88.

Rowell George P. 1873. *Geo. P. Rowell & Co's Gazetteer, Containing a Statement of the Industries, Characteristics, Population and Location of All Towns in the United States and British America, in which Newspapers are Published*. New York: G. P. Rowell & Co.

US Census Office. 1990. *Digest of Accounts of Manufacturing Establishments in the United States and of Their Manufactures: Made under Direction of the Secretary of State, in Pursuance of a Resolution of Congress, of 30th March, 1822*. Edited by Norman Ross, *Norman Ross Publishing series*, v. 6. New York: Norman Ross Publishing.

U S Congress, House; U S Army Corps of Engineers; U S War Department; and U S War Department, Engineer Department. 1871. *Engineer's Report of Certain Rivers and Harbors. Letter from the Secretary of War, Transmitting Reports of the Chief Engineer upon the Improvement of Certain Rivers and Harbors*, February 21.

Weber, Warren E. 2005. *Census of State Banks*. Federal Reserve Bank of Minneapolis. http://www.minneapolisfed.org/research/economists/wewproj.cfm.

————. 2008. *Balance Sheets for US Antebellum State Banks*. Federal Reserve Bank of Minneapolis. http://www.minneapolisfed.org/research/economic_research/bankarchive/info/homepage.html.

Whitford, Noble E. 1906. *History of the Canal System of the State of New York, Together with Brief Histories of the Canals of the United States and Canada. Supplement* to the *Annual Report of the Engineer and Surveyor of the State of New York*, vol. 2. Albany, NY: Brandow Printing Co.

Whitney, William Dwight, and Benjamin E. Smith. 1911. *The Century Dictionary and Cyclopedia, with a New Atlas of the World*, rev. and enl. ed., 12 vols. New York: The Century Co.

Williams, Alexander. 1854. *Telegraph and Rail Road Map of the New England States.* Boston: Redding & Co.

Wright, Carroll D. 1900. *History and Growth of the United States Census.* Washington, DC: GPO.

Sources of Credit and the Extent of the Credit Market
A View from Bankruptcy Records in Mississippi, 1929–1936

Mary Eschelbach Hansen

5.1 Introduction

Today banks and other financial institutions are a regular source of credit to firms (US Dept. of the Treasury 2014). The participation of financial institutions in credit markets serving business enterprise is generally believed to be essential for modern economic growth because financial institutions pool savings and channel the funds from low-value uses to high-value ventures.[1] Yet ventures with the highest potential value are often risky, and regulation of banks and other financial institutions has sought to limit risk-taking by banks. Although the success of regulation in this regard has been uneven,[2] over the course of American economic history the firms that have pushed the frontier of technology or the frontier of business organi-

Mary Eschelbach Hansen is associate professor of economics at American University.

Funding for the bankruptcy case file sample for Mississippi came from an American University Faculty Research Support Grant and a Mellon Grant from the AU College of Arts and Sciences. Funding for the collection of the Dun & Co. *Reference Books* came from the AU College of Arts and Sciences and Economics Department and the University of Iowa. Computing resources were provided through an NSF Major Research Instrumentation Program Grant (BCS-1039497). Thanks to the staff at the Atlanta Regional Branch of the National Archives for their enthusiasm and patience. Research assistance from Megan Fasules, Jess Chen, and Zach Duey was essential. Suggestions from Alan Dye, the editors, conference participants, and, of course, Jeremy Atack greatly improved the chapter. A complete list of research assistants and funders for the national sample of bankruptcy case files is available on the project home page (http://www.american.edu/cas/economics/bankrupt/). For acknowledgments, sources of research support, and disclosure of the author's material financial relationships, if any, please see http://www.nber.org/chapters/c13137.ack.

1. For a recent summary of the literature on the finance-growth nexus, see Barajas, Chami, and Yousefi (2013).

2. In addition to risky and complicated instruments at the center of the 2008 crisis, the traditional interpretation of the Panic of 1907 emphasizes the failure of regulation to limit risk taking (Hansen, 2014).

zation have seldom been able to obtain start-up funding through financial institutions. Instead, in the absence of family fortunes to invest, owners of innovative firms mainly obtained start-up funds directly from investors (Porter and Livesay 1971; Lamoreaux, Levenstein, and Sokoloff 2006; see also Levenstein 2013). Today, of course, these investors are known as "venture" capitalists.

Once the new frontier of technology or business organization has been established, firms that follow the innovators would seem to be less risky, though still potentially highly profitable. Similarly, firms that carry a known technology into new markets would seem profitable but not very risky. Yet less capital seems to have flowed through financial institutions to the more profitable manufacturing sector than one might expect: rates of return across the manufacturing and agricultural sectors were slow to equalize over the late nineteenth and early twentieth centuries (Atack, Bateman, and Weiss 1982; Epstein and Clark 1934).[3] This chapter demonstrates that the balance sheets of relatively few manufacturing firms included liabilities to financial institutions, even as recently as the 1930s. During the 1930s manufacturing firms were less likely to have banks or other financial institutions as creditors than merchants, farmers, or consumers. However, when a bank did provide credit to a manufacturing firm, it held a substantial stake, foreshadowing the patterns in business finance that came to dominate after World War II.

To document the sources of credit of manufacturers, farmers, merchants, and individual consumers, I use data on thousands of debt obligations recorded in the court records of 780 debtors who appeared in bankruptcy proceedings in Mississippi from 1929 to 1936. Under the Bankruptcy Act of 1898, debtors were required to submit to the court a complete and detailed listing of their debts. The court asked for the name of each creditor, the location of each creditor, the purpose of the debt, and the year the debt was contracted. The detail of the data permit a mapping of the sources of credit utilized by consumers and by different types of businesses.

---

3. Atack, Bateman, and Weiss (1982) use data from samples of the 1850, 1860, and 1870 manuscript censuses of manufactures to compute the ratio of net earnings to gross assets for each firm or farm. They compare rates in manufacturing to rates in agriculture (Bateman and Atack 1979) and in transportation (Atack et al. 1975; Mercer 1970). The rate of return in manufacturing enterprises was highest—higher even than the rate of return to steamboating on treacherous tributary rivers. They demonstrate that higher returns per unit of risk persisted for very small manufacturing firms in all regions, for middle-sized firms in the south, and for firms of all sizes in the east. Finally, they show that investment between census years did not flow toward those excess returns. They conclude that gaps in the rates of return between sectors were caused by differences in northern and southern attitudes toward risk and "the difficulties of small enterprises, particularly sole proprietorships, in obtaining external financing" (Atack et al., 150). Though it is not possible to extend the Atack-Bateman-Weiss methodology into the twentieth century because of the loss to fire of relevant manuscript census data, early tax records provide similar information. In 1928, the rate of return in manufacturing was still 1.6 times the rate in mining; the ratio of rates of return in these two sectors was just as large as the ratio between the rates in eastern manufacturing and agriculture had been seventy years earlier.

The data show the enduring importance of trade credit, and especially book credit, in the balance sheets of businesses of all kinds. They also show that the consumer loans that were new financial instruments in the early twentieth century were commonly held by the 1930s, even in the Deep South where the banking system has generally been considered backward. Much trade credit, including book credit, was offered at great distance. A considerable share of loans from financial institutions to consumers were offered at distances of more than one hundred miles as well.

In contrast, manufacturers had few banks among their creditors and even fewer loans from nonlocal banks. Most of the creditors of manufacturers were private individuals and commercial businesses. In sum, while financial intermediaries appear to have actively moved capital from areas of low to high rates of return *within* the agriculture and distribution sectors, during the 1930s they still did not regularly bring capital into the manufacturing sector.

5.2 A Brief History of Credit Markets

In every sector of the economy, there is a need for long-term capital to finance investment and a need for short-term capital to finance operating costs. Merchants were a key source of both long-term and short-term credit to other businesses throughout the nineteenth century. Banks did not much use the modern tools of business finance, such as term loans to finance equipment and loans on receivables, before World War II.

5.2.1   The Dominance of the Merchant

Throughout the nineteenth century, the source of long-term capital for most manufacturers was the savings of owners and, for successful firms, retained earnings. Partners were recruited from contacts upstream in the production process and, especially, downstream among the merchants who distributed the goods (Porter and Livesay 1971).

Sales of equity to the public did not play much of a role in long-term financing, except for railroads and the largest manufacturing firms, until well after the Civil War (Neal and Davis 2009). In 1860, for example, there were about 8,200 manufacturing firms in Massachusetts (University of Virginia 2004); 5 percent were incorporated, but only about fifty traded on the Boston Stock Exchange. Those fifty firms dominated the capitalization of their industries (Atack and Rousseau 1999). Major increases in listings of industrials did not occur until late in the 1890s (Navin and Sears 1955): Singer stock was not exchanged publicly until the 1890s, and Carnegie's steel operations did not incorporate until 1892. Innovative manufacturing firms in Ohio at the time did not use the Cleveland Stock Exchange to raise capital; instead, the exchange listings were mainly useful to local brokers who from time to time had small lots of these securities to offer the public. Smaller corporations tended to be privately held.

Banks also played a limited role in long-term finance. Scholars describe relations between manufacturers and financial institutions as insular and local (Cull et al. 2006; Lamoreaux 1996; Lamoreaux, Levenstein, and Sokoloff 2006). And, of course, the National Banking Act forbade national banks from issuing mortgages even to businesses, though banks could, and did, reissue debt with real estate as collateral.

The extent to which other financial institutions formed in the early nineteenth century (including savings banks, life insurance companies,[4] and investment banks) and later (such as trust companies and mortgage banks) stepped in to make long-term loans to manufacturers is not clear, but it is known that these institutions preferred to lend on strong collateral such as real estate (Porter and Livesay 1971; Hansen 2009). It seems unlikely that these firms invested substantially in manufacturing until they began participating in syndicates for the purchase of long-term securities around the turn of the twentieth century.

In the absence of a reliable source of long-term loans, when retained earnings fell short but the rate of return was high, manufacturers used short-term credit for both growth and operating costs. For manufacturers these needs could be substantial because often operating costs were about as large as total capital stock (Porter and Livesay 1971). While a small number of large industrial firms could secure short-term bank credit, direct lending from banks to manufacturers changed little over the course of the nineteenth and early twentieth centuries (Davis 1965; Jacoby and Saulnier 1947). Again, it was merchants—especially wholesalers—who were central to the system of short-term credit that had developed in the previous century.

Throughout the early modern era, general merchants restricted their dealings to well-known and often closed groups, occasionally groups bound by family or religious ties. They used credit instruments such as bills of exchange to finance trade. Between the American Revolution and the Civil War, the industrial revolution and the transportation revolution gave rise to markets in which a high volume of largely unbranded manufactured products were sold across geographically large markets through a system of specialized wholesalers (Chandler 1969; Porter and Livesay 1971). Specialized wholesalers worked closely with a small number of local banks (Richardson and Gou 2013). The short-term "commercial paper" market worked as follows: A wholesaler contracted with a manufacturer for future delivery of a product. The wholesaler's bank issued a letter of credit, which the manufacturer presented to its own bank. The manufacturer's bank discounted the letter of credit and provided cash to the manufacturer for operating expenses. To obtain payment, the manufacturer's bank could present the letter of credit

---

4. Life insurance companies did not make manufacturing loans: "It is the custom of our company, which has become practically a law with us, that we do not loan on manufacturing establishments" (Union Mutual Life Insurance Executive, quoted in Porter and Livesay 1971, 64).

for payment at the wholesaler's bank, or it could endorse the letter of credit, after which the letter of credit was called a "bankers' acceptance," and sell it on the "acceptance market."[5] The purchaser bought the bankers' acceptance at a discount (but presumably a smaller discount than the manufacturer's bank took) and redeemed it at maturity. Acceptance markets were widespread by the turn of the twentieth century in the United States, and until 1932 the regional Federal Reserve Banks were allowed to lend only against this sort of "eligible paper." In this system, then, the wholesaler was the debtor to a bank, while the manufacturer was a creditor.

In addition to liquid commercial paper, a large but largely unmeasured source of trade credit was the book account, which was secured only by the business owner's word of honor. The wholesaler would generally send goods ahead to retailers on book account. Suppliers of inputs would also sell to manufacturers on book account. Book accounts increased in importance at the end of the nineteenth century as merchants ceased making buying trips to major cities and bought instead from traveling representatives of wholesalers or the manufacturers who had begun direct-selling their widely used or complex products (Porter and Livesay 1971; Jacoby and Saulnier 1947).[6]

Trading across great a distance, which was made possible for an increasing number of products by a continual reduction in transportation costs, presented new problems for merchants and manufacturers using book accounts. If the debtor failed to pay, collection required the creditor to know the state collection law or to retain the services of a local lawyer who did. Moreover, state collection laws generally included a preference for local creditors. Thus large manufacturers with national markets, as well as specialized wholesalers, became influential as members of the The National Convention of Representatives of Commercial Bodies and were instrumental in the passage of the 1898 Bankruptcy Act, the law that gave rise to the documents used here (Hansen 1998).

5.2.2   Transition to Bank Lending

The banking system that was central to the system of commercial paper described above was highly developed and integrated. Markets in coastal cities were well integrated in the early national period, and the contours of continued integration after the Civil War are well known (Davis 1965; Sylla 1969; James 1976; Binder and Brown 1991). Recent work shows that complete integration may have slowed after the National Bank Acts of 1863

5. Jacoby and Saulnier (1947, 132) claim that in 1900 the single-name promissory note was still more common than the two-name bankers' acceptance. Richardson and Gou (2013) claim the bankers' acceptance was more important.

6. In the early twentieth century, commercial credit companies developed to discount notes and lend on receivables, and factoring companies were formed that bought receivables and lent on inventories. Commercial credit companies served manufacturers, wholesalers, and retailers (Jacoby and Saulnier 1947).

and 1864, which caused a redistribution of bank capital away from rural areas and toward industrial areas in the Old Northwest (Jaremski and Rousseau 2013). However, changes in state banking regulations and the Gold Standard Act of 1900 pushed markets closer to complete integration (Choi and Dupont 2007). The telegraph and telephone enhanced long-distance monitoring of more distant borrowers by banks, which supported increased competition between banks (Rousseau 1998). Though some places may have been left out,[7] in 1915 almost 30 percent of the loans of eastern reserve city banks were made interregionally (US Comptroller of the Currency 1915).

An integrated system of banks and other financial institutions began regularly lending to farmers and consumers during the late nineteenth and early twentieth centuries. Eastern and European banks and life insurance companies contracted with mortgage companies who provided local monitoring of farm mortgages (Beveridge 1985; Snowden 1995). In urban markets, interstate chains of small loan lenders extended unsecured loans through local agencies. These chains grew quickly over the first decades of the twentieth century, especially in states that passed uniform small loan laws (Easterly 2009; Carruthers, Guinnane, and Lee 2012). At the same time, installment loans became an important source of secured credit for consumers (Olney 1999).

Improvements in standards of accounting and disclosure by borrowers might have increased banks' confidence in loans to "outsiders" late in the nineteenth century (Rousseau 2011). The growth of business lending by banks was also facilitated, ironically, by two pieces of early twentieth-century legislation that were aimed at *limiting* the risks taken by banks. Under the Federal Reserve Act, banks were required to keep credit files on firms that presented notes for rediscounting. The Securities Act of 1933 greatly increased the formality of assessing long-term credit risk. As a result, investment banking departments and credit departments in banks merged and grew. These credit departments developed approval processes for four credit instruments "invented" by banks between 1920 and 1940: term loans, loans on accounts receivable, loans on warehouse receipts, and loans financing the purchase of equipment. At first, these services were offered only to large businesses, but between 1936 and 1941 banks began offering term loans to medium and small businesses. By 1941 more than half of term loans from

7. Dispersion remained between nonreserve cities at the turn of the twentieth century (Smiley 1975). Otherwise unexplained regional differences in bank profits persisted into the 1900s (Sullivan 2009), and local shocks far from New York dominated disturbances to regional interest rates until after World War II (Landon-Lane and Rockoff 2007). Remote areas may have been relatively disconnected: a network of banks was still forming around San Francisco (Odell 1989) and rural banks in the late 1800s had lower rates of return than urban banks (Keehn 1980), quite possibly because of high rates of bank failures in predominantly rural places (Rockoff 1977). The South was not fully integrated into the national system as late as the 1970s (Osborne 1988).

commercial banks were to firms with assets of less than $5 million (Jacoby and Saulnier 1947).

This chapter considers the sources of credit of firms, farms, and consumers during the years immediately prior to this expansion of bank-to-business lending, and it provides the first systematic comparison of the sources of credit across the various sectors of the economy and including consumers. To make these comparisons, it exploits a previously underused source: documents filed in the federal district courts subsequent to petitions for bankruptcy protection.

5.3 New Data from Bankruptcy Case Files

From 1898 (when the first permanent bankruptcy law was passed) through 1939, nearly 1.3 million petitions for bankruptcy protection were filed; 38 percent were cases in which the petitioner had primarily business debt (US DOJ, various years).[8] Although the bankruptcy statute required only that the files from certain bankruptcy cases be held permanently (railroad and municipal cases, for example), relatively few files from before 1945 have been destroyed or lost.

The court's file for each case contains detailed information on the assets, debts, incomes, and prefiling experiences of filers, as well as information on how the case progressed through the court. The case files are a rich source of long-run, microlevel data on the balance sheets of businesses and households. The documents used here are from a sample of 780 cases filed in the federal district courts in Mississippi from 1929 through 1936. The Mississippi sample constitutes a pilot project for a national sample of the bankruptcy case files covering the whole of the twentieth century.[9] As of this writing, documents have been photographed from more than 19,000 cases filed in eight states and the District of Columbia, and data have been transcribed for more than 7,000 of the cases. The appendix gives more information about the construction of the sample for Mississippi.

Given the rich data that the case files contain, it is surprising how little they have been used. Perhaps best known is the Consumer Bankruptcy Project, which has collected selected petitions filed since 1981 (see Sullivan, Warren, and Westbrook [1989] and their coauthors). As the project's title indicates, the project does not capture business bankruptcy.[10] Historical

---

8. The Constitution reserves for Congress the power to enact bankruptcy law. There were three temporary laws passed in the nineteenth century. The first permanent law was passed in 1898. Hansen and Hansen (2007) describe how business cases became a less important part of the bankruptcy case load after the Depression.

9. Depression-era Mississippi was chosen for a pilot project because of the possibility of using the natural experiment identified in Richardson and Troost (2009) to explore the impact of bank bailouts on the real economy; see Hansen (2012) and Hansen and Ziebarth (2014).

10. Some Consumer Bankruptcy Project cases do include small business debt, but businesses are not well represented.

samples of business bankruptcies have been collected by scholars in law, business history, and historical geography. Gross, Newman, and Campbell (1996) describe the occupations and circumstances of bankruptcies among women business owners under the laws in effect in the antebellum period. Balleisen (2001) considers antebellum bankruptcy in southern New York state, describing the evolution of credit connections and the tension between the admiration for entrepreneurship and the desire for steady middle-class salary. Cronon (1991) illustrates his hierarchies of cities using maps of the credit connections of 401 bankrupts in midwestern courts in the early 1870s. Of these works, only Cronon's maps of the locations of creditors to the bankrupt in Chicago and St. Louis utilize the details in the case files in a way that is similar to what is done here.

5.3.1   Data on Debtors

The data used here come from three documents: the petition that starts the case, the summary of debts and assets, and the detailed lists of debts, called "schedules." The petition has the name of the debtor, which may be the name of a person, a business, or both. From the name of the debtor I infer whether the case was a business case or a consumer case. For example, a name of "James Smith" indicates that the debts were consumer debts; "Smith's Store, a Corporation" indicates that the debts were entirely business debts; and "James Smith doing business as Smith's Store" indicates that the business was not incorporated and that the debts were mainly, but not exclusively, business debts. Table 5.1 gives the distribution of business and consumer cases in the sample. Business debtors are 59 percent of the entire sample, and nonbusiness debtors are 40 percent. In addition, there are five municipal entities (four drainage districts and one town) and one railway.

The ratio of business to consumer bankruptcy in the sample is consistent with what we know about the use of the bankruptcy law from other sources. The published statistics show that about two-thirds of those appearing in court under the bankruptcy law in Mississippi between 1929 and 1936 had business or professional debt (US DOJ, various years). The rate of consumer bankruptcy in Mississippi was just five per 100,000 in the 1920s and 1930s, compared to about seventeen per 100,000 nationally. This indicates that state laws governing collection from consumers, such as garnishment law, were viewed by many as relatively toothless. Creditors were slow to pursue Mississippi state remedies against individuals because action would not result in a quick collection to ease their own liquidity problems. As a result, debtors in Mississippi were unlikely to rush to federal bankruptcy court. In states with toothless collection laws, the consumer bankruptcy rate was not much affected by the Great Depression (Hansen and Hansen 2012).

To characterize the occupations of consumer debtors and the sector in which business debtors operated as shown in table 5.1, I use information on both the petition and the schedules. Consumer debtors include skilled

Table 5.1   **Summary of debtors in the sample**

	Number of debtors	Percent	Number of debts[b]	Average size of individual debts (1929$)[b]
Type of debtor				
Consumer debtor[c]	311	40.0	4,158	2,398
Business debtor	463	59.0	17,850	611
Municipal entity	5	0.6	16	72
Railway	1	0.1	n/a	n/a
Total	780	100.0	22,024	948
Occupation or type of business of debtor				
Not known	269	34.7	7,485	1,306
Unskilled blue collar[c]	37	4.7	479	1,400
Skilled blue collar	69	8.9	915	199
Unskilled white collar	37	4.7	437	766
Skilled white collar	16	2.1	192	637
Merchant	239	30.6	9,606	422
Manufacturer	27	3.5	1,781	1,286
Professional	34	4.4	733	1,724
Farmer	52	6.7	396	5,539
Total	780	100.0	22,024	948

Source: See text.

[a] Includes only observations for which amount of debt is reported.

[b] An observation is one debt obligation, which represents a debtor-creditor pair.

[c] There is an extreme outlier in the "unskilled blue collar" category. It is a mortgage note issued by a private person.

and unskilled blue-collar workers (13.6 percent of the sample), white-collar workers (6.8 percent), and farmers (6.5 percent). Merchants—including both wholesalers and retailers—are the largest group (30 percent of the sample). Professionals (4.9 percent) and manufacturers (3.5 percent) are smaller fractions of debtors in the sample. Insufficient information is available to categorize the occupations of 34.7 percent of the debtors in the sample. Despite the loss of this information, the proportions of merchants, manufacturers, professionals, and farmers in the sample are similar to the proportions reported in the published statistics of bankruptcy cases closed for Mississippi (US DOJ, various years). It is important to note that merchants dominate bankruptcy filings before World War II. Merchants were also a larger share of bankruptcy filers in Mississippi than they were nationwide, likely reflecting the state's position at the southern end of its eponymous river.

Among the twenty-seven manufacturers, ten milled lumber or made lumber-related materials such as veneer and plywood boxes. Five were food and beverage makers, and three were foundries or machine works. Eight firms were sole representatives of their industries. Examples are a neon sign maker, a headlight manufacturer ("Holliday Life-Saving Headlight Co."), a brick maker, and a manufacturer of suspenders.

5.3.2   Data on Debts and Creditors

Particularly critical to the current chapter are the detailed descriptions of debts provided on the documents titled "Schedule A-1" through "Schedule A-4." The first two schedules give priority debts (mainly taxes and wages owed) and secured debts. The last of the debt schedules lists liabilities on notes discounted; few debtors have any of these liabilities. Most debts owed are listed on Schedule A-3, which describes the unsecured, nonpriority debts owed. Almost all debts that can be discharged through the bankruptcy proceeding are listed on these schedules. Figure 5.1 shows the first page of Schedule A-3 for a proprietor of a retail store in Clarksdale, Mississippi, who filed in 1932.

On this schedule, as on the other detailed debt schedules, each creditor's name is given. The nature of each debt is described. Debts listed on Schedule A-3 and shown in figure 5.1 include stock purchased on book account, store fixtures purchased on credit, utility bills, and endorsed notes. Similar schedules for consumer debtors show personal loans from financial institutions and from personal acquaintances, doctors' bills, local open accounts, legal judgments, and the like.

Using the names of creditors and the information on the nature of the debt, I categorize creditors into the following types: private persons, commercial businesses, financial institutions, public entities, and civic associations. A creditor is coded as a commercial business if the creditor's name is a business name (such as a wholesale or retail store or manufacturer) or the creditor is associated with a debt taken for inventory or household goods. Financial institutions include banks, trust companies, building and loans, mortgage companies, and consumer loan or "small loan" companies. Federal land banks are treated as financial institutions. Public entities are primarily governments to which taxes are owed and court offices through which payments on legal judgments are made. Civic organizations include churches and fraternal organizations. The distribution of debts owed by type of creditor is shown in table 5.2. Just over 3,500 debts (16 percent) were owed to private persons, 16,000 debts (73 percent) were owed to commercial businesses, 729 debts (3 percent) were owed to financial institutions, and a small number of debts were owed to public entities and civic associations. It is not possible to identify the type of creditor for 1,571 of debts (7 percent).

The distribution of the various reasons for debt is also shown in table 5.2. It is not possible to determine the reason for 3,666 debts (17 percent). Twenty-one percent of debts were described only as "miscellaneous." Of clearly identified debts, the largest number financed the purchase of household goods (but not appliances) and inventory. Debt related to vehicle

Schedule A. (3)
Creditors Whose Claims Are Unsecured.

N. B.—When the name and residence (or either) of any drawer, maker, and indorser, or holder of any bill or note, etc., are unknown, the fact must be stated and also the name and residence of the last holder known to the debtor. The debt due to each creditor must be stated in full, and any claim by way of set-off stated in the schedule of property.
This sheet must be signed by the bankrupt at the end of the statement.

Names and residences of Creditors. If Residences Unknown, that fact must be stated.	When and Where Contracted.	Nature and consideration of the debt, and whether any judgment, bond, bill of exchange, promissory note, etc., and whether contracted as a partner or joint contractor with any other person; and if so, with whom?	Amount	
Ozark Pencil Co., St. Louis, Mo.	8/21/31 Drew, Miss.	Goods purchased open acct. individually	$18	70
Panno & Bossetta Inc. New Orleans, La.	3-5 to 10-14-31 Drew, Miss.	Goods purchased open Acct individually	41	30
Plough Chemical Co., Memphis, Tenn.	10-14-30 to 9-14-31; Drew, Miss.	Goods purchased open Acct individually	66	16
Procter & Gamble Dist. Co., Memphis, Tenn.	Aug. 6, 1931 Memphis, Tenn	Goods purchased open Acct individually	26	20
Rudolph Jacobs & Co. Cincinnati, Ohio	April 21, 1931 Drew, Miss.	Goods purchased open account individually	73	15
Rigo Mfg. Co., Nashville, Tenn.	April, 1930 to July, 1931. Drew, Miss.	Goods purchased open account individually	53	30
Standard Oil Co.	July 7th. to Oct. 3d.1931; Drew, Miss.	Goods purchased open account individually	46	75
Standard Candy Co., Nashville, Tenn.	Sept. 17., 1931 Drew, Miss.	Goods purchased open account individually	53	79
Tayloe Paper Co., Memphis, Tenn.	Aug. 4 to Sept. 22 1931; Drew, Miss.	Goods purchased open account individually	52	81
Yale University Press New York, N.Y.	Feb. 27, 1930 Drew, Miss.	Goods purchased open account individually	20	00
Miss. Power & Lt. Co. Drew, Miss.	Aug. Sept & Oct. 1931; Drew, Miss.	Light & Power for store individually	75	00
Sou. Bell Tel & Tel Co Drew, Miss.	Sept & Oct. 1931 Drew, Miss.	Telephone for store individually	3	50
Miller & Hart, Chicago, Ill.	Aug. 3, 1931 Drew, Miss.	Goods purchased open account individually	23	14
J.O. Lampkin, Receiver Drew, Miss.	December 1930 Drew, Miss.	Note due on demand individually endorsed by S.M. Ruscoe	$1.000	00
Burroughs Adding Mach. Co., Jackson, Miss.	June 1931 Drew, Miss.	Work on adding machine individually	2	50
Drew Insurance Agency Drew, Miss.	Sept. 1931 Drew, Miss.	Insurance on stock & fixtures; individually	11	92
C.C. Hay Drug Co., Como, Miss.	1930 Drew, Miss.	Goods purchased open account individually	12	36
Bob Cap Co., St. Louis Mo.	1931 Drew, Miss.	Goods purchased open account individually	5	63

Fig. 5.1 Schedule A-3 is an example of one of the detailed "schedules" on which individual debts owed by the bankrupt are listed

Source: MS Northern District, Clarksdale Division 1932, Accession 54A0463, Box 72x, Case no. 1410.

Table 5.2   **Summary of debts in the sample**

	Number of debts[a]	Average size of individual debts (1929$)[a]
Debts owed by type of creditor[b]		
Unknown	1,571	754
Private person	3,528	1,682
Commercial business	16,118	429
Financial institution	729	9,360
Public entity	70	191
Civic association	8	1,764
Total	22,024	948
Debts owed by reason for debt[a]		
Unknown (missing or invalid data)	3,666	1,843
Wages owed	560	228
Taxes	350	592
Domestic support	20	226
Total priority debt	436	1,197
Car (vehicle, accessories, repair)	486	350
Home (property, rent)	538	5,079
Household goods	5,506	339
Inventory	3,435	342
Miscellaneous (verbatim response)	4,552	1,113
Adverse judgments/legal settlement	379	1,190
Utilities	691	697
Household appliances	104	459
Fixtures and machinery	67	1,181
Food	194	323
Farm-related debt	33	2,343
Loans or losses in financial markets	23	2,067
Interest	51	1,813
Attorney & court fees	67	2,592
Medical	411	123
Insurance	113	3,619
Fees for other prof. services	140	648
Total	22,024	948

Source: See text.

[a] Includes only observations for which amount of debt is reported.

[b] An observation is one debt obligation, which represents a debtor-creditor pair.

[c] There is an extreme outlier in the "unskilled blue collar" category. It is a mortgage note issued by a private person.

purchase or maintenance and debts for mortgage or rent were each about 2 percent of debts.

Individual debts averaged $948 (in 1929 dollars); the standard deviation is $15,303. The largest debt recorded in the sample is $1.5 million. Debts as small as $0.10 are reported. The distribution of debts owed is heavily left-skewed: 10 percent are less than $10, the median is $68, and the 99th percentile is $11,880.

The individual debts owed by farmers were the largest of any occupation or business group. Similarly, the average debts owed by consumers were large compared to businesses because consumers owed money to relatively few creditors but tended to have a small number of large debts. In contrast, businesses—especially merchants—owed a large number of creditors but owed each creditor a relatively small amount.

The location of each creditor is noted so that the court could alert the creditor and publish an announcement in the local newspaper; this information is used in the final section below to map long-distance lending. The level of detail on the schedules provides much more information about the importance of different types of debt instruments, about the uses of credit, and about the geographic extent of credit markets than any other data currently available.

5.3.3   Representativeness of the Sample

There are three issues of representativeness to consider: Are the types of business in the sample representative of all businesses? Are the debts and creditors of bankrupts, especially bankrupts during a financial crisis, representative? Is Mississippi a representative state?

Type of business. In order to assess the representativeness of the businesses in the sample for Mississippi, I use information about all firms listed in the R. G. Dun & Co. *Reference Book of American Business* for January 1929 and 1931. Dun & Co. was one of the three major credit-reporting agencies established in the nineteenth century. By 1900, subscribers had access to basic information on the creditworthiness of nearly all business borrowers from across the United States (Sylla 2002). Dun & Co. used employee-reporters to gather and publish a brief description of the type of business (which I recharacterize as one of the major standard industrial classification [SIC] groups), an estimate of assets net of publicly recorded debts such as mortgages (in four categories), and an assessment of general creditworthiness (again in four categories). For additional information on the *Reference Books* and their contents, see Hansen and Ziebarth (2014).

There are 20,061 businesses listed in the 1929 *Reference Book* for Mississippi. In 1931, 18,695 firms are listed. I searched for all bankrupts in Mississippi in the *Reference Books* and successfully linked 54 percent of business cases.[11] Table 5.3 shows that the distribution of bankrupt firms across industries, estimated net worth, and credit-rating groups is similar to the distribution of all firms. About 70 percent were retail establishments, about 10 percent were wholesalers or manufacturers, and a small percentage fell into the other major SIC groups. Less than 15 percent of firms had assets valued at more than $10,000 and about 30 percent of firms had

---

11. For comparison, the success rate in matching between censuses seldom exceeds 40 percent (Ruggles 2002).

Table 5.3   Comparison of all firms to bankrupt firms

	All	Bankrupt	All	Bankrupt
SIC group				
Retail	70.42	77.22	69.54	76.57
Whole.	9.03	8.31	8.36	8.99
Constr.	1.61	1.57	0.99	1.23
Mfg.	10.62	8.87	10.04	9.54
Mining	0.01	0	0.01	0
AgForFish	3.26	2.36	4.45	1.09
Services	4.94	1.68	6.46	2.45
Transport	0.11	0	0.16	0.14
Assets (net of mortgages)				
More than $125K	3.62	4.60	3.5	1.63
$10K–$125K	9.13	7.74	9.39	9.63
$2K–$10K	26.19	33.74	27.46	27.95
Less than $2K	35.64	19.96	37.15	20.49
Not known	25.42	33.97	22.51	40.30
Credit rating				
High	3.07	2.24	3.04	2.04
Good	7.11	4.37	6.24	2.58
Fair	22.81	25.67	23.31	20.76
Limited	21.08	19.62	20.85	19.00
Not known	45.93	48.09	46.56	55.63

Source: See text.

assets between $2,000 and $10,000. The smallest firms are underrepresented among bankrupts, while the proportion of firms for which no estimate of assets is available is overrepresented. If Dun & Co. was unable to provide an estimate of assets, it may be because the firm was newly formed, and therefore likely that it was small. Adjusting for this makes the distribution of net worth more comparable. The *Reference Book* does not contain a judgment of creditworthiness for 45 percent of firms; creditworthiness of 48 percent of the matched bankrupt firms is not known. However, among firms with credit ratings, bankrupt firms are similar to all firms.

At first glance, the representativeness of bankrupt firms may be surprising. However, the extent to which the bankrupts are representative depends on whether the use of the law is "strategic" in the sense that debtors who use the law have knowingly leveraged up in order to take advantage of the discharge and exemptions in bankruptcy. If debtors who use the law are victims of sudden and unfortunate circumstances, representativeness is more likely. The extent of strategic filing in modern times is difficult to estimate (e.g., White 1998; Gan, Sabarwal, and Zhang 2012). Historians generally suspect that most bankrupts came to court because of unfortunate circumstances. For example, Balleisen (2001) notes that fire (especially the major New York City fire of December 1835), shipwreck, and flood were common reasons for bankruptcy in antebellum New York state. The data for the national project, for which this sample is a part, have the potential to allow for more systematic examination of the subject when the new data are compared to other sources data in addition to the Dun & Co. books. Sources for comparison include household expenditure and credit data collected by the Works Progress Administration (WPA) (US Department of Labor et al. 2009) and early Surveys of Consumer Finances (Economic Behavior Program 1999). Certainly, though, the representativeness of the Mississippi sample is enhanced by the fact that it is drawn from the Depression era: "If one looks at bankruptcies when large numbers of people are finding themselves unexpectedly insolvent because of broader changes in the economy as a whole . . . one might reasonably expect their circumstances to be more typical than at other times" (Cronon 1991, 270). Similarly Balleisen (2001, 26) writes that many of the bankruptcies filed in southern New York in 1842–1843 "stemmed from structural economic faults that were frequently difficult for foresee." Observers during the 1930s also attributed most consumer bankruptcies to bad luck: consumers filed for bankruptcy mainly because they experienced events such as job loss, medical problems, and automobile accidents (Hansen and Hansen 2012).

Type of debts and creditors. Whether we can expect the types of debts and creditors of the bankrupt to be representative of all debts is unclear.[12] On one hand, the demand for short-term credit is expected to increase as one's financial condition worsens. On the other hand, the supply of short-term credit might decrease. It seems likely, though, that the accounts of the bankrupt would contain more personal loans from nearby friends and relatives than the randomly selected firm's or consumer's. If this is true, then the accounts of the bankrupt would understate the extent of long-term and long-distance credit.

One might still be concerned about using Depression-era data because it is possible that the failure of banks during the credit crises of the 1930s creates a bias against finding banks as creditors in the sample. Figure 5.2

12. The existing literature on bankruptcy is not informative. Correlates of the consumer's decision to file have mainly been studied using the Panel Study of Income Dynamics (for example, White 1998), which (a) has only about 250 observations of filers for bankruptcy, (b) only separates mortgage debt from other debt, and (c) observes filers in the 1980s, at which time consumers were more like to be homeowners who took advantage of the option to restructure debt through Chapter 13, which the Chandler Act created. Cross-sectional studies, both historical and modern, emphasize that much of the spatial variation in bankruptcy rates is explained by variation in state collection law (Hansen and Hansen 2012; Lefgren and McIntyre 2009).

The correlates of bankruptcy filing among businesses have mainly been studied for modern publicly traded corporations. These studies, mostly of small samples in a single sector, over short-time horizons, and using data from company annual reports, tend to search for critical balance sheet ratios to predict bankruptcy in a one-year time horizon. For firms outside the financial sector, univariate models have nearly as much predictive power as more complicated models (Aziz and Dar 2006), suggesting little that would help us to understand selection biases. In summarizing the state of the literature on bankruptcy among modern unincorporated small business, Berryman (1993) concludes that "although a great deal of work has been done . . . there is not really an overriding theme."

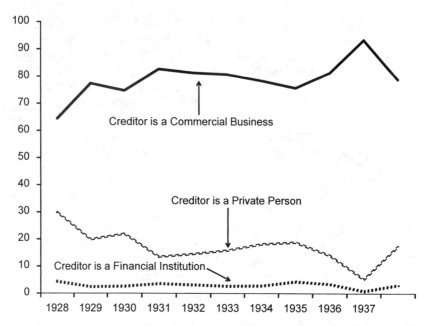

Fig. 5.2 The percent of debts owed to types of creditors, by year of the bankruptcy filing
Source: See text.

shows that this is unlikely to be a major concern: the percentage of all debts owed to financial institutions varied little over the period of the sample. In fact, it was lowest in calendar year 1929, before the start of the Depression, and at one of its higher points in 1935. The biggest change over time in the composition of creditors is from a decline in proportion of private individuals, which is offset by an increase in commercial businesses. A final reason that timing may have minimal impact on the results is that 70 percent of the sample comes from courts in the southern part of Mississippi, where there were fewer bank failures (Richardson and Troost 2009).

Location. The sample is taken from a southern state. It may be that debtors in the South were less likely than debtors elsewhere to have long-distance connections because the South was slow to be integrated into financial markets (Osborne 1988). Again, if this is the case, the results here understate the extent of long-distance credit networks. Future work will utilize samples from courts in a random sample of courts from across the country. The next samples to come online will be from courts in St. Louis and Kansas City.

5.4   Who Borrowed from Whom?

Despite the substantial literature on the development of the financial system and its integration summarized above, our pictures of credit networks have been biased toward banks and manufacturers. Until now it has not been possible to map fully the set of credit networks. This is a particularly interesting exercise during the first decades of the twentieth century as many of the financial institutions and credit instruments used today were developing. This section considers (a) the relative importance of financial institutions in consumer credit and farm mortgage markets, and (b) the relative importance of bank credit, trade credit, and personal credit for manufacturing firms compared to other businesses and to farmers.

5.4.1   Consumers and Farmers

As discussed above, traditionally most credit was extended to farmers and consumers by local retail merchants. However, by the first decades of the twentieth century, financial institutions began offering mortgages on good terms, finance companies formed to offer installment loans for consumer durables, and small loan companies spread. Table 5.4 shows the cross tabulation of the amount of the debts owed, by type of creditor, for nonbusiness debtors in the sample. Commercial businesses were owed 60 percent of debts, private persons were owed 30 percent of debts, and financial institutions were owed about 7 percent of debts. However, the debts owed to financial institutions were larger than the debts owed to private persons and more than five times the size of debts owed to commercial businesses. Debts owed by nonbusiness debtors to financial institutions averaged $3,414, at a time when nominal gross domestic product (GDP) per capita was about $600. Individual transactions between debtors and commercial businesses were just 8 percent of total debts. Individual transactions with financial institutions averaged 23 percent of debt owed by nonbusiness debtors.

Table 5.5 shows that three-quarters of debts owed to financial institutions were owed to traditional banks, trusts, and building and loans, and one quarter were owed to small loan companies. Unskilled blue-collar workers and farmers without any other kind of business debts were the most likely to borrow from a small loan company. The size of the debts owed to banks ($2,850 on average, in 1929 dollars) was more than five times the size of the debts owed to small loan companies ($125 on average). Table 5.5 also breaks down the debts owed to the different types of financial institutions by reasons for the debt. Fifty-two percent of debts owed to banks and 58 percent of debts owed to small loan companies are labeled as "miscellaneous" in the bankruptcy documents, indicating that these debts were taken on to consolidate other debt or to pay a variety of regular living expenses. Of course, loans for real estate or housing were more likely to come from banks than small loan companies, but to finance or refinance purchases of vehicles, household goods, and household appliances, or repairs of these items, debtors regularly obtained loans from small loan companies.

Table 5.4   **Amount of debt (1929$) and importance of sources of credit, consumers and farmers only**

		Private person	Commercial business	Financial institution	Public entity	Civic association	Total
Amount of debt (1929$)	Mean	2,576	638	3,414	5,124	6	1,497
	Std. dev.	17,834	5,838	7,307	12,436	0	11,110
This debt as percent of all debt	Mean	0.12	0.08	0.23	0.24	0.02	0.10
	Std. dev.	0.30	0.33	0.26	0.27	0.00	0.32
Number of debts		563	1,157	132	37	1	1,890

Source: See text.

Note: An observation is one debt obligation, which represents a debtor-creditor pair.

Table 5.5   **Debts owed to banks and small loan companies, consumers and farmers only**

	Percent of obligations to		Amount of debt (1929$)	
	Banks	Small loan co.	Banks	Small loan co.
Miscellaneous (unknown)	0.52	0.58	2,850	125
Housing & real estate	0.33	0.04	3,231	1,015
Adverse judgments	0.03	0.08	777	121
Attorney or court fees	0.03	0.02	649	16
Loans for financial mkt. trans.	0.03		1,043	
Insurance	0.02		966	
Household goods	0.02	0.08	385	41
Other farm-related debt	0.01		1,212	
Interest	0.01	0.02	3,336	9,785
Vehicles & related expenses	0.01	0.16	4,620	996
Household appliances		0.02		207
Total	1.00	1.00	2,717	486

Source: See text.

Note: An observation is one debt obligation, which represents a debtor-creditor pair.

5.4.2   Manufacturers, Merchants, and other Businesses

As discussed above, manufacturers traditionally obtained both equity and debt through personal relationships. The Mississippi sample demonstrates the enduring importance of personal relationships relative to "relationship banking": all manufacturers in the sample listed at least one private person among their creditors, but only half of manufacturers listed at least one financial institution among their creditors (table 5.6). Banks were clearly much more critical to merchants than to manufacturers. Just 42 of 265 debts owed to financial institutions (16 percent) are found in the case files of manufacturers. Of the forty-two loans from financial institutions to manufacturers, only five were secured by buildings or real estate. Moreover, this may overstate manufacturing financed by banks because the debtors may be sole proprietors and the mortgages may be for personal residences rather than business structures. Just one loan to a manufacturer—albeit the largest one, for about $21,000—was made for the purpose of purchasing equipment.

However, the data do indicate that some developments in bank-to-business lending that spread after World War II had already begun during the Depression. Of the forty-two loans between manufacturers and financial intuitions, about three-quarters were described as financing "miscellaneous" debts, indicating that the loans covered shortfalls in current operating expenses or facilitated the consolidation of other debts. Two were clearly made to finance the purchase of inventory.

The size of loans to manufacturers by banks was large: more than $12,000 per loan compared to about $6,500 per loan to professionals, $2,900 per loan

Table 5.6 Debts owed by business and farm debtors (1929 dollars)

	Private person	Commercial business	Financial institution	Public entity	Civic association	Total
Merchant						
Mean	1,209	224	2,877	1,654	3,155	398
Std. dev.	8,819	1,107	4,902	3,585	6,230	3,264
Percent of total	0.06	0.04	0.13	0.10	0.22	0.04
N	976	7,427	180	35	4	8,622
Manufacturer						
Mean	1,519	524	12,475	1,921	23	1,161
Std. dev.	13,225	2,840	31,275	5,900	4	9,544
Percent of total	0.02	0.01	0.14	0.05	0.00	0.02
N	604	1,102	42	18	2	1,768
Professional						
Mean	2,438	1,187	6,574	5,340	13	1,815
Std. dev.	8,693	6,600	13,000	8,135	3	7,680
Percent of total	0.06	0.03	0.12	0.06	0.00	0.05
N	180	536	39	12	2	769
Farmers						
Mean	1,989	2,530	1,714	10,473		2,701
Std. dev.	4,884	4,953	975	8,712		5,372
Percent of total	0.09	0.09	0.35	0.27		0.12
N	34	17	4	4		59
Total						
Mean	1,452	321	4,925	2,876	1,586	627
Std. dev.	10,451	2,158	14,319	5,887	4,410	5,189
Percent of total	0.04	0.03	0.13	0.09	0.11	0.04
N	1,794	9,082	265	69	8	11,218

Source: See text.

Note: An observation is one debt obligation, which represents a debtor-creditor pair.

to merchants, and $1,700 per loan to farmers. However, the importance of individual transactions with banks relative to the total of all debts owed was about the same for merchants, manufacturers, and professionals. Each transaction was just 12 to 14 percent of total debts. In contrast, the average debt owed by a farmer to a financial institution was 35 percent of the farmer's total debt.

Prominent in the balance sheets of the business debtors is debt to other commercial businesses—trade credit on book account. Manufacturers owed 1,100 of about 1,800 debts to other businesses. Merchants owed 7,400 of about 8,600 (86 percent) of their debts to other businesses. Even professionals had substantial book credit. While each obligation was small, in total book credit was nearly 30 percent of all credit for manufacturers, 45 percent for professionals, and nearly 50 percent for merchants. A significant portion of this business-to-business lending took place over long distances.

5.4.3   Who Borrowed at Long Distances?

There are 13,535 debts for which the distance between the debtor and creditor can be estimated and the amount of the debt is reported. (Distances are estimated using county centroids.) The average debt was owed to a creditor 130 miles from the debtor (table 5.7); the maximum distance between a debtor and one of his creditors was 1,927 miles. Half of debts were owed to creditors located in the same county as the debtor. Debts owed to out-of-state creditors tended to be smaller than debts owed to in-state creditors, although the standard deviations are large at all distances.

Figure 5.3 maps the locations of the creditors in the sample. The importance of debts, again mostly in the form of book credit, owed to businesses in freshwater and saltwater port cities is clear from the clustering of shaded areas along the Mississippi and the eastern and western seaboards.[13] Table 5.7 shows the underlying details. Although 28 percent of all debts were owed to creditors more than 100 miles away from the debtor, the average business creditor was just over 150 miles away from the business it lent to. Looking across types of businesses, the average distance between merchants and their creditors was 163 miles—twice the average distance between manufacturers and their creditors. Additionally, 34 percent of the creditors of merchants, but just 20 percent of the creditors of manufacturers, were more than 100 miles away. Manufacturers had credit networks that were similar in geographic scope to the networks of professionals and farmers.

Looking at the right-hand panel of table 5.7, it is evident that that credit extended by private persons, banks, and civic institutions tended to be to nearby debtors. Most consumer debts were owed to nearby creditors; only

---

13. The 1898 Bankruptcy Act that generated the data used here was the brainchild of trade "credit men" who sought to distribute goods more widely, but who found individual state laws giving in-state creditors preference in collections to be a major barrier to interstate operations (Hansen 1998). One of the areas for further research using the national sample is to explore whether the introduction of the Bankruptcy Act resulted in more interstate credit connections.

Table 5.7   **Distance between debtors and creditors**

	Average miles to creditor	Percent more than 100 miles	Number of debts
Type of debtor			
Consumer debtor	59	14.3	3,124
Business debtor	152	32.4	10,404
Municipal entity	295	42.8	7
Railway	n/a	n/a	n/a
Total	130	28.2	13,535
Occupation or type of business of debtor			
Not known	141	30.4	4,307
Unskilled blue collar	19	3.9	381
Skilled blue collar	25	7.2	812
Unskilled white collar	47	16.6	352
Skilled white collar	52	11.0	162
Merchant	163	34.4	5,998
Manufacturer	83	19.9	670
Professional	81	19.7	590
Farmer	88	19.0	263
Total	130	28.2	13,535
Debts owed by type of creditor[a]			
Unknown	47	11.1	270
Private person	43	10.6	2,422
Commercial business	158	33.7	10,183
Financial institution	58	17.7	605
Public entity	33	4.0	49
Civic association	63	14.3	6
Total	130	28.2	13,535
Debts owed by reason for debt[b]			
Unknown (missing or invalid data)	166	34.2	2,250
Wages owed	9	0.0	19
Taxes	12	0.0	2
Car (vehicle, accessories, repair)	29	7.1	402
Home (property, rent)	59	16.8	453
Household goods	161	34.2	3,341
Inventory	200	45.1	2,083
Miscellaneous (verbatim response)	90	19.9	3,230
Adverse judgments/legal settlement	107	21.2	269
Utilities	24	5.4	536
Household appliances	53	14.6	89
Fixtures and machinery	169	31.7	41
Food	30	6.2	161
Farm-related debt	116	15.8	19
Loans or losses in financial markets	78	33.3	19
Interest	117	26.5	34
Attorney & court fees	79	19.6	56
Medical	22	9.1	338
Insurance	225	25.0	82
Fees for other prof. services	88	18.0	111
Total	130	28.2	13,535

Source: See text.

Note: An observation is one debt obligation, which represents a debtor-creditor pair.

[a] An observation is one debt obligation, which represents a debtor-creditor pair.

[b] Includes only observations for which amount of debt is reported.

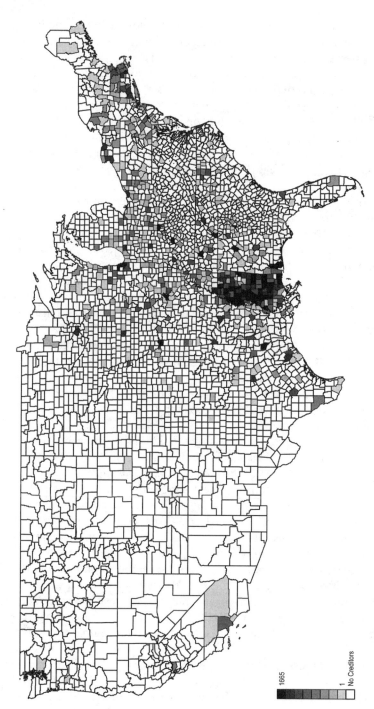

Fig. 5.3 The geographic distribution of creditors in the sample

Source: See text. Shading represents increasing number of creditors: no shading means no creditors, lightest gray means one creditor, and black means 1,665 creditors.

about 14 percent of consumer debts were owed to long-distance creditors. Consumer debts taken on at long distances included loans for household goods (34 percent of debts) and legal judgments or settlements (21 percent). Farmers had long-distance creditors for equipment, fertilizer, and other operating costs (16 percent). The creditors of municipal entities were farthest from their debtors, and municipal entities had the largest share of creditors (almost 43 percent) more than one hundred miles away. However, complete information is available for only seven debts of municipals.

Credit for insurance policies and inventory was extended at more than 200 miles distance on average. Fixtures and machinery for businesses were often bought on credit at long distances. Credit extended for inventory was extended over 200 miles on average, and just over 45 percent of debts owed for inventory were owed to creditors more than 100 miles distant.

Table 5.8 shows the cumulative amount owed by individual debtors to long-distance creditors, broken down by occupation of the debtor. Again, merchants dominate long-distance transactions: 172 merchants had more than eleven long-distance creditors on average, and the average merchant owed those long-distance creditors a cumulative $3,700. A total of sixteen manufacturers owed at least one creditor more than one hundred miles distant. The average number of long-distance creditors of manufacturers was about eight. The total debt owed to long-distance creditors by manufacturers was about $8,400, but that was just 18 percent of those manufacturers' total debts.

The long-distance debts to individuals were a larger percent of total debt than the long-distance debts of manufacturers. Fifty-five consumers (35 percent) owed long-distance creditors, but their debts were, naturally, smaller in size and number. The debts owed by twenty-six farmers (50 percent) to long-distance creditors were larger in size and of more importance to the individual debtors, but smaller in number.

If we limit our attention to debts owed *to financial institutions* at least one hundred miles distant from the debtor, there is an even greater difference in long-distance lending by occupation: 42 percent of all long-distance obligations to financial institutions were nonbusiness debt. At long distances, less than 1 percent of obligations (one debt) to a financial institution were owed by a manufacturer, while 38 percent were owed by merchants, and 17 percent by farmers.

Though the growth of small loan companies can be seen in the bankruptcy data, direct lending to farmers in Mississippi from a distance by private farm mortgage banks cannot. This may be explained by the structure of the mortgages: the debts were owed to local firms that were themselves financed from a distance. About six in ten farmers in the sample owed debts to financial institutions. Two-thirds of loans made to farmers by financial institutions were at distances of less than one hundred miles. Most loans to farmers came from local (within-county) banks. Though about one-third of loans made to farmers were at distances of one hundred miles, nearly all (81 percent) were loans from the Federal Land Bank of New Orleans.

Table 5.8   Cumulative debt owed to creditors at least one hundred miles from debtor

	Number of creditors		Cumulative owed (1929$)		Percent of all debt		Number of debtors
	Mean	Std. dev.	Mean	Std. dev.	Mean	Std. dev.	
Unskilled blue collar	1.6	0.8	10,161	22,070	0.31	0.33	10
Skilled blue collar	2.8	2.0	1,378	3,384	0.35	0.32	19
Unskilled white collar	3.3	4.1	3,004	6,307	0.36	0.29	19
Skilled white collar	1.7	1.3	1,602	2,329	0.21	0.35	7
Merchant	11.6	12.3	3,708	9,923	0.23	0.25	172
Manufacturer	7.9	7.2	8,415	17,573	0.18	0.20	16
Professional	5.3	4.3	16,453	25,873	0.23	0.29	25
Farmer	1.7	0.9	27,823	56,377	0.39	0.32	26

Source: See text.

Note: One observation per debtor.

5.5   Conclusion

Detailed data from the new sample of bankruptcy documents from courts in Mississippi document the importance of the interregional network of trade credit well into the twentieth century. Despite the disruptions of the Depression, during the years from 1929 to 1936, merchants in Mississippi continued to rely on long-distance creditors for inventory and fixtures.

The data show that the innovative financial firms that aimed to meet demand for credit of consumers had made inroads into the deep South by the 1930s. Consumer loans from financial institutions were relatively common and included a significant number made through small-loan lenders.

The bank-to-manufacturing lending channel that became important after World War II was only just emerging in the 1930s. While some short-term loans from banks for "miscellaneous" purchases were on the balance sheets of manufacturers, overall, manufacturers in Mississippi were unlikely to have credit from banks or other financial institutions. Although the manufacturers in Mississippi were mostly in well-established industries, their sources of credit were similar to the sources of credit of start-ups: private persons and other businesses. Thus, this study adds to the evidence that banks seldom brought capital into manufacturing, which helps to explain why rates of return across sectors converged only slowly.

This is not to say, of course, that banks are unimportant for economic growth. Though in the Mississippi example bank lending did not mainly support the local economy by funneling capital directly into production, it did support the local economy by facilitating the movement of goods to where they commanded the highest prices and by financing purchases by consumers. In fact, a modern distribution system was critical to manufacturers who hoped to take advantage of the economies of scale of modern industrial techniques and the spillovers associated with regional specialization. Yet cliometricans have focused on manufacturing and banking rather than distribution and trade credit. This production-oriented approach reflects available data. The new data from the bankruptcy documents will support a more balanced approach.

Appendix
Description of the Sample

More than thirty-four million businesses and consumers have used the federal bankruptcy law since the first permanent law was passed in 1898. The national sample of bankruptcy cases will consist of all cases in a random sample of boxes containing about 1 percent of cases from the permanent col-

Table 5A.1   **Sample size compared to extant dockets and published statistics**

	Published cases filed			Extant dockets			Sample		
	North	South	Total	North	South	Total	North	South	Total
							2	11	13
1929	125	273	398	135	301	436	39	89	128
1930	132	308	440	131	321	452	42	77	119
1931	139	376	515	102	362	464	24	67	91
1932	217	454	671	122	225	347	16	35	51
1933	227	414	641	80	168	248	34	56	90
1934	333	333	521	55	142	197	8	38	46
1935	105	210	315	106	107	213	23	85	108
1936	163	207	370	15	102	117	33	100	133
1937	143	178	321				0	1	1
Total	1,584	2,753	4,192	746	1,728	2,474	221	559	780
Dockets as % of published (1929–1936)				52	67	64			
Sample as % of published (1929–1936)							15	22	20

Sources: Published by United States Department of Justice, *Annual Reports of the Attorney General of the United States*, various years.

lection of the National Archives.[14] The Mississippi pilot contains an oversample to ensure a large enough number of observations for stand-alone analysis; the sample used here contains one box of records from each court selected at random for each year. If the selected box contained fewer than five cases, the next box was also selected.

For this time period in Mississippi, the boxes mostly contained consecutive case numbers; that is, the cases were boxed in the chronological order in which the cases commenced. The sample for each division court is therefore clustered in time, but the overall sample contains observations of cases filed in most months.

Table 5A.1 describes the size of the sample and provides comparisons to the totals in the extant docket sheets and published statistics of the Federal District Courts. The extant dockets include data on 64 percent of cases filed in the two federal court districts of Mississippi. Slightly more docket books have survived for the Southern District. The sample of case files represents 20 percent of all cases reported in the *Annual Report of the Attorney General.* The sample for the courts in the Northern District is 15 percent of cases; the sample for the Southern District is 22 percent of all cases.

There were six division (that is, local) courts in the two federal court districts in Mississippi (see figure 5A.1 for a map). Table 5A.2 shows the distribution

14. There are more than one million cubic feet of bankruptcy case files currently in the permanent collection of the National Archives. Additionally, approximately two million cubic feet of relatively recent case files are stored in the regional Federal Records Centers. Ownership of these records is being transferred from the Administrative Office of the US Courts to the National Archive and Records Administration (NARA). A 3 percent random sample of boxes will be added to the Archives' collection.

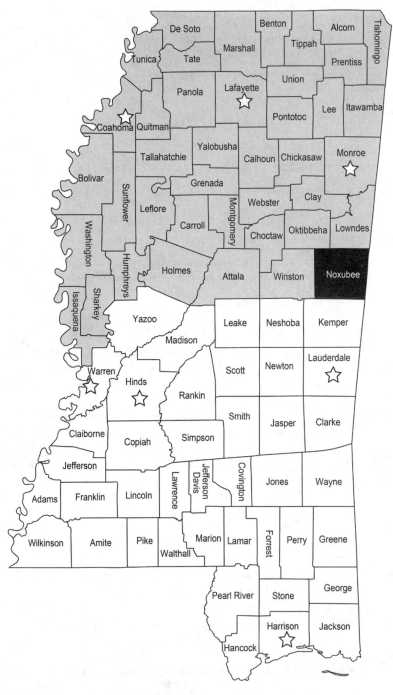

Fig. 5A.1 Map of Mississippi with district border and court locations

Table 5A.2   Distribution of sample across division courts

	Aberdeen	Biloxi	Clarksdale	Jackson	Meridian	Oxford	Vicksburg	Total
1928						2	11	13
1929		17	20	31	31	19	10	128
1930		24	23	23	16	19	14	119
1931		14	14	26	11	10	16	91
1932	1	2	0	10	6	15	17	51
1933		13	16	23	10	18	10	90
1934		9			7	8	22	46
1935		25	19	39	15	4	6	108
1936		18	18	42	23	15	17	133
1937							1	1
Total	1	122	110	194	119	110	124	780
Percent	0	16	14	25	15	14	16	100

Table 5A.3   Cases in sample compared to coverage of extant docket books by quarter

Year	1928		1929				1930				1931				1932			
Quarter	3	4	1	2	3	4	1	2	3	4	1	2	3	4	1	2	3	4
Aberdeen																**1**		
Biloxi			**9**	**8**			**14**	**4**	**5**	**1**	**11**	**2**	**1**		2			
Clarksdale			**19**			**1**	**6**	9	4	4				13				
Jackson			**25**	**6**			**2**	**1**		**20**	**25**	**1**			**7**	**1**	**1**	**1**
Meridian			**12**	**18**	1					15			10	1	6			
Oxford		2	**8**	**6**	**5**				**8**	**5**			**1**	**9**		**5**	**4**	**1**
Vicksburg	2	9	**10**		**5**			**6**	**8**	**14**	**1**	**1**	**6**	**8**	**16**	**5**	**1**	**6**

Year	1933				1934				1935				1936			
Quarter	1	2	3	4	1	2	3	4	1	2	3	4	1	2	3	4
Aberdeen																
Biloxi		15	8	5				9	10	3	5	7	3	6	4	5
Clarksdale			1						9	4	5	1	18			
Jackson	**23**								**6**	**16**	**16**	**1**	**16**	**21**	**5**	**2**
Meridian		1			7			0	1	4	7	3	15	5	1	
Oxford	**10**		**8**			**2**	**3**	**3**			**1**	**3**	**4**	**6**	**2**	**3**
Vicksburg	**1**	**8**	**1**			**5**	**3**	**14**	**5**		**1**		**4**	**6**	**4**	**3**

Note: Numbers describe the size of the sample for the quarter. Quarters covered by surviving docket books (bold):

Aberdeen, 1929:Q1 through 1935:Q4; Biloxi, 1929:Q1 through 1931:Q4; Clarksdale, 1929:Q1 through 1930:Q1; Jackson, 1929:Q1 through 1936:Q4; Meridian, 1929:Q1 through 1929:Q2; Oxford, 1929:Q1 through 1936:Q4; Vicksburg, 1929:Q1 through 1936:Q4.

of the 780 cases in the sample across the six division courts. The largest portion of the sample, 25 percent, comes from the court at Jackson. Four of the other courts each contribute 14 to 16 percent to the sample. Only one case in the sample comes from the court at Aberdeen. The Clerk of the Court at Aberdeen interfiled bankruptcy cases with civil and criminal cases. Except for one large case that was boxed separately, it was not feasible to separate the bankruptcy cases from the thousands of other cases filed in Aberdeen.

Table 5A.3 shows the overlapping periods covered by the extant docket books and the sample of cases for each division court. The shading represents the quarters for which docket books are available. The number in each cell gives the size of the sample for the quarter. As noted above, it was not feasible to collect a sample of case files for Aberdeen. Docket books for Aberdeen survived, however, as did docket books for Jackson, Oxford, and Vicksburg. Most docket books for Biloxi, Clarksdale, and Meridian, however, did not survive.

References

Atack, Jeremy, Fred Bateman, and Thomas Weiss. 1982. "Risk, the Rate of Return and the Pattern of Investment in Nineteenth-Century American Manufacturing." *Southern Economic Journal* 49 (1): 150–63.

Atack, Jeremy, Erik F. Haites, James Mak, and Gary M. Walton. 1975. "The Profitability of Steamboating on Western Rivers: 1850." *Business History Review* 49 (3): 346–54.

Atack, Jeremy, and Peter L. Rousseau. 1999. "Business Activity and the Boston Stock Market, 1835–1869." *Explorations in Economic History* 36 (2): 144–79.

Aziz, M. Adnan, and Humayon A. Dar. 2006. "Predicting Corporate Bankruptcy: Where We Stand?" *Corporate Governance* 6 (1): 18–33.

Balleisen, Edward J. 2001. *Navigating Failure: Bankruptcy and Commercial Society in Antebellum America.* Chapel Hill: University of North Carolina Press.

Barajas, Adolfo, Ralph Chami, and Reza Yousefi. 2013. "The Finance and Growth Nexus Re-Examined: Do All Countries Benefit Equally?" IMF Working Paper no. 13-130, International Monetary Fund.

Bateman, Fred, and Jeremy Atack. 1979. "The Profitability of Agriculture in 1860." *Research in Economic History* 4:87–125.

Berryman, Joyce E. 1993. "Small Business Failure and Bankruptcy: What Progress Has Been Made in a Decade?" *Small Enterprise Research* 2 (1–2): 5–27.

Beveridge, Andrew A. 1985. "Local Lending Practice: Borrowers in a Small Northeastern Industrial City, 1832–1915." *Journal of Economic History* 45 (2): 393–403.

Binder, John J., and David T. Brown. 1991. "Bank Rates of Return and Entry Restrictions, 1869–1914." *Journal of Economic History* 51 (1): 47–66.

Carruthers, Bruce G., Timothy W. Guinnane, and Yoonseok Lee. 2012. "Bringing 'Honest Capital' to Poor Borrowers: The Passage of the US Uniform Small Loan Law, 1907–1930." *Journal of Interdisciplinary History* 42(3): 393–418.

Chandler, Alfred D. 1969. "The Role of Business in the United States: A Historical Survey." *Daedalus* 98 (1): 23–40.

Choi, Kyongwook, and Brandon Dupont. 2007. "Revisiting Structural Change and Market Integration in Late 19th Century American Capital Markets." *Applied Economics* 39 (21): 2733–41.

Cronon, William. 1991. *Nature's Metropolis: Chicago and the Great West*. New York: Norton.

Cull, Robert, Lance E. Davis, Naomi R. Lamoreaux, and Jean-Laurent Rosenthal. 2006. "Historical Financing of Small- and Medium-Size Enterprises." *Journal of Banking & Finance* 30 (11): 3017–42.

Davis, Lance E. 1965. "The Investment Market, 1870–1914: The Evolution of a National Market." *Journal of Economic History* 25 (3): 355–99.

Economic Behavior Program, Survey Research Center, University of Michigan. 1999. *Survey of Consumer Finances, 1956*. ICPSR version. Ann Arbor, MI: Institute for Social Research, Social Science Archive [producer], 1973. Ann Arbor, MI: Inter-university Consortium for Political and Social Research [distributor], 1999. doi:10.3886/ICPSR03614.v1.

Easterly, Michael. 2009. "Your Job is Your Credit: Creating a Market for Loans to Salaried Employees in New York City, 1885–1920." *Enterprise and Society* 10 (4): 651–60.

Epstein, R. C., and F. M. Clark. 1934. *Industrial Profits in the United States*. New York: National Bureau of Economic Research.

Gan, Li, Tarun Sabarwal, and Shuoxun Zhang. 2012. "Personal Bankruptcy: Reconciling Adverse Events and Strategic Timing Hypotheses Using Heterogeneity in Filing Types." Manuscript, University of Kansas.

Gross, Karen, Marie Stefanini Newman, and Denise Campbell. 1996. "Ladies in Red: Learning from America's First Female Bankrupts." *American Journal of Legal History* 40 (1): 1–40.

Hansen, Bradley. 1998. "Commercial Associations and the Creation of a National Economy: The Demand for Federal Bankruptcy Law." *Business History Review* 72 (1): 86–113.

———. 2009. *Institutions, Entrepreneurs, and American Economic History*. New York: Palgrave Macmillan.

———. 2014. "A Failure of Regulation? Reinterpreting the Panic of 1907." *Business History Review* 88 (3): 545–69.

Hansen, Bradley A., and Mary Eschelbach Hansen. 2007. "The Role of Path Dependence in the Development of US Bankruptcy Law, 1880–1938." *Journal of Institutional Economics* 3 (2): 203–25.

Hansen, Mary Eschelbach. 2012. "Financial System Liquidity and Bankruptcy, 1929–1931." Manuscript presented at the Economic History Association Meetings, Vancouver, British Columbia, September 21.

Hansen, Mary Eschelbach, and Bradley A. Hansen. 2012. "Crisis and Bankruptcy: The Mediating Role of State Law, 1920–1932." *Journal of Economic History* 72 (2): 448–68.

Hansen, Mary Eschelbach, and Nicholas L. Zeibarth. 2014. "The Relationship between Banking and Business Distress: Evidence from Exits and Bankruptcies during the Great Depression." Unpublished Manuscript, American University.

Jacoby, Neil H., and Raymond J. Saulnier. 1947. *Business Finance and Banking*. New York: National Bureau of Economic Research.

James, John A. 1976. "The Development of the National Money Market, 1893–1911." *Journal of Economic History* 36 (4): 878–97.

Jaremski, Matthew, and Peter L. Rousseau. 2013. "Banks, Free Banks, and US Economic Growth." *Economic Inquiry* 51 (2): 1603–21.

Keehn, Richard H. 1980. "Market Power and Bank Lending: Some Evidence from Wisconsin, 1870–1900." *Journal of Economic History* 40 (1): 45–52.

Lamoreaux, Naomi R. 1996. *Insider Lending: Banks, Personal Connections, and Economic Development in Industrial New England.* Cambridge: Cambridge University Press.

Lamoreaux, Naomi R., Margaret Levenstein, and Kenneth L. Sokoloff. 2006. "Mobilizing Venture Capital during the Second Industrial Revolution: Cleveland, Ohio, 1870–1920." *Capitalism and Society* 1 (3): article 5.

Landon-Lane, John, and Hugh Rockoff. 2007. "The Origin and Diffusion of Shocks to Regional Interest Rates in the United States, 1880–2002." *Explorations in Economic History* 44 (3): 487–500.

Lefgren, Lars, and Frank McIntyre. 2009. "Explaining the Puzzle of Cross-State Differences in Bankruptcy Rates." *Journal of Law and Economics* 52 (2): 367–93.

Levenstein, Margaret. 2013. "Networks of Capital and Midwestern Industrialization: Cleveland, Ohio 1880–1914." Unpublished Manuscript, University of Michigan.

Mercer, Lloyd J. 1970. "Rates of Return for Land-Grant Railroads: The Central Pacific System." *Journal of Economic History* 30 (3): 602–26.

Navin, Thomas R., and Marian V. Sears. 1955. "The Rise of a Market for Industrial Securities, 1887–1902." *Business History Review* 29 (2): 105–38.

Neal, Larry, and Lance E. Davis. 2009. "Why Did Finance Capitalism and the Second Industrial Revolution Arise in the 1890s?" In *Financing Innovation in the United States, 1870 to the Present*, edited by Naomi R. Lamoreaux and Kenneth L. Sokoloff. Cambridge, MA: MIT Press.

Odell, Kerry A. 1989. "The Integration of Regional and Interregional Capital Markets: Evidence from the Pacific Coast, 1883–1913." *Journal of Economic History* 49 (2): 297–310.

Olney, Martha L. 1999. "Avoiding Default: The Role of Credit in the Consumption Collapse of 1930." *Quarterly Journal of Economics* 114 (1): 319–35.

Osborne, Dale K. 1988. "Competition and Geographical Integration in Commercial Bank Lending." *Journal of Banking & Finance* 12 (1): 85–103.

Porter, Glenn, and Harold C. Livesay. 1971. *Merchants and Manufacturers: Studies in the Changing Structure of Nineteenth-Century Marketing.* Chicago: Ivan R. Dee.

Richardson, Gary, and M. Gou. 2013. "Bank Failures Trigger Firm Bankruptcies." Unpublished Manuscript, University of California-Irvine.

Richardson, Gary, and William Troost. 2009. "Monetary Intervention Mitigated Banking Panics during the Great Depression: Quasi-Experimental Evidence from a Federal Reserve District Border, 1929–1933." *Journal of Political Economy* 117 (6): 1031–73.

Rockoff, Hugh. 1977. "Regional Interest Rates and Bank Failures, 1870–1914." *Explorations in Economic History* 14 (1): 90–95.

Rousseau, Peter L. 1998. "The Permanent Effects of Innovation on Financial Depth: Theory and US Historical Evidence from Unobservable Components Models." *Journal of Monetary Economics* 42 (2): 387–425.

———. 2011. "The Market for Bank Stocks and the Rise of Deposit Banking in New York City, 1866–1897." *Journal of Economic History* 71 (4): 976–1005.

Ruggles, Steven. 2002. "Linking Historical Censuses: A New Approach." *Computing and History* 14 (1–2): 213–24.

Smiley, Gene. 1975. "Interest Rate Movement in the United States, 1888–1913." *Journal of Economic History* 35 (3): 591–620.

Snowden, Kenneth. 1995. "The Evolution of Interregional Mortgage Lending Channels, 1870–1940: The Life Insurance-Mortgage Company Connection." In *Coordination and Information: Historical Perspectives on the Organization of Enterprise*, edited by Naomi R. Lamoreaux and Daniel M. G. Raff, 209–56. Chicago: University of Chicago Press.

Sullivan, Richard J. 2009. "Regulatory Changes and the Development of the US Banking Market, 1870–1914: A Study of the Profit Rates and Risk in National Banks." In *The Origins and Development of Financial Markets and Institutions from the Seventeenth Century to the Present*, edited by Jeremy Atack and Larry Neal, 262–93. Cambridge: Cambridge University Press.

Sullivan, Theresa A., Elizabeth Warren, and Jay L. Westbrook. 1989. *As We Forgive Our Debtors: Bankruptcy and Consumer Credit in America*. New York: Oxford University Press.

Sylla, Richard. 1969. "Federal Policy, Banking Market Structure, and Capital Mobilization in the United States, 1863–1913." *Journal of Economic History* 29 (4): 657–86.

———. 2002. "A Historical Primer on the Business of Credit Rating." In *Ratings, Rating Agencies and the Global Financial System*, edited by Richard M. Levich, Richard M. Giovanni Majnoni, and Carmen Reinhart, 19–40. New York: Springer.

US Comptroller of the Currency. 1915. *Annual Report*. Washington, DC: GPO.

US Department of Justice. Various years. *Annual Report of the Attorney General*. Washington, DC: GPO.

US Department of Labor. Bureau of Labor Statistics. Cost of Living Division, United States Department of Agriculture. Bureau of Home Economics. Economics Division, United States National Resources Committee. Consumption Research Staff. Industrial Section, United States Central Statistical Board, and United States Works Progress Administration. 2009. *Study of Consumer Purchases in the United States, 1935–1936*. ICPSR 8908–v3. Ann Arbor, MI: Inter-university Consortium for Political and Social Research[distributor], 2009–06–29. doi:10.3886/ICPSR8908.v3.

US Department of Treasury. 2014. *Bank Lending Surveys*. Last accessed April 12, 2014. http://www.treasury.gov/initiatives/financial-stability/TARP-Programs/bank-investment-programs/cap/lending-report/Pages/default.aspx.

University of Virginia, Geospatial and Statistical Data Center. 2004. Historical Census Browser. Last accessed April 12, 2014. http://mapserver.lib.virginia.edu/collections/stats/histcensus/index.html.

White, Michelle. 1998. "Why Don't More Households File for Bankruptcy?" *Journal of Law Economics and Organization* 14 (2): 205–31.

III

Scale Economies in Nineteenth-Century Production

6

Economies of Scale in Nineteenth-Century American Manufacturing Revisited
A Resolution of the Entrepreneurial Labor Input Problem

Robert A. Margo

6.1 Introduction

At the start of the nineteenth century the United States economy was overwhelmingly agricultural, well behind England in the development of a manufacturing sector. By the mid-nineteenth century the American industrial revolution was solidly underway, chiefly in the Northeast but spreading elsewhere in the country. By century's end labor productivity in US manufacturing substantially exceeded levels in Great Britain or continental Europe and the United States was rapidly becoming the leading industrial economy in the world (Wright 1990; Broadberry and Irwin 2006).

The conventional narrative of American manufacturing ascendancy emphasizes the "rise of big business" (Chandler 1977). At the start of the century American manufacturing was overwhelmingly the province of the "artisan shop" in which a craftsman, perhaps assisted by an apprentice or two, fashioned a custom product from start to finish using hand tools and no inanimate power source. The artisan shop was replaced by the factory, which employed more workers utilizing division of labor and, with increasing frequency over the century, powered machinery. By the end of the century the

Robert A. Margo is professor of economics at Boston University and a research associate of the National Bureau of Economic Research.

Comments from two referees, Jeremy Atack, William Collins, Stanley Engerman, Ian Keay, and workshop participants at Rennselaer Polytechnic Institute, the NBER-Vanderbilt "Enterprising America" conference, the 2014 Allied Social Science Association meetings in Philadelphia, the National Bureau of Economic Research, and the EH-Clio Lab in Santiago, Chile, are gratefully acknowledged. For acknowledgments, sources of research support, and disclosure of the author's material financial relationships, if any, please see http://www.nber.org/chapters/c13133.ack.

factory had already morphed into establishments that were both larger in terms of employment and more capital intensive.[1]

Central to the conventional narrative is a belief that large-scale production contributed substantially to productivity growth in manufacturing through the exploitation of economies of scale. For the very end of the century the existence of scale economies in manufacturing is not in question; as Chandler documents, there are abundant examples of scale economies in industries like steel production and meat packing. However, can the same be said for earlier in the century when industrialization was getting underway?

For many economic historians, convincing evidence that economies of scale were present early in the American industrial revolution is contained in a famous paper by Kenneth Sokoloff (1984). Using samples from the 1820 and 1850 manuscript censuses of manufacturing, Sokoloff estimated Cobb-Douglas production functions showing economies of scale. Very importantly he was able to demonstrate this for nonmechanized establishments, suggesting that pure division of labor, as hypothesized by Adam Smith, was a source of productivity gains.

A crucial piece of Sokoloff's analysis was an adjustment that he made to the census data for what has come to be known as the "entrepreneurial labor input problem."[2] Although the issue was first raised (and resolved in a particular way) by Atack (1976, chs. 3, 7; 1977), economic historians were made more broadly aware of the implications of the problem by Sokoloff's paper. Like the other nineteenth-century manufacturing censuses, those for 1820 and 1850 collected information on the number of individuals working in the establishment, classified by age or gender.[3] According to Sokoloff (1984), the reported count of workers in 1820 and 1850 generally excluded the labor input of the owner if he was a sole proprietor (or owners, if there was more than one); however, based on supplementary information for 1820,

---

1. "Continuous processing" techniques are an example in which raw materials are constantly in motion and being processed, with plants operating on multiple shifts; see Chandler (1977) and Goldin and Katz (1998).

2. In this chapter I treat the "entrepreneurial labor input problem" as a problem of measurement of the entrepreneurial labor input *per se* rather than a topic with its own economic history—that is, tracing over time, for example, long-term changes in the labor input provided by entrepreneurs. See Fishbein (1973) and Atack and Bateman (1999a) for a comprehensive discussion of the history of the nineteenth-century manufacturing censuses, the information collected, and available modern samples from the surviving manuscript schedules. There is a long history of doubts and disputes about the accuracy of the census manufacturing data, particularly for the earlier census years. Indeed, the census takers themselves expressed serious doubts about the data they collected. Francis A. Walker, the superintendent at both the 1870 and 1880 census, for example, described the data reported by the manufacturing censuses on capital invested as "entirely untrustworthy and delusive" and "wholly worthless." Nevertheless, such jaundiced views did not prevent others at the time or modern scholars from making extensive use of the data and drawing inferences from them.

3. The 1820 census collected information on the average number of boys, young women, and adult males working at the establishment separately. The 1850 census reports separately the average number of male and female workers.

Sokoloff believed that hired managers were generally counted. In effect, Sokoloff believed that the census collected information on the labor input of employees but not the employer(s) (see Atack [1976] for a similar argument).

Because the employer or "entrepreneurial" portion of the labor input was allegedly overlooked, the common census measure of labor productivity, value added per worker, is overstated because the denominator, the labor input, is too small. Critically, the degree of overstatement is not uniform across establishments with different numbers of workers. To the contrary, the upward bias in labor productivity is systematically greater for establishments with few workers because in such establishments the ratio of the entrepreneurial labor input to that of the other workers is greater than in larger establishments. According to Sokoloff, failure to correct for this bias systematically overstates labor productivity in smaller relative to larger establishments, thereby causing the usual measure of scale economies—for example, the sum of the labor and capital coefficients in a value-added Cobb-Douglas production function—to be biased downward. Sokoloff proposed specific and somewhat different solutions for this problem in 1820 and 1850. Once these were implemented, he was able to establish econometrically the existence of economies of scale.

The early response to Sokoloff's paper was favorable, as evidenced by Atack (1987), who adopted Sokoloff's proposed solution in his estimation of production functions using establishment-level data from the 1850–1870 manufacturing censuses.[4] In later work, however, Atack changed his mind, arguing that, in general, the census *did* include the labor input of the entrepreneur if it was economically relevant to do so.[5] As far as anyone knows Sokoloff never accepted Atack's criticisms, nor has there been a satisfactory resolution of the dispute, leaving economic historians in the lurch as to which point of view has more merit.[6] Unlike some debates over measurement in economic history this is far from a trivial dispute because, as mentioned in the original paper and as shown here, Sokoloff's proposed adjustment has a marked effect on measured productivity in small establishments relative to larger and therefore on the extent of measured economies of scale. It is thus fundamental to our understanding of the "treatment effect" of changes in establishment size and organizational form on labor productivity during early industrialization, as measured from census data of the era.

In this chapter I revisit the entrepreneurial labor input problem in a systematic way using data from the Atack-Bateman (1999a) samples from the

---

4. In this regard, Atack's (1987) analysis of the 1850 data differs from his 1977 analysis (see the discussion later in the chapter).

5. See Atack and Bateman (1999b), a revised version of which was later published as Atack and Bateman (2008).

6. The issue has also been considered for the case of the 1871 Canadian census of manufactures; in particular, Inwood and Keay (2012) conclude that the entrepreneurial labor input was properly counted and that no Sokoloff-like adjustment is necessary.

1850–1880 censuses of manufacturing along with textual material from the instructions to census enumerators. The conclusion I reach has two parts. First, Atack's revised position that the census did generally include the labor input of the entrepreneur when economically relevant has much to recommend it with regard to sole proprietorships; in particular, his claim is consistent with the textual evidence from the enumerator instructions as well as statistical evidence on the distribution of establishment sizes.[7] However, this is not to say that the census enumerators always included sole proprietors in the count of workers when they were supposed to, as I also uncover several examples that suggest a failure to do so, but such failures appear to be relatively uncommon.

Second, I extend Sokoloff's (1984) analysis of the effects of partnerships (versus sole proprietors) by using data on organizational form that Atack subsequently added to the original 1850–1870 Atack-Bateman samples. Consistent with Sokoloff's findings, I show in a regression analysis that partnerships had higher output than sole proprietorships after controlling for the reported number of employees. However, the effects are not statistically significant (and are relatively small), especially after controlling for industry, location, and capital invested. I conclude that Sokoloff's recommended blanket correction for any possible undercount in 1850 and, by inference, for the 1860–1880 censuses is not defensible.

That said, while it may be inappropriate to apply a correction in the particular manner that Sokoloff recommended, he was correct that the labor input was underenumerated in small establishments relative to large—but for an entirely different reason. The relative underenumeration occurs because the census data on the labor input refer not to the total quantity of labor used in the establishment over the course of the census year or even a literal average of the number of workers, as is often assumed (see, for example, Laurie and Schmitz 1981, 73). Rather, my analysis leads me to conclude that the data generally refer to the typical number of individuals at work at the establishment during the census year, where "typical" refers to the number usually present on a normal day of operation. This typical number does not take into account occasional periods of time when more labor might be at work as well as periods when fewer than typical were present. The failure to incorporate above or below typical numbers of workers would not necessarily introduce bias but, as it happens, there is a bias that is asymmetric with respect to establishment size. In effect, the census data on the labor input are more accurate for larger establishments and less accurate from smaller establishments, with the error being one-sided (too low) for smaller relative

7. In this regard, my argument is similar to that sketched in Atack and Bateman (1999b), who also argue on the basis of the distribution of establishment sizes that sole proprietors were generally counted correctly. Atack and Bateman's focus in their paper is on profitability in manufacturing; in particular, they argue that a Sokoloff adjustment leads to estimates of returns for small establishments that are systematically too low.

to larger establishments. This is the same type of bias that Sokoloff identified, albeit for a very different reason.

In support of this claim, I make use of novel data from the 1880 census that were included in the manuscripts but never tabulated and published. In 1880, as in 1870, the census ascertained the average numbers of adult males, adult females, and child workers separately. However, the census also included a new question on the maximum number of workers at the establishment at any point in time during the census year. I create a subsample of establishments in 1880 for which, if the census data on average numbers were literally correct, no establishment should have reported a maximum number of workers that exceed the sum of adult male, adult female, and child workers. However, as I show, almost half of the establishments in the particular subsample did so report. I argue that the most likely explanation is that these establishments gave the *typical* number at work in response to the enumerator, rather than a true average—a type of answer that the census instructions to enumerators permitted. I go on to show that the likelihood of this happening was decreasing in establishment size, which is the same pattern of bias alleged by Sokoloff.

The 1880 data also allow me to estimate whether the difference between the maximum and typical number of workers had a material effect on labor productivity. I show that it did. Under a set of reasonable assumptions it is possible to back out an adjustment factor to correct the reported average number of workers. This adjustment factor reduces labor productivity in small establishments relative to large establishments but to a much smaller extent than Sokoloff's adjustment and to an insufficient degree to generate a robust finding of increasing returns to scale.

6.2   The Emergence of Large-Scale Manufacturing in Nineteenth-Century America

In the early nineteenth century the overwhelming share of the labor force, approximately 76 percent in 1800, was engaged in agricultural production. Over the course of the century, a shift of labor out of agriculture occurred such that, by 1900, the share in agriculture had fallen by slightly more than half, to 36 percent (Weiss 1986, 1993). Although much of the reallocated labor went to the service sector, a significant portion went to manufacturing where labor productivity was substantially higher than on the farm. The growth of manufacturing employment in the nineteenth century was not neutral with respect to establishment size. In particular, the average number of workers per establishment increased (Atack 1987). Smaller establishments, especially sole proprietorships, decreased their share of the total number of establishments and of total employment in manufacturing—a process referred to by labor historians as the "displacement" of the artisan shop by the factory.

Table 6.1 documents the evolution of this process over the period from 1850 to 1880 by presenting employment size distributions in manufacturing, using the Atack-Bateman (1999a) manuscript census samples. In computing the distributions I have made some novel adjustments for the possible under-reporting of very small establishments prior to the Civil War. The details of these adjustments are described in the appendix.[8]

Panel A of table 6.1 shows the mean and median establishment size and proportion of establishments in five size categories: one to two workers, three to five workers, six to fifteen workers, sixteen to one hundred workers, and more than one hundred workers. These size categories are shown because within them the change over time in the proportions was monotonically decreasing (one to two workers), stable (three to five), or increasing (six or more). In the discussion below, I will refer to establishments with sixteen or more workers as "factories." While any specific cutoff, of course, is arbitrary, the substantive patterns evident in the table do not change for reasonable variations in this cutoff.

The basic finding of panel A is that the distribution of establishments shifted over time toward larger firm sizes—that is, the share of establishments in the smallest category (one to two workers) decreased over time while the shares of establishments with six or more workers increased. For establishments in the factory bin (sixteen or more workers) the increasing share reflects an upward trend in place before 1850 (Sokoloff 1984), but for the middle category (six to fifteen) the increase appears to have started after the Civil War.

The overriding impression from panel A is that change in the size distribution of establishments measured by employment was fairly slow. To be sure the estimated mean size grew by 73 percent between 1850 and 1880 but the average sizes—from 7.2 to 12.5 workers—were still small. Clearly, even as late as 1880 tiny establishments remained dominant in terms of numbers—approximately a quarter were sole proprietorships with the proprietor reported as the sole employee, while another 44 percent had between two and five workers. As a result of this dominance, the median establishment size in 1880 was three workers, having increased by just one worker from 1850 to 1880.

Panel A views the size distribution from the vantage point of the establishment as the unit of observation—one establishment, one observation. Panel

8. To be included in table 6.1, an establishment must be in the (a) "national" Atack-Bateman sample, (b) have reported value of output exceeding $500 nominal dollars (this was the cutoff used by the census), and (c) have positive reported employment. I have also excluded a small number (4) of establishments whose reported number of workers seems to be in error (too large to be credible). It is necessary to reweight the 1880 data in an attempt to correct for the underrepresentation of establishments in so-called "special agent" industries (see, for example, Atack, Bateman, and Margo 2004). My estimates of mean establishment size differ slightly from those implied by the figures on total number of establishments and total employment as published by the census; these differences are due to the fact that I am relying on sample evidence and, in particular, because of the adjustments discussed in the appendix.

Table 6.1   Establishment size distributions in manufacturing, 1850–1880 (Atack-Bateman sample evidence)

A. Establishments as the unit of observation

	Mean number of workers	Median number of workers	Percent with 1–2 workers	Percent with 3–5 workers	Percent with 6–15 workers	Percent with 16–100	Percent with 100 or more workers	Percent with 16 or more workers
1850	7.2	2	55.0	24.4	13.3	6.5	0.9	7.4
1860	8.3	2	54.6	23.1	13.8	7.3	1.2	8.5
1870	10.6	3	53.3	22.6	14.0	8.7	1.4	11.1
1880	12.5	3	45.3	25.0	17.1	10.1	2.4	12.5

B. Weighted by gross value of output

	Median	1–2 workers (%)	3–5 workers (%)	6–15 workers (%)	16–100 workers (%)	>100 workers (%)	16 or more workers (%)
1850	15	14.6	15.7	20.5	31.1	18.1	49.2
1860	25	11.9	14.4	16.3	32.8	24.7	57.5
1870	44	7.6	8.1	15.7	35.9	32.6	68.5
1880	42	6.6	8.6	13.9	38.4	32.5	70.9

Source: The Atack and Bateman (1999a) national samples of manufacturing establishments from the 1850–1880 manuscript censuses of manufacturing (panels A and B).

Notes: To be included in the table, observations (establishments) must meet certain criteria; see fn 6. The 1880 data are reweighted to correct for undersampling of establishments in special-agent industries (see fn 8); sample size in 1880 is the unweighted number of establishments, the weighted sample size is 7,184. For panel B, each establishment is weighted by its gross value of output. The number of workers in 1850–1860 is the sum of male and females; the number in 1870 and 1880 is the sum of adult males, adult females, and children. The 1880 data are reweighted (see above).

B offers a different look, in which establishments are weighted by the gross (nominal) value of their output.[9] Viewed in this manner, the shift toward larger firms was more dramatic (and continuous) over time. As early as 1850 almost half of the gross value of manufacturing output was produced in factories, as I have defined by the term. This increases to 70.9 percent in 1880 or by 21.7 percentage points from the level in 1850. The median establishment, judging by its contribution to total output, had fifteen workers in 1850, whereas its counterpart in 1880 had forty-two workers, or 2.8 times larger. Clearly, while larger establishments were not increasing their numbers all that quickly relative to small establishments, their relative share of gross output increased sharply after 1850.

The increase in size evident in table 6.1 could be due to shifts in industrial structure or geographic location—that is, to shifts in composition. To determine if this was the case, I estimated a panel regression in which the dependent variable takes the value one if the establishment was a factory (sixteen or more workers), and zero otherwise. I included dummy variables for the census year, three-digit standard industrial classification (SIC) code, the state in which the establishment was located, and urban status. The left-out census year dummy was 1850 and observations are weighted by gross value of output. The coefficient of the 1880 census year dummy in this regression was 0.197, or 19.7 percentage points, only slightly less than the increase shown in panel B of table 6.1 (21.7 percentage points). Thus, while compositional shifts played a role, most of the shift toward larger establishments was a general phenomenon.

For many, perhaps most economic historians, the shift toward larger-scale production, especially that shown in panel B, is prima facie evidence that economies of scale were present in some guise.[10] Fundamentally, economies of scale arise through division of labor and/or the use of indivisible inputs. Although there is no direct evidence of division of labor in the nineteenth-century American manufacturing censuses, there is indirect evi-

9. I do not report the weighted means in panel B as these are highly sensitive to the extreme values of the distribution of employment in any given year. The medians, however, are not sensitive in this sense and, as discussed in the text, these show a marked increase in size when establishments are weighted by gross value of output.

10. See Atack (1985). Atack applies the so-called "survivor method" in which the central concept is the "minimum efficient scale of production (MES)"—the smallest size establishment such that establishments larger than this were increasing (or nondecreasing) their share of aggregate production over time. If the MES is increasing over time, the presumption is that economies of scale are present. Atack frames his paper in terms of the debate over the "origins of the modern corporation" as told by Chandler (1977). According to Chandler, truly large scale production emerged late in the nineteenth century in response to fundamental changes in technology that were not in place until well after the Civil War. However, Atack (1985, 47) shows the typical plant at the end of the century was "little different from the scale required of an efficient plant in 1870" and that, with the exception of a few industries, the long-run growth in establishment size can be interpreted as a historical drift toward an equilibrium structure whose fundamental causes were put in play much earlier in the century.

dence suggested by differences in the demographic composition or in average wages by establishment size (Goldin and Sokoloff 1982; Atack, Bateman, and Margo 2004; Katz and Margo 2013). Evidence of indivisible inputs is suggested by the fact that the diffusion of the steam engine was positively correlated with establishment size, and that larger establishments generated greater labor productivity gains by using steam than did smaller establishments (Atack, Bateman, and Margo 2008).

A variety of causal factors contributed to the rise of large-scale production. As discussed by Hilt in this volume (chapter 2; see also Lamoreaux, chapter 1, this volume; Atack 2014) a changing legal and institutional environment made the corporate form increasing accessible, which may have eased access to the working and physical capital necessary for large-scale production. Such access was also enhanced by what was, for the era, a well-developed and vigorously expanding financial system (Rousseau and Sylla 2005). The "transportation revolution" (Taylor 1951)—canals, inland waterways and, especially, railroads—played a role; a recent econometric analysis (Atack, Haines, and Margo 2011) shows that factories became more prevalent when an area gained rail access. Technological advances in steam power—and, after 1880, in electrical power—were important. These advances enabled a more intricate division of labor, as well as dramatically raising labor productivity in larger establishments and associated levels of capital intensity (Goldin and Katz 1998; Atack, Bateman, and Margo 2008).

It is one thing to observe that scale economies were likely present because over time the average establishment had more workers and larger establishments were producing ever greater shares of total output. Pinning a number on these alleged scale economies is another thing entirely. The standard approaches to measuring economies of scale require the estimation of a cost or a production function. Because the census data provided only limited information on costs, most economic historians who have worked on this issue have chosen to estimate the production function. The first such studies were by Atack (1976, 1977) who reported estimates of production functions in 1850–1870 by industry-region cells. Using a variable scale parameter specification popular in econometrics at the time, Atack (1977) concluded that there were pervasive economies of scale present in 1850 but these were exhausted at relatively low levels of output and, consequently, in just five of the fourteen industry regions cells was the typical establishment operating in the range of increasing returns.[11] By 1860, however, the corresponding figure was nine of fourteen cells, suggesting that the optimal plant size was increasing before the Civil War.

---

11. A variable scale production function permits the econometrician to estimate the share of establishments operating in the region of decreasing returns. The most substantial evidence of decreasing returns is found for cotton textiles in 1850 in which 28 percent of establishments in the North and 19 percent in the South are deemed to be subject to (local) decreasing returns; see Atack (1977, 348).

Laurie and Schmitz (1981, 74–75) estimate Cobb-Douglas production functions using manuscript census data for Philadelphia in 1850 and 1880 and also some supplemental data for textiles in 1870. Laurie and Schmitz assume that workers reporting zero employees had, in fact, one employee, but this was the only adjustment they made to reported labor input. In eleven of seventeen industries in 1850 and thirteen of seventeen industries in 1880, Laurie and Schmitz reject the hypothesis of increasing or even constant returns to scale. Based on their regressions Laurie and Schmitz argue that American manufacturing in the nineteenth century was not characterized by scale economies, but rather the opposite. Later in the chapter I reproduce Laurie and Schmitz's general finding using the Atack-Bateman national samples, and also show that it is reversed if Sokoloff's proposed adjustment for entrepreneurial labor is implemented.

Sokoloff (1984) is next in line, but I defer detailed discussion until the next section except to note that Sokoloff argued that there were economies of scale in nonmechanized production in both 1820 and 1850 that typically were exhausted at relatively low levels of output. The implication of this finding, as previously noted, is that division of labor likely played some role in generating labor productivity growth in manufacturing after 1820 but truly large-scale production had to await fundamental advances in and widespread diffusion of steam power transmission and its associated machinery.

Finally, Atack (1987) is a comprehensive attempt to assess the extent of economies of scale using the census samples for 1820–1870 in their mid-1980s form.[12] This chapter, as previously, embraces Sokoloff's adjustment for the entrepreneurial input, although Atack later had second thoughts (see the next section). For the majority of industries in every census year that he examined, Atack found efficiency advantages to large-scale production—economies of scale—relative to small-scale production—artisan shops. Atack accounted for the persistence of small establishments by noting that many served markets that were protected from competition from more distant competitors by high shipping costs. Improvements in internal transportation and the diffusion of new technologies, such as steam, however, caused the market share of small establishments to erode over time.

Outside of the United States, the measurement of economies of scale in historical manufacturing has received the most attention by far in the French case. France is interesting because of the well-known hypothesis by Landes (1949, 1954) that nineteenth-century French manufacturing establishments were "too small" relative to their optimal size and that by failing to capture unexploited economies of scale, French economic growth suffered in the nineteenth century.

---

12. Subsequently, a census sample for 1880 was added and additional refinements made to the 1850–1870 samples; see Atack and Bateman (1999a). Currently the 1850–1880 samples and associated documentation are available to the public on Atack's Vanderbilt website.

Economic historians have evaluated the Landes hypothesis by attempting to estimate the extent of economies of scale using the two relevant French censuses from the nineteenth century, 1839–1845 and 1861–1865. Using a cost function approach applied to the census of 1861–1865, Nye (1987) found little evidence that there were economies of scale left to be exploited. However, using a production function approach, Sicsic (1994) does find evidence of unexploited scale economies in sectors where the average establishment size was small. The most recent study (Doraszelski 2004) splits the difference, arguing that there were some unexploited scale economies early in the nineteenth century but not in the second half of the century.

To summarize, census data for nineteenth-century US manufacturing indicated a pervasive shift toward larger establishments. The shift toward larger size strongly suggests the presence of economies of scale, but does not provide a "summary statistic" of their quantitative importance. With one exception (Laurie and Schmitz 1981), various studies using a production function approach find some evidence of economies of scale, although these were not always fully exploited. The strongest evidence of economies of scale is found by Sokoloff (1984) for as early as 1820. In the next section I argue that this evidence is not robust to the adjustment that he made for the alleged underreporting of the labor input by the census.

6.3   The "Entrepreneurial Labor Input Problem": Was the Labor Input of Entrepreneurs Properly Measured?

The measurement of economies of scale requires accurate information on factor inputs and outputs. In particular, if any inputs are systematically underreported in small versus large establishments, an econometric analysis that fails to correct for this might show evidence of decreasing returns even if the true production process exhibited increasing returns.

Sokoloff (1984) argued that just such a problem afflicted two nineteenth-century manufacturing censuses that he was analyzing, 1820 and 1850. Sokoloff was particularly interested in whether economies of scale were present in establishments that were nonmechanized or whether inanimate power was a precondition. If economies of scale were present in nonmechanized establishments, division of labor is the most likely explanation and factors that expanded market access—the transportation revolution—were critical for industrialization. But if scale economies generally required powered machinery, scholarly attention should shift to factors that made it easier for larger establishments to acquire such machinery—for example, improvements in financial markets or greater access to incorporation (Hilt, chapter 2, this volume).

Sokoloff (1984) argued that the labor input of entrepreneurs was not properly measured by the census in 1820 or 1850. There is sufficient information in the 1820 census to distinguish establishments that were sole proprietorships versus establishments that were two-person partnerships.[13] Sokoloff computed the difference in value added between sole proprietorships and two-person partnerships, controlling for the reported number of workers (but nothing else), for establishments reporting up to six workers. At each level of reported employment, output per worker was higher in partnership firms than in sole proprietorships. From this difference he concluded that the average number of workers reported in the census did not properly reflect the labor input of the partners relative to the sole proprietor; to correct for this it was necessary to inflate the labor input in small establishments. Otherwise, he observed, "firms with one worker would have the highest [measured] value added per worker" (Sokoloff 1984, 369, fn. 16).

For 1820, Sokoloff's correction was to add one to the count of workers if there was one owner listed or if the name of the firm was "Jones and Company"; two, if two owners listed; and three, if three or more owners were listed.[14] If the establishment was incorporated or a joint-stock company, Sokoloff assumed that it had a manager, and the manager was properly enumerated. In short, Sokoloff presumed that the owner(s) of the establishment, as a general rule, contributed their labor to production but were systematically excluded from the count of workers in 1820—in effect, that the census was measuring the labor input of employees, not that of the employers.

At the time Sokoloff wrote his paper he had no information on organizational form for the version of the 1850 sample that he analyzed, and thus he could provide no evidence similar to that for 1820 to convince the reader that the entrepreneurial labor input was not counted in 1850. Instead, he simply assumed this was so, and his correction for 1850 was simply to add one to the reported number of workers, on the theory that there was at least one owner per establishment (Sokoloff 1984, 375, fn. 21).[15]

As noted previously, Sokoloff was not the first economic historian to call attention to this alleged problem. Atack (1976; 1977, 344) asserted that

---

13. The key piece of information was the precise name of the establishment at the top of the census form. Atack (2014) uses similar information to measure the distribution of organizational forms for 1850–1870; see below where I use the 1850–1870 information to replicate Sokoloff's analysis of partnerships versus sole proprietorships.

14. In the 1850–1870 samples for which similar information has been inferred from the name of the establishment, some establishments were "family"-owned enterprises. Presumably there were also such establishments in 1820 but, if so, Sokoloff does not describe how he adjusted the labor input for these.

15. In their analysis of economics of scale in French manufacturing Sicsic (1994, 467) and Doraszelski (2004, 265) followed Sokoloff by adding one to their respective measures of the labor input; as best as can be determined from the published article, however, Nye made no adjustment for entrepreneurial labor. It is possible that this may explain why Nye found little or no evidence of scale economies in nineteenth-century France while Sicsic found the opposite; however, Doraszelski claims that the Sokoloff adjustment does not affect his substantive conclusions regarding scale economies and that a much more important issue is whether output is measured in value-added or gross value terms.

"proprietor and salaried managerial personnel" were "almost certainly excluded" in the 1850 and 1860 manufacturing census. Atack's proposed adjustment imputes managerial and supervisory workers based on the "ratio of [such] personnel to all employees reported in the 1890 census . . . subject to each firm being assigned at least one manager/proprietor[.]" According to Atack, the "returns to scale parameter" was "insensitive to changes in the labor input" induced by his adjustment (Atack 1976). Atack's adjustment is similar to Sokoloff's for 1850 (adding one to the count of workers) in that Atack's also adds at least one to each establishment count of workers, but for establishments with a sufficiently large number of employees, the adjustment will be greater than one because such establishments, based on the 1890 ratios, were more likely to employ managers and supervisors. Compared with Sokoloff's adjustment, therefore, which adds a uniform number—one—to each worker count, Atack's adjustment is closer to proportional, which may explain why he found no substantive effect on his estimates of returns to scale—unlike the case with Sokoloff's adjustment, as shown below.[16]

Every economic historian of the United States knows that nineteenth-century census data are fraught with error. With regard to the manufacturing censuses, the list of potential pitfalls is long and serious. Information on months of full-time operation is not reported prior to the Civil War, and information on daily hours of operation is not reported until 1880. As such, only in 1880 is it possible to construct even a rough estimate of annual labor input measured in hours (Atack and Bateman 1992; Atack, Bateman, and Margo 2002; Atack, Bateman, and Margo 2003). With the exception of some information on water and steam power, physical measures of the capital stock are not reported; instead, the capital figures, which are reported in dollars, refer to capital "invested" in the establishment, which could be book or market value or some combination of both, nor is it clear if the capital figures include or exclude working capital prior to 1890 (Gallman 1986; Atack 1977; Atack and Bateman 2008).

Given this laundry list of woes—which, to be clear, is just the highlights, not a complete list—why privilege the entrepreneurial labor input problem? Table 6.2, which reports parameters of Cobb-Douglas value-added production functions with and without Sokoloff's adjustment for the entrepreneurial labor input, provides the answer.[17] In panel A of table 6.2 I report the Cobb-Douglas scale

16. Even if one accepts Atack's reasoning, it is far from obvious that it is appropriate to apply 1890 employment ratios to the 1850 data. Unfortunately, the 1890 census was the first to separately report production and nonproduction workers.

17. The dependent variable in the regressions is the natural logarithm of value added. The independent variables are the logarithms of the labor input (variously defined, see the text), the logarithm of capital invested and dummy variables for three-digit SIC industry codes, urban status (= 1 if the establishment was located in an incorporated town or city with 2,500 or more population, 0 otherwise), and state. The purpose of including the geographic variables is to control for otherwise unexplained variation in value added due to variation in output prices (but see footnote 24).

Table 6.2   **Cobb-Douglas estimates of economies of scale, 1850–1880 (value-added production functions)**

A. Uses reported employment and capital

Sample	Number of observations	Scale parameter	Absolute value of t-statistic of scale parameter	Scale parameter	Absolute value of t-statistic of scale parameter
Sokoloff adjustment?		No		Yes	
1850	5,018	-0.056	5.54	0.093	7.45
1860	5,067	-0.007	0.69	0.131	10.29
1850–1860 pooled	10,085	-0.031	4.24	0.112	12.57
1870	3,858	-0.045	3.68	0.078	5.31
1880	7,178	-0.101	13.55	0.023	2.52
1870–1880 pooled	11,036	-0.081	12.70	0.042	5.53

B. Uses reported capital and demographically adjusted employment

Sample	Scale parameter	Absolute value of t-statistic of scale parameter	Scale parameter	Absolute value of t-statistic of scale parameter
Sokoloff adjustment?	No		Yes	
1850	-0.038	3.74	0.122	9.53
1860	0.011	1.05	0.163	12.48
1850–1860 pooled	-0.013	1.75	0.143	15.60
1870	-0.029	2.30	0.111	7.26
1880	-0.091	11.99	0.052	5.63
1870–1880 pooled	-0.068	10.58	0.073	9.20

C. Uses reported capital and demographically adjusted labor input, nonmechanized establishments

Sample	Number of observations	Scale parameter	Absolute value of t-statistic of scale parameter	Scale parameter	Absolute value of t-statistic of scale parameter
Sokoloff adjustment?		No	No	Yes	Yes
1850	2,814	-0.066	9.83	0.110	7.25
1860	1,595	-0.058	3.19	0.120	4.78
1850–1860 pooled	4,409	-0.061	5.64	0.115	8.70
1870	1,872	-0.096	4.89	0.071	2.81
1880	4,708	-0.149	15.28	0.023	1.87
1870–1880 pooled	6,580	-0.134	15.18	0.037	3.27

Source: For all panels, see text and Atack and Batemen (1999a).

Notes: For panel A, to be included in the regression the establishment has to meet the sample restrictions indicated in footnote 8 and, in addition, report positive values of capital invested, value of raw materials, and value added; in addition, establishments with unusually high or low estimated rates of return to capital invested are excluded. Dependent variable is logarithm of value added (value of outputs − value of raw materials). Scale parameter: sum of the coefficients of ln (labor) + ln (capital) − 1 from an OLS regression of ln (value added) on ln (labor) and ln (capital). Labor in 1850 and 1860 is the sum of reported male and female employees. Labor in 1870 and 1880 is the sum of adult men, adult females, and children. All regressions include dummy variables for urban status (= 1 if establishment is located in incorporated town or city with population of 2,500 or more, 0 otherwise), state, and three-digit SIC industry code. The 1880 data are reweighted to correct for undersampling of special agent industries. For panel B, demographically adjusted labor input without Sokoloff adjustment: men + 0.6*women in 1850 and 1860; men + 0.5*women + 0.33*children in 1870 and 1880. Sokoloff adjustment: add one to demographically adjusted labor input. For panel C, nonmechanized, 1850–1870: as indicated by the Atack-Bateman variable MPOWER = 3 (hand power) or MPOWER = 4 (animal power). In 1880: nonmechanized establishments are inferred from the absence of steam or water horsepower in production.

parameter, which is the sum of the coefficients of labor and capital minus one, along with its associated t-statistic. In column (2), the labor input is the sum of the number of male and female workers in 1850 and 1860, and the number of adult male, adult women, and children in 1870 and 1880. As can be seen in column (2), not only is there is no evidence for economies of scale, the evidence is overwhelmingly for the opposite—decreasing returns to scale. Column (2), in effect, replicates Laurie and Schmitz (1981) for the whole country rather than just Philadelphia and arrives at the same conclusion. The situation is very different in column (4) of panel A where I implement Sokoloff's adjustment, adding one to the count of workers. Now the evidence is strongly in favor of economies of scale and, with the exception of 1880, these are substantial.

Most economic historians who have estimated production functions from the nineteenth-century manufacturing data have preferred a modified total of the number of workers, which weights female and child workers less than male workers—that is, in "adult-male-equivalent" units. The presumption is that female and child workers were less skilled, on average, than male workers. Such an adjustment to the count of workers will also have implications for estimates of economies of scale because, as first demonstrated by Goldin and Sokoloff (1982; see also Katz and Margo 2013), the female/child share of workers was increasing in establishment size—larger establishments were more likely to employ women and children than small establishments.[18]

Accordingly, in panel B, I replicate the analysis in panel A using a demographically adjusted version of the labor input. Without the Sokoloff adjustment the scale parameter is now closer to zero than in panel A but it is still negative and significantly so, except in 1860 where the parameter is slightly positive (but insignificant). Applying the Sokoloff adjustment, the evidence for scale economies is stronger than in panel A.

In panel C, I replicate the analysis in panel B for the subsample of establishments that were nonmechanized—that is, made no use of water or steam power in production. This is as close as the census data permit of a test of pure division of labor in generating economies of scale. Again, the crucial effect of the Sokoloff adjustment is clearly evident on the magnitude of the scale parameter. If the adjustment is used, there is evidence of economies of scale even for nonpowered establishments, except perhaps in 1880. If it is not used, there are diseconomies of scale across the board.

---

18. Behind this adjustment is an assumption that larger establishments engaged in division of labor, substituting less skilled workers—women and children—and machines for the skilled male labor of the artisan. While the adjustment is plausible, it is also not fully adequate to account for differences in skill composition between small and large establishments because no adjustment is made for such differences among adult males. See Atack, Bateman, and Margo (2004) who argue that additional information on variations in skill composition by establishment size can be inferred from differences in average earnings (or what Atack, Bateman, and Margo call the "establishment wage").

The upshot of table 6.2 is that, for the 1850–1880 manufacturing samples, the presence of scale economies as an average treatment effect is not robust to Sokoloff's adjustment. Fundamentally, this nonrobustness arises because, as Sokoloff pointed out himself, measured labor productivity in very small establishments is high relative to very large establishments, making it difficult for any parametric procedure (e.g., OLS estimation of a Cobb-Douglas production function) to find economies of scale. Assuming this cross-sectional pattern to be a flaw in the census data rather than historical fact, one could imagine "corrections" for it other than Sokoloff's, but implementing these would either be difficult (or impossible) with the available information.[19]

Another alternative is to identify subsets of the census data for which a conclusion of economies of scale is robust without Sokoloff's adjustment. I explored this possibility using the 1870 sample.[20] There are two basic findings. First, if one is willing to restrict the econometrics to establishments with between two and fifty workers, there is robust evidence of economies of scale on average for powered (steam or water) establishments, but not for nonpowered establishments.[21] Second, at the two-digit industry level, there is robust evidence of economies of scale overall for powered establishments in the textile industry, but not otherwise. For an economic historian whose prior is that the emergence of large-scale production was a

---

19. For example, one could argue that some very small establishments had high output prices, either because they possessed local monopoly power or for other reasons; to correct for this, one could value output at national prices. In theory this could be done for 1850–1870 because the Atack-Bateman samples report physical output as well as values. But the enormous diversity of manufacturing output makes this conceptually as well as empirically difficult to implement. One could also argue that the effective labor input in large establishments was much lower than reported because of division of labor and that the demographic adjustment used in table 6.2 is very inadequate as a correction for this because a majority of establishments did not hire female or child workers (see Atack, Bateman, and Margo 2004). While this is certainly true, designing a defensible and robust correction for skill composition with respect to establishment size is arguably asking for more than the census data can deliver.

20. An appendix summarizing the results of the exploration in a table is available from Robert A. Margo on request. In brief, I estimate Cobb-Douglas value-added production functions like those reported in table 6.2, except that I restrict the analysis either to a subset of the data defined in terms of the reported number of workers by mechanization status (e.g., two to fifty workers, nonmechanized, or two to fifty workers using steam or water power) or at the two-digit (SIC code) industry level. The labor input in the regressions is adjusted for demographic composition as in table 6.2. The 1870 sample is good for this purpose because there is greater demographic detail on the labor input, allowing a better adjustment for skill than for the pre–Civil War censuses; unlike the 1880 data, no reweighting is necessary to correct for undersampling in particular industries (there were no "special agent" industries in 1870) and there is information about months of operation (allowing one to distinguish full- from part-year establishments; see Atack, Bateman, and Margo [2002]).

21. For nonpowered establishments with two to fifty workers, the scale parameter is –0.021 ($|t| = 0.70$). For mechanized establishments with two to fifty workers, the scale parameter is 0.114 ($|t| = 3.08$). However, if the regression for mechanized establishments is reestimated with a linear control for the number of months that the establishment operated, the scale parameter is 0.040 and is statistically insignificant. Larger establishments, in other words, were more likely to operate full year than part year (see Atack, Bateman, and Margo 2002).

major factor in American industrial ascendancy, these are disappointing results.[22]

Data problems in economic history range from the trivial to the highly consequential. The entrepreneurial labor input problem is an example of the latter. The beauty of Sokoloff's proposed adjustment is its simplicity; by itself, it generates strong evidence of economies of scale as an average treatment effect. In light of this, it is easy to see why the adjustment would have been favored by economic historians in the 1980s, given the prevailing wisdom at the time about census enumeration practices. In the next section, I argue that this prevailing wisdom was in error.

6.4   Is Sokoloff's Adjustment Warranted? Textual and Statistical Evidence

The analysis in the preceding section demonstrates that Sokoloff's proposed adjustment for the alleged undercount of entrepreneurial labor has a quantitatively large and significant effect on the estimated magnitude of the scale parameter in Cobb-Douglas production functions estimated from the Atack-Bateman nineteenth-century census manufacturing samples. As appealing as the results are when the adjustment is made, it cannot be justified on such grounds. Rather, the adjustment is justified if evidence, direct or circumstantial, may be found that the census did, in fact, fail to include the labor of entrepreneurs. In addressing this issue, it is useful to divide up the problem into two parts. Part one concerns the enumeration of labor in firms that are identified as sole proprietorships, while part two concerns the enumeration of the labor input of partnerships and other organizational forms.

One direct way to address whether an adjustment is warranted is to examine the written instructions to enumerators to see if these gave sufficient guidance as to whom to count as a worker (or not). To be sure, economic historians who hang their hats on the census instructions to enumerators do so at their own peril. The instructions were notoriously sketchy and there is no assurance that they were followed in the field—indeed, as I show below, there is evidence in the case at hand that they were not always followed. That said, the textural evidence does suggest that enumerators were expected to count

22. In addition to the findings for 1870, I also performed some additional regressions for 1850 and 1860. Specifically, if the analysis is restricted to mechanized establishments (steam or water power), there is evidence of economies of scale in 1850 and 1860 (pooled sample) if one includes industry dummies but not geographic controls (that is, the urban and state dummies; the scale parameter is 0.069 ($|t| = 5.11$)). Excluding the geographic dummies assumes, in effect, that geographic variation in value added unexplained by the labor and capital inputs or industry affiliation reflects true variation in total factor productivity (such as might be due to agglomeration economies in the case of an urban location) rather than variation in output prices. This seems a rather extreme assumption for the antebellum United States, in which there were large (albeit narrowing) regional differences in output and factor prices; see Berry (1943) and Margo (2000). It should also be kept in mind that it is not possible to control for months of operation in 1850 or 1860 and, judging from the 1870 analysis, this could explain the positive scale parameter.

sole proprietors as "workers"—that is, for sole proprietorships, the reported number of workers should be at least one.

The specific textual evidence comes from the instructions to enumerators that pertain to wages and to which establishments were at risk of being enumerated, and are taken from Wright's (1900) compilation. As to the former, consider for example, the instructions for questions no. 10 and no. 11 in 1850 and 1860, which reads as follows:

> 10, 11. Wages—Under 10, and 11, entitled Wages, is to be inserted the average Monthly amount paid for all the labor of all the hands, male and female, employed in the business or manufacture during the course of the year. In all cases where the employer boards the hands, the usual charge of board is to be added to the wages, so that cost of labor is always to mean the amount paid, whether in money or partly in money and partly in board; and the average number of hands and the average monthly wages to be returned, so that by dividing the latter by the former the result will show the average earnings of individuals. This is also to be included in the individual labor of a producer, working on his own account, whose productions are separately enumerated. (Wright 1900, 313–14)

A plausible reading of this paragraph is that, for sole proprietors working alone ("the individual labor of a producer, working on his own account, whose productions are separately enumerated") meeting the test for inclusion in the census, the labor input should have been reported at exactly one worker.[23] The test for inclusion, which is what the phrase "separately enumerated" at the end of the quotation is referring to, was specified in 1850 and 1860: separate enumeration was to occur as long as "annual productions" exceeded $500.00 in gross value. This was further clarified in 1870:

> The smallest shop must not be omitted, provided the production reaches $500 annually, including the cost of materials. It is believed that but few shops which employ the labor of one able-bodied artisan, fall short of this limit at the present prices of labor. Assistant Marshals will take pains to reach all the productive establishments, large and small, within their subdivisions. It is not necessary that there should be a distinct shop to constitute an establishment of productive industry in the meaning of the law. A room finished off in the barn, or a chest of tools kept in the corner of the house, may constitute a distinct establishment, provided the artisan does not habitually work in any other shop which could be separately enumerated. (Wright 1900, 162)

In sum, the census made provision for counting sole proprietors properly as workers if the owner, "working on his own account," was sufficiently pro-

---

23. Certainly there is no doubt that sole proprietorships were at risk of being enumerated because, at the top of the census form in, say, 1850, the "owner of the establishment, or business inquired into, either individual, company or corporation" was to be inserted.

ductive to have the establishment enumerated as a separate manufacturing entity.

Data on the distribution of establishment sizes from the 1850–1870 Atack-Bateman samples supports the conclusion that the labor input of sole proprietors in these circumstances was counted properly most of the time. As Atack and Bateman (1999b) first noted, if such workers were *not* counted even when their establishments met the condition to be enumerated—$500 in gross value—we should expect to see a great many zeroes in the distribution of employment across establishments, because sole proprietorships were ubiquitous in nineteenth-century manufacturing.[24] There is no question that there are "zeros" in the distribution of workers hired in the Atack-Bateman samples. These are more common after the Civil War—4.2 percent in 1870 and 5.2 percent in 1880—possibly because the census seems to have been more relentless in canvassing the "smallest shops," as the above instruction to enumerators suggests. Before the war, however, zeros are uncommon—in the 1850 and 1860 Atack-Bateman samples, less than 1 percent of the establishments report having zero workers.[25]

Obviously, zero is the wrong answer for any firm of any size. For sole proprietorships reporting zero workers, therefore, a plausible approach is to impute one worker.[26] For sole proprietorships already reporting one worker, however, it is not credible to change the one to two workers, because then the distribution of establishment sizes will have too few one-worker establishments.[27] This is the fundamental problem with Sokoloff's blanket adjustment.

That said, one can find instances of sole proprietorships with one worker in which the "worker" was probably not the proprietor. In the 1870 Atack-Bateman sample, there are six establishments that are identified as sole proprietorships with one worker—except that the worker is a child. Almost surely these are errors—the worker was an apprentice, not the owner.[28] For these establishments, the count of workers could be changed to "two" but

---

24. Atack (2014, table 17.1) estimates that 83 percent of manufacturing establishments in 1850 were sole proprietorships; the share declined over the next two decades, but was still very substantial at 78 percent in 1870.

25. The exact proportions are 0.65 percent in 1850 and 0.81 percent in 1860—that is, in both cases less than 1 percent of establishments report "0" as the number of workers. These figures pertain to the Atack-Bateman "national samples" and thus are nationally representative of the population of surviving manuscript schedules of manufacturing.

26. See Laurie and Schmitz (1981). Alternatively, one can simply exclude establishments with missing data on any relevant variable, such as employment; this is the procedure followed by Atack, Bateman, and Margo in their various papers.

27. See Inwood and Keay (2012) for a very similar analysis in the case of the 1871 Canadian census of manufactures. Inwood and Keay also argue that, in the case of the Canadian census, the enumerator instructions called for counting the labor input of entrepreneurs when it was economically relevant. Inwood and Keay find little evidence, as well, of establishments reporting zero workers in the Canadian data.

28. One can also find sole proprietorships in which the one worker is female. It is less clear whether these are errors.

the substantive effect is minimal because there are very few such observations in 1870.

I conclude that, on the basis of the textual and distributional evidence, it would appear that the labor input in sole proprietorships was enumerated correctly, at least most of the time. However, this leaves open the question of whether the census enumerated the labor input correctly in partnership or other types of establishments.

In particular, what are we to make of Sokoloff's observation that, in the 1820 census, establishments with two owners had higher value added per worker than sole proprietorships, controlling for the reported number of workers? Sokoloff showed this was the case in 1820 but was unable to investigate this issue for 1850. Subsequently, Atack added the information on ownership to the 1850–1870 samples, so it is possible to replicate Sokoloff's 1820 analysis for the later census years.[29]

Table 6.3 reports the coefficients of a dummy variable for dual (two-person) partnerships in a regression of the logarithm of value added for establishments with one reported worker. For each year I show the coefficient and its associated t-statistic with no additional controls in the regression, with controls for location and industry, and finally, capital invested. The results with no controls are intended to replicate the specification used by Sokoloff, which simply compared output per worker between the two organizational forms, holding the reported number of workers constant.

For 1850–1870 I find the same general pattern that Sokoloff did—namely, that output is higher in partnership establishments versus single proprietorships, even though ostensibly these are all establishments with just one worker. That said, all but one of the coefficients is statistically insignificant at conventional levels; even this is no longer the case once controls for industry, location, and capital invested are included. Note that the inclusion of these controls generally reduces the magnitude of the partnership effect, which suggests that the partnership dummy variable could easily be capturing unmeasured factors associated with higher output that had nothing to do with a higher level of the labor input. It is difficult to conclude on the basis of the statistical evidence in table 6.3 that an adjustment for the entrepreneurial labor input is warranted.

6.5   The Meaning of the Labor Input in the Nineteenth-Century Manufacturing Censuses: Evidence from 1880

I have argued that the textual, distributional, and statistical evidence does not favor the adjustment for entrepreneurial labor advocated by Sokoloff (1984). However, that does not end the matter because, rather surprisingly, there is evidence that the census understated the labor input in small

29. See Atack (2014) for further analysis of the ownership information.

Table 6.3   **The difference in value added: Sole proprietorships versus dual partnerships, one reported adult male worker (1850–1870)**

Year	Sample size (estab.)	Dual = 1	Controls	Coefficient of dual partnership dummy	Absolute value of t-statistic
1850	992	0.037	None	0.230	2.12
1850			Location + industry dummies	0.128	1.08
1850			Ln (capital) + location and industry dummies	0.130	1.24
1860	985	0.052	None	0.145	1.56
1860			Location + industry	0.163	1.76
1860			Ln (capital) + location + industry dummies	0.142	1.59
1870	615	0.031	None	0.319	1.64
1870			Location + industry dummies	0.314	1.59
1870			Ln (capital) + location + industry dummies	0.183	0.99
1870	390	0.041	Ln (capital) + location + industry dummies, full year establishments	0.160	0.83

Source: See text and Atack and Bateman (1999a).

establishments relative to large, although for a very different reason than claimed by Sokoloff.

In 1880 the census asked a question about employment that it had not asked previously and, to the best of my knowledge, has not asked since. This question ascertained the *maximum* number of workers employed at the establishment at any point in time during the census year. To understand why the answers to this question are useful in shedding light on whether a Sokoloff-like adjustment to the measured labor input is defensible, it is necessary to look again at the instructions to enumerators, this time at those pertaining specifically to the measurement of the labor input.

Consider, for example, the relevant instructions in 1850 and 1860. "These numbers"—male and female workers—"are to be estimated either by an average of the whole year, or by selecting a day when about an average number was employed, and inserting the number on such day as the average. You will observe that the enumeration of hands is not to apply to any particular day but to express the average number employed throughout the year." The instructions here were not changed for 1870 and 1880, except that in both years separate information was collected on adult males, adult females, and child workers.

Although it is certainly possible that some establishments reported a literally correct average of the number of workers, the answers to the additional question in 1880 suggest, rather, that the numbers reported were "typical"—that is, workers present on a day "when about an average number was employed." To see this, consider the subset of establishments in the 1880 Atack-Bateman sample with one reported worker who was an adult male that claimed to have been in operation for the full year (twelve full-time equivalent months). It is possible to identify such establishments because the 1880 census also asked (in detail) about months of full-time equivalent operation. By definition, these establishments did not shut down at any point during the year so they could not have experienced a period of time during which the number of workers fell (temporarily) to zero, the only integer below the average reported (one). If the one worker as reported was the true average, there should not be any establishments that report a maximum number of workers greater than one. However, 43 percent of these establishments claimed to have had a maximum number of workers greater than one at some point during the year (fully 15 percent reported a maximum of three or more). Conditional on reporting a maximum greater than one, the mean was 2.5 and the median was two.

The reporting of a maximum number of workers exceeding the average was not confined to the subset of one worker, full-year establishments just described. As the first row of panel A of table 6.4 shows, substantial fractions just short of a majority did so, regardless of size. But as the second row of panel A shows, the percentage difference between the maximum and the average declined sharply with the average number of workers.

Table 6.4   **Analysis of 1880 question on maximum employment**

A. Average versus maximum employment, sample statistics

Reported average number of workers	1	2–5	6–15	16 or more
Weighted sample mean of maximum number of workers	1.646	3.71	11.66	57.2
Weighted sample mean of average number of workers	1	2.83	8.96	47.6
Weighted sample mean of [(maximum – average)/average] × 100 percent	64.6	31.7	29.4	24.4
Percent reporting maximum > average	43.1	38.8	46.9	52.0
Number of establishments	1,102	1,719	475	207

B. Ln (value added) regressions, 1880 establishments hiring only adult males, full-year operation (by average number of workers reported)

Reported average number of workers	1	1	2–5	6–15	16 or more
Maximum number of workers	0.088	0.064	0.038	0.017	0.006
	(0.019)	(0.018)	(0.009)	(0.004)	(0.006)
Ln (capital)		0.169	0.221	0.216	0.247
		(0.019)	(0.016)	(0.030)	(0.037)
Ln (no. of workers)			0.631	0.618	0.616
			(0.058)	(0.118)	(0.103)
Adjusted R-square	0.262	0.317	0.517	0.452	0.768

Source: For both panels, see text and Atack and Bateman (1999a).

Notes: In panel A, in addition to standard sample inclusion criteria in table 6.1 (panel A), establishments had to operate for twelve full-time equivalent months and only employ male workers. Data are reweighted to correct for underreporting of special-agent industries (see text for panel A in table 6.1). In panel B, data are reweighted (see text for panel A in table 6.1).

The potential for bias, in other words, appears greater for the smallest establishments.[30]

In panel B, I report coefficients from a regression of the logarithm of value added for establishments in 1880 that operated for the full twelve months of the year. As in panel A, I only focus on establishments that hired adult males in order to avoid complications that arise because of adjustments to

---

30. Let $M(N)$ be the maximum number hired for establishments with an average number of workers equal to N. By definition (and empirically) the distributions of $M(N)$ are right-skewed. For the smallest establishments, the empirical distributions are smooth and steeply decreasing. For example, among firms hiring one worker on average and reporting M greater than one, fully two-thirds hired exactly one additional worker (that is, a maximum ever employed of two workers) and another 21 percent hired exactly two additional workers (a maximum of thirteen). But among firms with, say, fifteen workers on average but hiring additional workers during the year, the first mode was not sixteen but rather twenty—that is, five additional workers (the second mode was ten or a maximum of twenty-five). In other words, when larger establishments hired occasional workers, it appears these were added in discrete chunks or multiples of the average, which might reflect additional shifts.

worker characteristics. The regressions include dummies for urban status, state, and SIC industry code.

In the first column, I include the maximum number of workers in the regression for one-worker establishments, but do not control for capital invested. The marginal impact of an additional worker hired in this manner is to add about 8.8 percent to value added, and the effect is statistically significant. If we make the assumption that these additional workers were as productive *per day employed* as was the one average worker year round, the coefficient can be interpreted as the fraction of the year that the maximum was employed—in this case, 8.8 percent of the work year, or about one month. Economically speaking, this seems long enough to make a difference to measured output, but not long enough to warrant inclusion as a "typical" worker.

The current version of the 1880 Atack-Bateman sample does not include information on the organization of the firm, as do the 1850–1870 samples. However, if some of the firms reporting a maximum greater than two were partnerships, it stands to reason that they would have more capital invested, which could account for some of the effect of extra workers evident in column (1). As column (2) shows, when I control for capital invested, the effect diminishes to about 6.4 percent, but it is still statistically significant.

The remaining columns in the table repeat the same regression for establishments of larger size. For these regressions I also include the log of the number of average number of workers, since the bin sizes include establishments of different size, unlike the first two columns. As can be seen, having a maximum greater than the average contributes in a statistically significant way for establishments with two to five average workers, and even six to fifteen workers. But the effect is declining in size, and is entirely absent for establishments with sixteen or more workers.

The fact that the maximum number hired contributes less to output as size increases and eventually vanishes is consistent with an asymmetric measurement error interpretation. For a firm with, say, a reported average of twenty workers and a maximum of twenty-four, it is entirely possible—indeed probable—that at some point during the year, *fewer* than twenty persons were at work. That is, even if the larger establishments were also reporting the "typical" number of employees instead of a true average, the typical number for a large establishment is a better estimate—less biased, and possibly not at all—than it is for a small establishment.

Obviously, the evidence in table 6.4 pertains solely to 1880; it is simply not known (and probably unknowable) whether the same phenomenon was present in the early years. However, because the wording of the employment question did not change and because there is some association between organizational form and value added, as shown in table 6.4, it is quite plausible that the same bias is present in 1850 through 1870.

In summary, Sokoloff (1984) was correct that some adjustment to the reported labor input in manufacturing is needed, but was wrong about the reason. The adjustment is greater in size for smaller establishments, and thus serves to lower the level of labor productivity in such establishments relative to larger ones. The size of adjustment, however, is much smaller than Sokoloff advocated and, consequently, any correction for it has a much smaller effect on the estimated returns to scale.

A simple way to make this point is to add the term for the bias in percentage terms, (Maximum Labor – Average Labor)/Average Labor, to the conventional Cobb-Douglas value-added production for 1880, and to compare the returns to scale parameter with and without this additional variable. For this exercise, I adjust the labor input for its demographic composition, as in panel C of table 6.2, and I also include dummy variables for urban status, state, and SIC industry code. If the bias term is not included, the returns to scale parameter is –0.089 (as shown in panel C of table 6.2). If it is included, the returns to scale parameter is –0.072. Thus, correcting for the asymmetric measurement error in the labor input increases the estimated scale parameter by about 19 percent (in absolute value), but the parameter is still significantly (and well) less than one.

6.6   Concluding Remarks

In a famous paper Sokoloff (1984) argued that the labor input of entrepreneurs was not properly counted by the census and, therefore, labor productivity in small establishments, particularly those not using inanimate power, was considerably overstated. He proposed an elaborate correction for this alleged bias in 1820 but had to make do with a much simpler adjustment—adding one to the count of workers—in 1850. Initially, economic historians were favorably disposed to his correction (Atack 1987) but as research continued doubts set in, with no resolution. This chapter has taken a fresh look at the controversy using data that were not available to Sokoloff (1984) or his chief critics (Atack and Bateman 1999b) at the time. After evaluating textual and statistical evidence for the period 1850–1880, I conclude that Sokoloff's particular adjustment cannot be justified. Without the adjustment the evidence from the census for economies of scale on average in nineteenth-century American manufacturing adduced from production function estimates is not robust. That said, Sokoloff was correct that the labor input in very small establishments was biased upward, but not for the reason he thought. There is an upward bias because most establishments in nineteenth-century manufacturing appear to have reported the "typical" number of workers rather than a true average. Using novel data for 1880, I show that this tendency understates the labor input in small establishments relative to large. A correction for this is warranted but by itself does not deliver parametric evidence of returns to scale.

The findings of this chapter can be seen as half empty (negative) or half full (positive). On the half-empty side, the nineteenth-century manufacturing censuses are among the great historical documents of US economic history but the information in them does not seem up to the task to reliably summarize differences in productivity between small and large establishments in a parametric—that is, production function—framework. In particular, economic historians who believe that division of labor by itself generated significant widespread productivity gains from the very beginning of the American industrial revolution will likely have to forgo their systematic measurement from the census, relying instead on case studies or extrapolation back in time from much better, noncensus evidence from late in the century.[31]

On the half-full side, perhaps economic historians have made too much of the "rise of big business" as a crucial feature of the growth of American manufacturing in the nineteenth century. Taken at face value, the census data suggest that very small establishments remained quite productive throughout the nineteenth century even as the distribution of establishment sizes was shifting toward larger firms.[32] American manufacturing had its behemoths, but the success of the industrial sector in the nineteenth century may have owed much to having exceptionally productive artisan shops. Rather than dismissing these as data artifacts, future research might profitably concentrate on the underlying sources of differences in productivity across very small establishments at points in time as well as changes in their productivity over time.

31. An important example is the US Department of Labor (1899), an extraordinary study of differences in labor productivity between establishments using hand versus machine methods of production conducted by the department in the late nineteenth century. The department collected detailed data on each step in the production of a very specific product—manila envelopes, for example—when made entirely by hand versus machine, including the amount of time of each step, the number (and characteristics) of workers employed at each step, and the specific capital goods used. Atack (1987) provides some limited comparisons of hand and machine productivity using these data noting that they seem to imply a much larger effect of scale than the census manufacturing data do. Other than Atack (1987), these data have been almost wholly neglected by economic historians. See Atack, Margo, and Rhode (2014) for a preliminary analysis of these data. The unit of analysis is the product by type of labor (hand versus machine) and the dependent variable is the logarithm of the amount of time needed to produce one unit of the good. Atack, Margo, and Rhode (2014) estimate a regression of this dependent variable on the total number of workers that shows a large, negative coefficient—that is, establishments with more workers produce each unit of a product more quickly or equivalently, more units in a given period (the regression includes product fixed effects). This is much clearer evidence of economies of scale in nineteenth-century manufacturing than can be adduced from the census data. If a dummy variable for machine production is included in the regression, the coefficient on the number of workers is halved in size. Because the steps in production are known, it is possible to construct summary measures of the division of labor (number of tasks per worker, total number of tasks). Including these summary measures in the regression changes the sign of the number of workers to positive but the coefficient is no longer significant. The Atack, Margo, and Rhode (2014) preliminary analysis of the BLS data suggests, therefore, that larger establishments were more productive than smaller establishments, and that mechanization and division of labor both contributed to the productivity advantage.

32. Selection/survivor bias may be an important part of this story. Specifically, as very small establishments were being displaced, only the most productive remained in business. Small firms were very risky enterprises; this and selection bias could go some distance in explaining why their ex-post rates of return were quite high relative to larger establishments (see Atack and Bateman 2008). I am grateful to William Collins for this point.

Appendix

Beginning in 1850, it was the goal of the census to include the smallest establishments, those with one worker, in its enumeration of manufacturing, as long as the minimum cutoff of $500 of gross value of output was met. Its intentions aside, the census believed that its enumeration of very small establishments was less than complete before the Civil War, and it sought to improve coverage in 1870. Evidence that it was successful can be found in changes after the war in the relative distribution of one- versus two-worker establishments. In both the 1870 and 1880 Atack-Bateman samples, one-worker establishments are more numerous than two-worker establishments. However, the reverse is true in the 1850 and 1860 samples. It seems unlikely that the postbellum shift reflects underlying economic trends; a more likely explanation is that one-worker establishments were undercounted in 1850 and 1860. To estimate the missing one-worker establishments in 1850 and 1860, I assume that the ratio of establishments with two workers to establishments with one worker is the same as in the 1870 Atack-Bateman national sample, meeting the sampling criteria indicated in footnote 8; this ratio is 1.334. For panel A of table 6.1, I multiply 1.334 by the number of two-worker establishments in 1850 and 1860, to generate revised estimates of the total number (rounded to the nearest integer) of one-worker establishments and adjust the overall frequency distributions accordingly. I do the same in panel B, also assuming that the average gross output of the additional one-worker establishments is the same as for the one-worker establishments reported in the census.

References

Atack, Jeremy. 1976. "Estimation of Economies of Scale in Nineteenth-Century United States Manufacturing and the Form of the Production Function." PhD diss., Department of Economics, University of Illinois.
———. 1977. "Returns to Scale in Antebellum Manufacturing." *Explorations in Economic History* 14:337–59.
———. 1985. "Industrial Structure and the Emergence of the Modern Industrial Corporation." *Explorations in Economic History* 22:29–52.
———. 1987. "Economies of Scale and Efficiency Gains in the Rise of the Factory in America, 1820–1900." In *Quantity and Quiddity: Essays in Honor of Stanley Lebergott*, edited by P. Kilby, 286–335. Middletown, CT: Wesleyan University Press.
———. 2014. "America: Capitalism's Promised Land." In *The Cambridge History of Capitalism, Volume 1: The Rise of Capitalism from Ancient Origins to 1848*, edited by L. Neal and J. G. Williamson. New York: Cambridge University Press.
Atack, Jeremy, and Fred Bateman. 1992. "How Long was the Work Day in 1880?" *Journal of Economic History* 21:129–60.

————. 1999a. "Nineteenth-Century American Industrial Development through the Eyes of the Census of Manufactures: A New Resource for Historical Research." *Historical Methods* 32:177–88.

————. 1999b. "Profitability and Firm Size: The Small Firm Effect in the Nineteenth Century." Working Paper, Department of Economics, Vanderbilt University.

————. 2008. "Profitability, Firm Size, and Business Organization in Nineteenth-Century US Manufacturing." In *Quantitative Economic History: The Good of Counting*, edited by J. Rosenbloom, 54–77. New York: Routledge.

Atack, Jeremy, Fred Bateman, and Robert A. Margo. 2002. "Part-Year Operation in Nineteenth-Century American Manufacturing: Evidence from the 1870 and 1880 Censuses." *Journal of Economic History* 62:792–809.

————. 2003. "Productivity in Manufacturing and the Length of the Working Day: Evidence from the 1880 Census of Manufactures." *Explorations in Economic History* 40:170–94.

————. 2004. "Skill Intensity and Rising Wage Dispersion in Nineteenth-Century American Manufacturing." *Journal of Economic History* 64:172–92.

————. 2008. "Steam Power, Establishment Size, and Labor Productivity in Nineteenth-Century American Manufacturing." *Explorations in Economic History* 45:185–98.

Atack, Jeremy, Michael Haines, and Robert A. Margo. 2011. "Railroads and the Rise of the Factory: Evidence for the United States, 1850–1870." In *Economic Evolution and Revolution in Historical Time*, edited by P. Rhode, J. Rosenbloom, and D. Weiman, 162–79. Palo Alto, CA: Stanford University Press.

Atack, Jeremy, Robert A. Margo, and Paul W. Rhode. 2014. "The Division of Labor and Economies of Scale in Late Nineteenth-Century US Manufacturing: New Evidence." Unpublished working paper presented at the NBER Development of the American Economy Summer Institute, Cambridge, Massachusetts, July.

Berry, Thomas Senior. 1943. *Western Prices before 1861: A Study of the Cincinnati Market*. Cambridge, MA: Harvard University Press.

Broadberry, Stephen, and Douglas Irwin. 2006. "Labor Productivity in the United States and the United Kingdom during the Nineteenth Century." *Explorations in Economic History* 43:257–79.

Chandler, Alfred. 1977. *The Visible Hand: The Managerial Revolution in American Business*. Cambridge, MA: Harvard University Press.

Doraszelski, Ulrich. 2004. "Measuring Returns to Scale in Nineteenth-Century French Industry." *Explorations in Economic History* 41:256–81.

Fishbein, Meyer. 1973. *The Censuses of Manufactures, 1810–1890*. National Archives and Records Service Information Paper no. 67, General Services Administration. http://www.worldcat.org/title/censuses-of-manufactures-1810-1890/oclc/3880842/editions?referer=di&editionsView=true.

Gallman, Robert. 1986. "The United States Capital Stock in the Nineteenth Century." In *Long-Term Factors in American Economic Growth*, edited by S. Engerman and R. Gallman, 165–206. Chicago: University of Chicago Press.

Goldin, Claudia, and Lawrence F. Katz. 1998. "The Origins of Technology-Skill Complementarity." *Quarterly Journal of Economics* 113:693–732.

Goldin, Claudia, and Kenneth Sokoloff. 1982. "Women, Children, and Industrialization in the Early Republic: Evidence from the Manufacturing Censuses." *Journal of Economic History* 42:741–74.

Inwood, Kris, and Ian Keay. 2012. "Diverse Paths to Industrial Development." *European Review of Economic History* 16:311–33.

Katz, Lawrence F., and Robert A. Margo. 2013. "Technical Change and the Relative Demand For Skilled Labor: The United States in Historical Perspective." NBER Working Paper no. 18752, Cambridge, MA.

Landes, David. 1949. "French Entrepreneurship and Industrial Growth in the Nineteenth Century." *Journal of Economic History* 9:45–61.

———. 1954. "Social Attitudes, Entrepreneurship, and Economic Development: A Comment." *Explorations in Entrepreneurial History* 6:245–72.

Laurie, Bruce, and Mark Schmitz. 1981. "Manufacturing and Productivity: The Making of an Industrial Base, Philadelphia, 1850–1880." In *Philadelphia: Work, Space and Group Experience in the 19th Century*, edited by T. Hershberg, 43–92. New York: Oxford University Press.

Margo, Robert A. 2000. *Wages and Labor Markets in the United States, 1820–1860*. Chicago: University of Chicago Press.

Nye, John V. C. 1987. "Firm Size and Economic Backwardness: A New Look at the French Industrialization Debate." *Journal of Economic History* 47:649–69.

Rousseau, Peter L., and Richard Sylla. 2005. "Emerging Financial Markets and Early US Growth." *Explorations in Economic History* 2005:1–26.

Sicsic, Pierre. 1994. "Establishment Size and Economies of Scale in 19th Century France." *Explorations in Economic History* 31:453–78.

Sokoloff, Kenneth. 1984. "Was the Transition from the Artisan Shop to the Mechanized Factory Associated with Gains in Efficiency? Evidence from the US Manufacturing Censuses of 1820 and 1850." *Explorations in Economic History* 21:351–82.

United States Department of Labor. 1899. *Thirteenth Annual Report of the Commissioner of Labor: Hand and Machine Labor, Volumes 1 and 2*. Washington, DC: USGPO.

Weiss, Thomas. 1986. "Revised Estimates of the United States Workforce, 1800–1860." In *Long-Term Factors in American Economic Growth*, edited by S. Engerman and R. Gallman, 641–71. Chicago: University of Chicago Press.

———. 1993. "Long-Term Changes in US Agricultural Output per Worker, 1800–1900." *Economic History Review* 46:324–41.

Wright, Carroll D. 1900. *The History and Growth of the United States Census Prepared for the Senate Committee on the Census*. Washington, DC: US Government Printing Office.

Wright, Gavin. 1990. "The Origins of American Industrial Success, 1879–1940." *American Economic Review* 80:651–68.

7

Were Antebellum Cotton Plantations Factories in the Field?

Alan L. Olmstead and Paul W. Rhode

In his 1956 classic on American slavery, Kenneth Stampp wrote "each of the southern staples demanded its own kind of specialists. These agricultural enterprises, with their business directors, production managers, labor foreman, and skilled and unskilled workers, approached the organizational complexity of modern factories. Though agriculture was not yet mechanized, the large plantations were to a considerable extent 'factories in the field.'" Stampp (1956, 42). This identification of plantations with factories has since gained wide popularity.

Despite purported resonances to the nineteenth-century experience, the phrase "factories in the field" appears to be of mid-twentieth-century coinage. Carey McWilliams popularized the phrase in his 1939 book attacking large California farms.[1] McWilliams decried the exploitation of migrant labor,

Alan L. Olmstead is Distinguished Research Professor in the Department of Economics at the University of California, Davis, and a member of the board of directors of the National Bureau of Economic Research. Paul W. Rhode is Professor of Economics and Research Affiliate of the Population Studies Center at the University of Michigan and a research associate of the National Bureau of Economic Research.

We thank Jeremy Atack, Martha Bailey, Gregory Clark, Peter Coclanis, William Collins, Alan Dye, Stanley Engerman, Robert Follett, Barbara Hahn, Sumner La Croix, Naomi Lamoreaux, Margaret Levenstein, Robert Margo, Peter Richardson, Caitlin Rosenthal, Elyce Rotella, Richard Steckel, David Weiman, Thomas Weiss, Warren Whatley, and Gavin Wright for their comments and advice. For acknowledgments, sources of research support, and disclosure of the author's or authors' material financial relationships, if any, please see http://www.nber.org/chapters/c13134.ack.

1. McWilliams (1939). A text search reveals the combination of words appears earlier, but its meaning does not relate to agricultural operations. The heading "Factories in the Field" had first appeared over a series of articles by McWilliams and Belmont, aka Herbert A. Klein (1936a, 1936b, 1936c, 1936d, 1936e, 1936f). See Carey McWilliams Papers, Collection no. 1319, Box 64, Scrapbook XV, Department of Special Collections, Charles E. Young Research Library, University of California, Los Angeles. See also Richardson (2005, 75–92). In a 1982 interview, Klein claimed credit for suggesting the phrase. Critser (1983, 34–65, esp. 53).

the unequal distribution of wealth and power, and the violation of Jeffersonian agricultural ideals. McWilliams also tied the spread of power farming and extensive mechanization into his critique.[2] Both Stampp and McWilliams were contrasting large-scale agricultural enterprises with family farms and industrial factories.

On the family farms that prevailed in the East and Midwest, cultivators typically applied their labor to their own land to produce a mix of livestock, grains, and specialty crops. In *To Their Own Soil*, Jeremy Atack and Fred Bateman described how the availability of land coupled with the family farm organization influenced key demographic patterns and community development, leading to the widespread provision of public education and a relatively equal distribution of wealth (Atack and Bateman 1987, 11–12, 37–101). Industrialization in the North created both tensions and opportunities for family farmers. Atack and coauthors later provided a rich account of the rise of the factory in the United States (Atack, Haines, and Margo 2011). As with agriculture, the manufacturing sector was evolving, with small-scale artisanal shops being replaced by factories employing both power-driven machinery and a more extensive division of labor.

Stampp and McWilliams employed the term "factory" to large-scale agriculture enterprises with a clear purpose. Both sought to highlight the negative influences that they associated with factories: the depersonalization of work, the separation of workers from ownership and control, and the increasing social and economic inequalities. Both criticized the exploitation of disempowered, ethnically differentiated workers. Other scholars, including many cliometricians, have adopted and embellished Stampp's association of plantations with factories, but with a different purpose. The figure of speech now symbolizes modernity and efficiency. As an example, Jacob Metzer builds the case that plantations were rational modern business structures that like factories employed the division of labor to captured significant economies of scale and coordination (Metzer 1975). In *Time on the Cross*, Fogel and Engerman go beyond the previous uses of the "factories in the field" appellation to emphasize the assembly-line-driven efficiency of gang-labor plantations.[3] They note that "the ultimate objective of slave management was the creation of a highly disciplined, highly specialized, and well-coordinated labor force. Specialization and interdependence were the hallmarks of the medium- and large-sized plantations. On plantations, hands were rigidly organized as in a factory" (Fogel and Engerman 1974,

---

2. McWilliams (1941). Writing in roughly the same period as McWilliams, two leading scholars of agricultural history—Paul S. Taylor and Ulrich B. Phillips—drew parallels between the large-scale California farms and the southern slave plantation. See Taylor (1954) and Phillips (1925).

3. Nye (2013, 2) observes: "The assembly line emerged in a specific place (Detroit), at a specific time (between 1908 and 1913), in a specific industry (the automobile industry). But it also expressed trends in American society that can be discerned during the nineteenth century." Ford and his engineers took inspiration from Cincinnati pork-processing plants.

203). By Fogel's reckoning the owners of medium- and large-size planta-tions, through their perfection of the gang system, created a revolutionary advance worthy of mention alongside the "blast furnace, electricity, and medical surgery" (Fogel 2003, 46–47). Explaining his pathbreaking find-ings, Fogel observed: "A slave working on an assembly-line basis in cotton, sugar and tobacco—the Southern staples—produced as much output in 35 minutes as a traditional worker produced in an hour."[4]

It has become common to apply the "factories in the field" label to sugar plantations. In *Sweetness and Power*, Sidney Mintz characterized seventeenth- and eighteenth-century West Indian sugar plantations as "industrial enter-prises" due to the discipline and organization of the labor force as well as the high degree of time consciousness in production (Mintz 1985, 50–52). In his study of the Louisiana sugar plantations, Robert Follett also emphasizes the imposition of time-clock management and integration of field and mill work (Follett 2005, 92–117). The industrial nature of sugar-producing operations is strongly reinforced in the vivid images of their boiler houses, distilleries, and mills.

As noted above, many scholars have also applied the "factories in the field" metaphor to antebellum cotton plantations.[5] Some see the idea as sol-idly rooted in the nineteenth century, offering selected sources to support this lineage. One touch point is Michael Chevalier's 1839 account where he refers to the New South cotton plantation as "a sort of agricultural manufactory, in which [the planters] are obliged to exercise more or less of the activity, and to feel more or less of the hopes and fears of a manufacturer."[6] The 1884 Currier and Ives print, "A Cotton Plantation on the Mississippi" is another touch point. The chromolithograph depicts a postbellum harvest scene with a sky filled with smoke billowing from the plantation's steam-driven cotton gin and a distant steamboat.

In this chapter, we use census data, plantation records, and narrative evidence to investigate whether antebellum cotton plantations merit the title "factories in the field." Our focus is on cotton because it was the slave South's main cash crop and the leading user of enslaved labor. We also inquire whether management practices on cotton plantations were closely aligned with those of modern business enterprises associated with Frederick Taylor's scientific management prescriptions. We find that, by some measures, plantations were an intermediate form of enterprise located between the family farm and the contemporary factory, and in some ways, closer to the factory than to the farm. However, by other more important measures, plantations were very different from factories. We conclude that the analogies between cotton plantations and factories and

---

4. *Chicago Tribune*, February 25, 1994, p. 20.
5. Coclanis (2000, 59–78, esp. 61) labels "factories in the fields" a "nineteenth-century metaphor."
6. Chevalier (1839, 400). We thank Peter Coclanis for calling this source to our attention.

between slavery and "modern" management practices obscure more than they reveal.

The chapter has the following form. After defining key terms, we assemble the quantitative evidence on scale of production, labor force, and capital stock of plantations, family farms, and manufacturing establishments from the 1860 census in order to compare the operating characteristics of the three sets of organizations. Next, we investigate the extent of the division of labor, the seasonality of work, and regimentation at antebellum plantations, farms, and factories. We then question the relevance of analogies that liken slaves to machine parts and explore assertions that plantation practices were akin to modern management techniques. A fuller comparative analysis reveals substantial differences between plantations and factories.

7.1   Defining Terms

In his "Report on the Factory System" for the *Tenth Census of the United States*, Carroll D. Wright defined a factory as an "establishment where several workmen are collected for the purpose of obtaining greater and cheaper conveniences for labor than they could procure individually at their homes; for producing results by their combined efforts which they could not accomplish separately; and for preventing the loss occasioned by carrying the articles from place to place." The core principle was one of *association*: "each laborer, working separately . . . directs his producing powers to effect [sic] a common result." The more prominent is the "principle of association," the more the establishment is "entitled to the name of factory and the more generally does it receive the name in common parlance." (Wright 1882, 523). Wright drew on the writings of the British authority, Andrew Ure, for whom "the term factory system, in technology, designates the combined operation of many orders of work-people, adult and young, in tending with assiduous skill a series of productive machines continuously impelled by a central power." (Ure 1835, 13).

In courses on the Industrial Revolution, the "factory" is commonly defined as a manufacturing establishment utilizing a power source (water or steam) and employing a number of wage earners (the lower-bound cutoff is often around fifteen). Many scholars add the use of supervision (or what is known as "factory discipline") and the application of an extensive division of labor.[7] Applying the concept to census data, which are silent on the organization of work within establishments, requires modification. To do this we follow the guidance of Jeremy Atack, who defined a factory as "an inanimately powered plant," employing a large number of workers. "Factory production depended upon steam or water power to drive machinery. Arti-

---

7. Mantoux ([1928] 1961, 38–39). The definition has to be adjusted with the evolution of power technologies, including the introduction of electricity. See Devine (1983).

Table 7.1   **Percentage distribution of manufacturing activity by scale and power, 1850 and 1880**

		1850		1880	
	Scale	No power	Power	No power	Power
Establishments	Small	61.0	29.2	59.6	26.4
	Large	5.3	4.5	5.7	8.3
Workers	Small	28.2	12.7	16.8	9.3
	Large	26.0	33.2	24.5	49.4
Value added	Small	21.0	22.4	11.3	14.2
	Large	32.7	23.9	35.9	38.6

Source: Atack, Bateman, and Margo (2005, 593).
Notes: Small scale is fifteen or fewer employees, and large scale is sixteen or more. Power includes the use of steam or water power.

san shops, sweatshops, and manufactories, on the other hand, relied on hand tools. Human muscle was sufficient for their power needs."[8] Factory production also entailed specialization, which "could not be practiced extensively" unless the plant operated on a sufficient scale. In his recent work, Atack set the employment threshold at fifteen or more workers.[9] As table 7.1 shows, fewer than one in twenty (4.5 percent) of American manufacturing establishments in 1850 met the joint standard of employing sixteen or more workers and using water/steam power. Such establishments employed 33.2 percent of all workers and produced 23.9 percent of all value added. By 1880, the shares of establishments meeting the joint standard had increased to 8.3 percent of units, 49.4 percent of workers, and 38.6 percent of manufacturing value added (Atack, Bateman, and Margo 2005, 593).

In the southern history literature, the conventional dividing line separating plantations from yeoman farms is whether the operator owned twenty or more slaves. The degree of arbitrariness of this definition is widely acknowledged (Kolchin 1993, xiii). An alternative definition involved whether the operator worked in the field (Phillips 1906). The common practice in the economic history literature—one that we will follow—is to subdivide units into free farms (zero slaves), small-slave farms (one to fifteen), medium-sized operations (sixteen to forty-nine), and large plantations (fifty or more slaves).

In addition to comparing plantations to factories, a growing literature has associated antebellum cotton plantation operations with those of "modern

8. Mills also relied on inanimate power sources but did not utilize specialization or the division of labor as extensively as factories. Atack acknowledged the dividing line between mills and factories was "arbitrary," but he assumed "specialization could not be practiced extensively" unless the plant employed a large labor force. He initially set the threshold at twenty-five workers, but later lowered the number to fifteen (Atack 1987, esp. 287–88).

9. Atack, Bateman, and Margo (2005, 2008). This work adopted the fifteen-worker threshold and separated the power use and scale dimensions.

business enterprises," employing "scientific management" and "assembly lines." To separate reasonable claims from hyperbole requires yet more definitions. Alfred D. Chandler defined a "modern business enterprise" as a firm operating two or more distinct production/distribution units and run by a hierarchy of salaried managers who monitor and coordinate the activities at these units. This is contrasted with a "traditional business enterprise," a firm that is engaged in a single production activity, is owned and managed by family members, and bought its inputs from and sold its outputs to the market (Chandler 1977, 1–3). "Scientific management" was a set of management practices developed by Frederick Taylor and his followers to prevent "soldiering" and to improve work efficiency. The practices included implementing incentive pay and designing "optimal" work methods based on time-and-motion studies rather than "rules of thumb."[10]

The "assembly line," according to David Nye's recent book, was a production technique combining five key components—the subdivision of labor, interchangeable parts, single-function machines, the sequential ordering of machines, and the movement of work to workers by belts and slides. Work was divided "into small operations of nearly equal duration" and "every job could be learned quickly." Use of precision-made interchangeable parts allowed assembly to proceed smoothly without "any last-minute sanding, filing, or polishing." Each machine tool was designed to do one thing, and one thing only, as quickly as possible. The machines and tasks were arranged to ensure the smooth flow of the product through the assembly process, and this flow of parts and subassemblies through the production process was automated (Nye 2013, 22–27).

Henry Ford adds perspective: "[W]e began taking the work to the men instead of taking the men to the work. We now have two general principles in all operations—that a man shall never have to take more than one step . . . and that no man need ever stoop over. . . . [A]s nearly as possible, [a worker does] only one thing in only one movement" (Ford and Crowther 1923, 80). But Ford's efficiency-enhancing innovations were not universally applauded. The regularity and pace of work was so intense that the wife of one final assembler wrote to Ford in early 1914 complaining that the "chain system you have is a *slave driver*! *My God*! Mr. Ford. My husband has come home and thrown himself down & won't eat his supper—so done out."[11] Such statements illustrate the double-acting nature of this set of metaphors, which are used to assail modern management practices by equating industrial labor with slavery and to embellish the efficiency of slave labor by equating it with factory work. Our question is whether such analogies do justice to the realities of slave conditions.

---

10. Taylor (1913). "Soldiering" involves making a show of working in order to escape punishment.

11. Letter to Henry Ford, Jan. 23, 1914, assessed April 16, 2014 from http://www.thehenry ford.org/exhibits/smartfun/modelt/highlandpark/fivedollar/photo1big.html.

7.2   Assembling the Evidence

To compare antebellum cotton plantations with farms and factories in the same period, we can draw on the wealth of census-based microlevel data related to business organizations in 1860. These include the Parker-Gallman sample (ICPSR 7419), covering farms and plantations in cotton producing counties; the Bateman-Foust sample (ICPSR 7420), covering the rural North; and the Atack-Bateman sample (ICPSR 4048), covering manufacturing nationwide.[12]

A comparison of the data collected in the 1860 Censuses of Agriculture and Manufactures shows many similarities, but the significant differences suggest that the designers of the censuses thought of the two types of businesses as different entities. Both censuses collected data on location and the name of the operator (owner or manager). The censuses differed in the cutoff for inclusion. For farms and plantations, the threshold for coverage was annual production of $100 or more; for industrial establishments, the threshold was $500 annual output (US Census 1860a).

The manufacturing schedule noted the *value of total product* and the physical number of key outputs (for cotton: pounds of yarn, etc.). It also recorded the quantities, kinds, and *value of the raw materials* employed. This, in principle, allowed for calculating the value added produced by a given firm. The agricultural schedule collected the physical output of thirty-three commodities in the previous year—some important such as wheat and corn and others of minor significance such as silk cocoons. Some, including wine, butter, and cheese, were manufactured or processed on the farm. Output values were reported only for orchard and market garden products, home manufactures, and animals slaughtered. The failure to collect output values more generally may reflect that census designers thought that much of the output was consumed on the farm. The agricultural schedule did not collect data on raw material costs. Importantly, there is no information on the quantities or value of the inputs used to feed livestock. Computation of the value added for stock requires assumptions about feed costs and changes in inventories. We will calculate industrial output as value added—that is, the value of product minus the cost of raw materials. We gauge farm output as the value of all crops (at national prices) and the reported value of animals slaughtered, orchard products, and market garden products.[13] We

---

12. Parker and Gallman (1860) and Bateman and Foust (1860). For the Atack-Bateman sample, we use the 1860 national sample downloaded from my.vanderbilt.edu/jeremyatack/data-downloads/.

13. The national crop prices for 1860 are from Towne and Rasmussen (1960). We made no adjustment as in Elizabeth Field-Hendrey's work to reestimate meat production in the South or to include estimates for missing products. We did not include the value of home manufacturing or adjust for the differences in procedures used to create the Bateman-Foust and Parker-Gallman samples.

proceed with the sense that this procedure understates the output associated with the animal production. The instructions to the census marshals recognized that many agricultural data were likely to be imprecise. This concern was not emphasized in the instructions for manufacturing enumerators, suggesting that agricultural data were not as accurate as the manufacturing data.[14]

Another important distinction deals with the treatment of labor. The manufacturing schedule collected data on the "average number of hands employed," subdivided between males and females, by each firm and on the total wages, the "average cost." Perhaps reflecting the perception of the family nature of the farm enterprise, there are no comparable questions in agricultural schedule about the external (or internal) labor force or the expenditures for labor. Researchers must link demographic information on households in the population schedule to gauge the farm labor force. Hired workers were included only if they resided on the farm. A separate Census of the Slave Population did inquire about the number, ages, and gender, but offered no direct information about work.

To create comparable labor units across activities, we rely on established research. For manufacturing, Atack, Bateman, and Margo present total employment and an effective (or adult-male-equivalent) employment.[15] For northern agriculture, Lee Craig has created a set of weights to calculate adult-male equivalents.[16] For southern agriculture, we will use both the total labor force and the "adult-male-equivalent" labor force derived based on the weights of Fogel and Engerman.[17]

Both census schedules inquired about the sources of power and value of the *capital stock*. The agricultural schedule recorded the cash value of the farm, the value of livestock (some of which were capital and power sources),

---

14. US Census (1860b; 1864, viii-clxxii; 1865, ix-ccxvii), National Archives and Records Administration (1860), and Atack and Bateman (1999).

15. Atack, Bateman, and Margo (2005, 591). Total employment sums the males and females in the manufacturing labor force; adult-male-equivalent employment assigns a weight of 1 to males and 0.5 to females. We did not follow their practice of imputation entrepreneurial inputs by adding one worker. We did follow their practice of dropping observations for establishments reporting nonpositive value added (the value of product minus the cost of raw materials), raw materials, total employment, or capital.

16. Craig (1993, 80) provides regression results on the dollar value of household labor in northern agriculture that are consistent with prime-age-adult-male (age eighteen to fifty-four), weights of 0.67 for adult females (eighteen years and older), 0.77 for senior adult males (fifty-five years and older), 0.25 for teenage males (thirteen to seventeen years), and 0.10 for children (under thirteen years) and teenage females (thirteen to seventeen years).

17. Fogel and Engerman (1977). These weights exceed unity in some cases, allowing equivalent labor to exceed raw labor. Our labor force numbers cover the ages twelve years and older. Our calculations assign one-half of those in the ten to fourteen age category to the total labor force, which in some cases results in estimates with fractions. Wright (2006, 106) highlights the sensitivity of the empirical outcomes regarding the relative efficiency of slave plantations and free farms to the labor weights assumed. He also points to the difficulties arising from the valuation of land (102–06).

and the value of farm implements and machinery. (The "cash value" of the farm included "the actual cash value of the whole number of acres returned by you as improved and unimproved." It is unclear whether farm buildings were included, although it is commonly assumed that they were.[18]) The manufacturing schedule recorded the value of the capital, specifically the "dollars invested, in real and person estate, in the business." Both schedules inquired about an establishment's machinery. However, the manufacturing schedule gathered information on the number of specific types of power sources and machines, that is, on the "kind of motive power, machinery, structure, or source." The agricultural schedule asked for the value of "all implements and machinery used to cultivate and produce crops and fit the same for market or consumption." It also collected information on the number of horses, mules, and working oxen (on 1 June of the year of enumeration).

The capital stock ratios in agriculture can thus be subdivided into various categories. Most agricultural units used mobile power sources (such as draft animals) rather than fixed power sources (such as steam engines or water wheels) when driving machinery. To measure the extent of substitution away from tools powered by human muscles, we will include statistics on capital invested in draft animals and implements.[19] Census enumeration procedures in 1860 unfortunately do not allow the manufacturing capital stock to be subdivided in an equivalent way at the establishment level. According to Robert Gallman's aggregate estimates for 1860, equipment made up 22 percent of the aggregate manufacturing capital stock, buildings 23 percent, and land 24 percent.[20]

We calculate the capital-to-labor ratios using both the total labor force and the adult-male-equivalent labor force. We treat slaves as labor, not as capital; their value is not included in the capital stock. One can derive a broad sense of the differing gender-and-age compositions of the labor forces by comparing the results for total labor and adult-male-equivalent labor. The ratios will be similar in activities where men made up the bulk of the labor force and different in activities where women and children were important.

A number of previous studies, which have investigated these samples separately, raise salient comparisons to examine. The rise of the factory in the late-nineteenth-century United States has been associated with capital deepening and the growth of the capital-to-labor ratio. In their analysis of 1880 manufacturing data, Atack, Bateman, and Margo showed that the

18. The agricultural schedule also inquired about the acreage of "improved" and "unimproved" land.

19. We calculate the value of capital in draft stock by multiplying the sum of horses, mules, and oxen (weighted by 0.5) times the national equine price of $59 per head from Towne and Rasmussen (1960, 286). The one-half weight on oxen roughly captures the typical price ratio between bovine and equine draft power sources. See Olmstead and Rhode (2008b, 364).

20. Gallman based the estimates on figures in the US Census (1902, xcvii).

capital-to-labor ratio and capital-to-effective-labor ratio were higher for those establishments employing sixteen or more workers than those employing fifteen and fewer and much higher for those establishments using inanimate power than those that did not (Atack, Bateman, and Margo 2005, 591). Focusing on the antebellum agricultural sector, Heywood Fleisig contrasted differences in the use of specific forms of capital, most notably implements, on plantations and free farms (Fleisig 1976). He argued plantations could expand output by adding slave workers whereas free farms, facing a family labor constraint, could expand output only by mechanizing, that is, by adopting machinery *and* draft power to increase the land-to-labor ratio. Wright shows that the value of implements per unit of labor rose sharply in the North by 1860 as the scale of operations (as measured by acres of improved land) rose; however, the ratio fell on Virginia Piedmont farms as scale (here measured by the number of slaves) increased (Wright 2006, 119–21). A more systematic comparison of the scale of operations and the capital-to-labor ratios of plantations, farms, and manufacturing establishments promised to shed more light on the relevance of the "factories in the field" appellation.

7.3   Comparing Plantations, Farms, and Factories

Figure 7.1 graphs the distribution of output in manufacturing and agricultural samples by size of operation in 1860. Size is measured in two ways: the total number of workers per establishment and the number of adult-male-equivalent workers. By either measure, agricultural production is concentrated in far larger units in the Cotton South than in the North. This is no surprise. The larger production units in the South, which were almost exclusively slave plantations, had no real counterparts in northern agriculture. In our sample drawn from the Bateman-Foust data set, the largest northern farm, measured by the total number of workers, has a labor force of twenty-eight. (This Iowa farm accounted for a negligible share of total output.) In our sample drawn from the Parker-Gallman data set, 4 percent of units, accounting for 32 percent of output, are of this size or larger. In this sample, the largest enterprise, a Rapides, Louisiana, plantation, had 257 workers.

Comparing the cotton farms and plantations with manufacturing establishments puts the "factories in the field" idea into perspective. The very large units in the cotton sample account for a far smaller share of output than their counterparts in the manufacturing sample. The top 5 percent of manufacturing units (on a workers-per-establishment basis) employed forty-six or more workers and accounted for 45 percent of total output. (The largest industrial establishment in the sample was a water-powered textile mill in Maine that employed 1,825 workers.) The top 5 percent of units in the cotton sample had twenty-five or more workers and accounted for 36 percent

a. Number of Workers

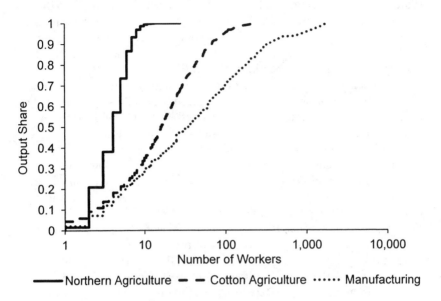

b. Number of Adult Male Equivalent Workers

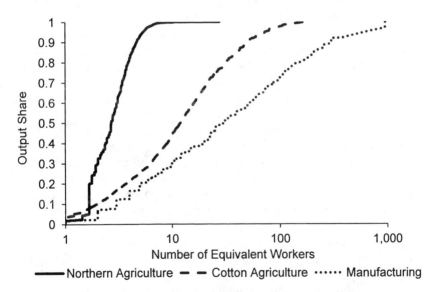

Fig. 7.1 Distribution of output by size of operation, 1860

Source: Data from Bateman-Foust, Parker-Gallman, and Atack-Bateman samples.

Note: See text for weights used to calculate equivalent workers.

of total output. The top 5 percent in the northern farm sample had seven or more workers and accounted for only 10 percent of total output. So by this measure, large plantations were much more akin to factories than to large northern farms. But there were large differences between large plantations and factories, as seen in table 7.2, which describes how output varied across the organization units in the different sectors.

The top panel of table 7.2 reports summary statistics including the mean and standard deviation of the log of output for the different categories of activities. Here, a "factory" is defined as an establishment with an inanimate power source and sixteen or more employees, a "mill" is an establishment with an inanimate power source and fifteen or fewer employees, a "manufactory" is defined as an establishment with no inanimate power source and sixteen or more employees, and an "artisanal shop" is an establishment with no inanimate power source and fifteen or fewer employees. Operations in the cotton sample are also distinguished by the size of the slave population. Output per unit was ranked from highest to lowest: factories, manufactories, and plantations with fifty or more slaves; those with sixteen to forty-nine slaves; mills, artisanal shops, and operations in the cotton sample with one to fifteen slaves; northern free farms; and free operations in the cotton sample. The bottom panel of table 7.2 reports regression results placing the three sectors into a common framework. It presents two sets of standard errors, those that correct for heterogeneity alone and those that are clustered by sector. Even the largest category of slave plantations—those with fifty or more slaves—produced less output than the average factories (the omitted category in the regression).

Table 7.3 investigates variations in the output-to-labor ratios across the organizations in the different samples. Here the differences between the total and adult-male-equivalent labor are more pronounced, especially within the agricultural operations in the cotton sample. In the regressions reported, slave operations in all three categories—those with one to fifteen slaves, sixteen to forty-nine, and fifty or more—have lower output-to-labor ratios than factories. Another notable result is that mills and manufacturing establishments with power sources, but with fifteen or fewer employments, have output-to-labor ratios above (in raw terms) or roughly equal (in adult-male equivalents) to factories. Manufactories also have lower output-to-labor ratios than artisanal shops. Such patterns may arise from the use of the labor variable to categorize the units, and its inclusion in the denominator of the output-to-labor ratio.

Table 7.4 presents statistics on the capital-to-labor ratio in manufacturing and agricultural samples. These data reveal that the difference in the aggregate capital-to-labor ratios across these broad activities was not large. However, greater differences at the more fine-grained level are apparent. In the 1860 sample, manufacturing establishments (a) powered by water or steam

Table 7.2   **Comparing output across organization forms**

Summary statistics	Mean	Std. Dev.	Min.	Max.	Obs.
Log(output)	6.426	1.217	−0.879	13.560	19,371
Northern agriculture	0.559	0.496	0	1	19,371
Log(output)	6.094	0.787	0.507	10.437	10,662
Cotton free	0.131	0.337	0	1	19,371
Log(output)	5.555	0.906	−0.879	9.793	2,529
Cotton slave 1–15	0.091	0.288	0	1	19,371
Log(output)	6.562	0.969	0.219	9.707	1,764
Cotton slave 16–49	0.033	0.179	0	1	19,371
Log(output)	7.994	0.887	1.962	11.189	643
Cotton slave 50+	0.008	0.087	0	1	19,371
Log(output)	9.146	0.888	4.449	11.669	148
Manufacturing	0.183	0.386	0	1	19,371
Log(output)	7.621	1.389	3.219	13.560	3,466
Mill	0.065	0.247	0	1	19,371
Log(output)	7.441	1.232	3.219	11.963	1,261
Artisanal shop	0.093	0.290	0	1	19,371
Log(output)	7.219	0.985	4.317	11.626	1,796
Manufactory	0.010	0.100	0	1	19,371
Log(output)	9.628	1.014	6.751	13.137	196
Factory	0.011	0.104	0	1	19,371
Log(output)	10.234	1.102	6.380	13.560	213

Explaining log(output)

Full specification	Coeff.	RSE	Cl. SE
Northern agriculture	−4.141	(0.076)	(1.43E–11)
Cotton free	−4.680	(0.077)	(1.43E–11)
Cotton slave 1–15	−3.673	(0.079)	(1.43E–11)
Cotton slave 16–49	−2.240	(0.083)	(1.43E–11)
Cotton slave 50+	−1.089	(0.104)	(1.43E–11)
Mill	−2.794	(0.083)	(1.93E–11)
Artisanal shop	−3.016	(0.079)	(1.21E–11)
Manufactory	−0.607	(0.104)	(1.63E–11)
Constant	10.234	(0.061)	(1.43E–11)
R^2	0.47		
Obs.	19,371		

Notes: Robust standard errors correct for heterogeneity only; clustered standard errors are clustered at the sector level. A "factory" is defined as an establishment with an inanimate power source and sixteen or more employees, a "mill" is an establishment with an inanimate power source and fifteen or fewer employees, a "manufactory" is defined as an establishment with no inanimate power source and sixteen or more employees, and an "artisanal shop" is an establishment with no inanimate power source and fifteen or fewer employees.

Table 7.3   Comparing output/labor ratios across organization forms

Summary statistics	Mean	Std. Dev.	Min.	Max.	Obs.
Log(output/labor)	5.165	0.971	−1.978	10.354	19,371
Log(output/equiv. labor)	5.434	0.901	−1.788	10.354	19,371

	Log(output/labor)			Log(output/equiv. labor)		
Full specification	Coeff.	RSE	Cl. SE	Coeff.	RSE	Cl. SE
Northern agriculture	−1.490	(0.059)	(8.6E–12)	−1.261	(0.056)	(4.6E–12)
Cotton free	−1.294	(0.061)	(8.6E–12)	−1.246	(0.058)	(4.6E–12)
Cotton slave 1–15	−1.320	(0.062)	(8.6E–12)	−1.164	(0.059)	(4.6E–12)
Cotton slave 16–49	−1.168	(0.066)	(8.6E–12)	−0.982	(0.064)	(4.6E–12)
Cotton slave 50+	−1.125	(0.087)	(8.6E–12)	−0.944	(0.084)	(4.6E–12)
Mill	0.112	(0.063)	(9.2E–12)	−0.003	(0.061)	(5.2E–12)
Artisanal shop	−0.106	(0.061)	(9.2E–12)	−0.198	(0.058)	(4.7E–12)
Manufactory	−0.421	(0.084)	(8.2E–11)	−0.342	(0.078)	(4.6E–12)
Constant	6.324	(0.058)	(8.6E–12)	6.453	(0.056)	(4.6E–12)
R^2	0.30			0.22		
Obs.	19,371			19,371		

Notes: Robust standard errors correct for heterogeneity only; clustered standard errors are clustered at the sector level. See table 7.2 for definitions.

Table 7.4   Capital/labor ratios in manufacturing and agriculture, 1860 (log of ratio in dollars/worker)

	All labor		Equiv. labor		
	Mean	SD	Mean	SD	Obs.
All manufacturing	6.182	1.133	6.226	1.111	3,466
Artisanal shop	5.791	1.001	5.828	0.993	1,796
Manufactory	5.260	1.204	5.468	1.126	196
Mill	6.839	0.962	6.852	0.958	1,261
Factory	6.435	0.962	6.564	0.936	213
Northern farms	6.544	0.854	6.903	0.838	10,821
Cotton sample	6.418	0.822	6.651	0.811	5,084
Cotton free	6.385	0.899	6.561	0.880	2,529
Cotton slave	6.450	0.736	6.741	0.726	2,555
Slave, 1 to 15	6.470	0/744	6.752	0.733	1,764
Slave, 16 to 49	6.384	0.696	6.699	0.688	643
Slave, 50 plus	6.491	0.803	6.801	0.793	148

had higher capital-to-labor ratios than those that were not, and (b) those in the larger employment scale category had lower capital-to-labor ratios than establishments in the small-scale category. This is consistent with increasing scale saving capital by spreading a fixed stock over a larger employment base. The result (a) is consistent with the findings of Atack, Bateman, and Margo

Table 7.5   Comparing capital/labor ratios across organization forms, controlling for output

Summary statistics	Mean	Std. Dev.	Min.	Max.	Obs.
Log(capital/labor)	6.498	0.880	1.708	10.451	18,953
Log(capital/equiv. labor)	6.672	0.894	2.54	10.449	18,953

	Log(capital/labor)			Log(capital/equiv. labor)		
Full specification	Coeff.	RSE	Cl. SE	Coeff.	RSE	Cl. SE
Log(output)	0.327	(0.008)	(0.110)	0.339	(0.008)	(0.116)
Northern agriculture	1.462	(0.072)	(0.449)	1.742	(0.072)	(0.478)
Cotton free	1.479	(0.074)	(0.508)	1.583	(0.074)	(0.541)
Cotton slave 1–15	1.235	(0.071)	(0.399)	1.433	(0.071)	(0.424)
Cotton slave 16–49	0.681	(0.071)	(0.243)	0.894	(0.071)	(0.259)
Cotton slave 50+	0.412	(0.089)	(0.118)	0.606	(0.089)	(0.126)
Mill	1.316	(0.073)	(0.303)	1.235	(0.073)	(0.323)
Artisanal shop	0.341	(0.072)	(0.327)	0.286	(0.072)	(0.348)
Manufactory	−0.977	(0.106)	(0.066)	−0.890	(0.106)	(0.070)
Constant	3.091	(0.104)	(1.111)	3.094	(0.104)	(1.182)
R^2	0.19			0.24		
Obs.	19,371			19,371		

Notes: Robust standard errors correct for heterogeneity only; clustered standard errors are clustered at the sector level. See note to table 7.2 for definitions.

for 1880, and the result (b) is inconsistent with their results for 1880.[21] The differences may be due to inclusion in their analysis of the rich set of controls for location and three-digit SIC industry, which we omit.

These results suggest that we compare farms, plantations, and manufacturing establishments controlling for the level of output. Table 7.5 reports regressions examining whether, controlling for output in a common way, the organizational forms had measurably different capital/labor ratios. It presents two sets of standard errors, those that correct for heterogeneity alone and those that are clustered by sector. The cotton plantations with a greater numbers of slaves have progressively lower capital-to-labor ratios than cotton producers with fewer slaves. If one takes into account controls for sectors, slave plantations have higher capital-to-labor ratios than factories. Thus, the null hypothesis that the intercepts are the same may be rejected. The differences are statistically significant at conventional levels using either set of standard errors. It is clearly desirable to investigate the expansion paths of the capital-labor ratios in a more flexible way, allowing variation across type of unit. And it is undesirable to continue using

21. Atack, Bateman, and Margo (2005, 591) report that, controlling for power use, manufacturing operations in 1880 in the higher employment category have higher capital-labor and capital-effective-labor ratios than those with fewer employees. In their sample, the "mechanical" inverse relationship between the capital-labor ratio and employment does not hold.

categorical variables (dummy variable for factories, large plantations, etc.) that are defined by labor force numbers that also enter into the capital-labor ratios under investigation.

To help address these concerns, figure 7.2 graphs the expansion paths of the total capital-labor ratio as estimated by locally weighted regression separately for northern farms, free farms in the cotton sample, slave operations, and manufacturing establishments.[22] Panel A shows the relationship between the log of the capital-labor ratio to the log of output. The series for adult-male-equivalent labor (not shown here) has the same general pattern. The graph presents results for ranges of output where all four types of establishments coexisted, thus allowing for reasonable comparisons. Northern farms are the most capital intensive, followed by free cotton farms, slave operations, and finally, at a much lower level, by manufacturing establishments. (At lower levels of output, the relationships between the agricultural units are reversed.) Not only are the levels different, but so are the slopes of the expansion paths. The capital-labor ratio rises sharply with output for northern farms. For manufacturing establishments and slave operations, the increase is much more muted. The overall patterns suggested in the locally weighted regressions are reenforced by the results of ordinary least squares (OLS) regressions (not reported). The total capital-to-labor ratio grew rapidly with output on free farms in both the northern and southern samples, but in a more moderate way on slave operations or in manufacturing establishments.

Panel B graphs the expansion path for machinery and power. The agricultural series shows the log of the ratio of value of the capital in implements and draft stock to the number of laborers. Limitations in the manufacturing data prevent us from calculating an exact analogue; instead, for the manufacturing series we graph the fraction of establishments with steam or water power (as displayed on the right axis). While the manufacturing series obviously cannot be compared directly with the series for the agricultural units, the relationship between the fraction with power and output is informative. The manufacturing series follows a U-shaped pattern. The minimum for the manufacturing series occurs near a log(output) value of 6.71. Over 71 percent of manufacturing establishments, accounting for 98 percent of total manufacturing output, produced to the right of this point—that is, on the upward sloping portion of the manufacturing curve.

On free farms in the northern agricultural and cotton sample, the ratio of capital invested in machinery and power sources relative to labor increases sharply with output. The growth is especially rapid for northern farms,

22. The regressions were run using the lowess command in Stata. The bandwidth was 0.8 for all but the manufacturing power series, where 0.4 was used. To avoid distracting clutter, we have trimmed the observations accounting for 1 percent of output at the top and bottom ends from each of the graphed series.

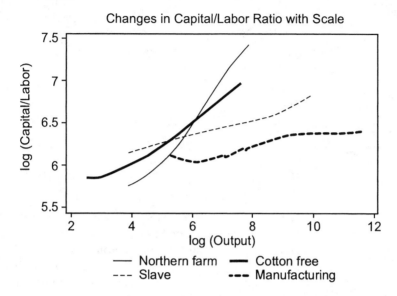

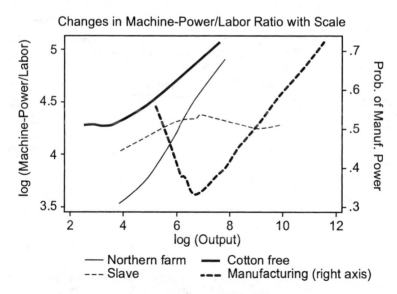

Fig. 7.2 Expansion paths as revealed by locally weighted regressions

Notes: The figures are for "all labor"; the analogues for "adult-male-equivalent labor" are similar. The observations accounting for the top and bottom 1 percent of output are trimmed from each series.

Table 7.6   Composition of agricultural capital stock

	Land and buildings (%)	Livestock (%)	Implements (%)	Implements and draft stock (%)
Northern	83.4	13.4	3.1	9.2
Cotton	80.1	16.3	3.6	10.7
Free	69.5	26.8	3.7	18.5
Slave	81.7	14.7	3.6	9.6
Slave, 1 to 15	76.8	19.6	3.5	12.1
Slave, 16 to 49	81.0	15.6	3.5	9.4
Slave, 50 plus	87.2	9.1	3.7	7.3

Notes: "Implements and draft stock" include the value of work animals, not all livestock.

mirroring the increase in total capital to labor for these units. For slave operations, the machinery and power ratio increases at low scale and then declines at higher scales. Overall, the expansion path of slave plantations follows a shallow inverted U-shaped pattern. This contrasts with both free farms and with manufacturing establishments. The maximum point for the slave power series occurs near a log(output) value of 6.93. Over 53 percent of slave operations, accounting for over 90 percent of the output of such units, produced at a scale greater than this. Whereas an upward-sloping part of the expansion path was relevant for the overwhelming bulk of manufacturing units, the downward-sloping segment was relevant for most slave operations. Once again, the overall patterns suggested in the locally weighted regressions are reenforced by the results of OLS regressions (not reported). The machinery-to-labor ratio grew rapidly with output on free farms in both the northern and southern samples, but not on slave operations. In summary, large cotton plantations differ from free farms because the plantation total capital-labor does not increase rapidly with scale; they differ from free farms and manufacturing establishments (including factories) because the plantation power-and-machine intensity does not increase rapidly with scale.

The evidence on the composition of the agricultural capital stock displayed in table 7.6 points to a core difficulty with the "factory in the field" appellation. The capital mix of large cotton plantations was heavily weighted to "fields"—over 87 percent for land—and not to the accoutrements of "factories"—only 7 percent for machinery and power sources. The low ratio of equipment was not due to the inherent incompatibility of slavery with industrial production or mechanized farming as the example of sugar plantations shows. Instead, it was a product of the cotton regime. The owners of the largest cotton plantations often sought to occupy the richest and most valuable lands and to accumulate a stock to hold in reserve.

7.4   Division of Labor, Regimentation, and Seasonality of Work

What about other attributes of the factory system, such as the use of the division of labor? By most accounts, the harvest was the binding constraint in cotton production. Stampp asserted this view and added that during the peak of harvest season almost all able-bodied hands, including those skilled in a craft and working in the big house, were sent to the field to pick (Stampp 1956). In our investigation of plantation production activities, we are exploring the allocation of the labor force over the harvest season. The surge of laborers into the picking work during September and October is plainly evident. It was all hands on deck, or rather, into the fields. This difference is in part rooted in the different nature of the annual production process. Cotton plantations produced a marketable output once a year. Factories likely produced marketable commodities every day or week. Each stage of production of the cotton crop depended on the success of all prior stages. There was little parallel to this annual cycle of production in manufacturing.[23]

Large plantations maintained specialized slaves trained as smiths, wrights, and carpenters and thus were like factories, which coordinated the division of labor within the enterprise. But care must be taken in concluding that the existence of such slave specialists implied greater efficiency.[24] This presumes northern farmers actually performed similar work (instead of purchasing such specialized services in local towns and villages) or that northern farmers, who did perform some of these tasks for themselves, were less efficient than slave craftsmen. No evidence has been offered that slave crafts workers were more adept than free farmers or townspeople.

Vertical disintegration was a hallmark of northern industrialization. Factories regularly performed tasks internally in the early phases of an industry, but over time external specialists emerged to provide the services more cheaply. Agglomeration economies allowed northern factories to specialize in what they did best. Northern farmers followed the same route. The existence of such markets was typically a sign of an increase in the division of labor and greater efficiency. The literature arguing self-sufficient plantations were somehow more efficient or like factories because they failed to evolve and specialize misses this fundamental element of northern industrialization. The mirror image of the supposed efficiency of plantation craftsmen was the absence of small- and medium-size towns compared to northern agricultural regions.[25] Herein lay an important source of the broader negative impacts of the plantations internalizing craft activities.

23. We thank Gavin Wright for this point.
24. Anderson and Gallman (1977, 32) note that in "most of the cases examined, the planter attempted to satisfy his requirements for artisan and construction work with resident slave labor."
25. Wright (1986, 21–24, 39–43) and Weiman (1990, 135).

According to the conventional view, work in factories was regular and freed from dependence of seasonal conditions. Factories were indoor spaces where external forces could largely be controlled. In practice this ideal took time to be fully realized, and many industrial workplaces in mid-nineteenth-century America reduced their hours of operation in the winter due to weather conditions, inadequate light, and lack of flowing water to drive power equipment. In the early nineteenth century, industrial work had been "from sun to sun." In addition, many early industrial activities involved processing agricultural products, which were available on a seasonal basis. By the early postbellum period (1870 and 1880) when the relevant data on the seasonality of manufacturing activity first became available, "the typical establishment (weighted by the value of its capital stock or by employment) . . . operated for 12 months on a full-time-equivalent basis." Part-time establishments had not disappeared, but they were smaller and less capital intensive (Atack, Bateman, and Margo 2002, 793, 807).

Historians have debated the role of natural time and clock time in the antebellum South. Eugene Genovese, reflecting the dominant view, argued that the southern plantation "setting remained rural, and the rhythms of work followed seasonal fluctuations. Nature remained the temporal reference point for the slaves" (Genovese 1974, 291). Mark M. Smith has pushed a revisionist perspective, asserting that after 1830 southerners came to view the clock as the "legitimate arbiter of time" (Smith 1997, 240). To address the regularity, seasonality, and duration of work on slave plantations, we have surveyed about 800 slave narratives and oral histories. Of these, about one in four gave an indication of the daily hours of work, including both starting and ending times. Of this latter group, 90 percent were consistent with the notion that the hours extended from "sunrise to sunset," from "kin to can't," from "before daylight to dark" (or "almost dark" or "after dark"), or "all day." Clearly the plantation work schedule depended on natural conditions, such as the seasonal variability of light. The same was undoubtedly true of northern farms (although the seasonal variation obviously increased with latitude).[26]

Work and life on slave plantations were far more regimented than on northern farms. The regimentation was crucial for the mobilization of all able-bodied hands for field work, especially during the picking season. The laborers on a given plantation were awakened by the same horn and sent into the fields under the same supervisors. The provision of food, clothing, and housing was also centrally controlled. In early American textile factories, many workers lived in dormitories and ate in communal facilities. Many

---

26. Our search of slave narratives is still ongoing. To date, we have examined narratives posted online by the Library of Congress, *Born in Slavery: Slave Narratives from the Federal Writers' Project*, 1936–1938, http://memory.loc.gov/ammem/snhtml/snhome.html; we have also mined information found in numerous published slave narratives.

labored under factory discipline subject to explicit work rules.[27] Hence, there were some parallels with the slave labor force (we emphasize *some*). But this regimentation of factory housing gave way to more dispersed and presumably more efficient living arrangements as the composition of the labor force evolved and as suppliers of housing and food supplanted factory provision as a part of the general process of vertical disintegration. The continuing extent of regimentation of slaves on plantations exceeded that prevailing in factories.

7.5 Slaves as Machine Parts

In 1956, Martin Luther King, Jr. observed that under slavery African Americans were "considered a thing to be used, not a person to be respected. He was merely a depersonalized cog in a vast plantation machine" (King 1986, 136). King was neither the first nor last to conjure the image of slaves working like machines or being treated as parts of a larger mechanism. The "Rules" of Bennet H. Barrow's Highland Plantation read "A plantation might be considered as a piece of machinery, to operate successfully, all of its parts should be uniform and exact, and the impelling force regular and steady; and the master . . . should be their impelling force."[28] In his *Journey in the Back Country*, Frederick Law Olmsted characterized slaves on Mississippi Valley cotton plantations as laboring in a "stupid, plodding, machine-like manner." As an example, he noted the case of "nearly two hundred hands . . . moving across the field in parallel lines, with a considerable degree of precision." Even when he and others charged by on horse, the slaves toiled without "the smallest change or interruption" (Olmsted 1860, 81–82).

The immediate victims of slavery often invoked a different analogy, one that was more organic and less mechanical.[29] Frederick Douglass described slaves as being treated akin to livestock. Upon his master's death and the division of the estate: "We were all ranked together at the valuation. Men and women, old and young, married and single, were ranked with horses, sheep, and swine. There were horses and men, cattle and women, pigs and children, all holding the same rank in the scale of being, and were all subjected to the same narrow examination . . . the same indelicate inspection" (Douglass [1845] 1963, 47–48). In *Twelve Years a Slave*, Solomon Northup referred to slaves in transport and trade as being treated like "human cattle" (Northup 1975, 134, 138). Slave owners were deeply interested in the rate of

---

27. Ware (1931, 263–66). These conditions invoke complaints such as "Some of the Beauties of Our Factory System—Otherwise Lowell Slavery," in *Factory Tracts* (1845, *Factory Life As It Is*, no. 1. Lowell, MA).

28. Barrow and Davis (1967, 406–10). Barrow maintained a system of punishment inconsistent with treating his slaves as mere machine parts.

29. Davis (2014, 15–44) provides an insightful analysis of the treatment of slaves as brute animals.

increase of their slave populations and exerted extensive control over family life and the raising of children. Northup repeatedly emphasized the widespread use of corporal punishment on plantations (Northup 1975). In the passage mentioned above, Olmsted observed that the hoe hands were being threatened by a driver brandishing a whip. The sound of the whip cracking was intimation enough. Threats and displays of violence matter only for conscious beings making choices.

Apologists for the plantation system also emphasized its living and personal dimensions, including its penetration into almost every aspect of the slave's life. In 1918, Ulrich Phillips noted that on southern plantations there was "little of that curse of impersonality and indifference which too commonly prevails in the factories of the present-day world where power-driven machinery sets the pace, where the employers have no relations with the employed outside of work hours, where the proprietors indeed are scattered to the four winds, where the directors confine their attention to finance, and where the one duty of the superintendent is to procure a maximum output at a minimum cost" (Phillips [1918] 1966, 307). In 1929, Phillips opined that contemporary urban industry "did not give work to women, their administration did not facilitate a cherishing of health or a training of the youth, and their limitations of capital excluded investment in persons who were not laborers. These, in short . . . were masculine enterprises conveniently ignoring family complications" (Phillips 1929, 173).

Phillips did note that as an enterprise, either agricultural or industrial, grew in scale, eventually its owner could "no longer combine manual work with supervision. . . . [W]here full differentiation of administration from labor occurs, the shop becomes a factory, the farm changes into a factory, whatever the number of its operatives may be."[30] But in keeping with his general perspective, Phillips applied the factory analogies to West Indian plantations but found them less appropriate for the American South. Phillips wrote: "On the generality of the [West Indian sugar] plantations the tone of the management was too much like that in most modern factories. The laborers were considered more as work-units than as men, women, and children. Kindliness and comfort, cruelty and hardship, were rated at balance-sheet value; births and deaths were reckoned in profit and loss, and the expense of rearing children was balanced against the cost of new Africans. These things were true in some degree in the North American slave-holding communities, but in the West Indies they excelled" (Phillips [1918] 1966, 52). The slave owner in the American South often lived on the farm or plantation where his bondmen and bondwomen worked. Even the owners of the largest estates usually resided on or nearby their holdings. By Phillips's reckoning, they were not absentees but rather styled themselves as the heads of large plantation families.

30. Phillips (1929, 305). For commentary, see Metzer (1975, 124–25).

The correspondence of Israel E. Trask, who lived in both the industrial and plantation worlds, offers valuable insights into the differences. Trask resided in Springfield, Massachusetts, and ran the Brimfield Cotton and Woollen Manufacturing Company. He also owned a cotton plantation near Natchez, Mississippi, which he regularly visited in the winter. Trask's letters home speak in familiar terms about the individual slaves, their health, and living conditions. He wrote of the slaves' frequent inquires about his wife and children—the "Missis" and "Massa Wm. and Ed"—and of sharing food with the "young negroes." James Trask, a brother who managed the family's extensive Mississippi holdings, spoke of "our Black family." The labor force at the Massachusetts mills is never discussed in such personal terms.[31]

The southern plantations went beyond even the company towns associated with some manufacturing and mining enterprises. In a company town, the firm served as the employer, landlord, storekeeper, and local government. (As Price Fishback notes, the broad scope of the company's domain bred resentment and protest [Fishback 1992, 166].) The plantation owner controlled or sought to control family life, education, and religious life. More fundamentally, the plantation owner determined the slave's geographic location and, together with the surrounding community, prevented his or her escape. Even the most paternalistic manufacturing employer of the 1910s and 1920s when Phillips wrote did not exercise these powers.

These issues are related to the question about whether plantation agriculture was a business or a way of life. Whether it was a capitalist profit-seeking enterprise or a system for social control? For the apologist Phillips, the social control motives—maintaining white supremacy over African Americans—was the dominant consideration. For most economic historians, the profit motive dominated the calculus. As Conrad and Meyer famously asserted, investing in a slave was like investing in any other capital asset (Conrad and Meyer 1958). But it does not impoverish one's historical analysis to acknowledge that both motives were likely at play.

7.6   Modern Management

A number of scholars have equated systematic exploitation of slave labor to factory discipline and to later doctrines of scientific management. R. Keith Aufhauser argued that in their administration of labor, southern slaveholders anticipated and conformed to F. W. Taylor's principles of scientific management. As an example, planter George Fitzhugh shared many of Taylor's precepts regarding the lack of motivation, self-discipline, and intelligence among workers and about the need for constant supervision.

31. Israel E. Trask papers, Mss. 899, Baker Library Special Collections, Harvard Business School. Israel E. Trask to Eliza C. Trask, 18 Jan. 1819, 26 Nov. 1821, 4 Dec. 1824, 31 Jan. 1825, 5 Dec. 1827, 21 Dec. 1827, 26 Dec. 1828; James Trask to Israel E. Trask, 1 Feb. 1835.

Both Taylor and southern slaveholders sought through routine, task design, job enrichment, and physical coercion to secure greater work effort (Aufhauser 1973).

Drawing such connections has a long history. Lewis Gray reads in George Washington's 1769 description of his wheat harvest an account that "savors a sort of Scientific Management."[32] Washington sought to reduce his use of hired cradlers and rely solely on his own enslaved labor force. To this end, he proposed to stagger his planting to spread out the harvest demands and to separate his cradler-binder crews into individual teams to speed up the pace of work above that achieved when all the cradlers worked together. Surely, concerns about work effort in groups long preceded Frederick Taylor.

Taylor attributed slow work to two causes. The first cause, associated with so-called "natural soldiering," was the "natural laziness" or the "natural instinct and tendency of men to take it easy." Taylor believed this characterized "the average man (in all walks of life)" and only "men of unusual energy, vitality, and ambition" choose on their own to work hard. The second cause, associated with so-called "systematic soldiering," was due to the "fallacy, which has from time immemorial been almost universal among workmen, that a material increase in the output of each man or each machine in the trade would result in the end in throwing a large number of men out of work" (Taylor 1913, 22–24). The first cause has been the subject of great debate in the literature on slavery. One observer's "laziness" is another observer's "slave resistance and exercise of agency." The second cause is irrelevant, or largely so, in the operation of slavery. The fear of losing work was not an issue, and Taylor's remedies do not apply. Slaves had other concerns. House slaves feared being moved to harder labor in the field, but this is explained by greater effort inducing disutility rather than a fear of unemployment. Slaves in general feared that if they were more energetic and more productive, their owners might ratchet up their allotted tasks. Taylor understood the ratchet effect, but he studied a world in which workers received a wage in a competitive economy. Workers could quit if management increased its demands, and managers had to worry about voluntary turnover. Such concerns were far less salient for slave owners (Brown [1855] 1971, 128).

The dean of American business historians, Alfred D. Chandler, offered a mixed opinion on appellation of "factories in the field" to antebellum southern plantations. In his 1977 classic, *The Visible Hand*, he argued that southern plantations were not in any meaningful way precursors to the development of modern business enterprise in America (Chandler 1977, 64–67). True, southern plantations were larger than contemporary family farms, but they were not as large as New England textile factories. Chandler (incorrectly) asserted that plantation owners did not commonly employ white overseers and that management was not widely separated between ownership. When

32. Gray (1933, 550). See also Metzer (1975) and Collins (2001).

the plantation owners did employ overseers, their instructions (as reflected in the plantation rules) typically dealt with the treatment of slaves rather than other forms of capital. According to Chandler, the plantation books did not allow the comparison of performance of individual workers or the entire operation over meaningful stretches of time.

Other scholars have disagreed, pointing out that numerous plantations met Chandler's definition of modern business enterprise. Historian Bill Cooke goes so far as to say the "visible hand was holding a whip" (Cooke 2002, 2003). Many plantation owners did utilize overseers and drivers to manage their operations.[33] Furthermore, a considerable number of plantation owners had multiple units. Those operating plantations within the same region—for example, with a home plantation and a bottomland plantation—often decided how to allocate the combined labor force, draft stock, and supplies (food, seed, and feed) across the units. In a technical sense, these plantations did fit Chandler's bill as employing salaried managers to allocate resources across distinct operating units without using market mechanisms. In addition, accounting historians describe plantation bookkeeping practices as being as sophisticated as those employed in the industrial North.[34]

We have spent more than a decade scouring archives for plantation accounts, chiefly with an eye to investigating work activities. The most popular cotton account book was produced by Thomas Affleck of Mississippi, and later Texas (Williams 1957). The first edition of the *Affleck Plantation Journal and Account Book* appeared in 1847. Within a few years, he offered different volumes for small, medium, and large plantations. In addition to space for a journal of daily activities, Affleck provided forms for listing the slaves' names, ages, and values, births and deaths, stock and equipment inventories, the weight of individual cotton bales, the pounds of cotton picked daily by individual slaves, and other valuable information (Olmstead and Rhode 2008a, 1144–46). According to one source, Affleck sold between two and three thousand books per year.[35]

Thomas Affleck was the most famous, but hardly the only or first producer of preprinted cotton books.[36] In the 1850s, W. H. Fox of Natchez, Missis-

33. Scarborough (1966); Bassett, *Southern Plantation Overseer*. In a chapter entitled "Factories in the Fields: The Managerial Ideal and Plantation Realities," Oakes goes so far as to call the ideal plantation a "bureaucracy" achieving worker obedience and community harmony through the systematic imposition of rules by a managerial hierarchy. See Oakes (1982, 153–58).

34. In interesting new work focusing on the use of preprinted account books, Caitlin Rosenthal builds on the theme that plantations were modern business enterprises (Rosenthal, forthcoming). See also Flesher and Flesher (1981), Barney and Flesher (1994), and Fleischman and Tyson (2004).

35. Touchstone (1988, 99–126, 213–29, esp. 224).

36. B. M. Norman also printed and sold Affleck books. See Robinson Papers (LSU 1413), RASP, series I, part 2, reel 20, frame 701. RASP is *Records of Ante-Bellum Southern Plantations: From the Revolution through the Civil War*, edited by Kenneth M. Stampp (Frederick, MD: University Publications of America, various dates after 1985).

sippi, sold a similar product under the title "Statement of Cotton."[37] Other publishers released what were copycat versions with a similar general appearance as the Affleck books.[38] In the early 1850s, J. W. Randolph of Richmond, Virginia, produced a "Plantation & Farm Instruction, Regulation Record, Inventory & Account Book" with preprinted pages for "Manager's Journal or Daily Record" as well as larger editions with "Daily Record of Cotton Picked."[39] There were a variety of earlier cotton books printed by others.[40] Even in the absence of preprinted forms, planters and overseers often kept records in other, more generic, bound volumes. We agree with the accounting historians who argue that plantation record keeping represented signs of modernity and acquisitiveness, but we caution against overstating the case.

The "factories in the field" notion runs into a problem in the plantation account books. For all the attention given to labor, "fields" have little role in preprinted account books. None of the books that we have studied offered any specific form relating to fields, their size, use, improvements, crop rotation, daily activities, or production. There are no forms for fertilizer use, land cleared, drainage, and other important activities on plantations. The layout of the Affleck ledgers and other account books are in accord with Gavin Wright's depiction of southern masters as being first and foremost labor lords rather than landlords (Wright 1986, 17–50). The record keepers sometimes mentioned what happened in specific fields, but the books are not structured to extract such information from the users or to make an organized accounting of activities easy. In the account books that we have surveyed, a small fraction of record keepers occasionally crafted their own schedules summarizing production (output and acreage) by field by year. Some kept separate diaries or logs of daily activities. Most did not.

The preprinted plantation books were not set up to record the systematic use of incentives, negative or positive. Neither Thomas Affleck nor his competitors provided specific sheets for tallying whippings, for example. A few record keepers did note lashing in the "Daily Record of Passing Events," but most were silent. The books did not include pages to enumerate payments to slaves for the produce grown on slave plots; there are no pages or prompts to document contest or tournament results. Again, surviving evidence depends

37. Robert Stewart, Account Books, Ms. 404, 4732, Louisiana and Lower Mississippi Valley Collections, Louisiana State Univ. Libraries (Baton Rouge, LA).

38. Lewis papers at Univ. of North Carolina (Southern Historical Collection 2528) and A. F. Smith plantation records (Western Reserve Historical Society).

39. Robinson Papers (RASP, series I, part 2, reel 20, frame 546) and Branch family (SHC 2718, RASP, series J, part 4, reel 46, frame 689). Randolph's books date to 1852 at the latest.

40. James H. Hammond (RASP, series A, part 1, reel 14). LeBlanc family papers (RASP, series I, part 2, reel 17, frame 678) has a 1830s plantation book with sheets similar to an Affleck book. The South Carolina Historical Society collections contain a preprinted cotton account used during the 1812 crop year by the Plantations Hope and Experiment in British Guiana. See also Wilberforce, Box 9/1 , Hope and Experiment, June 1812, Slavery, Abolition, & Social Justice, http://www.slavery.amdigital.co.uk/Contents/ImageViewerPage.aspx?documentid=35657 &sectionid=5184.

on what the record keepers chose to add. Many scholars have touted picking contests as an important example of modern incentive practices. However, the records that we have seen suggest picking contests were rare events and of minor significance in the overall scheme of plantation life. Picking on Sundays, a practice that Affleck discouraged, was far more common than offering prizes to stimulate production.[41] Our reading of the plantation records and slave narratives suggests that the primary methods of incentivizing slaves were terror, corporal punishment, and the threat of family breakup.

While plantation bookkeeping was far more common than one might think, it was rarely meticulous for long periods. Even in the preprinted books, practices were typically idiosyncratic and often incomplete. We have examined thousands of archival plantation records. This search allowed us to assemble a database of individual-level picking records for some 113 antebellum plantations covering 396 crop years (or parts thereof).[42] In our sample, the number of years covered for individual plantations ranged from one (the modal coverage with forty-three cases) to twenty-two (in the remarkable records of Francis Terry Leak in Tippah, Mississippi). The mean coverage was 3.5 years, the standard deviation was 3.64 years, and the median coverage was 2.0 years. Among those sixty-seven plantations with individual picking records covering more than a single year, thirty (or about 45 percent) have a break in the middle of the available records of one crop-year or more. The short span covered and the breaks in some of the records are undoubtedly, in part, due to destruction, loss, and failure of books to be archived. But chronological gaps in the coverage within the surviving volumes—starting in one year, stopping, and then picking up again after months or even years—indicate lapses in the recording were common. Making long-run comparisons for individual plantations is difficult now and would have been hard even in the antebellum period.

Accounting historian Jan Hierer found that in a sample of over fifty antebellum plantation books from Alabama and Mississippi, the record keepers deviated significantly from the protocols that Affleck had established (Hierer 1988). The data enumerated and the accompanying diaries describing daily activities are very valuable for some purposes, but they fail to provide much information now considered central to modern accounting. It is important to recall that decades of research by historians with access to such records could not even resolve the fundamental debate about whether antebellum southern plantations were profitable. Systematic generalization on this issue from the individual cases has proved elusive. The alternative approach of Conrad and Meyer to addressing the profitability question is celebrated with good reason.

---

41. Slaves likely viewed contests with trepidation, fearing that higher output levels might incite overseers to ratchet up their daily quotas.

42. This sample differs from that discussed in Olmstead and Rhode (2008a). Here we include only the subset of documents that identify the amount of cotton picked by individual slaves.

Showing that the managerial practices of these southern plantations actually affected practices at large industrial enterprises in the nineteenth and early twentieth centuries remains to be demonstrated. But the lack of evidence suggests that this line of causality was weak at best. A fair assessment is that many plantation owners desired an accounting of farm activities to judge the work of their overseers and to reckon how their business affairs changed over time, but the records kept (by design and practice) and the actual operations in the fields were far removed from the dictates of Taylor and other apostles of modern business management.

7.7   Conclusion

A formalist comparative history approach requiring constant definitions and standards shows plantations had some similarities and many differences with factories. Plantations used considerable labor—more than the median factory; plantations also had a high capital/labor ratio (counting land but not slaves as capital); many plantations employed professional managers as did many factories; and many plantation owners operated at more than one location. On the other hand, there was a high turnover rate in plantation overseers and their oft described character flaws does not elicit visions of modern efficient supervisors; plantations carried on their primary business outdoors and were more susceptible to the conditions of daylight, the elements, and the season; and they used relatively little machinery.[43] Plantations kept records, but these were in many cases unsystematic and incomplete (we lack the expertise to compare these accounts to those kept by contemporary factories). The analogy of slaves and machines appears not to work; the victims of the system compared their treatment to that of draft animals. The management of offspring, along with the doling out of whippings and rationing of food, had little parallel with machines in a factory. Cotton plantations did not employ anything approaching an assembly line or even the large-batch system found in northern factories. In this key area the evidence does not support the popular claims.

Our overall assessment is that the notion that slave plantations operated as "factories in the field" was adapted from its original negative connotation to help conjure a powerful but unwarranted image of modernity and efficiency. Even the most modern, progressive planters faced production and management challenges and employed managerial methods that were different in fundamental ways from those confronted in managing a factory. The view from the workers' perspective was also dramatically different. Although the term "factories in the field" may have a nice ring to it, southern plantations were not akin to the emerging northern factories.

---

43. Scarborough notes that the tenure of overseers was "notoriously" brief and that the turnover problem was particularly acute in the New South. Scarborough (1966, 38–40, 125–27, 197, 200).

References

Anderson, Ralph V., and Robert E. Gallman. 1977. "Slaves as Fixed Capital: Slave Labor and Southern Economic Development." *Journal of American History* 64 (1): 24–46.

Atack, Jeremy. 1987. "Economies of Scale and Efficiency Gains in the Rise of the Factory in America, 1820–1900." In *Quantity & Quiddity: Essays in US Economic History*, edited by Peter Kilby, 286–335. Middletown, CT: Wesleyan University Press.

Atack, Jeremy, and Fred Bateman. 1987. *To Their Own Soil: Agriculture in the Antebellum North*. Ames: Iowa State University Press.

———. 1999. "Nineteenth-Century US Industrial Development through the Eyes of the Census of Manufactures." *Historical Methods* 32 (4): 177–88.

Atack, Jeremy, Fred Bateman, and Robert A. Margo. 2002. "Part-Year Operations in Nineteenth-Century American Manufacturing: Evidence from the 1870 and 1880 Censuses." *Journal of Economic History* 62 (3): 792–809.

———. 2005. "Capital Deepening and the Rise of the Factory: The American Experience during the Nineteenth Century." *Economic History Review* 58 (3): 586–95.

———. 2008. "Steam Power, Establishment Size, and Labor Productivity Growth in Nineteenth-Century American Manufacturing." *Explorations in Economic History* 45:185–98.

Atack, Jeremy, Michael R. Haines, and Robert A. Margo. 2011. "Railroads and the Rise of the Factory: Evidence for the United States, 1850–70." In *Economic Evolution and Revolution in Historical Time*, edited by Paul W. Rhode, Joshua Rosenbloom, and David Weiman, 162–79. Stanford, CA: Stanford University Press.

Aufhauser, R. Keith. 1973. "Slavery and Scientific Management." *Journal of Economic History* 33 (4): 811–43.

Barney, D., and Dale L. Flesher. 1994. "Early Nineteenth-Century Productivity Accounting: The Locust Grove Plantation Ledger." *Accounting, Business and Financial History* 4 (2): 275–94.

Barrow, Bennet Hilliard, and Edwin Adams Davis. 1967. *Plantation Life in the Florida Parishes of Louisiana, 1836–1846: As Reflected in the Diary of Bennet H. Barrow*. New York: AMS Press.

Bateman, Fred, and James D. Foust. 1860. "Agricultural and Demographic Records for Rural Households in the North, 1860." ICPSR07420–v1. Ann Arbor, MI: Inter-University Consortium for Political and Social Research [distributor], 1976. doi:10.3886/ICPSR07420.v1.

Brown, John. (1855) 1971. *Slave Life in Georgia: A Narrative of the Life, Suffering, and Escape of John Brown, a Fugitive Slave, Now in England*, 2nd ed. Edited by L. A. Chamerovzow. Reprint, London: W. M. Watts.

Chandler, Jr., Alfred D. 1977. *The Visible Hand: The Managerial Revolution in American Business*. Cambridge, MA: Harvard University Press.

Chevalier, Michael. 1839. *Society, Manners, and Politics in the United States; Being a Series of Letters on North America*. Translated from 3rd Paris ed. Boston: Weeks, Jordan.

Coclanis, Peter A. 2000. "How the Low Country Was Taken to Task: Slave-Labor Organization in Coastal South Carolina and Georgia." In *Slavery, Secession, and Southern History*, edited by Robert L. Paquette and Louis A. Ferleger, 59–78. Charlottesville: University Press of Virginia.

Collins, Steven G. 2001. "System, Organization, and Agricultural Reform in the Antebellum South, 1840–1860." *Agricultural History* 75 (1): 1–27.

Conrad, Alfred H., and John R. Meyer. 1958. "The Economics of Slavery in the Ante Bellum South." *Journal of Political Economy* 66 (2): 95–130.

Cooke, Bill. 2002. "The Visible Hand was Holding a Whip: The Denial of Slavery in Management Studies." Discussion Paper no. 68, July. Institute for Development Policy and Management, University of Manchester.

———. 2003. "The Denial of Slavery in Management Studies." *Journal of Management Studies* 40 (8): 1895–918.

Craig, Lee A. 1993. *To Sow One Acre More: Childbearing and Farm Productivity in the Antebellum North.* Baltimore, MD: Johns Hopkins University Press.

Critser, Greg. 1983. "The Political Rebellion of Carey McWilliams." *UCLA Historical Journal* 4:34–65.

Davis, David Brion. 2014. *The Problem of Slavery in the Age of Emancipation.* New York: Alfred A. Knopf.

Devine, Jr., Warren D. 1983. "From Shafts to Wires: Historical Perspective on Electrification." *Journal of Economic History* 43 (2): 347–72.

Douglass, Frederick. (1845) 1963. *Narrative of the Life of Frederick Douglass, an American Slave.* Garden City, NY: Doubleday.

Fishback, Price V. 1992. *Soft Coal, Hard Choices: The Economic Welfare of Bituminous Coal Miners, 1890–1930.* New York: Oxford University Press.

Fleischman, Richard K., and Thomas N. Tyson. 2004. "Accounting in Service to Racism: Monetizing Slave Property in the Antebellum South." *Critical Perspectives on Accounting* 15:376–99.

Fleisig, Heywood W. 1976. "Slavery, the Supply of Labor, and the Industrialization of the South." *Journal of Economic History* 36 (3): 572–97.

Flesher, Dale L., and Tonya K. Flesher. 1981. "Human Resource Accounting in Mississippi before 1865." *Journal of Accounting and Business Research* 10 (Supplement): 124–29.

Fogel, Robert W. 2003. *The Slavery Debates, 1952–1990: A Memoir.* Baton Rouge: Louisiana State University Press.

Fogel, Robert W., and Stanley L. Engerman. 1974. *Time on the Cross: The Economics of American Negro Slavery*, vol. 1. Boston: Little, Brown and Co.

———. 1977. "Explaining the Relative Efficiency of Slave Agriculture in the Antebellum South." *American Economic Review* 67 (3): 275–96.

Follett, Robert J. 2005. *The Sugar Masters: Planters and Slaves in Louisiana's Cane World, 1820–1860.* Baton Rouge: Louisiana State University Press.

Ford, Henry, and Samuel Crowther. 1923. *My Life and Work.* Garden City, NY: Garden City Publishing Co.

Genovese, Eugene. 1974. *Roll, Jordan, Roll: The World the Slaves Made.* New York: Pantheon.

Gray, Lewis C. 1933. *History of Agriculture in the Southern United States to 1860*, vol. 1. Washington, DC: Carnegie Institution.

Hierer, Jan R. 1988. "A Content Comparison of Antebellum Plantation Records and Thomas Affleck's Accounting Principles." *Accounting Historians Journal* 15 (2): 131–50.

King, Jr., Martin Luther. 1986. *A Testament of Hope: The Essential Writings of Martin Luther King, Jr.*, edited by James M. Washington. San Francisco: Harper & Row.

Kolchin, Peter. 1993. *American Slavery 1619–1877.* New York: Hill and Wang.

Mantoux, Paul. (1928) 1961. *The Industrial Revolution in the Eighteenth Century: An Outline of the Beginnings of the Modern Factory System in England.* New York: Harper & Row.

McWilliams, Carey. 1939. *Factories in the Field: The Story of Migratory Farm Labor in California.* Boston: Little, Brown and Co.

———. 1941. "Farms into Factories: Our Agricultural Revolution." *Antioch Review* 1 (4): 406–31.

McWilliams, Carey, and Clive Belmont, Jr. (aka Herbert A. Klein). 1936a. *Pacific Weekly*, March 30, 105–07.

———. 1936b. *Pacific Weekly*, April 6, 131–33.

———. 1936c. *Pacific Weekly*, April 13, 199–201.

———. 1936d. *Pacific Weekly*, April 27, 231–32.

———. 1936e. *Pacific Weekly*, May 4, 247–49.

———. 1936f. *Pacific Weekly*, May 11, 265–67.

Metzer, Jacob. 1975. "Rational Management, Modern Business Practices, and Economies of Scale in Antebellum Southern Plantations." *Explorations in Economic History* 12 (2): 123–50.

Mintz, Sidney. 1985. *Sweetness and Power: The Place of Sugar in Modern History*. New York: Viking Penguin.

National Archives and Records Administration. 1860. "1860 Agricultural Census Schedule." NA Form 14131e (6/03). www.archives.gov.

Northup, Solomon. (1853) 1975. *Twelve Years a Slave*, edited by Sue Eakin and Joseph Logsdon. Baton Rouge: Louisiana State University Press.

Nye, David. 2013. *America's Assembly Line*. Cambridge, MA: MIT Press.

Oakes, James. 1982. *The Ruling Race: A History of American Slaveholders*. New York: Alfred A. Knopf.

Olmstead, Alan L., and Paul W. Rhode. 2008a. "Biological Innovation and Productivity Growth in the Antebellum Cotton Economy." *Journal of Economic History* 68 (4): 1123–71.

———. 2008b. *Creating Abundance: Biological Innovation and American Agricultural Development*. New York: Cambridge University Press.

Olmsted, Frederick Law. 1860. *A Journey in the Back Country*. New York: Mason.

Parker, William N., and Robert E. Gallman. 1860. Southern Farms Study. [Computer file]. ICPSR07419–v1. Ann Arbor, MI: Inter-university Consortium for Political and Social Research [distributor], 1991. doi:10.3886/ICPSR07419.

Phillips, Ulrich B. 1906. "The Origin and Growth of the Southern Black Belts." *American Historical Review* 11 (4): 798–816.

———. 1925. "Plantations with Slave Labor and Free." *American Historical Review* 30 (4): 738–53.

———. 1929. *Life and Labor in the Old South*. Boston: Little, Brown and Co.

———. (1918) 1966. *American Negro Slavery*. Baton Rouge: Louisiana State University Press.

Richardson, Peter. 2005. *American Prophet: The Life and Work of Carey McWilliams*. Ann Arbor: University of Michigan Press.

Rosenthal, Caitlin C. Forthcoming. "Slavery's Scientific Management: Accounting for Mastery." In *Slavery's Capitalism*, edited by Seth Rockman, S. Beckert, and D. Waldstreicher. Philadelphia: University of Pennsylvania Press.

Scarborough, William Kauffman. 1966. *The Overseer: Plantation Management in the Old South*. Baton Rouge: Louisiana State University Press.

Smith, Mark M. 1997. *Mastered by the Clock: Time, Slavery, and Freedom in the American South*. Chapel Hill: University of North Carolina Press.

Stampp, Kenneth. 1956. *The Peculiar Institution: Slavery in the Ante-Bellum South*. New York: Vantage Books.

Taylor, Frederick W. 1913. *The Principles of Scientific Management*. New York: Harper & Brothers.

Taylor, Paul S. 1954. "Plantation Agriculture in the United States: Seventeenth to Twentieth Centuries." *Land Economics* 30 (2): 141–52.

Touchstone, Blake. 1988. "Planters and Slave Religion in the Deep South." In *Masters & Slaves in the House of the Lord: Race and Religion in the American South, 1740–1870*, edited by John B. Boles. Lexington: University Press of Kentucky.

Towne, Marvin W., and Wayne D. Rasmussen. 1960. "Farm Gross Product and Gross Investment in the Nineteenth Century." In *Trends in the American Economy in the Nineteenth Century*, Studies in Income and Wealth, vol. 24, edited by William Parker, 255–316. Princeton, NJ: Princeton University Press.

Ure, Andrew. 1835. *Philosophy of Manufacturers*. London: Charles Knight.

US Census. 1860a. *Instructions to US Marshals; Instructions to Assistants*. Washington, DC: Bowman.

———. 1860b. *Instructions to US Marshals; Instructions to Assistants*. Washington, DC: Bowman.

———. 1864. *Agriculture of the United States in 1860 Compiled from the Original Returns of the Eighth Census*. Washington, DC: GPO.

———. 1865. *Manufactures of the United States in 1860 Compiled from the Original Returns of the Eighth Census*. Washington, DC: GPO.

———. 1902. *Twelfth Census of the United States*, vol. 7, pt. 1. Washington, DC: GPO.

Ware, Caroline F. 1931. *The Early New England Cotton Manufacture: A Study in Industrial Beginnings*. Boston: Houghton Mifflin.

Weiman, David F. 1990. "Staple Crops and Slave Plantations: Alternative Perspectives on Regional Development in the Antebellum Cotton South." In *Agriculture and National Development: Views on the Nineteenth Century*, edited by Louis Ferleger, 119–61. Ames: Iowa State University Press.

Williams, Robert W. 1957. "Thomas Affleck: Missionary to the Planter, the Farmer, and the Gardener." *Agricultural History* 31 (3): 40–48.

Wright, Carroll D. 1882. "Report on the Factory System of the United States." In *Tenth Census of the United States: Manufactures, 1880*, US Census Office. Washington, DC: GPO.

Wright, Gavin. 1986. *Old South, New South: Revolutions in the Southern Economic Since the Civil War*. New York: Basic Books.

———. 2006. *Slavery and American Economic Development*. Baton Rouge: Louisiana State University Press.

Contributors

Jeremy Atack
Department of Economics
Vanderbilt University
VU Station B #351819
2301 Vanderbilt Place
Nashville, TN 37235–1819

Howard Bodenhorn
John E. Walker Department of
  Economics
College of Business and Behavioral
  Science
201–B Sirrine Hall
Clemson University
Clemson, SC 29634

William J. Collins
Department of Economics
Vanderbilt University
VU Station B #351819
2301 Vanderbilt Place
Nashville, TN 37235–1819

Mary Eschelbach Hansen
Department of Economics
American University
4400 Massachusetts Avenue NW
Washington, DC 20016

Eric Hilt
Department of Economics
Wellesley College
106 Central Street
Wellesley, MA 02481

Matthew S. Jaremski
Department of Economics
Colgate University
13 Oak Drive
Hamilton, NY 13346

Naomi R. Lamoreaux
Department of Economics
Yale University
Box 208269
New Haven, CT 06520–8269

Robert A. Margo
Department of Economics
Boston University
270 Bay State Road
Boston, MA 02215

Alan L. Olmstead
University of California, Davis
Department of Economics
One Shields Ave.
Davis, CA 95616–8617

Claudia Rei
Department of Economics
Vanderbilt University
VU Station B #351819
2301 Vanderbilt Place
Nashville, TN 37235–1819

Paul W. Rhode
Economics Department
University of Michigan
205 Lorch Hall
611 Tappan St.
Ann Arbor, MI 48109–1220

Peter L. Rousseau
Department of Economics
Vanderbilt University
Box 1819, Station B
Nashville, TN 37235

Eugene N. White
Department of Economics
Rutgers University
75 Hamilton Street
New Brunswick, NJ 08901–1248

Author Index

Subject Index

Page numbers followed by *f* or *t* refer to figures or tables, respectively.

Agency problem, 122–23

American credit markets, 13

American economy: accounting for growth of, 2–3; domestic perspective of, 2; global perspective of, 2; understanding history of growth of, 2

American exceptionalism: about, 25–28; economists and, 26

American manufacturing: economies of scale and, 216; emergence of large-scale, in nineteenth-century, 219–25; rise of, 215–16; Sokoloff's analysis of, 216–19. *See also* Economies of scale

Antebellum bank failures, 151–55. *See also* Railroads

Antebellum cotton plantations, 249–50; comparing farms and factories with, 254–62; data sources, 251–54; division of labor and, 263–65; modern management and, 267–72; regimentation and, 263–65; seasonality of work and, 263–65; slaves and, 265–67

Assembly line, defined, 250

Bank boards of directors, 109–10; data sources for study of, 124–28; evidence on separation of ownership and control and ownership concentration, 128–31; evidence on size of, 131–34; multivariate

analysis of size of, 134–40; "optimum," 122–24. *See also* New York State

Bank failures, antebellum, 151–55. *See also* Railroads

Bank of North America, 35–36

Bankruptcy Act of 1898, 180

Bankruptcy case files, data from, 185–94

Bankruptcy laws, description of sample for, 204–9

Bessemer Steel Company, 52

Board of directors. *See* Bank boards of directors

Boston Manufacturing Corporation, 77

Britain. *See* United Kingdom

Buckalew, Charles R., 45

CAMELS ratings, 162, 162n22

Canals, bank failures and, 154

Carey, Henry C., 42–43, 49

Carnegie, Andrew, 52, 52n48

Carnegie Steel Company, 3, 52

Closed banks, defined, 152–53

Corporate governance, 108–9; New York State banking law and, 110–11

Corporate ownership, history of American, 73–74

Corporations: distinctive character of, in United States, 28–35; state statutes in US and, 30–35, 32t. *See also* Limited partnerships